Leveraged Marketing Communications

This comprehensive book features recent works on leveraged marketing communications (LMC)—an intentional pairing of a brand to benefit from the associations the target audience has with the object. LMC conceptually binds a wide range of marketing communication strategies previously studied in isolation: celebrity endorsements, sponsorship, product placements, cause-related marketing, and cobranding. LMC strategies assume that an entity (e.g., Michael Jordan) can be paired with a brand (e.g., Nike) to evoke associations that ultimately enhance brand awareness and evaluations.

The collection of chapters in this book examines the association between brands and entities, ideas, and contexts and combines theory and practice to offer new perspectives to help academics, practitioners, and policymakers better understand and apply LMC research. The chapters collectively provide a theoretical framework for building brand equity via linking brands to people, places, and things; examine how marketers can best leverage brand alliances; explore ways to maximize the effectiveness of sponsorship, product placement, corporate social responsibility (CSR), and cause-related marketing; and summarize our knowledge of the various forms of LMC.

The chapters in this book were originally published in the *International Journal of Advertising*.

Sukki Yoon is Professor of Marketing, Bryant University. Previously he taught at Cleveland State University. He was a visiting scholar at Grey Worldwide, Harvard University, and Southern Methodist University and a consultant at U.S. and Korean firms and government agencies. He has published articles in many international journals and has served on editorial boards.

Yung Kyun Choi (Ph.D., Michigan State University) is Professor in the Department of Advertising and Public Relations at Dongguk University in Seoul, Korea. His research interests are in advertising effects and consumer behaviour in digital media such as social media, mobile media, and AR/VR. He has published articles in many international journals including *Journal of Advertising*, *International Journal of Advertising*, and *Journal of Business Research*, serving on editorial boards in these journals.

Charles R. Taylor is John A. Murphy Professor of Marketing at Villanova University. He currently serves as Editor-in-Chief of *International Journal of Advertising*. Taylor has published extensively and has received the Ivan L. Preston Award for Outstanding Contribution to Research from the American Academy of Advertising and the Flemming Hansen Award for long-term impact on the advertising field from the European Advertising Academy.

Leveraged Marketing Communications

The Importance of Studying the Transfer of Object-to-Brand Associations

Edited by
Sukki Yoon, Yung Kyun Choi and Charles R. Taylor

Routledge
Taylor & Francis Group

LONDON AND NEW YORK

First published 2021
by Routledge
2 Park Square, Milton Park, Abingdon, Oxon OX14 4RN

and by Routledge
605 Third Avenue, New York, NY 10158

Routledge is an imprint of the Taylor & Francis Group, an informa business

Introduction, Chapters 1–4 and 6–9 © 2021 Advertising Association
Chapter 5 © 2020 Jos Bartels, Machiel J. Reinders, Chrissie Broersen and Sarah Hendriks. Originally published as Open Access.
Chapter 10 © 2019 Sarah Desirée Schaefer, Ralf Terlutter and Sandra Diehl. Originally published as Open Access.
Chapter 11 © 2019 Alexander P. Schouten, Loes Janssen and Maegan Verspaget. Originally published as Open Access.

British Library Cataloguing in Publication Data
A catalogue record for this book is available from the British Library

ISBN: 978-0-367-72546-4 (hbk)
ISBN: 978-0-367-72547-1 (pbk)
ISBN: 978-1-003-15524-9 (ebk)

Typeset in Myriad Pro
by Newgen Publishing UK

Publisher's Note
The publisher accepts responsibility for any inconsistencies that may have arisen during the conversion of this book from journal articles to book chapters, namely the inclusion of journal terminology.

Disclaimer
Every effort has been made to contact copyright holders for their permission to reprint material in this book. The publishers would be grateful to hear from any copyright holder who is not here acknowledged and will undertake to rectify any errors or omissions in future editions of this book.

Contents

Citation Information

The following chapters were originally published in different issues of *International Journal of Advertising*. When citing this material, please use the original page numbering for each article, as follows:

Chapter 1

Leveraging secondary associations to build brand equity: theoretical perspectives and practical applications
Kevin Lane Keller
International Journal of Advertising, volume 39, issue 4 (2020), pp. 448–465

Chapter 2

Leveraged brand evaluations in branded entertainment: Effects of alliance exclusivity and presentation style
Hyejin Bang, Dongwon Choi, Tae Hyun Baek, Sang Do Oh and Yeonshin Kim
International Journal of Advertising, volume 39, issue 4 (2020), pp. 466–485

Chapter 3

The effects of sensory fit on consumer evaluations of co-branding
Jungyong Ahn, Ahyeon Kim and Yongjun Sung
International Journal of Advertising, volume 39, issue 4 (2020), pp. 486–503

Chapter 4

Legitimacy and sincerity as leveraging factors in social sponsorship: an experimental investigation
Alain d'Astous, François Anthony Carrillat and Audrey Przybysz
International Journal of Advertising, volume 39, issue 4 (2020), pp. 504–522

Chapter 5

Communicating the fair trade message: the roles of reputation and fit
Jos Bartels, Machiel J. Reinders, Chrissie Broersen and Sarah Hendriks
International Journal of Advertising, volume 39, issue 4 (2020), pp. 523–547

For any permission-related enquiries please visit:
www.tandfonline.com/page/help/permissions

Notes on Contributors

H. Aghakhani, Rowe School of Business, Faculty of Management, Dalhousie University, Halifax, Canada.

Jungyong Ahn, Department of Psychology, Korea University, Seoul, Korea.

Tae Hyun Baek, Department of Integrated Strategic Communication, College of Communication and Information, University of Kentucky, Lexington, Kentucky, USA.

Hyejin Bang, School of Journalism and Mass Communication, The University of Kansas, Lawrence, Kansas, USA.

Jos Bartels, School of Communication, Department of Communication Studies, Hong Kong Baptist University, Hong Kong.

Lars Bergkvist, College of Business, Zayed University, Dubai, United Arab Emirates.

Chrissie Broersen, MeMo2, Amsterdam, the Netherlands.

François Anthony Carrillat, University of Technology Sydney, Ultimo, Australia.

S. W. Carvalho, Kenneth C. Rowe Management Building, Halifax, Canada.

Dongwon Choi, Department of Advertising and Public Relations, College of Social Sciences, Kookmin University, Seoul, Korea.

Sejung Marina Choi, School of Media and Communication, Korea University, Seoul, Korea.

Yung Kyun Choi, Department of Advertising and Public Relations, Dongguk University, Seoul, Republic of Korea.

P. H. Cunningham, Rowe School of Business, Faculty of Management, Dalhousie University, Halifax, Canada.

Alain d'Astous, HEC Montreal, Montreal, Quebec, Canada.

Sandra Diehl, Department of Media and Communications Science, Alpen-Adria Universitaet, Klagenfurt am Woerthersee, Austria.

Sarah Hendriks, Department of Communication and Cognition, Tilburg University, Tilburg, the Netherlands.

Loes Janssen, Department of Communication & Cognition, Tilburg University, Tilburg, the Netherlands.

Kevin Lane Keller, Tuck School of Business, Dartmouth College, Hanover, NH, USA.

Ahyeon Kim, Department of Psychology, Korea University, Seoul, Korea.

Yeonshin Kim, Department of Business Administration, College of Business, Myongji University, Seoul, Korea.

Yoojung Kim, Department of Media and Communication, Konkuk University, Seoul, Korea.

Sang Do Oh, Management Division, Maeji School of Business, Yonsei University, Wonju, Korea.

Audrey Przybysz, CSA France, Paris, France.

Machiel J. Reinders, Wageningen Economic Research, Subdivision Consumer and Chain, Wageningen, the Netherlands.

Sarah Desirée Schaefer, Department of Human Resource Management, Leadership and Organizational Behavior, Alpen-Adria Universitaet, Klagenfurt am Woerthersee, Austria.

Alexander P. Schouten, Department of Communication & Cognition, Tilburg University, Tilburg, the Netherlands.

Yongjun Sung, Department of Psychology, Korea University, Seoul, Korea.

Charles R. Taylor, Villanova University, PA, USA.

Ralf Terlutter, Department of Marketing and International Management, Alpen-Adria Universitaet, Klagenfurt am Woerthersee, Austria.

Maegan Verspaget, Department of Communication & Cognition, Tilburg University, Tilburg, the Netherlands.

Sukki Yoon, Marketing Department, Bryant University, Smithfield, RI, USA.

Kris Qiang Zhou, College of Business, The University of Texas at San Antonio, San Antonio, TX, USA.

Preface
Why Leveraged Marketing Communications is a Critically Important Topic in Marketing

The concept of celebrity endorsement and a basic understanding of the logic behind it is well known to the general public. The basic idea is that a brand can benefit from being associated with the celebrity. The idea seems pretty simple. However, as is well known to both managers and researchers, how to best transfer positive associations from one entity (e.g., a celebrity, sports team, charity, television show brand) to another can be complex, and such practices have been studied for many years. In 2003, Kevin Lane Keller observed that marketing communications strategies such as sponsorships and celebrity endorsements essentially try to *leverage* knowledge consumer associate with one object in order to benefit a brand (Keller 2003).

Indeed, several marketing communications practices engage in leveraging consumer knowledge, including celebrity endorsements, sponsorship, product placement, cause-related marketing, some corporate social responsibility advertising, and branded entertainment/branded content. As defined by Bergkvist and Taylor (2016, p.158), leveraged marketing communication (LMC) is defined as a brand building strategies that are "an intentional pairing of a brand to benefit from the associations the target audience has with the object." The authors pointed out that for a holistic theoretical understanding of LMC, it is important to recognize that these practices have important commonalities as a result of associations being transferred. In this way, a deeper understanding of when and how associations transfer from a branded object to another branded entity can arise, as LMC research can integrate diverse perspectives into theoretically coherent explanations unique to marketing communications. For example, information processing and meaning transfer models, along with research findings from studies using these models allows us to understand how to better design communications via executional factors such as length of appeal, attractiveness level, "fit" of object and brand, length, and format.

It is with this need for a deeper understanding of leverage communications in mind that the *International Journal of Advertising* ran a special issue on Leveraged Marketing Communications. We had the good fortune of having prominent marketing communications scholars Sukki Yoon and Yung-Kyun Choi agree to edit the issue. In addition, best papers submitted to the Global Marketing Conference, a premier marketing conference run by the Global Alliance of Marketing and Management Association, held in Tokyo in Summer, 2018, were chosen to be entered into the review process for the issue. We have also supplemented the special issue with a few additional key articles from recent issues of the journal in order to provide holistic coverage of leveraged marketing communications. We believe that the result is a book that both examines LMC holistically and provides new, cutting-edge insights on individual practices. We are particularly fortunate to have contributions from Kevin Lane Keller and Lars Bergkvist, both leading thinkers in the LMC area in this volume.

In closing I would like to thank special issue editors Sukki Yoon and Yung-Kyung Choi for their hard work, along with Anveshi Gupta of Routledge, Taylor and Francis for her assistance. Gratitude is also due to Global Alliance of Marketing and Management Association President Eunju Ko and Executive Secretary Kyung Hoon Kim for their collaboration in this effort.

References

Bergkvist, L. and Taylor, C.R. (2016). Leveraged marketing communications: a framework for explaining the effects of secondary brand associations. *Academy of Marketing Science Review*, 6(3), 157–175.
Keller, K.L. (2003). Brand synthesis: the multidimensionality of brand knowledge. *Journal of Consumer Research*, 29(4), 595–600.

Introduction
Leveraged Marketing Communications

Leveraged marketing communications (LMC) refers to brand-building strategies that are "an intentional pairing of a brand to benefit from the associations the target audience has with the object" (Bergkvist and Taylor 2016, p. 158). LMC conceptually binds a wide range of marketing communication strategies previously studied in isolation: celebrity endorsements, sponsorship, product placements, cause-related marketing, and cobranding.

LMC strategies basically assume that an entity (e.g., Michael Jordan) can be paired with a brand (e.g., Nike) to evoke associations that ultimately enhance brand awareness and evaluations. In the past decades, psychological studies have increasingly investigated association processes in theoretical contexts such as associative networks, schema theory, dual-process models, affect transfer, classical conditioning, and attribution theory (e.g., Yoon, Choi, and Song 2011).

LMC research conceptually integrates findings from diverse literatures into a theoretically coherent story unique to marketing and advertising. For example, LMC uses conventional information processing and meaning transfer models to show how marketing communications could strengthen or weaken brand–entity leverage through factors such as format, length, attractiveness, and celebrity endorsement.

In this special issue and corresponding book, under the broad rubric of LMC, we feature recent works examining the association between brands and entities, ideas, and contexts. To that end, we introduce papers combining theory and practice to offer new perspectives to help academics, practitioners, and policymakers better understand and apply LMC research.

The original LMC issue comprises seven original research articles most of which were among the best papers presented at the 2018 Global Marketing Conference in Tokyo, and all of which were rigorously selected after a regular IJA peer review process. The edited book was supplemented with a few additional key articles from recent issues of the journal. The articles collectively contribute to LMC research by 1) providing a theoretical framework for building brand equity via linking brands to people, places, and things (Bergkvist and Zhou 2016; 2019; Keller 2020); 2) examining how marketers can best leverage brand alliances (Ahn, Kim and Sung 2020; Bang, et al. 2020; Janssen and Verspaget 2020); and 3) exploring ways to maximize the effectiveness of sponsorship, corporate social responsibility (CSR), and cause-related marketing (Aghakhani, Carvalho and Cunningham 2020; Bartels et al. 2020; d'Astous, Carrillat, and Prezybysz 2020; Kim and Choi 2020; Schouten, Janssen and Verspaget 2020).

The authors use various samples and methods, which increases the validity of findings, as strengths and weaknesses are mutually complementary. The Keller (2000) and Bergkvist and Zhou (2016; 2019) articles review a theoretical model that can be readily applied to

LMC. The d'Astous, Carrillat, and Prezybysz (2020) article reports results of a door-to-door, paper-and-pencil field survey. The Schaefer, Terlutter and Diehl (2020) article surveys a large European energy provider. The Aghakhani, Carvalho and Cunningham (2020) article focuses on a survey of online consumers. The Ahn, Kim and Sung (2020), Bang et al. (2020), Bartels et al. (2020), Kim and Choi (2020), and Schouten, Janssen and Verspaget (2020) articles report experimental data collected from laboratory settings. Collectively, the studies represent consumers from Asia, North America, and Europe, the three continents with the largest buying powers and GDPs (IMF 2019).

Keller (2020) reviews and applies the brand resonance model, a comprehensive, cohesive model of brand building, to theoretically delineate associations between brands (e.g., Wilson) and people (e.g., a celebrity tennis player), places (e.g., a professional tennis club), and things (e.g., a sports magazine). By applying the model to real-world examples, Keller identifies and discusses practical brand planning and measurement. Bergkvist and Zhou (2016; 2019) review celebrity endorsement research and cause-related marketing (CRM) persuasion research. Their first article (Bergkvist and Zhou 2016) identifies six areas of research on celebrity endorsements: celebrity prevalence, campaign management, financial effects, celebrity persuasion, non-evaluative meaning transfer, and brand-to-celebrity transfer. Their second article (Bergkvist and Zhou 2019) proposes the two paths by which CRM affects brand evaluations: the indirect transfer path which is mediated by attribution of motives and the direct transfer path in which attitude towards the cause is transferred to the brand.

Bang et al. (2020) combine brand alliance and presentation style, important elements of LMC, to show that when an unfamiliar brand is simultaneously paired with a well-known brand in branded entertainment, consumers evaluate the brand more favorably. However, when the brand is paired with multiple ally brands with time intervals between the pairings, consumers evaluate focal brands more favorably. Credibility is identified as a mediator underlying the interaction. Ahn, Kim, and Sung (2020) highlight the importance of sensory fit to show that cobranding is more effective when logo color themes match (e.g., orange with yellow) rather than mismatch (e.g., orange with green) cobranded logo color themes. The effect is more pronounced for low rather than high involvement products. Schouten, Janssen and Verspaget (2020) investigate the impact of celebrity versus influencer endorsements on advertising effectiveness. They report that participants identify more with influencers than celebrities, feel more similar to influencers than celebrities, and trust influencers more than celebrities.

The remaining five papers address the efficacies of social sponsorship, CSR, and cause-related marketing. d'Astous, Carrillat, and Prezybysz (2020) find that consumers have increased purchase intentions when they perceive that the sponsoring brand has legitimacy and sincerity, based on its philanthropic investments, especially if the cause is congruent with the sponsor's activities and image. Relatedly, Bartels et al. (2012) show that when companies communicate fair trade initiatives, consumers are more trusting and supportive if the companies are known for fair-trade. Aghakhani, Carvalho and Cunningham (2020) demonstrate that consumers have reduced brand perceptions and purchase intentions when a sponsoring firm terminates a cause-related-partnership, but the impact is mitigated if the firm switches support to a new cause. Kim and Choi (2020) show that previous CSR initiatives protect company images for companies faced with competence-related rather than morality-related crises. Issue congruence between CSR and the nature of the crisis affects consumer reactions. Schaefer, Terlutter and Diehl (2020) show that liking of the company's CSR advertisements, message credibility, and cause-company fit influence employees' evaluation of their organization's CSR engagement, which in turn relates to employees' job satisfaction, organizational pride, and word-of-mouth about CSR.

We, the guest editors, thank the authors who submitted their work and endured multiple rounds of revisions for this special issue. We also thank reviewers who provided constructive comments on the submissions. In addition, we thank Charles "Ray" Taylor, the journal editor; Kyung Hoon Kim, the Executive Secretary of Global Alliance of Marketing and Management Associations; and Eunju Ko, the Organizing Committee Chair of 2018 GMC, for encouraging us to submit our proposal for this special issue and for trusting us to edit it.

References

Aghakhani, H., Carvalho, SW. & Cunningham, PH. 2020. When partners divorce: Understanding consumers' reactions to partnership termination in cause-related marketing programs, *International Journal of Advertising*, 39 no. 5: 548–570.

Ahn, J., Kim, A. & Sung, Y. 2020. The effects of sensory fit on consumer evaluations of co-branding, *International Journal of Advertising*, 39 no. 5: 486–503.

Bang, H., Choi, D., Baek, TH., Oh, SD. & Kim, Y. 2020. Leveraged brand evaluations in branded entertainment: Effects of alliance exclusivity and presentation style. *International Journal of Advertising*, 39 no. 5: 466–485.

Bartels, J., Reinders, MJ., Broersen, C. & Hendriks, S. 2020. Communicating the fair trade message: The roles of reputation and fit, *International Journal of Advertising*, 39 no. 5: 523–547.

Bergkvist, L., Taylor, CR. 2016. Leveraged marketing communications: A framework for explaining the effects of secondary brand associations. *AMS Review*, 6: 157–175.

Bergkvist, L. & Zhou, KQ. 2016. Celebrity endorsements: A literature review and research agenda, *International Journal of Advertising*, 35 no. 4: 642–663.

Bergkvist, L. & Zhou, KQ. 2019. Cause-related marketing persuasion research: an integrated framework and directions for further research, *International Journal of Advertising*, 38 no. 1: 5–25.

d'Astous, A., Carrillat, FA. & Przybysz, A. 2020. Legitmacy and sincerity as leveraging factors in social sponsorship: An experimental investigation, *International Journal of Advertising*, 39 no. 5: 504–522.

International Monetary Fund 2019. *IMF DataMapper*. Washington, D.C: International Monetary Fund, Retrieved 30 June 2019.

Keller, KL. 2020. Leveraging secondary associations to build brand equity: Theoretical perspectives and practical applications, *International Journal of Advertising*, 39 no. 5: 448–465.

Kim, Y. & Choi, SM. 2020. When good becomes bad: The role of corporate crisis and issue congruence, *International Journal of Advertising*, 39 no. 5: 571–586.

Schaefer, SD., Terlutter, R. & Diehl, S. 2020. Talking about CSR matters: Employees' perception of and reaction to their company's CSR communication in four different CSR domains, *International Journal of Advertising*, 39 no. 2: 191–212.

Schouten, A. Janssen, L. & Verspaget, M. 2020. Celebrity vs. Influencer endorsements in advertising: The role of identification, credibility, and product-endorser fit, *International Journal of Advertising*, 39 no. 2: 258–281.

Yoon, S., Choi, YK., & Song, S. 2011. When intrusive can be likable: Product placement effects on multitasking consumers. *Journal of Advertising*, 40 no. 2: 63–75.

Leveraging secondary associations to build brand equity: theoretical perspectives and practical applications

Kevin Lane Keller

ABSTRACT

One potentially valuable strategy for companies to build brand equity for their products and services is to actually link their brands to other people, places and things. By linking their brands to these other entities, consumers may change how they think, feel or act towards the company's brands. To help understand how these secondary associations can transform brand knowledge, a comprehensive, cohesive model of brand building – the brand resonance model – is reviewed and applied. Theoretical insights are generated and practical issues are identified and discussed to aid brand planning and measurement.

Brands can build meaning with consumers in many different ways (Keller and Lehmann 2006; Schmitt 2012). Although a positive personal experience with a product or service is an invaluable way to establish strong, favorable and unique associations for a brand, marketing communications – in their broadest form – often play a critical role in brand building too. One important way that brands can build meaning through marketing communications is by using them to tap into or borrow meaning from another entity – another person (e.g., celebrity endorser), place (e.g., country of origin), or thing (e.g., a cause).

Leveraged marketing communications can be thought of in terms of leveraging secondary associations – "secondary" because they are associations linked to another entity that in some way changes the meaning of the brand for consumers (Bergkvist and Taylor 2016). In other words, consumer knowledge for a brand may be created or changed by linking it to some other person, place or thing with its own identifiable node and knowledge in memory that consumers feel conveys some relevant information or meaning about the brand (Keller 1993).

Brands thus may themselves be linked to other entities that have their own associations, creating "secondary" brand associations. Because the brand becomes identified with another entity, even though this linked entity may not directly relate to the product or service performance of the brand in any way, consumers may infer that the brand shares certain associations or meaning with that entity, thus producing indirect or secondary associations for the brand. In essence, the marketer is borrowing or "leveraging" some associations and knowledge from the other entity to create or enhance some associations and knowledge to help to build its own brand equity.

There may be many different types of entities with which to be linked and, and as will be outlined below, many different types of associations which could potentially transfer. For example, the brand may be linked to certain source factors, such as the company, countries or other geographical regions, and channels of distribution, as well as to other brands, characters, spokespeople, sporting or cultural events, causes, or some other third party sources (through awards or reviews). All of these different entities could have a myriad of different kinds of associations of potential value to leverage.

As an example of some of the branding issues involved, assume Nike – the highly successful makers of shoes, clothing and equipment in a wide variety of sports – decided to introduce a new tennis racquet called, "The Avenger." Although Nike sells tennis shoes and apparel, they have yet to introduce a tennis racquet. In creating the marketing program to build brand equity for the new Avenger racquet, Nike could attempt to leverage secondary brand knowledge in a number of different ways, as follows.

1. Nike could leverage associations to its corporate brand by "sub-branding" the product, e.g., by calling it the "Nike Avenger" or "The Avenger by Nike." Consumer evaluations of the brand extension would be influenced by the extent to which consumers: a) held favorable associations about Nike as a company or brand because of their other athletic shoes, clothing and equipment; and b) felt that such knowledge was predictive of a tennis racquet that the company made.
2. Nike could try to sell through upscale, professional tennis shops and clubs in a hope that their credibility would "rub off" on the Avenger brand.
3. Nike could attempt to co-brand by identifying a strong ingredient brand for their grip, frame, or strings (e.g., as Wilson did by incorporating Goodyear tire rubber on the soles of their ProStaff Classic tennis shoes).
4. Nike could use one or more of its top professional players to also endorse or become an advertising spokesperson for the racquet (e.g., Rafael Nadal or Serena Williams), or they could choose to become a sponsor of select tennis tournaments or even the entire ATP men's or WTA women's professional tennis tour.
5. Nike could attempt to secure and publicize favorable ratings from third party sources (e.g., *Tennis* magazine).
6. Nike could try to rely on Oregon and its West Coast roots, although such a location would not seem to have any special relevance to tennis.

Thus, independent of the associations created by the racquet itself, its Avenger brand name, or any other aspects of the marketing program, Nike may be able to build equity by linking the brand to these other entities in these various ways. We next consider the nature of brand knowledge that marketers can attempt to transfer or leverage from other entities and the process by which marketers can try to do so.

Theoretical perspectives

In this section, we outline some basic considerations before delving into the details of a model application. Our assumption is that the target brand under study is a product or service brand. Even if it comes in the form of a corporate brand, it is assumed that products and services of some kind are its core and the foundation of its meaning.

Basic considerations

In general, two factors may be particularly important in predicting how much leverage might result from linking the brand to another entity:

1. *Nature of the knowledge about the linked entity* - If consumers have no familiarity with or knowledge of the other entity, then obviously there is nothing that can be transferred (John et al. 2006). Ideally, as will be developed below, consumers would be aware of the entity, hold some strong, favorable, and perhaps even unique associations towards the entity, have positive judgments and feelings about the entity, and have developed an intense, active loyalty relationship with it (Keller 2003).
2. *Impact of the knowledge about the linked entity* - Assuming that consumers have some potentially valuable knowledge about the other entity, to what extent is this knowledge evoked in the context of the brand? In what ways does it change knowledge about the brand? How does it change behavior towards the brand? Thus, a key issue is the extent to which knowledge about the linked entity will become positive – when considered *in the context of the brand* – such that consumers update their knowledge about the brand in some positive way and act more favorably towards it as a result.

In other words, the two crucial questions with transferring secondary knowledge from a linked entity to a product or service brand are: 1) What do consumers know about the linked entity; and 2) Does any of this knowledge affect what consumer think or feel about the brand and how they act towards it? Affirmative answers to the first question are the necessary, but not sufficient condition for affirmative answers to the second question. In other words, some knowledge about an entity has to exist before it can be inferred or transferred to the brand.

A number of issues come into play in understanding this two-step process and how the two factors might operate differently depending on the different types of entities and the different dimensions of knowledge potentially involved. We next turn to another model to help us with that analysis.

Nature of the knowledge

The brand resonance model describes how to create intense, active loyalty relationships with customers for a brand (Keller 2001; Keller and Swaminathan 2020). The model considers what consumers think, feel, and do and the degree to which they

Brand Resonance Pyramid

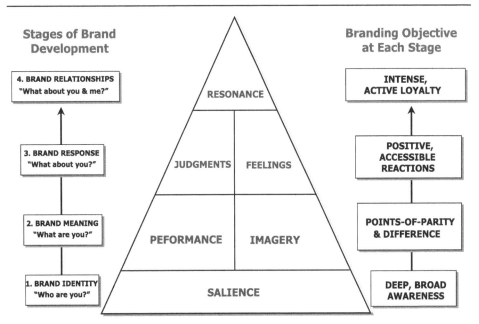

Figure 1. Brand resonance pyramid.

connect or "resonate" with a brand. Brand resonance is defined as the intensity of customers' psychological bond with the brand and the level of activity it engenders.

The brand resonance model views brand building as an ascending series of steps, from bottom to top, as: (1) ensuring customers identify the brand and associate it with a specific product class or set of needs; (2) firmly establishing the brand meaning in customers' minds by strategically linking a host of tangible and intangible brand associations; (3) eliciting the proper customer responses in terms of brand-related judgment and feelings; and (4) converting customers' brand responses to intense, active loyalty. Each step is contingent on successfully achieving the objectives of the previous one.

According to this model, enacting the four steps requires establishing a pyramid of six "brand building blocks" as illustrated in Figure 1, with stages of brand development and branding objective at each stage also shown. The model emphasizes the duality of brands—the rational route to brand building is on the left side of the pyramid and the emotional route is on the right side. Creating significant brand equity requires reaching the top of the brand pyramid, which occurs only if the proper building blocks are put into place.

- *Brand salience* is how easily and often and in what ways customers think of the brand under various purchase or consumption situations – the depth and breadth of brand awareness.
- *Brand performance* is how well the product or service meets customers' more functional needs.

Brand Resonance Pyramid Sub-Dimensions

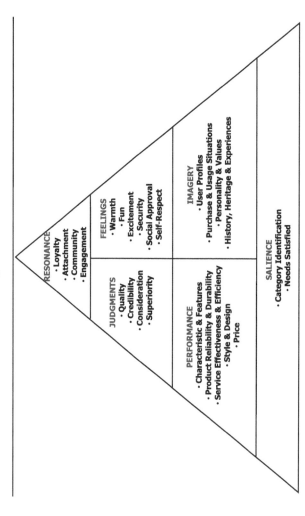

Figure 2. Sub-dimensions of brand resonance pyramid.

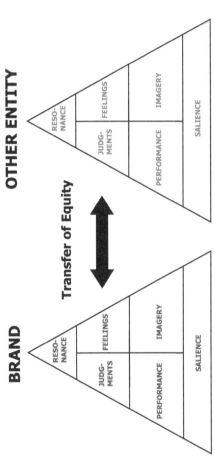

Figure 3. Brand resonance model as a guide to knowledge transfer.

- *Brand imagery* describes the extrinsic properties of the product or service, including the ways in which the brand attempts to meet customers' more psychological or social needs.
- *Brand judgments* focus on customers' own personal opinions and evaluations.
- *Brand feelings* are customers' emotional responses and reactions with respect to the brand.
- *Brand resonance* describes the relationship customers have with the brand and the extent to which they feel they're "in sync" with it.

Each of the six building blocks has a number of different sub-dimensions that provide richness and diagnostic insight (see Figure 2). As a whole, the brand resonance model provides a comprehensive, cohesive understanding of brand building in the marketplace, i.e., what consumers think and feel about a brand and how they act towards it.

Because it captures the full range of brand development – from a new brand just trying to establish itself in the marketplace to a mature brand seeking to deepen and broaden relationships with its current customer base – the brand resonance model is a helpful tool for understanding how brands at different stages of development can leverage secondary associations to build or maintain their brand equity.

In applying the brand resonance model to understand secondary associations, the key is to recognize that the linked entity can itself be viewed as a brand. It has a name and perhaps even other brand elements, and it may take on some – or even a lot of – meaning with consumers in the marketplace. As with a product or service brand, brand knowledge of the linked entity consist of all the thoughts, feelings, images, beliefs, experiences, behaviors etc. that a consumer stores in memory and associates with the linked entity.

The flexibility of the brand resonance model is that it applies equally well to any type of brand and thus any type of entity that can be thought of as a brand, e.g., a person, place or thing. The question then becomes, *how do the brand resonance pyramids of the brand and the other linked entity relate in the minds of consumers*? In particular, how does consumer knowledge of the brand – defined broadly in terms of the brand resonance pyramid – change as a result of the knowledge about the other entity (see Figure 3).

From a brand resonance model point of view, there are several considerations to keep in mind in understanding this transfer or updating process. Obviously, the more resonance that has been created for the other entity – and thus the corresponding salience, performance and imagery, and judgments and feelings that also exist – the more opportunity there is to have the target brand impacted by the linked entity. Moreover, in general, those transfer or leveraging effects are often likely to be "parallel" such that imagery associations for the linked entity are more likely to affect or create imagery associations for the product or service brand; feeling associations for the linked entity are more likely to affect or create feeling associations for the product or service brand; and so on.

Nevertheless, it is also possible that "halo effects" occur such that "crossover effects" prevail and one type of knowledge about the linked entity affects multiple types of knowledge for the brand. For example, positive affect for a linked celebrity spokesperson or popular cause or event may not only create positive feelings or judgments towards the brand, it may also even color specific perceptions or beliefs about the brand's performance or imagery.

Beyond these general observations, more specific insights can come from considering each of the six building blocks, as follows.

Salience

Salience concerns how easily and often a brand is thought of and in what ways – is it thought of at all the right times, in all the right places and in all the right ways? Salience reflects the depth and breadth of brand awareness. Certainly by linking a brand to an entity that is better known, there may be an opportunity to increase the depth of brand awareness so that more people recall the brand more easily and more often. The breadth of brand awareness could also be enhanced if the association changes how – or at least when and where – consumers think of a brand, although that may be harder to have happen in general.

That is, given the linked entity, as a person, place or thing, is typically not directly related to the the product or service performance, it may be harder for its meaning to somehow change the way consumers think of when, where, and how the brand performs. Nevertheless, such broadening can happen. For example, assume an insurance brand wanted to be thought of more broadly as a "financial service brand" that helps consumers "establish a firm financial foundation." By securing a well-known financial expert, supporting a financial literacy non-profit, and/or (especially) co-branding with another financial service brand, consumers may form new associations that increase the salience of the brand in other financial domains beyond insurance.

Performance

Performance describes how well the product or service meets customers' more functional needs. How well does the brand rate on objective assessments of quality? To what extent does the brand satisfy functional needs and wants and provide utilitarian, aesthetic, and economic benefits to customers in the product or service category? Five important types of attributes and benefits often underlie brand performance:

1. Primary ingredients and supplementary features
2. Product reliability, durability, and serviceability
3. Service effectiveness, efficiency, and empathy
4. Style and design
5. Price

Similar to the issues noted with breadth of awareness and salience, because performance relates so much to the actual functioning of the product or service, the meaning of other entities can often be more removed from how the brand works or performs and potentially be seen by consumers as less relevant. Nevertheless, as was also noted above, even performance may be impacted by secondary associations. For example, linking to country of origin may change the fashionability of Italian suits, the taste of French wines, the driving performance of German automobiles, etc. In general, however, secondary associations are probably more likely to impact imagery than performance associations, as discussed next.

Imagery

Brand imagery depends on the extrinsic properties of the product or service, including the ways in which the brand attempts to meet customers' psychological or social needs. It is the way people think about a brand abstractly, rather than what they think the brand actually does. Thus, imagery refers to more intangible aspects of the brand. By its very definition, imagery is more dependent on extrinsic factors resulting from marketing communications and thus potentially leveraged entities.

Many kinds of intangibles can be linked to a brand, but four main ones are:

1. User profiles
2. Purchase and usage situations
3. Personality and values
4. History, heritage, and experiences

Leveraged entities offer much opportunity to add or change the imagery meaning for brands. By virtue of their human characteristics, linking a brand to a person, event, organization or can have the potential to affect personality, values and user imagery for the brand (Aaker 1997; Chernev, Hamilton, and Gal 2011; Mathur, Jain, and Maheswaran 2012).

Because many different entities are likely to have personality characteristics or values themselves, secondary associations from linked entities are particularly useful for establishing or enhancing personality dimensions for a brand. For example, if a brand wants to be seen as "fun and playful," it can use a comedic actor or actress in advertising and/or sponsor a comedy festival. If the brand wants to be seen as "sincere and competent," it can instead use a dramatic actor or actress, perhaps known for playing roles as a political leader or CEO and/or sponsor more civic-minded events or organizations.

Formally, Aaker (1997) examined 60 brands and found they fell into five main clusters or dimensions of brand personality: sincerity, excitement, competence, sophistication and ruggedness. Depending on the brand personality dimension(s) a brand aspires to embody, a brand can choose to align with entities that have the desired personality. In terms of brand these personality dimensions, some events, like the Ironman Triathlon in Hawaii, can be described as "rugged." Other sponsored events, like New York's Metropolitan Opera, are likely to be seen as "sophisticated." Still others, like NCAA "March Madness" post-season basketball tournament, are all about "excitement." As another example, charities such as the World Wildlife Fund would be considered to exhibit "sincerity." Along these lines, brands that aspire to personalities of ruggedness and/or excitement might be more likely to sponsor these types of sporting events, whereas brands aspiring to personalities of sophistication and/or sincerity might be more likely to sponsor these types of arts organizations or causes.

Additionally, linked entities with experiential components, such as events, can also be expected to add experiences to a brand. For example, if a brand wants to be seen as more edgy and daring, it can sponsor action sports; if wants to be seen as more youthful and energetic, it can sponsor youth-oriented events and activities such as musical concerts or craft beer festivals; and so on. In general, linked entities offer the greatest potential to affect imagery associations in these and other different ways.

Judgments

Brand judgments are customers' personal opinions about and evaluations of the brand, which consumers form by putting together all the different brand performance and imagery associations. Customers may make all types of judgments with respect to a brand, but four types of judgments are particularly important for a brand: judgments about the quality, credibility, consideration, and superiority of the brand.

Although all four major types of judgments for the linked entity may affect brand knowledge, given its more abstract nature, credibility would seem like the one for the brand most likely to be directly affected by the linked entity. Brand credibility is the extent to which consumers believe that a firm can design and deliver products and services for a brand that satisfy customer needs and wants. Credibility itself has three dimensions – expertise, trust and likability. By associating with a highly credible entity known or seen as being expert, trustworthy and/or likable, there may more halo effects impacting the brand on those same dimensions.

Celebrities can exemplify one or more of these dimensions. The success of various celebrities such as Oprah Winfrey, George Clooney or Bono as a spokesperson is in large part due to the fact that they are viewed favorably by many on all three dimensions. As another approach, likeability can be enhanced by sponsoring events that consumers enjoy, because they may be more likely to feel positive about the brand as a result. Additionally, sponsoring a well-liked event may contribute to perceptions that the brand is more customer-oriented and can enhance trustworthiness.

Consideration and superiority may similarly benefit from the linked entity if it helps the brand to be seen as more relevant and differentiated. On the other hand, quality may be the least likely to be directly affected, depending on the performance implications of the linked entity, as noted above. Brand quality judgments are more likely to result from direct experience or usage of the brand. Nevertheless, a sponsored person or event may be able to contribute to perceptions of quality, for example, if the sponsorship can be used to showcase aspects of the brand that contributes to quality judgments.

Feelings

Brand feelings are customers' affective and emotional responses to the brand (Pham, Geuens, and De Pelsmaker 2013; Coleman and Williams 2013). Brand feelings also relate to the social currency evoked by the brand. What feelings are elicited by the marketing program for the brand or by other means? How does the brand affect customers' feelings about themselves and their relationship with others? These feelings can be mild or intense and can be positive or negative. The brand resonance model highlights six important types of brand-building feelings.

1. Warmth
2. Fun
3. Excitement
4. Security
5. Social approval
6. Self-respect

These six feelings can be divided into two broad categories: The first three types of feelings are experiential and immediate, increasing in level of intensity; the latter three types of feelings are private and enduring, increasing in level of gravity.

There are many different types of feelings that may be established or accentuated for the brand as a result of a linked entity. By their very nature, events may be particularly effective with more experiential and immediate feelings. Still, sponsors can generate private and enduring feelings such as social approval, since consumers may attend an event such as a concert or a sports game to earn social approval and build social currency. Certain people may also be particularly effective as endorsers by evoking feelings of warmth, fun and excitement. In these and many other ways, secondary associations can have a significant effect on different brand-related feelings.

Resonance

Brand resonance focuses on the ultimate relationship and level of identification that the customer has with the brand and describes the extent to which customers feel that they are "in sync" with the brand. Resonance is characterized in terms of intensity, or the depth of the psychological bond that customers have with the brand (Thomson, MacInnis, and Park 2005), as well as the level of activity engendered by this loyalty (e.g., repeat purchase rates and the extent to which customers seek out brand information, events, and other loyal customers). These two dimensions of brand resonance can be broken down into four categories:

1. Behavioral loyalty
2. Attitudinal attachment
3. Sense of community
4. Active engagement

As with all of the other building blocks for brand resonance, linked entities could potentially impact any of these four categories. Attachment could occur as a result of direct affect transfer – affection and admiration for the linked entity may transfer directly to the brand. If, at the lower levels of the resonance pyramid, an association with another entity builds positive brand imagery, judgments and feelings, it may be more likely to elicit stronger attitudinal attachment. A sense of community could also follow if the brand is able to tap into the community and fandom associated with a popular celebrity or event. For example, one of the selling points of NASCAR for years was that its fans felt part of a special community and supported any brands that sponsored NASACAR. Active engagement with the brand can also be established if the event sponsorship has experiential components, like product trials or demos, or if the sponsor plays a key role in bringing the event to the public and earns credit from consumers.

Behavioral loyalty is difficult to influence through the linkage to another entity alone, since consumers are typically not directly experiencing or using the brand as a result. It is possible to build behavioral loyalty, however, by extending the linkage the other entity. For example, if a marketer integrates its brand into an event, or builds a promotional campaign around the event that encourages product usage, these can yield opportunities to generate behavioral loyalty.

True brand resonance may be difficult to achieve as a direct consequence of sponsorship of a person or event or through the linkage of other entities. It typically occurs as the result of a series of direct, positive interactions with the brand. With a event sponsorship, for example, a sponsoring brand is rarely the focal point for the participant, which is why it is essential for sponsors to do more than simply sign a sponsorship deal. They must support and enhance the sponsorship with other marketing activities that occur outside the bounds of the event itself. Many sponsors do not take full advantage of their sponsorship programs by complementing them with robust external marketing to create more direct brand interactions.

In general, the more consumers feel an intense, active loyalty relationship with the linked entity, the more likely they might be to notice a brand affiliation. Although that realization could potentially lead to changes in knowledge for the brand, ultimately many of the other factors noted above would also come into play to determine how much brand awareness, image, response or relationships were affected.

Impact of the knowledge

The brand resonance model is particularly well-suited to address the first step in the leveraging process – understanding the breadth and depth of the knowledge that consumers have for both the linked entity and the brand itself. As outlined some above, it can also be helpful with the second step in the leveraging process and whether knowledge of the linked entity is deemed by consumers as potentially relevant and meaningful for the brand. In this section, we consider several additional issues related to that second step of the process, i.e., how brand knowledge and judgments and decision-making might actually change for consumers as a result of knowledge of the linked entity.

Effects on Brand knowledge
When consumers recognize that a brand is linked to another entity, they may implicitly or explicitly infer that some of the particular associations, judgments, or feelings that characterize the other entity may also characterize the brand. That is, by using communications in some form to make a connection between the brand and another entity, consumers may form a mental association from the brand to the linked entity

and, consequently, knowledge for that linked entity may therefore "transfer" in some form over to the brand.

Assuming some potentially relevant and meaningful knowledge exists for the linked entity, connecting the brand to that other entity may: 1) affect existing brand associations or 2) potentially create some new brand associations. The degree of transferability will depend, in part, on the intensity (how much people think about the other entity) and direction (how much of this thinking is also directed at the brand) of processing. This transfer can be either positive, if the knowledge being transferred is beneficial to the brand, or negative, if the knowledge is detrimental to the brand.

The meaningfulness of the knowledge about the linked entity may vary depending on the brand and product context. Some knowledge about the other entity may seem relevant and applicable to the brand, whereas other knowledge may seem to have little connection or importance. The inferencing process will depend largely on the strength of the relationship in consumers' minds between the brand and other entity. The more consumers see similarity – of some kind – between the brand and the linked entity, the more likely it is that consumers will infer similar knowledge between the two. If the other entity is seen as wholly dissimilar and not sharing any features or connections, then consumers may be more likely to compartmentalize the two and not transfer any knowledge or associations.

If consumers do see some basis of similarity, in theory, essentially any aspect of knowledge may be inferred from other entities to the brand. In general, however, it may be more likely for higher level judgments or feelings to transfer from the entity than more specific lower level performance or imagery associations. Although possible exceptions were noted above, in general, many specific performance or even imagery associations about the linked entity may be more likely to be seen as irrelevant or too strongly connected to the original entity to transfer to the brand.

The transferability process is a function of other factors too beyond the fit between the brand and other entity. For example, transferability may depend on consumers' level of engagement with different marketing activities associated with the other entity. Other brands linked to the other entity also may affect transferability, depending on how much of the other brand's brand associations and activities are connected to the other entity.

Linking the brand to some other entity may not only affect existing brand knowledge, this linkage may also establish new knowledge about the brand. New brand knowledge may be created if the linked entity conveys meaning or elicits responses which do not currently exist for the brand. If consumers feel this meaning or responses are relevant for the brand too, they may become also linked as a result. These new associations may be particularly valuable to enrich the meaning of the brand and establish its positioning in important ways, as discussed further below.

Effects on consumer judgments and Decision-Making

There are two main ways by which a leveraged entity can affect judgments and choice for the brand, as suggested by the theorizing with respect to central vs. peripheral routes of persuasion (Petty and Cacioppo 1986) or System 1 vs. System 2 thinking (Kahneman 2011).

The more direct effect on consumer decision-making (akin to the central route or System 1 thinking) is when knowledge of the linked entity changes brand knowledge such that the actual inputs into decisions – specific attributes or benefits – are evaluated or weighted differently. In other words, *consumers just assess and use specific considerations for the brand differently because of the existence of the linked entity*. If the linked entity changes beliefs or weight for performance or imagery considerations, then consumer judgments and decisions can potentially change too as a result.

The indirect effect on consumer decision-making (akin to the peripheral route or System 2 thinking) is when knowledge of the linked entity – by itself – drives consumer decision-making. In other words, attributes or benefits are not evaluated nor weighted differently, *just the mere knowledge of the association with the other entity becomes a factor in making judgments or choice with respect to the brand*. In other words, consumers may adopt an affect referral decision rule that leads them to base brand judgments and opinions strictly or largely on their judgments and opinions of the other entity.

In general, this indirect effect on judgments and decision-making for the brand is most likely when consumers lack either the motivation or ability to evaluate more product-related concerns. In other words, when consumers either don't care much about choosing a particular brand or don't feel that they possess the knowledge to evaluate particular brands, they may be more likely to make brand decisions on the basis of such secondary considerations as how they think or feel about the celebrity endorsing it, other brands associated with it, etc.

In summary, the important consideration here is that there multiple routes by which secondary associations can either directly or indirectly influence consumer decision-making. The two routes are not mutually exclusive, and different routes may be used by different consumers or even by the same consumer at different times.

Conclusions

Companies can build or strengthen brand equity for their products and services by linking their brands to other entities – other people, places and things – and changing how consumers think, feel or act towards these brands in the process. To understand how these "secondary associations" can potentially transform brand knowledge, a well-established model of brand building, the brand resonance model, was applied, yielding a number of theoretical and managerial insights. We conclude by summarizing some practical applications that follow from our analysis and by highlighting some directions for future research.

Implications

In theory, any aspect of knowledge may be inferred from linked entities to the brand, although some types of entities are perhaps more likely to create or affect certain kinds of brand knowledge than would other types of entities. For example, as suggested above, events may be especially conducive to the creation of experiences; people may be especially effective for the elicitation of feelings; other brands may be especially well suited for establishing particular attributes and benefits; and so on. At the same time, any one entity may be associated with multiple dimensions of know-ledge, each of which may impact brand knowledge directly or indirectly.

For example, consider the effects on knowledge of linking a brand to a cause. Take Pampers, P&G's multi-billion dollar diaper brand positioned on the basis of "Caring for Baby's Development." Identification of Pampers with a particular cause (e.g., Autism Speaks) could have multiple effects on brand knowledge for consumers. A cause mar-keting program could build brand awareness via recall and recognition; enhance brand image in terms of attributes such as user imagery (e.g., kind and generous) and brand personality (e.g., sincere); evoke brand feelings (e.g., social approval and self-respect); establish brand attitudes (e.g., credibility judgments such as trustworthy and likable); and create brand experiences (e.g., through a sense of community and partici-pation in cause-related activities).

Choosing which other entities to become associated with and what knowledge to try to leverage should be based on thoughtful, careful analysis. For example, a *second-ary association audit* can be conducted which would: 1) characterize the knowledge structures of the brand and all other entities (people, places and things) currently or potentially linked to the brand; and 2) evaluate the other entities in terms of their actual or potential ability, respectively, to affect brand equity according to the two fac-tors of knowledge and impact.

In the remainder of this section we consider how the brand resonance model and other concepts might be used to conduct such an audit and discuss some other planning and analysis issues in choosing other entities and leveraging secondary associations.

Characterizing knowledge about the Brand and linked entities

In terms of conducting a secondary association audit, a good start point would be a deep, rich understanding of consumer knowledge structures for the brand itself, as well as those for other entities. Given its comprehensive nature, using the brand res-onance model to guide the audit increases the likelihood that the full range of pos-sible leveraged effects are identified and explored. The resonance model could be used to profile knowledge for both the brand and all the currently linked entities, as well as potentially linked entities.

Profiling these brand knowledge structures should reveal critical sources of brand equity. In terms of the brand itself, what types of thoughts, feelings, images, percep-tions, experiences, attitudes, and so on does the brand elicit? This understanding pro-vides a point of reference by which the brand building contribution of linked entities and secondary associations can be interpreted. Comparing the two resonance models would then be helpful to understand what potentially might transfer. Specifically, sec-ondary associations can then be critiqued on how much they might add or embellish brand awareness, enhance brand image, generate positive consumer judgments and feelings, and help to forge strong consumer bonds.

Assessing impact

Evaluating actual or potential impact, however, is more difficult. Survey work can be done based on test and control conditions with the other entity in question becoming linked – or not – to the brand. Comparing the brand knowledge structures in the two conditions should yield some baseline insight into how the linked entity might change knowledge for the brand

In doing so, however, several points should be recognized. One, the actual marketing and communications program would undoubtedly highlight the linkage of the other entity in a much different way. The survey comparison would only provide a fairly limited view of what might actually happen in the marketplace. Two, the impact may not be all positive and some associations may weaken or become less favorable, and negative associations may actually be created. Recommendations would then center on how to maximize the desired and minimize the undesired equity transfer.

The most important consideration in evaluating other entities is how consumers perceive the relationship of the brand to the other entity. As noted above, the inferencing process associated with leveraging secondary associations largely depends on the strength of the connection in consumers' minds between the brand and the other linked entity. The more consumers see similarity of the entity to the brand, the more likely it is that consumers will infer similar knowledge about the brand.

Entities may be chosen for which consumers have some or even a great deal of similar associations. A *commonality* leveraging strategy makes sense when consumers have associations in memory to another entity that are congruent with desired brand associations. For example, consider Dawn dish soap with its "tough on grease, but gentle on hands" positioning. By linking the brand to the cause of cleaning and rescuing birds affected by oil spills, Dove is able to reinforce its positioning and strengthen key brand associations of "strong" but "gentle."

On the other hand, there may be times that entities may be sought which represent a departure for the brand and where, by choice, there are few if any common or similar associations. Such *complementarity* leveraging strategies can be strategically critical in terms of delivering the desired position. For example, assume that Dawn dish soap was seen as strong but not gentle. Dove's cause marketing efforts to clean and rescue birds may be critical to actually even establish a "gentle" brand association.

As suggested by that example, leveraging is often designed to provide complementary brand knowledge in an attempt to shore up a negatively correlated attribute. As an actual real-world example, consider the comparatively youthful Matthew McConaughey endorsement of the aging Lincoln brand of automobiles to make it seem modern and contemporary. The challenge with a complementary strategy, however, is to ensure means of transferability such that the less congruent knowledge for the entity has either a direct or indirect effect on existing brand knowledge. This may require skillfully designed marketing programs that overcome initial consumer confusion or skepticism.

Even if consumers "buy into" the desired secondary associations one way or another, leveraging secondary brand knowledge may be risky because some control of the brand image is given up. The source factors or related person, place, or thing will undoubtedly have a host of other associations of which only some smaller set will be of interest to the marketer. Managing the transfer process so that only the relevant secondary knowledge becomes linked to the brand may be difficult. Moreover, this knowledge may change over time as consumers learn more about the entity, and new associations, judgments, or feelings may or may not be advantageous for the brand.

Directions for future research

There are a whole host of research questions that the above analysis suggests. In general, additional research should examine both steps in our process model of leveraging secondary associations more closely. First, there needs to be a deeper, richer understanding of the knowledge structures typically associated with different types of entities. What differences commonly exist in consumer knowledge of different types of people, places and things? How might measures of brand resonance be adapted for different types of entities? Using the resonance model to compare and contrast knowledge of different types of entities can illuminate the potential types of secondary associations that may be leveraged by a brand.

Second, there also needs to be a better understanding of the leveraging process itself and how these different knowledge structures for other entities impact brand knowledge for products and services when linked. How easily are different types of associations or knowledge added or impacted? When are direct vs. indirect effects on judgments and choice likely to be manifested?

Multiple methods should be employed to explore both steps. For example, experimental and survey research can be used to profile consumer knowledge structures for different entities and how brand knowledge structures change as a result of a brand being linked to those entities; econometric analysis can be used to understand sales and market share shifts over time as a result of a brand being linked to different entities in different ways; From a more qualitative social and cultural point of view, CCT methods can be used to view how brands leverage secondary associations. In these and other ways, a more complete view can be achieved as to how marketing and communications can affect brand building by leveraging secondary associations.

Disclosure statement

No potential conflict of interest was reported by the author.

References

Aaker, J.L. 1997. Dimensions of Brand personality. *Journal of Marketing Research* 34, no. 3: 347–57.

Bergkvist, L., and C.R. Taylor. 2016. Leveraged marketing communications: a framework for explaining the effects of secondary Brand associations. *AMS Review* 6, no. 3-4: 157–17. (December),

Chernev, A., R. Hamilton, and D. Gal. 2011. Competing for consumer identity: Limits to self-expression and the perils of lifestyle branding. *Journal of Marketing* 75, no. 3: 66–82.

Coleman, N.V., and P. Williams. 2013. Feeling like my self: emotion profiles and social identity. *Journal of Consumer Research* 40, no. 2: 203–22.

John, D.R., B. Loken, K. Kim, and S.B. Monga. 2006. Brand concept maps: a methodology for identifying Brand association networks. *Journal of Marketing Research* 43, no. 4: 549–63.

Kahneman, D. 2011. *Thinking, fast and slow*. New York: Farrar, Straus and Giroux.

Keller, K.L. 1993. Conceptualizing, measuring, and managing customer-based Brand equity. *Journal of Marketing* 57, no. 1: 1–22.

Keller, K.L. 2001. Building customer-based brand equity: a blueprint for creating strong brands. *Marketing Management* 10, no. 2: 15–9.

Keller, K.L. 2003. Brand synthesis: the multi-dimensionality of Brand knowledge. *Journal of Consumer Research* 29, no. 4: 595–600.

Keller, K.L., and V. Swaminathan. 2020. *Strategic brand management*. 5th ed., Upper Saddle River, NJ: Pearson Prentice-Hall.

Keller, K.L., and D. Lehmann. 2006. Brands and branding: research findings and future priorities. *Marketing Science* 25, no. 6: 740–59.

Mathur, P., S.P. Jain, and D. Maheswaran. 2012. Consumers' implicit theories about personality influence their Brand personality judgments. *Journal of Consumer Psychology* 22, no. 4: 545–57.

Petty, R.E., and J.T. Cacioppo. 1986. The elaboration likelihood model of persuasion. *Advances in Experimental Social Psychology* 19: 123–205.

Pham, M.T., M. Geuens, and P. De Pelsmacker. 2013. The influence of ad-evoked feelings on Brand evaluations: empirical generalizations from consumer responses to more than 1,000 TV commercials. *International Journal of Research in Marketing* 30, no. 4: 383–94.

Schmitt, B. 2012. The consumer psychology of brands. *Journal of Consumer Psychology* 22, no. 1: 7–17.

Thomson, M., D.J. MacInnis, and C.W. Park. 2005. The ties that bind: measuring the strength of consumers' emotional attachments to brands. *Journal of Consumer Psychology* 15, no. 1: 77–91.

Leveraged brand evaluations in branded entertainment: effects of alliance exclusivity and presentation style

Hyejin Bang, Dongwon Choi, Tae Hyun Baek ⓘ, Sang Do Oh and Yeonshin Kim

ABSTRACT

The authors study how marketers can best leverage brand alliances in branded entertainment. The study shows that alliance exclusivity and presentation style influence how consumers make brand-to-brand associations and ultimately evaluate a focal brand. When an unfamiliar focal brand is paired with a single well-known ally brand, consumers tend to evaluate the focal brand more favorably when the two brands are simultaneously presented (i.e., massed presentation). On the other hand, when the focal brand is paired with multiple ally brands, the spaced presentation evokes a more favorable evaluation of the focal brand. Brand credibility plays a mediating role underlying the interactions. Theoretical and managerial implications are discussed.

Introduction

The past decade has seen rapid growth in various forms of leveraged marketing communications (LMC), which are brand-building strategies for pairing individual brands with other entities and causing audiences to form favorable associations (Bergkvist and Taylor 2016). Leveraged entities include celebrities (McCracken 1989), sports events (Olson 2010), nonprofit organizations (Varadarajan and Menon 1988), and well-established brands (Cunha, Forehand, and Angle 2015). Cross-category brand alliance, a brand-pairing strategy in which advertisers link two or more brands from different categories (Smarandescu, Rose and Wedell 2013), has been widely adopted in brand extension (Aaker and Keller 1990; Dacin and Smith 1994), bundling (Harlam et al. 1995), and marketing communications (Smarandescu et al. 2013). For instance, in 2004, the athletic brand Nike and the tech company Apple synced the Apple iPod and Nike + and enabled users to track fitness activities. Such co-brandings and brand alliances tend to generate positive brand evaluations (Simonin and Ruth 1998).

With the development of digital media, branded entertainment has grown twice as fast as traditional advertising to provide new opportunities for brand alliances (Haberman 2018). As marketers gain more control over content production and distribution, brand alliances between two or more brands have rapidly moved beyond mere product integration to include content co-creation (Bernazzani 2018). For instance, the energy drink Red Bull and the tech company GoPro have collaborated in creating a series of high-flying videos such as "Stratos," a video of Felix Baumgartner's 2012 sound-breaking freefall from space. The video has garnered more than 40 million YouTube views, and has created synergy for both brands (Griner 2014). Also, Dodo, a digital media brand for animal lovers, partnered with Samsung to create emotional videos encouraging pet adoptions (Grimm 2017).

Such cross-category brand alliances are typically established when (a) a relatively new brand pay well-established brands to form LMC alliances or (b) both parties expect to benefit from the alliance. Relatively new brands are particularly challenged to overcome many obstacles preventing them from generating awareness and establishing brand credibility. They often use LMC strategies to jumpstart founding their new brand (Cunha, Forehand, and Angle 2015). Thus, we examine how LMC generates consumer perceptions about relatively new or unfamiliar "focal" brands that have formed partnerships with one or more well-established "object" brands in branded entertainment ventures (Bergkvist and Taylor 2016). In this study, we refer to a brand leveraged by another LMC object as a "focal brand" and a brand that already has strong associations and is thus used to leverage a relatively new brand as an "object brand" (Bergkvist and Taylor 2016).

Do LMC partnerships always have positive outcomes? Consumers have been shown to positively evaluate brands that are allied with known brands, and to negatively evaluate the same unknown brands if they lack ally support (Gammoh, Voss, and Fang 2010; Ruekert and Rao 1994; Rao, Qu, and Ruekert 1999), but LMC can be risky. For instance, when an object brand has both positive and negative associations, consumers are more likely to transfer their negative rather than positive associations to the focal brand (Campbell and Warren 2012). Situational factors such as brand/product category characteristics, marketing context, perceived fit, and consumer/cultural characteristics are known to moderate brand alliance success (e.g., Bluemelhuber, Carter and Lambe 2007; Gammoh, Voss, and Chakraborty 2006; Ruekert and Rao 1994; Simonin and Ruth 1998), but we lack research regarding the impact of executional strategies. In this study, we examined how two executional factors —alliance exclusivity and presentation style— interact to enhance or inhibit the effect of brand alliance in a branded entertainment venture.

Among many factors, alliance exclusivity (i.e., the number of object brands allied) might directly impact consumer ability to pair brands. Although numerous brand associations might benefit focal brands by increasing the number of brand associations, consumers might encounter difficulty in trying to remember the pairing because consumers have limited cognitive processing ability and memory; they cannot process too much information at once (Petty and Cacioppo 1986). Thus consumers exposed to multiple associative information may be unable to process it all, and each individual brand association is weakened (Weisberg and Reeves 2013). For instance, Feeding

America, a charitable organization, partners with more than 150 companies and organizations. All involved should gain enhanced status and credibility from so many alliances, but actually the links between so many partners are so extreme that they may be weakened. Thus, we postulate that the number of ally brands (i.e., alliance exclusivity) in branded entertainment content would influence how consumers respond to an unfamiliar focal brand by modulating the amount of associative information.

Presentation style is another executional factor that might influence consumer ability to process and integrate branded entertainment content. Massed presentation occurs when unfamiliar focal brands are simultaneously paired with familiar object brand(s). Indeed, simultaneous presentation of multiple cues in one scene tends to facilitate comparison, category acquisition, and generalization (Gentner et al. 2009; Oakes and Ribar 2005). In contrast, separately spaced presentations give viewers time to consolidate the concepts that were presented first and then make stronger connections with concepts presented after the interval (Bjork and Allen 1970; Dempster 1996). Therefore, a time interval between the presentation of a focal brand and one or more object brands might enhance or inhibit consumer ability to transfer meanings from one brand to another. We suggest that massing and spacing presentation styles are boundary conditions that determine the effectiveness of alliance exclusivity in branded entertainment content. In particular, we expect that massing presentation would increase the effectiveness of brand alliance with a single object brand as it enhances category generalization and association processes so that consumers can better associate two brands. In contrast, we expect spacing to allow a more successful meaning transfer by giving consumers time to connect cues between multiple associations.

Furthermore, we examine brand credibility as a mediator underlying the interactive effect. Signaling theory explains that successful brand alliances can make consumers perceive that unknown brands are similar to well-reputed brands in having quality and credibility (Gammoh et al. 2006). To extend the discussion of signaling theory in the context of cross-category brand alliance, we examine how the match between brand alliance exclusivity and presentation style can heighten the credibility of an unfamiliar brand and ultimately yield more favorable brand evaluations (Baek, Kim and Yu 2010).

Literature review and hypotheses

Co-created branded entertainment content as a form of LMC

LMC strategies include celebrity endorsements (Kang and Herr 2006; Rice, Kelting and Lutz 2012), sponsorships (Gwinner and Eaton 1999), product placements (Brennan, Dubas and Babin 1999), cause-related marketing (Lafferty and Goldsmith 2005), and co-branding (Simonin and Ruth 1998; Smarandescu et al. 2013). Branded entertainment is known to build strong consumer–brand relationships and to increase ROI (Riess 2018) by incorporating products or brand messages into audience-pleasing blogs, video clips, infographics, and news articles (e.g., Chen and Lee 2014; Hudson and Hudson 2006). Branded entertainment gives marketers more control over production and distribution of advertising content that blurs the line between entertainment and marketing communication (Boerman, Van Reijmersdal, and Neijens 2014; Choi et al. 2018; IAB 2018). Consequently, branded entertainment has become a promising venue for brand partnerships (Riess 2018; Lundqvist et al. 2013).

The direct affect transfer model explains that consumers tend to directly transfer emotional states evoked from stimuli in evaluating a subsequent situation or object (Allen and Madden, 1985). Branded entertainment differs from LMC strategies such as co-branding or co-production (Mitchell 2014) in that both partnering brands are placed into the entertainment content and both benefit in that consumers can easily associate their positive emotions with brand evaluations. Consequently, the partnering of two brands potentially maximizes direct affect transfer. Furthermore, brand alliances through branded entertainment could have a more expansive reach because people tend to share positive emotional experiences (Phelps et al. 2004; Walsh, Gwinner, and Swanson 2004). An example of using branded entertainment to powerfully amplify LMC effects is the previously mentioned exclusive content partnership between Red Bull and Go Pro for producing highly popular cutting-edge videos about extreme sports such as mountain biking, water skiing, and skydiving (Griner 2014).

Branded entertainment partnerships are rapidly increasing, but scholarly focus has been limited to how situational factors such as brand prominence, placement, and sponsorship disclosure relate to persuasion, knowledge, referral decisions, and content enjoyment (Boerman, Van Reijmersdal, and Neijens 2012; Choi et al. 2018; Matthes and Naderer 2016). Among diverse possibilities for investigating how brand alliances in the context of branded entertainment affect evaluations of focal brands, we focused on how alliance exclusivity and presentation style, two executional factors, affect consumer evaluations of an unfamiliar focal brand.

Signaling theory and brand alliance

Signaling theory is often used to show how new brands signal product quality by leveraging the positive reputations of respected brands through exclusive alliances, rather than forming alliances with other new or unfamiliar brands (Gammoh et al. 2006; Ruekert and Rao 1994; Rao et al. 1999). Companies know more than consumers know about the inherent quality of products or brands; instead, customers have asymmetric information and uncertainty about product quality (Baek and King 2011; Spence 1973).

To decrease consumer uncertainty, sellers often use signals that transmit credible information "about unobservable product quality" (Rao et al. 1999, 259) through marketing elements such as advertising, prices, and warranties. Some companies have well-established credibility reputations associated with their brand names (Erdem, Swait and Valenzuela 2006). Consequently, unknown brands often try to signal credibility by forming alliances with reputable brands (Gammoh et al. 2006; Ruekert and Rao 1994; Washburn, Till and Priluck 2004). The theoretical explanation aligns with the meaning transfer model, which states that cultural meanings are transferred from brand to brand, from brand to celebrity, and from brand to consumer (McCracken 1989).

Applying signaling theory, scholars have shown that LMC strategies tend to improve brand evaluation (Batra and Homer 2004; Gwinner and Eaton 1999; Lafferty and Goldsmith 2005; Simonin and Ruth 1998). Relatively new or unfamiliar brands particularly need to reduce consumer uncertainty and establish strong brand equity or images by partnering with brands that have already established positive associations or values (Aaker and Keller 1990; Boush and Loken 1991; Broniarczyk and Alba 1994). Indeed, studies have shown that unknown brands can enhance their credibility by pairing with well-known, reputable brands (Fang and Mishra 2002) and that brands with a high degree of product fit can co-brand and improve consumer evaluations of both brands (Simonin and Ruth 1998).

However, situational factors may affect whether brand alliances send positive signals (Campbell and Warren 2012; Farquhar 1994; Janiszewski and van Osselaer 2000). For instance, brand order in brand partnerships could signal the relative power of partnering brands and determine whether the object brand has strong signaling power. That is, co-branding efforts are likely to send stronger signals by placing the well-established brand first (Li and He 2013). Also, if a focal brand partners with an object brand that evokes both positive and negative associations, the focal brand could suffer from spillover negative signals as negative signals are more easily transferred (Campbell and Warren 2012). Such findings call for in-depth research investigating contextual factors that could amplify signaling effects in brand alliances. In particular, we expect that signal effectiveness may depend on whether the focal brand partners with one or multiple partner brands, and on how they present the brand alliances.

Alliance exclusivity: Effects of alliances with single versus multiple brands

Single or multiple partnerships may have varying effects on brand evaluations (Kang and Herr 2006; Kirmani and Shiv 1998; Rice et al. 2012). In highly exclusive partnerships, the focal brand associates with the unique attributes of only one object brand. In less exclusive brand alliances, the focal brand is associated with valued attributes of multiple object brands (Rodrigue and Biswas 2004). In general, alliances with one or only a few brands have been shown to evoke stable and consistent images (Tripp, Jensen and Carlson 1994), while alliances with many partners are more likely to evoke inconsistent associations, unclear positioning, and uncertainty (Keller 1993; Simmons and Becker-Olsen 2006). Thus, brands that have few rather than many LMC partners might gain fewer but stronger associations.

In low involvement situations, however, consumers tend to be "cognitive misers" (Burnkrant 1976). Indeed, for low involvement situation, study participants formed more favorable brand attitudes and stronger purchase intentions in response to an ad featuring multiple rather than single celebrity endorsers (Rice et al. 2012; Saleem 2007). For high involvement situation, however, single and multiple celebrity endorsers evoked equally favorable brand attitudes and purchase intentions. Thus, numerous brand associations might provide heuristic cues for forming brand attitudes in low involvement conditions (Rice et al. 2012).

Furthermore, multiple brand alliances were shown to be better than no alliances for evoking favorable brand evaluations, but single and multiple alliances were shown to have equal effects (Voss and Gammoh 2004). Thus, findings are mixed regarding whether single or multiple partner brand alliances are superior. We propose that alliance presentation style is a contextual moderator that may determine the effects of focal and object brand partnerships.

Presentation style: Spacing versus massing as moderator

Conventional wisdom holds that partnerships between unknown brands and well-known brands will positively impact the former because, having yet to establish a strong image, they are blank slates ready to benefit from an association with a well-established brand (Aaker and Keller 1990; Broniarczyk and Alba 1994; Levin and Levin 2000). Two lines of research suggest that the presentation of different concepts can influence one's ability to integrate them.

In simultaneous presentation, or massing, multiple cues or objects are presented at once; in spacing, cues or objects are presented separately across time intervals (Gentner et al. 2009; Oakes and Ribar 2005). A considerable number of findings provide support for the massing effect. Massing enables viewers to compare, categorize, and generalize (Gentner et al. 2009; Oakes and Ribar 2005) while spacing may prevent them from retaining and integrating information cues because succeeding cues disperse their recall (Gagné 1950). Supporting this view, previous findings show that when consumers observed co-appearing brands, they made associational transfers without in-depth deliberation (Dimofte and Yalch 2011; Galli and Gorn 2011; Perkins and Forehand 2012).

However, spacing has also been shown to have robust effects (Cepeda et al. 2006). Consumers tend to learn better and have longer recall when time or space separate their exposure to information (Dempster 1996; Glenberg 1979). Spaced presentation gives time to form an abstract mental representations regarding unified, central features rather than the surface characteristics of individual concepts (Vlach, Sandhofer and Kornell 2008). In other words, spacing provides more time to consolidate given information, strengthening the integration of concepts (Bjork and Allen 1970).

In branded entertainment contexts, consumers may be able to make easier associations when unfamiliar focal brands are allied with well-known, single object brands (Aaker and Keller 1990; Boush and Loken 1991). When the two brand allies are simultaneously massed rather than spaced, consumers may create stronger associations through stronger meaning transfer. That is, consumers can easily create vivid and strong links between both brands that are presented adjacently (Gentner et al. 2009; Oakes and Ribar 2005). Thus, for single-brand alliances, we propose that massing rather than spacing presentation causes more successful affect transfer and more favorable focal brand evaluation.

In contrast, consumers may form more favorable evaluations of focal brands allied with multiple object brands if the presentation is spaced. Although multiple sponsoring or endorsing object brands may positively affect focal brand evaluations in low involvement situations (Rice et al. 2012; Saleem 2007), we must consider the possibility of cue competition, or competitive interference (Cunha, Forehand, and Angle 2015; Kumar 2000; Kumar and Krishnan 2004), occurring when consumers are exposed to too much information, overly complicated information, or information from similar object categories, which hinders information processing and the ability to recall additional, related information (Burke and Srull 1988; Kelting and Rice 2013; Kent and Allen 1994; Kumar 2000; Kumar and Krishnan 2004). For example, when multiple products of an unfamiliar focal brand and a well-known partner brand were presented simultaneously, the cue competition effect occurred and damaged evaluation of the unfamiliar brand; but when a time interval separated the two sets of information, the co-branding improved subsequent evaluation (Cunha, Forehand, and Angle 2015). Similarly, we expect that when a focal brand and multiple object brands are presented simultaneously, cue competition would nullify the leveraging effect, but spacing should allow consumers to process multiple object brands as a unitary representation and process the focal brand as a separate entity, leaving two sets of information to be paired (Vlach et al. 2008).

We suggest that massing versus spacing presentation styles determine whether alliance exclusivity is effective in branded entertainment. A meta-analysis suggested that learning a simple task is easiest when information is massed or presented at very brief time intervals, while learning a complex task is easiest when information is introduced over long intervals (Donovan and Radosevich 1999). That rationale motivated our predictions that brand alliance is more effective when an unfamiliar focal brand is massed with a single object brand or spaced with multiple object brands.

Taken together, we expect that massed or spaced presentation moderates the effect of alliance exclusivity on leveraged brand evaluations, and hypothesize:

H1: In single brand alliances, massed presentation will allow the focal brand to acquire more favorable (a) attitudes and (b) credibility.

H2: In multiple brand alliances, spaced presentation will allow the focal brand to acquire more favorable (a) attitudes and (b) credibility.

Mechanism underlying the interaction

We also expected perceived credibility to mediate the interaction effect between alliance exclusivity and presentation styles on focal brand evaluations. Signaling theory (Gammoh et al. 2006; Rao et al. 1999) explains that when unfamiliar brands are allied with one or more reputable brands, the positive attributes and perceived value of reputable brands serve as a cue for inferring the quality of the unfamiliar brands. Consequently, unfamiliar brands and products can use their associations with well-established brands to gain credibility (Fang and Mishra 2002) and increase consumer certainty (Gammoh et al. 2006; Ruekert and Rao 1994).

Signaling theory suggests that a fundamental element of any brand signal is brand credibility indicating that brands are willing and able to meet their promises (Tirole 1988). Marketing communication strategies are designed to build cumulative brand credibility, reduce consumer uncertainty, and create salient brand associations (Baek and King 2011). Thus marketers use alliances to establish strong brand associations that will enhance brand credibility and lead to more favorable product evaluations (Hillyer and Tikoo 1995). Consistent with the signaling perspective (Spence 1973), brand credibility mediates the relationship between endorser credibility and consumer-based brand equity (Spry, Pappu and Cornwell 2011).

Brand alliance will have signaling value depending on how effectively consumers integrate cues and successfully associate the focal brand with the object brand (Geylani et al. 2008; Walchli 2007).When alliance exclusivity is matched with presentation style, the credibility of the object brand(s) should successfully transfer to the focal brand.

Perceptions of brand credibility should also increase perceptions regarding product quality and should decrease perceptions that an unknown brand is risky to purchase, use, or consume (Baek et al. 2010). Thus, brand credibility is likely to enhance brand evaluation (Baek et al. 2010; Erdem and Swait 1998).

We hypothesize that when brand alliance exclusivity is matched with presentation style, brand credibility is heightened, and the focal brand will have more favorable evaluations:

> **H3**: Alliance exclusivity will interact with presentation style to affect focal brand evaluation, mediated by perceived credibility of the focal brand (interaction → perceived credibility of the focal brand → attitude toward the focal brand).

Methods

We designed a lab experiment to examine the overall effect of a cross-category brand alliance in branded entertainment content and to investigate how alliance exclusivity and presentation style jointly interact to influence the effectiveness of the brand alliance strategy. We used a 2 (alliance exclusivity: alliance with a single brand vs. alliance with multiple brands) × 2 (presentation style: massing vs. spacing) between-subjects design.

Pretest

Before we conducted our main experiment, we conducted a series of pretests (1) to select a product category that would have a high level of perceived fit with milk, our focal product category; (2) to choose an unfamiliar focal milk brand; (3) to check the brand familiarity of the object brands that we would embed in the branded entertainment content

For the first pretest, we recruited 56 students (60.7% women; $M_{age} = 19.4$) enrolled in undergraduate courses at a large southeastern university to participate in exchange for extra course credit. The co-branding literature has shown that consumers tend to evaluate alliances more positively when they perceive that the allied brands fit together (Simonin and Ruth 1998). Thus, we controlled for a high level of perceived fit by using two brands from well-matched product categories. Based on GfK Mediamark and Research Intelligence, we chose milk, a product frequently purchased by consumers 18–24 years-old (index = 109). On a 7-point Likert-type scale (1 = strongly disagree, 7 = strongly agree), participants indicated perceived fit between "milk" and ten other product categories such as cereal, yogurt, and waffles. The results indicate that "milk-cereal" was the best product pair ($M_{product\_fit} = 5.67$).

Aligned with our objective to examine how brand partnership between a well-established object brand and an unfamiliar focal brand will leverage attitudes toward the unfamiliar brand, we conducted the second pretest to choose an unfamiliar milk brand for our focal brand and to choose several well-known cereals as object brands. We recruited 59 undergraduates (52.5% men; $M_{age} = 19.8$) who indicated their familiarity with five milk brands and twelve cereal brands (i.e., "I am familiar with [brand name]."). Based on the pretest, we chose our focal brand to be Kapiti, an unfamiliar foreign milk brand ($M_{familiarity} = 2.67$), and chose five well-known cereal brands to be our object brands: Kellogg's ($M_{familiarity} = 5.91$), Cheerios ($M_{familiarity} = 5.81$), General Mills ($M_{familiarity} = 5.60$), Post ($M_{familiarity} = 5.42$), and 365 Everyday Value ($M_{familiarity} = 4.47$). Since participants' attitudes or associations toward object brands can influence the meanings they transfer to focal brands (Campbell and Warren 2012), we measured participants' existing attitudes toward the each of the cereal brands to confirm participants have favorable attitudes toward the brands. Participants showed relatively favorable attitudes toward the five chosen cereal brands: Kellogg's ($M_{Ab} = 5.32$), Cheerios ($M_{Ab} = 5.34$), General Mills ($M_{Ab} = 5.20$), Post ($M_{Ab} = 4.86$), and 365 Everyday Value ($M_{Ab} = 4.46$).

Stimulus and manipulation

Based on the pretest results, we created four versions of branded entertainment content co-sponsored by the unfamiliar focal milk brand, Kapiti, and the familiar cereal brands. We designed the content to be entertaining and to elicit favorable emotions that might transfer to the focal brand. We chose a popular, general online magazine platform for the presentation (Dool 2018). Participants clicked through pages featuring images of nine types of cereal and to complete a quiz titled "Can You Identify Cereals Just by Looking at Them"? The final screen provided information for each cereal brand (Appendix).

We manipulated alliance exclusivity by presenting Kapiti, the focal brand, with either one or five cereal brands. The pretest indicated that Kellogg's scored highest on brand familiarity, so we used Kellogg's for the single alliance condition, and used all five cereal brands for the multiple brands alliance condition. Finally, we manipulated presentation style by including or excluding spacing between exposures to the focal and object brands. In the massing condition, we presented the focal brand simultaneously with the object brand(s) on the second page of the online magazine. In the spacing condition, we presented the focal brand on the first page and the object brand(s) on the second page (Cunha, Forehand, and Angle 2015). Participants could proceed to the second page 15 seconds after landing on the first page.

Participants and procedure

A total of 132 students (53% women; $M_{age} = 19.8$) enrolled in undergraduate courses at either a large southeastern university or a large northeastern university participated in exchange for extra course credit. We conducted the experiment in a controlled laboratory setting in individual 15-minute lab sessions in which participants were randomly assigned to one of the four conditions in a 2 (alliance exclusivity: alliance with a single brand vs. alliance with multiple brands) × 2 (presentation style: massing vs. spacing) between-subjects experimental design. We asked participants to imagine entertaining themselves by browsing an online magazine and then randomly showed them one of the four branded entertainment content stimuli. We asked them to browse the content as they would in real life before indicating their attitude toward the focal brand and their perceptions of its brand credibility.

Measures

Dependent measures included attitude toward the focal brand (A_b) and brand credibility. We measured A_b using four 7-point semantic-differential scale items: unfavorable/favorable, bad/good, negative/positive, and dislikable/likable (Lee and Aaker 2004). We averaged the four items to form an index for A_b ($\alpha = .95$, M = 4.09, SD = 1.26). We measured brand credibility using three 7-point Likert scale items adopted from Mackenzie and Lutz (1989) (1 = strongly disagree, 7 = strongly agree): "I found this brand credible/believable/convincing."($\alpha = .89$, M = 4.22, SD = .95).

Results

Tests of hypotheses

To test how alliance exclusivity and presentation style impacted the effect of brand alliance in the branded entertainment context, we performed a 2 (alliance exclusivity: alliance with a single brand vs. alliance with multiple brands) × 2 (presentation style: massing vs. spacing) MANOVA on A_b and perceived credibility of the focal brand. Following Hair et al. (1998), we checked the assumptions of MANOVA. First, Box's M test revealed that homogeneity of the variance and covariance matrices were met (Box's M = 9.35, p = .43). Second, Bartlett's test of sphericity revealed significant inter-correlation between the dependent variables (r = .61, p < 0.01). Thus, MANOVA assumptions were met.

As predicted, a significant two-way interaction effect on A_b (F (1, 128) = 15.13, p < .001) and perceived credibility (F (1, 128) = 11.84, p < .001) emerged (Wilks' λ =.89, F (1, 127) = 8.26 p < .001). However, alliance exclusivity (Wilks' λ =.98, F (1, 127) = 1.58, p =.21) and presentation style had nonsignificant main effects on combined DVs (Wilks' λ =.99, F (1, 127) = .53 p =.59) (Table 1).

To better understand the two-way interaction, we ran subsequent contrast tests. Figure 1 shows that when the focal brand was paired with a single object brand, participants showed more favorable A_b when the focal brand and object brand were presented simultaneously (i.e., massing) rather than spaced ($M_{massing}$ = 4.57 vs. $M_{spacing}$ = 3.78; t(64) = -3.38, p < .001). Similarly, participants perceived higher brand credibility when the focal brand and object brand were presented simultaneously rather than spaced ($M_{massing}$ = 4.44vs. $M_{spacing}$ = 3.86; t(64) = -2.51, p < .05). Thus, H1 was supported.

Table 1. MANOVA Results.

Source	Dependent Variable	df	Mean Square	F	Sig.
Corrected Model	Ab	3	4.84	5.37	.002
	Perceived Credibility	3	3.59	4.033	.01
Intercept	Ab	1	2248.50	2496.36	.001
	Perceived Credibility	1	2354.32	2836.86	.001
Presentation Style	Ab	1	.72	.80	.37
	Perceived Credibility	1	.03	.03	.86
Alliance Exclusivity	Ab	1	.28	.31	.58
	Perceived Credibility	1	.74	.90	.35
Interaction	Ab	1	13.63	15.13	.001
	Perceived Credibility	1	9.83	11.84	.001
Error	Ab	128	.90		
	Perceived Credibility	128	.83		
Total	Ab	132			
	Perceived Credibility	132			
Corrected Total	Ab	131			
	Perceived Credibility	131			

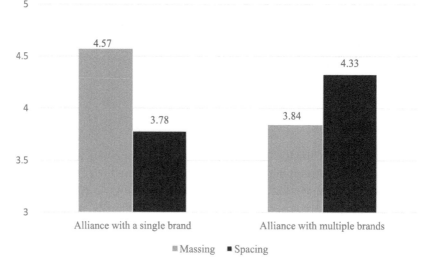

Figure 1. Attitude toward the Less-known Brand (7-point scale).

In contrast, when the focal brand was paired with multiple familiar object brands, participants showed more favorable A_b under spaced rather than simultaneous presentation ($M_{massing} = 3.84$ vs. $M_{spacing} = 4.33$; t(64) = 2.12, p < .05). The same pattern emerged for brand credibility ($M_{massing} = 4.04$ vs. $M_{spacing} = 4.56$; t(64) = 2.36, p < .05). Thus, H2 was also supported (Figure 2).

Mechanism underlying the interactive effect

To investigate how alliance exclusivity and presentation style influenced attitudes toward the focal brand, we used the PROCESS Macro with 5,000 bootstrap samples (Model 8, Hayes, 2013) to perform a moderated mediation analysis with perceived credibility as the mediator. Bootstrapping procedures generated a bias-corrected 95% confidence interval [CI] of the indirect effect.

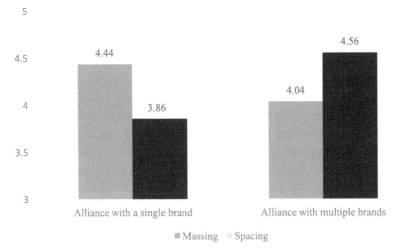

Figure 2. Brand Credibility of the Less-known Brand (7-point scale).

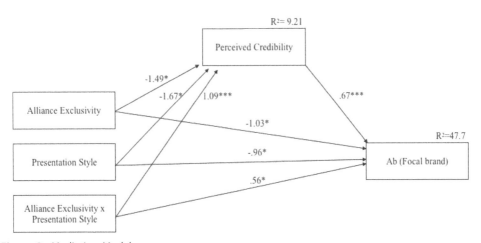

Figure 3. Mediation Model.

Figure 3 shows that mediation analyses indicated that the model explained 9.21% of the variance in the focal brand's perceived credibility. All three variables included as potential predictors yielded significant coefficients: alliance exclusivity (b = -1.49, t=-2.94, p < .05), presentation style (b = -1.67, t=-3.32, p < .05), and the interaction term (b = 1.09, t = 3.44, p < .001). Also, the model explained 47.7% of the variance in attitude toward the focal brand. A significant direct effect of alliance exclusivity (b = -1.03, t=-2.45, p < .05), presentation style (b = -.96, t=-2.30, p < .05), and the interaction term on A_b emerged (b = .56, t = 2.09, p < .05). Furthermore, perceived credibility positively influenced A_b (b = .67, t = 9.43, p < .001), confirming the significant indirect effect through perceived credibility to attitude toward the focal brand (95% CI from to .28 to 1.26). Following Baron and Kenny's procedures (Baron and Kenny 1986), as the independent variables had significant direct effects on attitude toward the focal brand, the result confirms that perceived credibility was a partial mediator, supporting H3.

Discussion

Theoretical and managerial implications

Brand partnership in the context of branded entertainment is a new and promising LMC strategy, but we lack understandings regarding boundary conditions that may boost or damage focal brand evaluations. Consequently, we conducted this study to examine whether the executional factors of alliance exclusivity and presentation style determine whether partnerships are successful in branded content. In particular, we show that when focal brands ally with single object brands, consumers can easily transfer their stored brand images or attitudes to the focal brand, without cue interference (Kelting and Rice 2013). Consequently, we suggest that massing strategies are more efficient for transferring meaning. However, in one-to-multiple brand partnerships, we confirm that spacing better counters cue competition (Burke and Srull 1988; Kent and Allen 1994). Similar to Cunha, Forehand, and Angle (2015), we show that when focal brands are presented simultaneously with multiple object brands, cue competition or overload can inhibit LMC. However, if focal brands and multiple object brands are presented separately, participants have time to generalize, form abstract associations, and more efficiently transfer the associations to the focal brand. Furthermore, brand credibility is a partial mediator in the interaction. The results are consistent with signaling theory in confirming that object brand credibility indeed signals the values or quality of focal brands by eliminating uncertainty about unfamiliar focal brands (Gammoh et al. 2006; Ruekert and Rao 1994).

Our findings show that even when the object brands were relatively well-established, merely increasing their number did not always increase positive meaning transfer to the focal brand. The elaboration likelihood model (ELM) explains that people can change their attitudes through central or peripheral cognitive routes. People who are highly involved, highly able, or highly motivated tend to use central, deliberative, cognitive processing routes. In contrast, people who lack motivation and ability tend to use peripheral routes involving the use of heuristic principles, such as simple cues present in the information (Petty and Cacioppo 1986). ELM indicates that consumers who have low involvement and low motivation will base their brand attitudes on peripheral cues, such as the number of object brands in a co-branding context (Rice et al. 2012). Indeed, an experiment showed that consumers who had low involvement were favorably impressed by the number of endorsing celebrities, but the experimenters used three different celebrities in three sequential ads rather than having all three celebrities in a single ad for the multiple endorsement condition (Rice et al. 2012). Thus the stimulus exemplified a spaced rather than a massed presentation. Although the study did not consider presentation style, the experimental procedure indicates that presentation style played a potential role. The findings strongly indicate that the mere co-appearance of focal and object brands in branded entertainment cannot guarantee a leveraging effect, even when product categories have a good fit. Instead, object-related executional factors (e.g., length, duration, format, and size of brand logo presentation) may be possible moderators of LMC effectiveness (Bergkvist and Taylor 2016).

Furthermore, we found that brand credibility partially mediated the interaction effect. Consistent with signaling theory, we confirm that brand credibility eliminates uncertainty by signaling that unfamiliar brands have value and quality (Gammoh et al. 2006; Ruekert and Rao 1994). Our findings invite further discussion about how brand alliance strategy impacts brand credibility, an important consumer-based brand equity that affects perceived benefits and purchase intentions (Baek et al. 2010). Thus we show that marketers should strive to build strong brand credibility.

Our findings make three contributions to the advertising and marketing literature. We examined the effect of a cross-category brand alliance in the context of branded entertainment, which has been overlooked in the previous studies. Extending previous findings on LMC, we confirm that brand alliance in branded entertainment content can favorably impact evaluations of focal brands. Second, although LMC studies have paid little attention to executional factors (Bergkvist and Taylor 2016), we filled the gap by examining the interactive effect of alliance exclusivity and presentation style. Furthermore, alliance research has generally used only one focal brand and one object brand (Ruekert and Rao 1994; Rao et al. 1999; Simonin and Ruth 1998), although alliances have involved multiple brands for a long time. Accordingly, we investigated how alliance exclusivity and presentation style, which are executional factors that marketers can easily control, shape the strength and direction of brand alliances.

Our findings have practical implications for marketers. Relatively unfamiliar brand(s) or start-up companies encounter difficulty in establishing their brands, especially in industries that have high market entry barriers. For marketers of new or relatively unfamiliar brand(s), however, our findings show that brand alliances with well-established brand(s) and co-branding strategies can be powerful in branded entertainment. Thus, marketers of new brand(s) should go beyond integration of actual products or brand extensions by investing in co-created branded entertainment. They must be careful, however, about placement when associating new brands with multiple established brand partners or multiple celebrities. Brief delays can change the impact of cues, from competition to facilitation (Cunha, Forehand, and Angle 2015). Thus, new brands might be placed at the beginning of the content, and the familiar partnering brand(s) or famous endorsers might be placed at the end to maximize leveraging effects. In contrast, if marketers are integrating an unfamiliar focal brand with a single established brand partner, they should present the two brands simultaneously, so that viewers develop stronger associations between the two. Marketers can directly control branded entertainment content, so they might maximize the efficiency of brand alliance by controlling presentation style. Although we conducted our study in the online magazine context, marketers could effectively use the presentation style guidelines for designing online video content as well.

Previous researchers have primarily examined the effect of co-branding on overall *attitudes* toward focal or object brand(s) (Lafferty 2009; Simonin and Ruth 1998). However, we delved into a cognitive mechanism underlying effects of co-branding, which has been overlooked in prior studies, by investigating the mediating role of brand credibility. Brands establish credibility by presenting clear brand information in a mix of marketing strategies over time and by fulfilling the promises they made to consumers (Erdem and Swait 1998), but marketers of relatively new brands struggle to establish brand equity. We suggest that brand partnerships in branded entertainment are a powerful way to enhance credibility and subsequently build reputable brands.

Limitations and future research

Although our study has significant theoretical and practical implications, it also has several limitations that future research could address. First, we focused on the interaction between alliance exclusivity and presentation style for enhanced evaluations of an unfamiliar focal brand, but brand alliances might actually undermine the value of well-known brands (Janiszewski and van Osselaer 2000; Simonin and Ruth 1998). Thus, future research should examine how LMC strategies might boost or damage reputations of well-established object brands. Second, our experiment measured brand familiarity and brand attitudes regarding the well-established object brand(s), but we did not measure other brand perceptions or associations. However, negative associations with familiar brands could damage leveraging effects (Campbell and Warren 2012). Thus, future research should measure and control for more diverse dimensions of object brands, such as brand image(s), reputation, attractiveness, and credibility. Third, in the spaced presentation condition, we presented the focal brand first and the object brand(s) later. Although research has paid scant attention to the effect of brand order in brand alliances, previous findings on the co-branding suggested that brand order could indicate relative powers among brands and subsequently moderate evaluations of partnering or ally brands (Li and He 2013). Thus, future research should examine how presentation order affects brand alliances in branded entertainment. Finally, our study aligns with most studies about cross-category brand alliances in focusing on brand alliances between unfamiliar and well-established brands (Cunha, Forehand, and Angle 2015), but scholars should investigate the effect of brand alliances between two or more well-established brands to possibly replicate our results.

Funding

This work was supported by the National Research Foundation of Korea Grant funded by the Korean Government (NRF-2017S1A2A2041723).

ORCID

Tae Hyun Baek ⓘ http://orcid.org/0000-0003-2000-698X

References

Aaker, D.A., and K.L. Keller. 1990. Consumer evaluations of Brand extensions. *Journal of Marketing* 54, no. 1: 27–41.

Grimm, J. 2017. The 10 best branded content partnerships of 2017. *Adage*, https://adage.com/article/agency-viewpoint/10-branded-content-partnerships-2017/311725/

Riess, D. 2018. New study reveals the emotional impact of branded content increase ROI. *Adage*, https://adage.com/article/turner-ignite/biometric-research-proves-purchase-power-branded-content-ad-age-turner-ignite/315635/

Griner, D. 2014. GoPro's super bowl ad looks a lot like red bull, Circa 2012. *AdWeek*, https://www.adweek.com/creativity/gopros-super-bowl-ad-looks-lot-red-bull-circa-2012-155386/

Allen, C.T., and T.J. Madden. 1985. A closer look at classical conditioning. *Journal of Consumer Research* 12, no. 3: 301–15.

Baek, T.H., J. Kim, and J.H. Yu. 2010. The differential roles of Brand credibility and Brand prestige in consumer Brand choice. *Psychology & Marketing* 27, no. 7: 662–78.

Baek, T.H., and K.W. King. 2011. Exploring the consequences of Brand credibility in services. *Journal of Services Marketing* 25, no. 4: 260–72.

Baron, R.M., and D.A. Kenny. 1986. The moderator–mediator variable distinction in social psycho-logical research: Conceptual, strategic, and statistical considerations. *Journal of Personality and Social Psychology* 51, no. 6: 1173–82.

Batra, R., and P.M. Homer. 2004. The situational impact of Brand image beliefs. *Journal of Consumer Psychology* 14, no. 3: 318–30.

Bergkvist, L., and, and C.R. Taylor. 2016. Leveraged marketing communications: a framework for explaining the effects of secondary Brand associations. *AMS Review* 6, no. 3–4: 157–75.

Bernazzani, S. 2018. 13 examples of successful co-branding partnerships. *HubSpot*, https://blog. hubspot.com/marketing/best-cobranding-partnerships.

Bjork, R.A., and T.W. Allen. 1970. The spacing effect: Consolidation or differential encoding? *Journal of Verbal Learning and Verbal Behavior* 9, no. 5: 567–72.

Bluemelhuber, C., L.L. Carter, and C.J. Lambe. 2007. Extending the view of Brand alliance effects. *International Marketing Review* 24, no. 4: 427–43. no.

Boerman, S.C., E.A. Van Reijmersdal, and P.C. Neijens. 2012. Sponsorship disclosure: Effects of duration on persuasion knowledge and Brand responses. *Journal of Communication* 62, no. 6: 1047–64.

Boerman, S.C., E.A. Van Reijmersdal, and P.C. Neijens. 2014. Effects of sponsorship disclosure tim-ing on the processing of sponsored content: a study on the effectiveness of European disclos-ure regulations. *Psychology & Marketing* 31, no. 3: 214–24.

Boush, D.M., and B. Loken. 1991. A process-tracing study of Brand extension evaluation. *Journal of Marketing Research* 28, no. 1: 16–28.

Brennan, I., K.M. Dubas, and L.A. Babin. 1999. The influence of product-placement type & expos-ure time on product-placement recognition. *International Journal of Advertising* 18, no. 3: 323–37.

Broniarczyk, S.M., and J.W. Alba. 1994. The importance of the Brand in Brand extension. *Journal of Marketing Research* 31, no. 2: 214–28.

Burke, R.R., and T.K. Srull. 1988. Competitive interference and consumer memory for advertising. *Journal of Consumer Research* 15, no. 1: 55–68.

Burnkrant, R.E. 1976. A motivational model of information processing intensity. *Journal of Consumer Research* 3, no. 1: 21–30.

Campbell, M.C., and C. Warren. 2012. A risk of meaning transfer: Are negative associations more likely to transfer than positive associations? *Social Influence* 7, no. 3: 172–92.

Cepeda, N.J., H. Pashler, E. Vul, J.T. Wixted, and D. Rohrer. 2006. Distributed practice in verbal recall tasks: a review and quantitative synthesis. *Psychological Bulletin* 132, no. 3: 354–80.

Chen, T., and H. Lee. 2014. Why do we share? the impact of viral videos dramatized to sell: How microfilm advertising works. *Journal of Advertising Research* 54, no. 3: 292–303.

Choi, D., H. Bang, B.W. Wojdynski, Y. Lee, and K.M. Keib. 2018. How Brand disclosure timing and Brand prominence influence consumer's intention to share branded entertainment content. *Journal of Interactive Marketing* 42: 18–31.

Cunha, M., M.R. Forehand Jr, and J.W. Angle. 2015. Riding coattails: When co-branding helps ver-sus hurts less-known brands. *Journal of Consumer Research* 41, no. 5: 1284–300.

Dacin, P.A., and D.C. Smith. 1994. The effect of Brand portfolio characteristics on consumer eval-uations of Brand extensions. *Journal of Marketing Research* 31, no. 2: 229–42.

Dempster, F.N. 1996. Distributing and managing the conditions of encoding and practice. In *Memory*. 317–344. Boston: Academic Press.

Dimofte, C.V., and R.F. Yalch. 2011. The mere association effect and Brand evaluations. *Journal of Consumer Psychology* 21, no. 1: 24–37.

Donovan, J.J., and D.J. Radosevich. 1999. A Meta-analytic review of the distribution of practice effect: Now you see it, now you don't. *Journal of Applied Psychology* 84, no. 5: 795–805.

Erdem, T., and J. Swait. 1998. Brand equity as a signaling phenomenon. *Journal of Consumer Psychology* 7, no. 2: 131–57.

Erdem, T., J. Swait, and A. Valenzuela. 2006. Brands as signals: a cross-country validation study. *Journal of Marketing* 70, no. 1: 34–49.

Farquhar, P.H. 1994. Strategic challenges for branding. *Marketing Management* 3, no. 2: 8–15.

Fang, X., and S. Mishra. 2002. The effect of Brand alliance portfolio on the perceived quality of an unknown Brand. *Advances in Consumer Research* 29: 519–20.

Dool, G. 2018. As branded content moves to the forefront, trust and accountability remain key. *Folio*. https://www.foliomag.com/hearstus-weekly-branded-content/

Gagné, R.M. 1950. The effect of sequence of presentation of similar items on the learning of paired associates. *Journal of Experimental Psychology* 40, no. 1: 61–73.

Galli, M., and G. Gorn. 2011. Unconscious transfer of meaning to brands. *Journal of Consumer Psychology* 21, no. 3: 215–25.

Gammoh, B.S., K.E. Voss, and G. Chakraborty. 2006. Consumer evaluation of Brand alliance signals. *Psychology and Marketing* 23, no. 6: 465–86.

Gammoh, B.S., K.E. Voss, and X. Fang. 2010. Multiple Brand alliances: a portfolio diversification perspective. *Journal of Product & Brand Management* 19, no. 1: 27–33.

Gentner, D., J. Loewenstein, L. Thompson, and K.D. Forbus. 2009. Reviving inert knowledge: Analogical abstraction supports relational retrieval of past events. *Cognitive Science* 33, no. 8: 1343–82.

Glenberg, A.M. 1979. Component-levels theory of the effects of spacing of repetitions on recall and recognition. *Memory & Cognition* 7, no. 2: 95–112.

Geylani, T., J.J. Inman, and F.T. Hofstede. 2008. Image reinforcement or impairment: the effects of co-branding on attribute uncertainty. *Marketing Science* 27, no. 4: 730–44.

Gwinner, K.P., and J. Eaton. 1999. Building Brand image through event sponsorship: the role of image transfer. *Journal of Advertising* 28, no. 4: 47–57.

Haberman, R. 2018. Branded entertainment growing branded entertainment growing twice as fast as advertising spend, study finds. *Skyword*. https://www.skyword.com/contentstandard/creativity/branded-entertainment-growing-twice-as-fast-as-advertising-spend-study-finds/

Hair, J. F., W. C. Black, B. J. Babin, and R. E. Anderson. 1998. *Multivariate data analysis*. London: Pearson.

Harlam, B.A., A. Krishna, D.R. Lehmann, and C. Mela. 1995. Impact of bundle type, price framing and familiarity on purchase intention for the bundle. *Journal of Business Research* 33, no. 1: 57–66.

Hayes, A.F. 2013. *Introduction to mediation, moderation, and conditional process analysis: A regression-based approach*. New York: Guilford Press.

Hillyer, C., and S. Tikoo. 1995. Effect of cobranding on consumer product evaluaitons. *Advances in Consumer Research* 22, no. 1: 123–7.

Hudson, S., and D. Hudson. 2006. Branded entertainment: a new advertising technique or product placement in disguise? *Journal of Marketing Management* 22, no. 5–6: 489–504. no.

IAB. 2018. Branded Content Creation & Distribution Guide Steps for Success. https://www.iab.com/wp-content/uploads/2018/04/IAB_Branded_Content_Creation_and_Distribution_Guide_2018-04_FINAL.pdf

Janiszewski, C., and S.M. Van Osselaer. 2000. A connectionist model of Brand–quality associations. *Journal of Marketing Research* 37, no. 3: 331–50.

Kang, Y., and P.M. Herr. 2006. Beauty and the beholder: toward an integrative model of communication source effects. *Journal of Consumer Research* 33, no. 1: 123–30.

Keller, K.L. 1993. Conceptualizing, measuring, and managing customer-based Brand equity. *Journal of Marketing* 57, no. 1: 1–22.

Kelting, K., and D.H. Rice. 2013. Should we hire David Beckham to endorse our Brand? Contextual interference and consumer memory for brands in a celebrity's endorsement portfolio. *Psychology & Marketing* 30, no. 7: 602–13.

Kent, R.J., and C.T. Allen. 1994. Competitive interference effects in consumer memory for advertising: the role of Brand familiarity. *Journal of Marketing* 58, no. 3: 97–105.

Kirmani, A., and B. Shiv. 1998. Effects of source congruity on Brand attitudes and beliefs: the moderating role of issue-relevant elaboration. *Journal of Consumer Psychology* 7, no. 1: 25–47.

Kumar, A. 2000. Interference effects of contextual cues in advertisements on memory for ad content. *Journal of Consumer Psychology* 9, no. 3: 155–66.

Kumar, A., and S. Krishnan. 2004. Memory interference in advertising: a replication and extension. *Journal of Consumer Research* 30, no.4: 602–11.

Lafferty, B.A. 2009. Selecting the right cause partners for the right reasons: the role of importance and fit in cause-Brand alliances. *Psychology and Marketing* 26, no. 4: 359–82.

Lafferty, B.A., and R.E. Goldsmith. 2005. Cause–Brand alliances: does the cause help the Brand or does the Brand help the cause? *Journal of Business Research* 58, no. 4: 423–9. no.

Lee, A.Y., and J.L. Aaker. 2004. Bringing the frame into focus: the influence of regulatory fit on processing fluency and persuasion. *Journal of Personality and Social Psychology* 86, no. 2: 205–18.

Levin, I.P., and A.M. Levin. 2000. Modeling the role of Brand alliances in the assimilation of product evaluations. *Journal of Consumer Psychology* 9, no. 1: 43–52.

Li, Y., and H. He. 2013. Evaluation of international Brand alliances: Brand order and consumer ethnocentrism. *Journal of Business Research* 66, no. 1: 89–97.

Lundqvist, A., V. Liljander, J. Gummerus, and A.V. Riel. 2013. The impact of storytelling on the consumer Brand experience: the case of a firm-originated story. *Journal of Brand Management* 20, no. 4: 283–97.

MacKenzie, S.B., and R.J. Lutz. 1989. An empirical examination of the structural antecedents of attitude toward the ad in an advertising pretesting context. *Journal of Marketing* 53, no. 2: 48–65.

Matthes, J., and B. Naderer. 2016. Product placement disclosures: Exploring the moderating effect of placement frequency on Brand responses via persuasion knowledge. *International Journal of Advertising* 35, no. 2: 185–99.

McCracken, G. 1989. Who is the celebrity endorser? cultural foundations of the endorsement process. *Journal of Consumer Research* 16, no. 3: 310–21.

Mitchell, T. 2014. Branded entertainment in emotional scenes: excitation transfer or direct affect transfer? PhD diss., University of Illinois at Urbana-Champaign.

Oakes, L.M., and R.J. Ribar. 2005. A comparison of infants' categorization in paired and successive presentation familiarization tasks. *Infancy* 7, no. 1: 85–98.

Olson, E.L. 2010. Does sponsorship work in the same way in different sponsorship contexts? *European Journal of Marketing* 44, no.1/2: 180–99.

Perkins, A.W., and M.R. Forehand. 2012. Implicit self-referencing: the effect of nonvolitional self-association on Brand and product attitude. *Journal of Consumer Research* 39, no. 1: 142–56.

Petty, R.E., and J.T. Cacioppo. 1986. The elaboration likelihood model of persuasion. In *Communication and persuasion*, 1–24. New York: Springer.

Phelps, J.E., R. Lewis, L. Mobilio, D. Perry, and N. Raman. 2004. Viral marketing or electronic word-of-mouth advertising: Examining consumer responses and motivations to pass along email. *Journal of Advertising Research* 44, no. 4: 333–48.

Ruekert, R.W., and A. Rao. 1994. Brand alliances as signals of product quality. *Sloan Management Review* 36, no. 1: 87–97.

Rao, A.R., L. Qu, and R.W. Ruekert. 1999. Signaling unobservable product quality through a Brand ally. *Journal of Marketing Research* 36, no. 2: 258–68.

Rice, D.H., K. Kelting, and R.J. Lutz. 2012. Multiple endorsers and multiple endorsements: the influence of message repetition, source congruence and involvement on Brand attitudes. *Journal of Consumer Psychology* 22, no. 2: 249–59.

Rodrigue, C.S., and A. Biswas. 2004. Brand alliance dependency and exclusivity: an empirical investigation. *Journal of Product & Brand Management* 13, no. 7: 477–87.

Saleem, F. 2007. Effect of single celebrity and multiple celebrity endorsement on low involvement and high involvement product advertisements. *European Journal of Social Sciences* 5, no. 3: 125–32.

Simmons, C.J., and K.L. Becker-Olsen. 2006. Achieving marketing objectives through social sponsorships. *Journal of Marketing* 70, no. 4: 154–69.

Simonin, B.L., and J.A. Ruth. 1998. Is a company known by the company it keeps? assessing the spillover effects of Brand alliances on consumer Brand attitudes. *Journal of Marketing Research* 35, no. 1: 30–42.

Smarandescu, L., R. Rose, and D.H. Wedell. 2013. Priming a cross-category Brand alliance: the moderating role of attribute knowledge and need for cognition. *Psychology & Marketing* 30, no. 2: 133–47.

Spence, M. 1973. Job market signaling. *The Quarterly Journal of Economics* 87, no. 3: 355–74.

Spry, A., R. Pappu, and T.B. Cornwell. 2011. Celebrity endorsement, Brand credibility and Brand equity. *European Journal of Marketing* 45, no. 6: 882–909.

Washburn, J.H., B.D. Till, and R. Priluck. 2004. Brand alliance and customer-based Brand-equity effects. *Psychology and Marketing* 21, no. 7: 487–508.

Tirole, J. 1988. *The theory of industrial organization*. Cambridge: MIT press.

Tripp, C., T.D. Jensen, and L. Carlson. 1994. The effects of multiple product endorsements by celebrities on consumers' attitudes and intentions. *Journal of Consumer Research* 20, no. 4: 535–47.

Varadarajan, P.R., and A. Menon. 1988. Cause-related marketing: a coalignment of marketing strategy and corporate philanthropy. *Journal of Marketing* 52, no. 3: 58–74.

Vlach, H.A., C.M. Sandhofer, and N. Kornell. 2008. The spacing effect in children's memory and category induction. *Cognition* 109, no. 1: 163–7.

Voss, K.E., and B.S. Gammoh. 2004. Building brands through Brand alliances: does a second ally help? *Marketing Letters* 15, no. 2/3: 147–59. no.

Walchli, S.B. 2007. The effects of between-partner congruity on consumer evaluation of co-branded products. *Psychology & Marketing* 24, no. 11: 947–73.

Walsh, G., K.P. Gwinner, and S.R. Swanson. 2004. What makes mavens tick? exploring the motives of market mavens' initiation of information diffusion. *Journal of Consumer Marketing* 21, no. 2: 109–22.

Weisberg, R.W., and L.M. Reeves. 2013. *Cognition: from memory to creativity*. Hoboken: John Wiley & Sons.

Appendix

Sample Stimuli (Single Object Brand & Massed Presentation Condition)
(Page 1)   (Page 2)

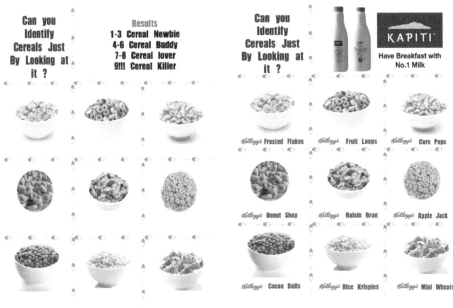

Sample Stimuli (Multi Object Brands & Spaced Presentation Condition)
(Page 1)   (Page 2)

The effects of sensory fit on consumer evaluations of co-branding

Jungyong Ahn, Ahyeon Kim and Yongjun Sung

ABSTRACT

While previous co-branding research sheds light on the effects of perceived fit between partner brands, the findings have been limited to only two types of perceived fit: product category and brand image fit. This research suggests the importance of sensory fit and examines how it affects evaluations of co-branding. Three experiments were conducted to reveal the effects of sensory fit on consumer evaluations of co-branding. The findings demonstrate that sensory fit significantly influences the evaluation of co-branding (Experiments 1, 2, and 3). In addition, it shows stronger effects when the co-branded product is a low- (vs. high-) involvement product (Experiment 2). Further, the findings suggest that the sensory fit effect is stronger for high-involvement and hedonic products (Experiment 3). These findings provide additional empirical evidence for the theoretical explanations of the fit effect in the branding literature and managerial insights into the design of effective collaboration between brands.

Introduction

H&M, a mid-priced global SPA fashion brand that offers affordable fashion items, has launched an annual collaboration with prestigious fashion brands such as Versace, Moschino, Alexander Wang, and Balmain. Since 2004, H&M's co-branding partnerships have attracted not only H&M loyalists but also huge queues of fashion fans who are eager to purchase items of high-end designer clothing for relatively affordable prices. Consumers camp outside H&M stores overnight to purchase the limited edition of such co-branded items. As a result, H&M can marginally increase overall sales and attract significant media attention. More importantly, H&M can be associated with high-end prestigious luxury brands, thereby enabling it to build a sophisticated brand image and personality, which is quite important for fashion brands.

This collaboration is just one of many successful co-branding partnerships. Co-branding is not limited to the same product/service categories. In fact, brands across a variety of industries have collaborated with artists, musicians, cartoon characters, and commercial brands. However, co-branding does not always guarantee success.

Findings of previous research show that for successful co-branding, perceived fit between brands should be considered (Bluemelhuber, Carter, and Lambe 2007; Keller 1993; Lanseng and Olsen 2012; Leuthesser, Kohli, and Suri 2003; Mazodier and Merunka 2014; Walchli 2007). For example, Lanseng and Olsen (2012) found that consumers show more positive attitudes in the high product category fit condition (e.g. battery brand: Energizer × electronic brand: Philips) than in the low fit condition (e.g. battery brand: Energizer × toothpaste brand: Clinomyn). In addition, the prestigious beer brand Corona received better evaluation when partnered with Gucci, a prestigious fashion brand, than with a popular coffee brand, illy (Lanseng and Olsen 2012).

Although the literature provides plenty of explanations of the effect of perceived fit in the context of co-branding, it is yet to be fully understood as it has focused mainly on two types of perceived fit: product category and brand image fit. In this present study, we suggest that another type of perceived fit between brands (so-called sensory fit) should be further explored. Sensory fit can be defined as a congruency of sensory attributes of brands such as colour, shape, size, and font style between partner brands. Not only product category or brand image, but sensory attributes too affect consumers' perception of the brand (Lefkoff-Hagius and Mason 1993). Sensory attributes of brands is a very important factor in determining the first impression of any brand (Tversky and Kahneman 1974) as consumers infer the characteristics of the brand via its name (Buttle and Westoby 2006), colour (Singh 2006), and shape of logo (Henderson and Cote 1998) in the absence of any other information about product quality, reputation, and more. Thus, if two partner brands share the same sensory attributes, consumers might feel the two brands have something in common, thereby perceiving a high fit between the brands just as the other two types of fit (i.e. category and brand image fits) did.

Nevertheless, the effect of sensory fit in the context of co-branding is yet to be fully investigated by academic research. To fill this gap in the literature, the present research investigated the effects of sensory fit in determining co-branding effectiveness. Moreover, this research tested the interplays between product involvement and the sensory fit. Three experiments empirically examined this tenet. More specifically, Experiment 1 investigated the sensory fit effect by employing colour as a sensory attribute of brands. In Experiment 2, the same postulation was further investigated but with another type of sensory fit (i.e. phonetic attribute). In addition, the product involvement was examined as a potential moderating variable. Finally, Experiment 3 further replicated the findings of previous experiments across two different product types (i.e. hedonic vs. utilitarian).

Two factors illustrate the contribution that this study makes to marketing and consumer psychology literature. First, drawing upon the recent advances in the theoretical development and empirical evidence of the effect of perceived fit on co-branding, the present research extends and deepens our understanding of another form of perceived fit (sensory fit) and adds to our understanding of the interplay between sensory fit and product involvement in co-branding persuasion. In addition, sensory fit in the context of co-branding is of critical importance and relevance to marketing researchers and practitioners. Brands' sensory attributes such as colour, shape, size, and font style influence consumers' perceptions, beliefs, and attitudes toward the co-branding and co-branded products. This study's findings suggest that sensory fit of co-branding should be considered in the investigation of co-branding effectiveness and provide managerial insights into the design of effective collaboration between brands.

Theoretical background

Co-branding

Co-branding is defined as a marketing strategy in which 'two brands are deliberately paired with one another in a marketing context such as in ads, products, products placements, and distribution outlets' (Grossman 1997). The practice of co-branding has been around for a long time and remains a popular brand strategy such that the share of co-branded products in the U.S. market almost doubled from 3.5% in 2013 to 6% in 2014 (Schultz 2014). Brands like H&M, Coca-Cola, and Apple have proved countless times that co-branding can bring advantages to brands. H&M's sales in December 2015 increased by 10% compared with figures from 2014. In the same period, Marks & Spencer, a competitor of H&M, announced that their sales fell 0.5%. The sales of the two brands differed because of the success of H&M's co-branding strategy (Telegraph 2016). Successful co-branding not only increases revenue but also broadens market reach and repositions brand image with more elevated appeal, so it is very natural that many brands favour co-branding (Desai and Keller 2002; Leuthesser et al. 2003). Co-branding is a win–win strategy for partner brands with synergy, where 'the whole is greater than the sum of its parts', to use Aristotle's words.

The popularity of co-branding encourages academic researchers to conduct empirical studies to identify some key factors for effective co-branding persuasion. For example, when consumers have a positive view of the partner brands, they have a favourable attitude toward co-branding (Dickinson and Heath 2006; Helmig, Huber, and Leeflang 2007). This perception is influenced by the consumers' prior attitudes toward the partner brands (Helmig et al. 2007). When brand A (which consumers regard positively) collaborates with brand B (which lack consumer awareness and preference), the consumers' prior positive attitude toward brand A spills over to brand B, leading to a positive evaluation of the co-branding between A and B. In a similar vein, brand reputation also affects the expectancy of co-branding (Dickinson and Heath 2006). If either one or both the co-branding partner brands are well-known, consumers generally have high expectations from the co-branding regardless of the attitudes toward the partner brands. While there are many variables that influence the success of co-branding, perhaps one of the most well-researched factors that plays a primary role in consumer evaluations of co-branding is perceived fit between the partner brands (Bluemelhuber et al. 2007; Helmig et al. 2007; Keller 1993; Lanseng and Olsen 2012; Simonin and Ruth 1998; Walchli 2007).

Between-partner fit

Perceived fit between co-branding partner brands refers to how well the two brands fit together for a co-branded product (Helmig et al. 2007; Lanseng and Olsen 2012). The automobile brand BMW and luxury fashion brand Louis Vuitton launched a tailor-made set of luggage in 2014. A car is well matched with travel, and Louis Vuitton has built their reputation with their signature travel bags. Thus, both brands fit well with the co-branded product (i.e. product category fit). Furthermore, both BMW and Louis Vuitton are associated with a luxurious, sophisticated, and upscale brand image (i.e. brand image fit). As such, BMW and Louis Vuitton share many common attributes, so consumers perceive the two brands as well matched.

Existing co-branding studies suggest that between-partner fit (similarity) among partner brands is a crucial factor for determining evaluations of co-branding (i.e. Bluemelhuber et al. 2007; Helmig et al. 2007; Keller 1993; Lanseng and Olsen 2012; Simonin and Ruth 1998; Walchli 2007). Among various potential theoretical explanations for the fit effect, cognitive consistency is the most well-accepted explanation in existing branding literature. According to cognitive psychology theories such as balance theory (Heider 1946) and the matchup hypothesis (Kamins 1990), when consumers believe that two objects fit harmoniously, they show a favourable attitude toward the objects. This is because when people deal with two well-fitting objects, it is easy to cognitively integrate the two objects and recognize them as one, but when processing two completely different objects at once, more cognitive effort is needed and they find it difficult to integrate the objects (Abelson et al. 1968; Cummings and Venkatesan 1976; Park, Milberg, and Lawson 1991). In summary, easy interpretation of an object leads to positive feelings toward the object.

Previous co-branding research indicates that consumers evaluate co-branded products with high product category fit more positively than those with low product category fit (i.e. Delgado-Ballester and Hernandez-Espallardo 2008; Park, Jun and Shocker 1996; Simonin and Ruth 1998; Walchli 2007). The brand image fit can also affect consumer attitudes toward co-branded products (Mazodier and Merunka 2014; Simonin and Ruth 1998; Thompson and Strutton 2012; Walchli 2007). In the area of co-branding, the brand image fit indicates that there is a congruence of abstract images (i.e. luxury, sincere) between co-branding partner brands (Simonin and Ruth 1998). The brand image fit between such brands can affect the consumer's evaluation of co-branded products without any product fit between partner brands (Mazodier and Merunka 2014). Aaker and Keller (1990) proved that if consumers feel that a parent brand's personality (or image) and the extended brands' personalities match, consumers generate a more positive attitude toward the extended brands than when they do not match. Consequently, consumers may wonder why two brands collaborated for a new product if brand image fit is not well-matched (Simonin and Ruth 1998). Hence, the consumer's perceived fit between co-branding partner brands is a parameter that predicts consumers' evaluation of co-branding (Helmig et al. 2007; Lanseng and Olsen 2012).

Sensory fit

As discussed, previous research proved that the perceived fit is a crucial factor for generating positive consumer attitudes toward co-branding. However, the aforementioned research has focused on either the product category or brand image fit. In this study, we suggest that sensory attributes in co-branding play a significant persuasive role.

Sensory attributes include sensory factors such as colour, shape, and size. According to Lefkoff-Hagius and Mason (1993), sensory attributes are key factors used to distinguish a brand from its competitors in the same way product benefits and brand images are. Thus, it is crucial to examine the impact of sensory attributes as co-branding is an influential marketing strategy for corporates in terms of their 'market territory extensions'.

Imagine, for example, that fashion brand 'Uniqlo' collaborates with automobile brand 'Honda' or 'Volkswagen'. Looking at their brand logo, Uniqlo's sensory attributes are red colour and square shape. Honda has the same attributes, but Volkswagen has blue colour and round shape. When two objects share common attributes, individuals tend to easily integrate the two objects into one (Abelson et al. 1968; Cummings and Venkatesan 1976; Park, Milberg, and Lawson 1991). Therefore, when Uniqlo and Honda (vs. Volkswagen) work together, consumers are more likely to integrate the two brands into one due to their high perceived sensory fit. In fact, sensory fit in the context of co-branding is yet to be fully investigated by academic research. Few studies have attempted to reveal the effectiveness of sensory fit in the context of brand extensions and the field of cause-related marketing. For example, Zhang and Sood (2002) revealed that children use sensory fit (i.e. phonetic attributes) to evaluate their preference for a brand extension product (i.e. Coca-Cola 'Gola' iced tea). Kuo and Rice (2015) also found that the role of sensory fit is important for successful cause-related marketing. In their experimental study, they manipulated the colour of lemonade to either pink or yellow. They then created two charity campaigns that donate some of the profits from the lemonade sales, one for breast cancer patients and the other for leukemia patients. They found that donators favoured the campaign more when the pink lemonade was associated with the breast cancer campaign than when the yellow lemonade was used. In contrast, using yellow lemonade induced the opposite result. The authors explained the reason for this as follows: a pink ribbon is the symbol of a breast cancer charity while a yellow ribbon is the symbol of a leukemia charity. Donators in the experiment either explicitly or implicitly felt that the pink lemonade was a better fit with the breast cancer campaign than the leukemia campaign.

In light of the aforementioned discussion, sensory fit of co-branding partner brands is expected to influence consumer evaluations of co-branding. Specifically, a high sensory fit between two brands enhances positive affect transfer from one to another, resulting in favourable attitude toward the co-branding. Thus, the preceding discussion suggests the following hypothesis:

> **Hypotheis 1**: A sensory fit will positively affect attitude toward the evaluation of co-branding.

Experiment 1

Overview and design

Experiment 1 aimed to test the effects of sensory fit on co-branding evaluation. To that end, we manipulated the colours of co-branded brands. Thus, each participant was presented with one of two co-branding conditions: high sensory fit (i.e. two brands with similar colours) or low sensory fit (i.e. two brands with different colours).

Stimuli

Fictitious brands were created and used to minimize any potential confounding effects of the participants' previous brand exposures and related experiences. We selected a tumbler as the co-branded product for experiment because: (a) it is relevant to the student sample of the study and (b) it is not a gender-specific product. Since product category fit between brands can affect co-branding evaluation (Delgado-Ballester and Hernandez-Espallardo 2008; Park et al. 1996; Simonin and Ruth 1998), we conducted a series of pretests. Participants were asked to evaluate several product categories in terms of similarity and comparability with the tumbler product. As a result, the pair of bottle × chair was chosen, as the bottle received the highest score and the chair received the lowest score. Thus, we used the pair of low fit between-partner brands to control for the effects of product category fit. In addition, to control for the effects of other sensory attributes (i.e. alphabet, pronunciation, etc.), two fictitious brand names were created: 'AAKER' and 'TROPE'.

To manipulate the sensory attributes of Experiment 1 (i.e. colour), a total of eight pairs of colours were pre-tested. The pairs of colours were chosen based on proximity of the colours on the spectrum wheel. For example, orange is closely located with red or yellow, but far from blue or green on the spectrum wheel. Participants were asked to rate the pairs in terms of the similarity as well as the degree of likability. As a result, orange and yellow were chosen for the high sensory fit condition, whereas orange and green were selected for the low fit condition.

Finally, at the top of all stimuli is the co-branding logo with emphasis on the brand colour of 'AAKER' and 'TROPE'. Below that, the advertising messages are placed. The messages read, 'The thermos brand "AAKER" and the chair brand "Trope" collaborated to launch the new tumbler "Lunar"' and 'Let's enjoy "Lunar" with its lightweight, compact and stylish designs'. The brand name in the messages is filled with colours. At the bottom is the image of the co-branded product (see Appendix 1).

Sample and procedure

Sixty college students at a large university in Seoul, Korea (mean age = 25.21 years; 59% female), participated in an online experiment in exchange for a $2 coupon. Participants were first asked to carefully read the co-branding advertisement; they then answered questions including manipulation check and dependent variables. Three dependent variables assessed the effectiveness of the advertisement: attitude toward the advertisement (AA; 1 = negative, bad, unfavourable; 7 = positive, good, favourable; $\alpha = .93$), attitude toward the co-branded product (PA; 1 = negative, bad, unfavourable; 7 = positive, good, favourable; $\alpha = .94$), and attitude toward co-branding (CA; 1 = negative, bad, unfavourable, unsuccessful; 7 = positive, good, favourable, successful; $\alpha = .94$). A single index for each dependent variable was formed by averaging the corresponding items.

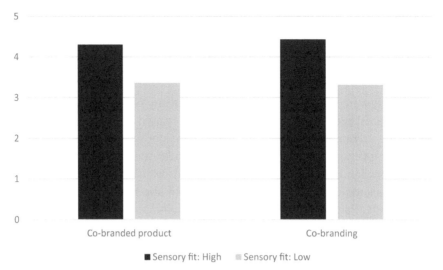

Figure 1. Experiment 1: attitude toward the co-branded product and co-branding.

Results

Manipulation checks

To assess the co-branding partner brands' similar-colour effect on the perceived over-all fit of co-branding, we asked the participants to rate how well the brands fit together (1 = poor, unconnected, different; 7 = well, connected, similar; α = .87). As expected, participants in the high sensory fit condition reported higher scores (M = 4.52) than those in the low condition (M = 2.70) (p < .001).

Hypotheses testing

The results showed that participants in the high sensory fit condition showed a more favourable attitude toward the co-branding advertisement (M_{AA} = 4.10, η^{p2} = .417), co-branded product (M_{PA} = 4.30, η^{p2} = .441), and co-branding (M_{CA} = 4.43, η^{p2} = .595) than those in the low fit condition (M_{AA} = 3.43; M_{PA} = 3.36; M_{CA} = 3.32) (ps < .01), supporting H1 (Figure 1).

Discussion in brief

The results of Experiment 1 demonstrated that sensory fit generates a positive impact on co-branding. When participants saw a co-branding in which two partner brands shared the same sensory attributes (i.e. colour), they felt the brands fit better and evaluated the co-branding more positively than the brands that did not share sensory attributes. Nevertheless, some issues need further investigation. First, in Experiment 1, we manipu-lated the sensory fit with brand colour, which is associated with brand images (Bottomley and Doyle 2006; Kirmani and Zeithami 1993). Both orange and yellow in the high sensory fit condition are typically associated warmth and energy, while green in the low condition symbolizes calm and rejuvenation (Aslam 2006). Therefore, there is a possibility that par-ticipants in the high condition perceived the brand image fit between the co-branding partner brands more highly than those in the low condition.

Second, we did not consider product-related variables such as product involvement and perceived product fit. In Experiment 1, we employed only low product fit to control for the effects of the product category fit and a relatively low-involvement product as a cobranded product (i.e. tumbler). According to the Elaboration Likelihood Model (ELM), if consumers are highly involved with a product, they process the product information through the central route. Consumers with high product involvement focus on the information about product functions and performance, and they show positive attitudes when the information is salient and clear. In contrast, if consumers display low product involvement, they interpret the product through the peripheral route and focus on the peripheral information about the product such as a model, sales person, and background music (Petty and Cacioppo 1986).

Applying the ELM to co-branding, it is reasonable to suggest that for a high-involvement co-branded product (vs. low-involvement co-branded product), consumers will consider the product category fit more because product fit is considered a primary attribute of the product. However, consumers will not place too much emphasis on the sensory fit (i.e. brand logo's colour, shape) because it is a secondary attribute of the product. As a result, for a low-involvement co-branded product, the sensory fit (vs. product fit) is more likely to be used as a basis of the evaluation of co-branding. The following hypothesis addresses this issue by examining the interplay between the sensory fit and product involvement in determining the effectiveness of co-branding.

Hypothesis 2: The sensory fit effect will be stronger in the low-involvement co-branded product condition (vs. high-involvement co-branded product condition).

Experiment 2

Overview and design

Experiment 2 was designed to identify not only the main effect of the sensory fit, but also the interplay between sensory fit, product category fit, and product involvement. We manipulated the similarity between brand names for the sensory fit and the relevance of product category between brands for the product category fit. Thus, a 2 (sensory fit: high vs. low) × 2 (product involvement: high vs. low) × 2 (product fit: high vs. low) between-subjects design was employed.

Stimuli

First, pre-tests were conducted to select the types of co-branded product representing either high or low involvement. As a result, a laptop was selected for the high-involvement condition whereas a tumbler was chosen for the low-involvement condition.

In Experiment 2, the similarity between partner brand names was used to manipulate the sensory fit. In the high sensory fit condition, participants were shown a co-branded co-branding advertisement for 'Aaker' and 'Aamer'. On the other hand, participants who are assigned to the low sensory fit condition were exposed to a co-branded advertising for 'Aaker' and 'Trope'. To manipulate the product category fit, we provided information regarding two different co-branding collaborations. In the high product category fit condition, participants were given information about a fictitious brand of personal computer collaborating with an audio brand to create a laptop. In the low condition, participants were given a laptop collaborated by a fictitious personal computer brand and a chair brand.

Sample and procedure

A total of 200 individuals (mean age = 24.17 years; 54% female) were recruited online to participate in this experiment and were offered a cell phone coupon (equivalent to $3) as compensation for their time. The experiment was administered online, and prospective participants were randomly assigned to one of eight experiment conditions. After being shown an advertisement, participants answered a series of questions that were designed to capture their evaluation of the advertisement, product, and co-branding. In the final stage, certain demographic information was collected.

The same dependent variables as in Experiment 1 were used: attitude toward the advertisement (AA; α = .91), attitude toward the co-branded product (PA; α = .94), and attitude toward co-branding (CA; α = .96). A single index for each dependent variable was formed by averaging the corresponding items.

Results

Manipulation checks
To assess the co-branding partner brand's similar-name effect on the perceived overall fit of co-branding, we asked the participants to rate how well the brands fit together (1 = poor, unconnected, different; 7 = well, connected, similar; α = .91). Participants in the high sensory fit condition reported higher scores (M = 4.42) than those in the low condition (M = 2.67) ($p < .001$). We also measured the effectiveness of the relevance of product category between brands. High product category fit scored higher (M = 4.77) than the low-fit condition did (M = 1.87) ($p < .001$). Finally, we examined the level of product involvement for each condition with four questions (1 = unimportant, not interested, low risk for choice, easy decision; 7 = important, interested, high risk for choice, hard decision; α = 78) (Zaichkowsky 1994). Participants in the high-involvement product condition showed higher scores (M = 5.81) than those in the low-involvement condition (M = 3.01) ($p < .001$). Thus, all factors were successfully manipulated.

Hypothesis testing
A $2 \times 2 \times 2$ ANOVA was conducted for the three dependent variables. The results supported H1 as the main effect of sensory was significant (F_{AA} = 17.25, $p < .001$, η^{p2} = .082; F_{PA} = 10.02, $p < .01$, η^{p2} = .050; F_{CA} = 20.55, $p < .001$, η^{p2} = .097). Although we did not hypothesize the main effect of product fit, we found a significant main effect of the product fit for the three dependent variables (F_{AA} = 15.06, $p < .001$, η^{p2} = .073; F_{PA} = 25.80, $p < .001$, η^{p2} = .118; F_{CA} = 32.81, $p < .001$, η^{p2} = .366), which is consistent with the findings of previous research (Delgado-Ballester and Hernandez-Espallardo 2008; Park et al. 1996; Simonin and Ruth 1998; Walchli 2007). A main effect of product involvement was not found. More important, consistent with our

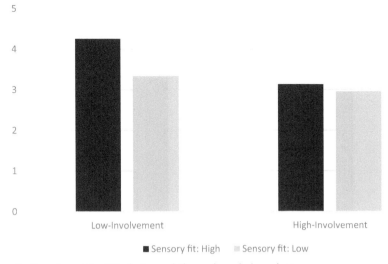

Figure 2. Experiment 2: attitude toward the co-branded product.

prediction, the sensory fit × product involvement interaction effect was significant (F_{AA} = 4.85; F_{PA} = 4.62, F_{CA} = 4.87) ($ps < .05$). Planned one-tailed comparisons revealed that when the co-branded product was a low-involvement product, participants in the high sensory fit condition showed a significantly higher attitude toward the advertisement (M_{AA} = 4.02), co-branded product (M_{PA} = 4.25), and co-branding (M_{CA} = 3.94) than the low sensory fit participants (M_{AA} = 3.09; M_{PA} = 3.34; M_{CA} = 2.81) ($ps < .001$). However, the same pattern was not significant when the co-branded product was a high-involvement product (high sensory fit M_{AA} = 3.15; M_{PA} = 3.13, M_{CA} = 3.27 vs. low sensory fit M_{AA} = 2.86; M_{PA} = 2.95, M_{CA} = 2.88) ($p < .23$, $p < .53$, $p < .22$, respectively), lending support for H2. The three-way interaction effect was not significant. However, in the low-involvement product condition, when both sensory fit and product fit were high, participants scored higher for PA ($M = 4.60$, $SD = 1.07$) than for the product fit 'high' condition ($M = 3.52$, $SD = 1.28$) ($p < .01$). No additional significant interaction effects were observed (Figures 2 and 3).

Discussion in brief

Through Experiment 2, the effects of sensory fit were again supported. More specifically, the prediction that sensory fit showed stronger effects when the co-branded product is a low-involvement product (vs. high-involvement product) was supported. That is, sensory fit due to similarity of co-branding partner brands can cause positive feelings for consumers, but this feeling is less important for high-involvement products. One possible explanation for the strong sensory fit effects for the low- (vs. high-) involvement co-branded product is that the products employed in Experiment 2 were both utilitarian products (i.e. tumbler and laptop). The utilitarian value of products is perceived through consumption, and product functions and performance are important. According to an FCB Grid (Foote, Cone, and Belding Grid) model, high involvement is classified into two domains, high-involvement/thinking and high-involvement/

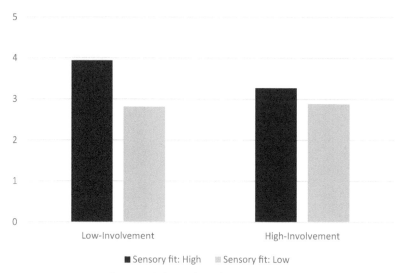

Figure 3. Experiment 2: attitude toward the co-branding.

feeling (Vaughn 1980). The characteristic of high-involvement/thinking is that consumers rely on information about a product's function or performance when purchasing products in that domain (Vaughn 1980). The other domain, high-involvement/feeling, contains high-involvement and hedonic products such as fashion items, cosmetic products, and jewellery. When consumers shop for these kinds of products, they rely on attitudes or overall feeling toward the products rather than its function or performance, even though they are highly involved with the products (Vaughn 1980).

Therefore, it seems plausible that the sensory fit effect can be observed under the high-involvement condition if the co-branded product is a hedonic product. To address this issue, we attempted to compare high-involvement and utilitarian products (HU) with high-involvement and hedonic products (HH). The following hypothesis formally states the prediction.

> *Hypothesis 3*: When a co-branded product is a high-involvement product, the sensory fit effect will be stronger in the hedonic product condition (vs. utilitarian product).

Experiment 3

Overview and design

To replicate and extend the results of previous experiments, a 2 (sensory fit: high vs. low) × 2 (product type: high involvement and utilitarian vs. high involvement and hedonic) between-subjects design was employed. In the HU condition, as in Experiment 2, participants evaluated an advertisement for a laptop. Participants in the HH condition evaluated an advertisement for sunglasses.

Stimuli

First, a pre-test was conducted to select the types of co-branded product representing either high involvement utilitarian or high involvement hedonic products with 44 participants (54% female, age $M = 23$). The participants were given several different product categories and were asked to answer a set of six questions (1 = effective, functional, practical, unenjoyable, not fun, dull; 7 = ineffective, not functional, impractical, enjoyable, fun, exciting; $\alpha = .74$) (Crowley, Spangenberg, and Hughes 1992). In addition, we examined the level of product involvement for each product (Zaichkowsky 1994). As a result, a laptop was selected for the high-involvement utilitarian condition ($M = 3.01$) whereas a sunglass was chosen for the high-involvement hedonic condition ($M = 5.08$; $p < .001$). Both products did not show any significant differences in terms of product involvement (laptop $M = 5.52$ vs. sunglass $M = 5.34$; $p = .38$).

Next, the congruence of the font style of co-branding partner brand names was manipulated to distinguish sensory fit conditions. In the high sensory fit condition, participants were shown the brand names 'Aaker' and 'Trope' written in the Futura font. In the low sensory fit condition, participants were shown 'Aaker' written in the Vivaldi font and 'Trope' written in the Futura font (see Appendix 2).

Sample and procedure

A total of 120 individuals (mean age = 24.22 years; 45% female) were recruited online to participate in this experiment and were offered an online gift card (equivalent to $3) as compensation for their participation. Prospective participants were first asked to view an advertisement for a newly launched co-branded product. Then, participants responded to a series of questions regarding their evaluation of the advertisement, product, and co-branding.

The same set of dependent variables was used: attitude toward the advertisement (AA; $\alpha = .91$), attitude toward the co-branded product (PA; $\alpha = .94$), and attitude toward co-branding (CA; $\alpha = .91$). A single index for each dependent variable was formed by averaging the corresponding items.

Results

Manipulation checks

To assess the font congruence effect of the co-branding partner brand names on the perceived overall fit of co-branding, we asked the participants to rate how well the two partner brands fit together. Participants in the high sensory fit condition scored higher ($M = 4.77$) than those in the low sensory fit condition ($M = 3.80$) ($p < .001$). Regarding the level of product involvement, there was no difference between HU ($M = 5.86$) and HH ($M = 5.69$) ($p < .19$). Finally, product type manipulation was examined (1 = effective, functional, practical, unenjoyable, not fun, dull; 7 = ineffective, not functional, impractical, enjoyable, fun, exciting; $\alpha = .74$) (Crowley, Spangenberg, and Hughes 1992). Participants in the HU condition reported lower scores ($M = 3.21$) than those in the HH condition ($M = 4.87$) ($p < .001$), suggesting that participants in the HU condition viewed the laptop as a utilitarian product and those in the HH condition viewed the sunglasses as a hedonic product. Therefore, all factors were successfully manipulated.

Hypothesis testing

The results showed that sensory fit had a significant main effect ($F_{AA} = 12.55$, $p < .01$, $\eta^{p2} = .098$; $F_{PA} = 14.24$, $p < .001$, $\eta^{p2} = .109$; $F_{CA} = 24.77$, $p < .001$, $\eta^{p2} = .129$). We also confirmed the main effect of product type ($F_{AA} = 5.28$, $p < .05$, np2 $= .044$; $F_{PA} = 6.82$, $p < .05$, np2 $= .056$; $F_{CA} = 9.92$, $p < .01$). More importantly, as predicted, the interaction effect between sensory fit and product type was significant ($F_{AA} = 7.64$, $p < .01$, $F_P = 9.79$, $p < .01$; $F_{CA} = 10.22$, $p < .01$). The results of planned contrasts showed that participants who viewed the co-branding advertisement for HH gave more positive ratings with high sensory fit between co-branding partner brands ($M_{AA} = 4.21$; $M_{PA} = 4.42$; $M_{CA} = 5.10$) compared with the low sensory fit condition ($M_{AA} = 3.31$; $M_{PA} = 3.23$; $M_{CA} = 3.68$) ($p < .001$). In the HU condition, there was no significant difference for sensory fit on AA *(high sensory fit $M_{AA} = 3.49$; $M_{PA} = 3.43$; $M_{CA} = 4.00$ vs. low sensory fit $M_{AA} = 3.38$; $M_{PA} = 3.32$; $M_{CA} = 3.70$)* ($p < .59$, $p < .66$, $p < .24$, respectively). Thus, H3 was supported.

General discussion

Due to its success in the marketplace, co-branding represents a well-researched topic for marketing scholars and practitioners. The objective of the current study is to systematically test the effects of a new form of perceived fit (i.e. sensory fit) on consumer evaluations of co-branding. Across the three experiments of the study, we demonstrated that sensory fit significantly and positively influences co-branding evaluations. In particular, sensory fit has a greater effect on co-branding evaluations for low-involvement compared with high-involvement products (Experiment 2). To further examine the limited effect of sensory fit for high-involvement products, Experiment 3 tested the moderating role of product type (i.e. hedonic vs. utilitarian) in the relationship. Findings demonstrate that the effect of sensory fit holds for the high-involvement and hedonic product condition only.

This research contributes to the literature on several fronts. Our research is one of the first demonstrations of sensory fit as an important factor of co-branding evaluations. By conceptualizing the perceived fit as sensory fit, the findings from the three experimental studies with different types of sensory cues suggest that sensory fit effects hold for co-branding evaluations. Consumer attitudes toward co-branding as well as co-branded products are more positive when two partner brands' sensory attributes (i.e. colour, font type) are congruent than when they are unmatched with each other. Our findings suggest that both colour and brand name are particularly relevant sensory cues that play a central role in co-branding evaluations. Such findings are also in line with past research that classified rhyme as consisting more of sensory attributes, as opposed to semantic attributes in product evaluations (McQuarrie and Mick 1996). As we predicted, these sensory attributes were more important for low-involvement co-branded products as well as hedonic products. Co-branding of high-involvement and utilitarian products (e.g. laptop) appear to require a high category fit and similarity between partner brands. Consumers may not be as sensitive to sensory similarity as they are to category similarity, suggesting that affective information processes can result in more persuasive outcomes depending upon product type and involvement.

For marketing practitioners, the findings of this study offer important managerial implications. The findings suggest that consumers may rely more on 'sensory' cues such as brand colours, brand names, font type, shape, and so on, rather than on category similarity as a basis for co-branding evaluations, especially for low-involvement or hedonic products. That is, when marketers attempt to develop low-involvement or hedonic co-branded products, they need to pay more attention to sensory similarity between partner brands. In fact, co-branding strategies such as this have begun to emerge, as in the case of the recent UNIQLO × Disney collaboration. UNIQLO is a clothing brand, and one of the Disney's main products is animation movies. There appears to be no product category or brand image fit between the two brands, but they created sensory fit in their co-branding. They created a new Mickey Mouse logo that was red, Uniqlo's identity colour, to stress their collaboration. Another example includes a luxury hedonic brand, Fendi, that collaborated with a sportswear brand, Fila, not because of their brand image fit, but due to sensory fit (i.e. the same initial 'F' for their brand names). These co-branding examples and their phenomenal success in the marketplace suggest that both the colour and linguistic characteristics of brand names can directly contribute to consumers' evaluations of co-branding. In addition, sensory fit is relatively easier for marketers to manipulate in real marketing situations compared with both product category and brand image fit.

Although this study addresses important aspects of sensory fit and its role in co-branding evaluations, it has some limitations to be addressed in future research. First, while this study used two different types of sensory cues, additional sensory attributes should be further considered and tested to increase the generalizability of our findings. Second, this study relied on a limited number of co-branded product categories (i.e. laptop and tumbler). Further research with a larger set of product or service categories is needed. Since the service industry deals with intangible products, it should approach customers with other factors rather than attributes of the product itself. Thus, the impact of sensory fit may appear larger in the service product. Another avenue that merits future exploration is to identify other variables that may further explain or change the results obtained in the three experiments presented herein. Some of the variables may reflect individual or cultural differences. For example, Zhang and Sood (2002) found that children and adults evaluate brand extension differently. Their findings indicate that adults tend to consider brand category similarity while children tend to use surface cues such as brand names and name characteristics for brand extension evaluations. Furthermore, as noted by Monga and John (2006), previous literature suggests that individuals in Western cultures are more likely to pay attention to category similarity and cues than individuals in East Asian cultures. Thus, to ascertain if there are significant differences among these cultural and age groups, future research should incorporate both cultural orientation and age variables in a variety of co-branding contexts and expand the body of knowledge regarding this marketing tactic.

Disclosure statement

No potential conflict of interest was reported by the authors.

Funding

This study was supported by a faculty research grant from the College of Liberal Arts at Korea University in 2017.

References

Aaker, D.A., and K.L. Keller. 1990. Consumer evaluations of brand extension. *Journal of Marketing* 54, no. 1: 27–41.

Abelson, R.P., E.E. Aronson, W.J. McGuire, T.M. Newcomb, M.J. Rosenberg, and P.H. Tannenbaum. 1968. *Theories of cognitive consistency: A sourcebook.* Chicago, IL: Rand McNally.

Aslam, M.M. 2006. Are you selling the right colour? A cross-cultural review of colour as a marketing cue. *Journal of Marketing Communications* 12, no. 1: 15–30.

Bluemelhuber, C., L.L. Carter, and C.J. Lambe. 2007. Extending the view of Brand alliance effects: An integrative examination of the role of country of origin. *International Marketing Review* 24, no. 4: 427–43.

Bottomley, P.A., and J.R. Doyle. 2006. The interactive effects of colors and products on perceptions of Brand logo appropriateness. *Marketing Theory* 6, no. 1: 63–83.

Buttle, H., and N. Westoby. 2006. Brand logo and name association: It's all in the name. *Applied Cognitive Psychology* 20, no. 9: 1181–94.

Crowley, A.E., E.R. Spangenberg, and K.R. Hughes. 1992. Measuring the hedonic and utilitarian dimensions of attitudes toward product categories. *Marketing Letters* 3, no. 3: 239–49.

Cummings, W.H., and M. Venkatesan. 1976. Cognitive dissonance and consumer behavior: A review of the evidence. *Journal of Marketing Research* 13, no. 3: 303–8.

Desai, K.K., and K.L. Keller. 2002. The effects of ingredient branding strategies on host Brand extendibility. *Journal of Marketing* 66, no.1: 73–93.

Delgado-Ballester, E., and M. Hernández-Espallardo. 2008. Building online brands through Brand alliances in internet. *European Journal of Marketing* 42, no. 9/10: 954–76. DOI:10.1080/14241277.2011.568305.

Dickinson, S., and T. Heath. 2006. A comparison of qualitative and quantitative results concerning evaluations of co-branded offerings. *Journal of Brand Management* 13, no. 6: 393–406.

Grossman, R.P. 1997. Co-branding in advertising: Developing effective associations. *Journal of Product & Brand Management* 6, no. 3: 191–202. DOI:10.1108/10610429710175709.

Helmig, B., J.A. Huber, and P. Leeflang. 2007. Explaining behavioural intentions toward co-branded products. *Journal of Marketing Management* 23, no. 3–4: 285–304.

Heider, F. 1946. Attitudes and cognitive organization. *The Journal of Psychology* 21, no. 1: 107–12. no.

Henderson, P.W., and J.A. Cote. 1998. Guidelines for selecting or modifying logos. *Journal of Marketing* 62, no. 2: 14–30.

Kamins, M.A. 1990. An investigation into the "match-up" hypothesis in celebrity advertising: When beauty may be only skin deep. *Journal of Advertising* 19, no.1: 4–13.

Keller, K.L. 1993. Conceptualizing, measuring, and managing customer-based brand equity. *Journal of Marketing* 57, no.1: 1–22.

Kirmani, A., and V. Zeithaml. 1993. *Advertising, perceived quality, and Brand image.* Hillsdale, NJ: Lawrence Erlbaum Associates.

Kuo, A., and D.H. Rice. 2015. The impact of perceptual congruence on the effectiveness of cause-related marketing campaigns. *Journal of Consumer Psychology* 25, no. 1: 78–88.

Lanseng, E.J., and L.E. Olsen. 2012. Brand alliances: The role of Brand concept consistency. *European Journal of Marketing* 46, no. 9: 1108–26. DOI:10.1108/03090561211247874.

Lefkoff-Hagius, R., and C.H. Mason. 1993. Characteristic, beneficial, and image attributes in consumer judgments of similarity and preference. *Journal of Consumer Research* 20, no.1: 100–10.

Leuthesser, L., C.C. Kohli, and R. Suri. 2003. 2 + 2= 5? A framework for using co-branding to leverage a Brand. *Journal of Brand Management* 11, no.1: 35–47.

Mazodier, M., and D. Merunka. 2014. Beyond brand attitude: Individual drivers of purchase for symbolic cobranded products. *Journal of Business Research* 67, no.7: 1552–8.

McQuarrie, E.F., and D.G. Mick. 1996. Figures of rhetoric in advertising language. *Journal of Consumer Research* 22, no.4: 424–38.

Monga, A.B., and D.R. John. 2006. Cultural differences in Brand extension evaluation: The influence of analytic versus holistic thinking. *Journal of Consumer Research* 33, no.4: 529–36.

Park, C.W., S. Milberg, and R. Lawson. 1991. Evaluation of Brand extensions: The role of product feature similarity and Brand concept consistency. *Journal of Consumer Research* 18, no.2: 185–93.

Park, C.W., S.Y. Jun, and A.D. Shocker. 1996. Composite branding alliances: An investigation of extension and feedback effects. *Journal of Marketing Research* 33, no.4: 453–66.

Petty, R.E., and J.T. Cacioppo. 1986. *The elaboration likelihood model of persuasion. Communication and persuasion,* 1–24. New York: Springer.

Schultz, E.J. 2014. *Uptick in co-branding brings some unusual combos* (accessed November 15, 2017).

Simonin, B.L., and J.A. Ruth. 1998. Is a company known by the company it keeps? Assessing the spillover effects of Brand alliances on consumer Brand attitudes. *Journal of Marketing Research* 35, no.1: 30–42.

Singh, S. 2006. Impact of color on marketing. *Management Decision* 44, no.6: 783–9.

Telegraph. 2016. Did Balmania help boost H&M's December sales? *Telegraph*, January 15. https://www.telegraph.co.uk/fashion/brands/did-balmania-help-boost-hms-december-sales (accessed November 30, 2018).

Thompson, K., and D. Strutton. 2012. Revisiting perceptual fit in co-branding applications. *Journal of Product & Brand Management* 21, no. 1: 15–25. DOI:10.1108/10610421211203079.

Tversky, A., and D. Kahneman. 1974. Judgment under uncertainty: Heuristics and biases. *Science* 185, no. 4157: 1124–31. DOI:10.1126/science.185.4157.1124.

Vaughn, R. 1980. How advertising works: A planning model. *Journal of Advertising Research 20, no. 5: 27-33.*

Walchli, S.B. 2007. The effects of between-partner congruity on consumer evaluation of cobranded products. *Psychology & Marketing* 24, no.11: 947–73. DOI:10.1002/mar.20191.

Zaichkowsky, J.L. 1994. The personal involvement inventory: Reduction, revision, and application to advertising. *Journal of Advertising* 23, no. 4: 59–70.

Zhang, S., and S. Sood. 2002. Deep" and "surface" cues: Brand extension evaluations by children and adults. *Journal of Consumer Research* 29, no. 1: 129–41.

Appendix 1. Stimuli of experiment 1

Sensory fit high: Orange with Yellow

Senosry fit low: Orange with Green

보온병 브랜드 AAKER와 의자 브랜드 TROPE가 함께 손을 잡고 새로운 텀블러 라인 LUNAR를 출시하였습니다

가볍고 콤팩트하면서, 세련된 디자인으로 시선을 사로잡는 LUNAR를 지금 만나보세요

보온병 브랜드 AAKER와 의자 브랜드 TROPE가 함께 손을 잡고 새로운 텀블러 라인 LUNAR를 출시하였습니다

가볍고 콤팩트하면서, 세련된 디자인으로 시선을 사로잡는 LUNAR를 지금 만나보세요

Appendix 2. Stimuli of Experiment 3

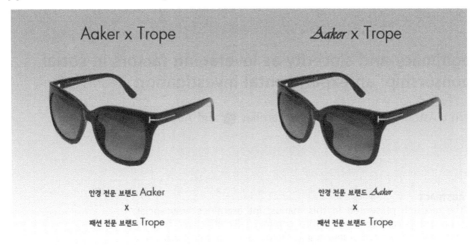

Legitimacy and sincerity as leveraging factors in social sponsorship: an experimental investigation

Alain d'Astous, François Anthony Carrillat (iD) and Audrey Przybysz

ABSTRACT

The research presented in this manuscript examines how social sponsorship can be made more commercially effective. To this end, the effects of two leveraging factors are explored by means of an experiment: the extent to which the social sponsorship is seen by consumers as legitimate, and that to which the sponsor is perceived as sincere. The results show that these two factors have a positive and statistically significant impact on consumers' intentions to purchase the sponsor's products. In addition, they show that the sponsor's perceived sincerity increases when the sponsorship is combined with philanthropic investments, either in sequence (i.e. philanthropy followed by sponsorship) or simultaneously, and that the legitimacy of a sponsorship is enhanced when the cause and its sponsor are congruent. These results are discussed in the context of the literature on social sponsorship, and managerial implications for firms that contemplate using social sponsorship as a marketing communication strategy are derived.

Introduction

The use of social sponsorship as a marketing communication tool to help a firm reach commercial objectives (e.g. improving brand image, increasing sales) has been on the rise for several years. Relevant and high-visibility examples include Ben & Jerry's support of the 'Lift the Ban' campaign to allow asylum seekers to work while waiting for their claim, and Coca-Cola's ongoing partnership with the World Wildlife Fund aimed at ensuring the salubrity of freshwater basins in several areas of the world.

While global spending on social sponsorship was estimated at 816 million of dollars in 2002, it amounted to about 1.92 billion in 2015 (IEG 2015). In North America alone, it reached 2.13 billion in 2018 and is expected to amount to 2.23 billion in 2019, representing about 9% of total spending in sponsorship (IEG 2019). Therefore, spending on social sponsorship corresponds to a significant portion of many firms' integrated marketing communication investments.

The interest of firms in social sponsorship – that is, 'a cash and/or in-kind fee that a company pays to a social cause or non-profit organization in return for advertising potential' (Daw 2011) – lies primarily in the presumption that consumers generally like to patronize companies that support social causes (Cone 2004; Diehl, Terlutter, and Mueller 2016; Lafferty and Goldsmith 2005; Matin, Ruiz, and Rubio 2009; Taylor 2018). However, consumers' positive reactions to social sponsorship are not assured since they depend on the extent to which the sponsor and the social cause are perceived as fitting well together. As shown by Simmons and Becker-Olsen (2006), when this is not the case, consumers may elaborate on the reasons why the firm has engaged in the sponsorship and are likely to generate negative thoughts which, ultimately, will lower their intention to purchase the sponsor's products as well as to recommend them.

The objective of the research presented in this paper is to investigate how a firm may augment its chances of generating brand benefits, in terms of consumer purchase intentions, in the context of a social sponsorship. This is done by examining whether certain variables have a positive impact on consumers' intentions to purchase the sponsor's products. More precisely, it is argued that this may first be accomplished by combining the social sponsorship program with philanthropic investments to the benefit of the cause, thus increasing consumers' perception that the sponsor is truly motivated by the desire to support the organization. Research in the domain of social sponsorship has shown that consumers are inclined to attribute motivations to sponsors that are either intrinsic (i.e. the firm's support for the cause is sincere) or extrinsic (i.e. the firm's support is driven by profit-seeking objectives) (Rifon et al. 2004). These two motivations may be seen as motive-inferred endpoints of a firm-cause collaboration continuum that goes from philanthropic (i.e. one-sided transfer of resources) to transactional (i.e. reciprocal exchange of resources) activities (Austin 2000; Austin and Seitanidi 2012). Because philanthropic partnerships lead to more positive consumer reactions (e.g. d'Astous and Bitz 1995), social sponsorship programs should therefore benefit from being perceived as a natural evolution in the context of such collaborative continuum.

Second, the effectiveness of social sponsorship may also be enhanced by selecting a cause-related organization that is perceived by consumers as being congruent with the sponsoring firm (e.g. its activities, its image). This proposition is consistent with the research findings of Simmons and Becker-Olsen (2006), but also with numerous studies in the sponsorship domain that have documented the positive impact of sponsor-sponsee congruence on consumer responses (e.g. Becker-Olsen and Hill 2006; Fleck and Quester 2007; Pappu and Cornwell 2014; Wakefield and Bennett 2010). According to this stream of research, congruence is beneficial because it facilitates the association of the sponsor and the organization in consumers' minds. In turn, this ease-of-processing, in and of itself, generates some positive affect that spreads to the sponsoring brand as well as to the sponsored entity. In the context of a social sponsorship however, a high level of congruence between the firm and the cause also provides a justification for the fact that a cause-related organization engages in a partnership with a commercially-oriented firm; in other words, congruence should also impact the content of consumer cognitions as it relates to the legitimacy of the sponsorship itself (e.g. Rifon et al. 2004; Simmons and Becker-Olsen 2006). Hence, congruence should not only attenuate the cognitive effort needed to associate the two entities, but should also increase consumers' perception that the partnership is legitimate and, therefore, positively influence their intention to purchase the sponsor's products (Fleck and Quester 2007; Suchman 1995).

Conceptual model and research hypotheses

The conceptual model of this research is presented in Figure 1. In this model, it is proposed that the effectiveness of social sponsorship increases as consumers' perceptions that the sponsor is sincere (H1) and that the sponsorship is legitimate (H2) are enhanced. Sponsorship effectiveness in this model refers to consumers' intentions to purchase the sponsor's products. In addition, the sponsor's perceived sincerity is shown to depend on how the social sponsorship strategy is implemented. More precisely, it is hypothesized that consumers' perceptions of the sponsor's sincerity are the lowest when social sponsorship is implemented as a single strategy, higher when social sponsorship is combined with philanthropy, and at their highest when philanthropic initiatives precede the sponsorship (H3). It is also hypothesized that consumers' perceptions that the social sponsorship is legitimate are positively affected by the degree to which the sponsor and the cause-related organization are perceived as being congruent (H4). In addition, the conceptual model posits that the perceived sincerity of the sponsor (H5a) and the perceived legitimacy of the sponsorship (H5b) act as mediators in the relationships between the independent and dependent variables. These research hypotheses are justified in the next two sections.

Social sponsorship implementation strategy and sponsor's sincerity

As argued by Rifon et al. (2004), consumers may see the involvement of a firm in the sponsorship of a cause as a strategy to reach commercial objectives rather than a sincere form of support. Consequently, the goodwill benefits usually associated with partnering with a social cause (Bhattacharya and Sen 2004) may not come to life if the firm is not seen as being sincere in its endeavor.

Austin and Seitanidi (2012; see also Austin 2000) contend that the ultimate objective of business/non-profit collaboration is the creation of value. They propose that this can be best achieved through a collaborative continuum comprising three stages. The first stage is *philanthropic collaboration*, where the partnership is essentially unilateral (i.e. the firm transfers resources to the cause). The second stage is *transactional*

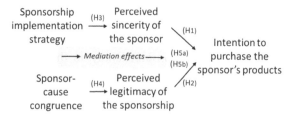

Figure 1. The conceptual model.

collaboration, where the firm and the cause exchange resources through different joint initiatives, such as sponsorship and cause-related marketing. The final stage is *integrative collaboration*, where the firm and the non-profit entity work actively together with the purpose of co-creating value.

While Austin and Seitanidi (2012) do not envision their collaborative-stage model as a fixed sequence in either a normative or descriptive sense (for instance, it is frequent that firms engage directly in stage-2 partnerships), they suggest that this sequential approach provides benefits in terms of value creation. The collaboration continuum implies that the effectiveness of social sponsorship (stage 2) should be greater when it is preceded by philanthropic collaboration (stage 1), because the sponsorship then represents a natural, logical evolution in the context of a changing collaborative relationship among two partners. This is consistent with the research findings of Lii and Lee (2012) which suggest (it was not formally tested) that engaging in philanthropic activities with causes *before* turning to sponsorship should lower consumers' skepticism as regards the firm's motivations as well as enhance the degree to which they identify with the sponsor.

Because 'substantive' philanthropy – as opposed to 'symbolic' philanthropy, see e.g. Zajac and Westphal (1995) – is fundamentally an altruistic, charitable, selfless enterprise, it is likely to affect positively the firm's image and generate perceptions that the firm's commitment to a cause is sincere (Cuypers, Koh, and Wang 2016). Therefore, simply combining sponsorship with philanthropy should, in itself, have a positive impact on consumer responses. Uhrich, Koenigstorfer, and Groeppel-Klein (2014) have shown, for instance, that linking sponsorship with corporate social responsibility initiatives may increase the brand's credibility and consumers' attitude toward the brand (see also Lacey, Close, and Finney 2010). Hence, leading consumers to believe that a firm's interest in a cause in the context of a social sponsorship is sincere should be easier to accomplish when it is combined with philanthropic actions to the benefit of the cause, especially if it precedes – rather than being simultaneous with – the sponsorship. Consequently, it is also hypothesized that the sincerity of the sponsor mediates the impact of the sponsorship implementation strategy on consumers' intentions to purchase the sponsor's products (see Figure 1).

Sponsor-cause congruence and sponsorship's legitimacy

According to Suchman's (1995) classic definition, legitimacy corresponds to the 'perception or assumption that the actions of an entity are desirable, proper, or appropriate within some socially constructed system of norms, values, beliefs, and definitions' (p. 574). Because consumers perceive congruent sponsorships to form an expected and relevant combination (Fleck and Quester 2007; Geue and Plewa 2010), the extent to which a firm is perceived as being congruent with a cause should logically positively impact consumers' judgments that the firm's engagement is aligned with expectations, that it corresponds to social norms. Consequently, congruent firm-cause combinations should be considered more legitimate than incongruent ones.

The positive impact of the perceived congruence between a firm and a sponsored entity on consumer responses toward the sponsor is often explained using an ease-of-processing argument (e.g. Fleck and Quester 2007; Jagre, Watson, and Watson 2001; McDaniel 1999). When a sponsor and its sponsored entity are perceived as fitting well together (e.g. Simmons and Becker-Olsen 2006), or having image-based or attribute-based commonalities (e.g. Gwinner and Eaton 1999), or forming an expected and relevant combination (Fleck and Quester 2007), or making up a strategic match (Becker-Olsen and Hill 2006), their association in consumers' minds is facilitated. Through the process of spreading activation (Collins and Loftus 1975; Wyer and Carlston 1979), the affect (thoughts, sentiments, feelings, etc.) that the sponsored entity generates is therefore transferred to the sponsor, which leads to positive consumer responses.

Although the ease-of-processing argument meets the approval of a majority of sponsorship researchers, it is noteworthy that it overlooks the content of the cognitions experienced by consumers, which can play an important role in their response to sponsorship stimuli. Several studies have shown that the impact of congruence on consumer responses to sponsorship is not only contingent on ease-of-processing effects but also on the type of inferences that consumers make – that is, on their cognitive content. Rifon et al. (2004) have argued that a high level of perceived congruence between a firm and a sponsored cause leads consumers to infer that the motivations of the sponsor are altruistic, thereby enhancing its perceived credibility, which ultimately induces more favorable attitudinal responses. Simmons and Becker-Olsen (2006) for their part have shown that the degree of fit between a firm and its sponsored cause has a positive impact on the degree to which the sponsor's image (or positioning) is clear and on consumers' attitude toward the sponsorship. Using a variety of research methods, Bhattacharya and Sen (2004) have shown that consumers are less skeptical of companies that are involved in causes with which they have a good fit. The role of cognitive content, as illustrated by the aforementioned studies, seems particularly relevant in the case of social sponsorship where consumers are likely to perceive a disconnect between the objectives of the sponsor (i.e. to make profits – basically, a 'receiving' schema) and those of the cause (i.e. to support – basically, a 'giving' schema). Such disconnect may generate perceptions that the partnership is not appropriate, and therefore that the sponsor's involvement with the cause is not legitimate.

Interestingly, the proposed impact of perceived congruence on perceived legitimacy can be contrasted with Rifon et al.'s (2004) claim that congruence leads to enhanced perceptions among consumers that the sponsor's motivations are altruistic. Indeed, even if consumers admit that a firm's motivations behind a given social sponsorship are not altruistic – that the firm is not primarily concerned by the cause's best interest – the sponsorship could nevertheless be seen as legitimate as long as the sponsorship is consistent with what consumers expect from firms engaged in social sponsorship (i.e. supporting causes even if not for entirely selfless reasons). Accordingly, it is hypothesized that the perceived legitimacy of a social sponsorship mediates the relationship between the extent to which the sponsor and the cause are seen as congruent and consumers' intentions to purchase the sponsor's products (see Figure 1).

Method

Overview

An experiment was conducted in which a firm's *sponsorship implementation strategy* (sponsorship only, philanthropy and sponsorship simultaneously, philanthropy and sponsorship in sequence) and degree of *congruence* with a cause-related organization (low, high) were manipulated by means of fictitious newspaper articles.

Pretest

A pretest was designed to select appropriate experimental stimuli; that is, a sponsor, and a less congruent and a more congruent cause-related organizations. In the selection process, it was important to make sure that the participants had at least a moderate level of appreciation and familiarity for the sponsor and the organizations. Six sponsor-organization combinations were identified which *a priori* differed with respect to their level of congruence (three congruent, three incongruent). For each combination, 20 adult consumers (13 females, seven males) forming a convenience sample were asked to rate their familiarity with the sponsor and the cause-related organizations (two items from Kent and Allen 1994; e.g. 'X is a brand/organization that I do not know at all/I know very well' – Cronbach's alphas ranging from 0.61 to 0.97 with a mean of 0.85), their attitude toward each entity (two items from MacKenzie and Lutz 1989; e.g. 'X is a brand/organization that I do not like/I like' – alphas ranging from 0.78 to 0.98 with a mean of 0.82), the perceived realism of the combination (three items specific to this study; e.g. 'It is difficult to believe in this partnership' – totally disagree/totally agree – alphas ranging from 0.81 to 0.97 with a mean of 0.88), and the perceived congruence between the entities (three items adapted from Speed and Thompson 2000; e.g. 'Brand X and organization Y go well together' – totally disagree/ totally agree – alphas ranging from 0.69 to 0.91 with a mean of 0.82). For each concept, the mean of the items was computed to create an indicator (all seven-point scales).

Based on the pretest results, *L'Oréal* – a global firm operating in the cosmetics market – was chosen as the sponsor; the *Canadian Breast Cancer Foundation* as the congruent cause-related organization, and *L'Itinéraire* – a Canadian organization devoted to helping homeless people – as the incongruent counterpart. The chosen sponsor and organizations had good levels of familiarity (means ranging from 4.30 to 6.23) and were evaluated quite positively (means ranging from 4.83 to 6.20). The congruent combination was perceived as more realistic (mean = 5.77) and more congruent (mean = 4.43) than the incongruent one (means = 2.92 and 1.98, respectively) (all differences statistically significant at $p < .05$).

Design and experimental stimuli

A 3 (sponsorship implementation strategy: sponsorship only, philanthropy and sponsorship simultaneously, philanthropy and sponsorship in sequence) × 2 (sponsor-cause congruence: low, high) completely factorial design was used to test the conceptual

framework. Fictitious newspaper articles were prepared that announced the partnership of *L'Oréal* with either the *Canadian Breast Cancer Foundation* or *L'Itinéraire*,
depending on the congruence conditions. The partnership consisted in *L'Oréal* sponsoring a 'Run for the Cure' event in the case of the congruent dyad, or a 'One-day
newsperson' event in the other case. In the sponsorship only conditions, the article
mentioned that *L'Oréal* had become the sponsor of the event for the current year. In
the simultaneous philanthropy and sponsorship conditions, it said that *L'Oréal* was
involved with the organization through its philanthropic corporate program as well as
the sponsorship of the event. Finally, in the philanthropy and sponsorship in sequence
conditions, the article mentioned that becoming the sponsor of the event was not
L'Oréal's first partnership with the organization since it had supported it during the
previous year through its philanthropic corporate program. An experimental stimulus
example (philanthropy and sponsorship in sequence/congruent) is presented in
the Appendix.

Measures

After having been exposed to the newspaper article, the participants filled in a questionnaire containing measures of the theoretical and manipulation check variables (all
items rated on seven-point bipolar scales). *Purchase intention* was assessed with two
different measures to test the robustness of the results. The first comprised three
items taken from Carrillat, Lafferty, and Harris (2005): 'Taking into account the information contained in this article, and assuming that you have someday the intention of
buying a cosmetic product, for a man or for a woman, how likely are you to buy products from *L'Oréal* rather than from its competitors:' improbable/probable, impossible/
possible, unlikely/likely. The second intention measure was a an eleven-point percentage scale (0%, 10%, …, 100%) to rate the respondent's estimated chances of buying
a *L'Oréal* product if needed. *Perceived sincerity* was measured with three items adapted
from Speed and Thompson (2000): 'The main reason why *L'Oréal* sponsors the (event)
is because it thinks (the organization) deserves to be supported'; 'As a sponsor, *L'Oréal*
seems to have the best interests of (the organization) at heart'; and '*L'Oréal* would
support the event even if it would bring few benefits'. The *perceived legitimacy* measure comprised two items that were specifically designed for this study: 'The fact that
L'Oréal sponsors this event is legitimate', and 'Given the context, it makes sense that
L'Oréal sponsors this event'. The first item refers directly to the concept to be assessed
whereas the second item attempts to map in a simple and short way Suchman's
(1995) definition: 'perception or assumption that the actions of an entity are desirable,
proper, or appropriate (i.e. it makes sense that L'Oréal sponsors this event) within
some socially constructed system of norms, values, beliefs, and definitions (i.e. given
the context). *Perceived sponsor-cause congruence* was measured with six items adapted
from existing scales: 'L'Oréal and (the organization) go well together', 'There is a logical
connection between *L'Oréal* and (the organization)', 'It makes sense to me that *L'Oréal*
is associated with issues that concern (the organization)' (Speed and Thompson 2000);
'The ideas I associate with *L'Oréal* are related to the ideas I associate with (the organization)' (Gwinner and Eaton 1999); 'The association of the *L'Oréal* brand with (the

organization) does not make sense given the activities of this brand', 'The association of the *L'Oréal* brand with (the organization) is not pertinent given the activities of this brand' (Ellen, Mohr, and Webb 2000). Finally, *L'Oréal's commitment to the organization* was assessed with two items adapted from Ellen, Mohr, and Webb (2000): '*L'Oréal* is truly involved with (the organization)', '*L'Oréal* strongly committed itself through its association with (the organization)'.

Data collection

The data were collected by means of a drop-off questionnaire delivery survey. This method which consists in delivering questionnaires to a sample of households and planning with the respondents a time for later collection is particularly well suited for complex questionnaires (such as those used in this study). Streets in some residential areas of a major North-American city were selected for the distribution of question-naires. Interviewers knocked on the door of every two dwellings on these streets, asked for the resident's participation, and transmitted orally the instructions for filling in the questionnaire, which was picked-up later at a time that was convenient for the participant. From a total of 418 attempted contacts, 301 could be made (contact rate = 72.0%) and 223 residents accepted to participate (acceptance rate = 74.1%). The interviewers picked up 192 questionnaires (completion rate = 86.1%), from which 183 were deemed usable.

Results

Sample description

The sample comprises a slightly greater number of female respondents (57.4%).[1] Most of the participants belong to the 25–34 age category (18–24: 24.0%; 25–34: 43.2%; 35–44: 12.6%; 45–54: 12.6%; 55 and more: 7.7%). They are in general well educated since 64.4% have some university education. About three-fourth of the participants (74.9%) were currently employed (14.2% are students).

Psychometric assessment of the measures

The items of each additive scale were subjected to a factor analysis. In all cases, a single factor emerged that explained a fair proportion of the total variance (minimum = 62.58%). As shown in Table 1 which displays the mean, standard

Table 1. Correlations among the study variables, with their mean, standard deviation, and reliability.

Variable	M	SD	1	2	3	4
1 Perceived sincerity of the sponsor	4.12	1.40	(.82)			
2 Perceived legitimacy of the sponsor	4.68	1.50	.47	(.76)		
3 Purchase intention (3 items)	4.26	1.48	.43	.31	(.96)	
4 Purchase intention (percentage)	51.65	23.66	.39	.36	.59	—

Notes: Minimum $n = 181$. All correlations statistically significant at $p < .001$.
Reliability coefficients (Cronbach's alpha) are reported within parentheses on the diagonal (excluding the purchase intention percentage).

deviation, and Cronbach's alpha coefficient of the theoretical variables as well as their inter-correlations, the reliability of the scales is generally very good (minimum alpha = 0.76). A factor analysis conducted on the set of all items measuring the theoretical concepts (3-item intention, percentage intention, legitimacy, and sincerity – 9 items altogether) led to three factors, as expected, with all items loading strongly on their appropriate concept (explained variance = 79.41%; mean intra-factor loading = 0.83; mean absolute extra-factor loading = 0.18). These results provide strong empirical evidence for the discriminant validity of the scales.

The reliability of the manipulation check scales is also very good (perceived sponsor-organization congruence: alpha = 0.90; sponsor's perceived commitment: 0.93). In addition, two factors emerged from a factor analysis of the manipulation check items (congruence, commitment – 8 items altogether), with all items loading properly on their concept (explained variance = 70.87%; mean intra-factor loading = 0.79; mean absolute extra-factor loading = 0.23). These results also provide strong empirical evidence for the discriminant validity of the scales. For each additive scale, the average of the items was used to test the empirical predictions. In the case of the percentage purchase intention measure, the indicated response was used.

Manipulation checks

An analysis of variance (ANOVA) using *perceived sponsor-organization congruence* as dependent variable, and the two experimental factors as independent variables, resulted in a statistically significant effect of *congruence* ($F(1, 177) = 44.18$, $p < .001$). No other effect was statistically significant. As expected, the participants perceived the partnership between *L'Oréal* and the *Canadian Breast Cancer Foundation* as more congruent (mean = 4.06, SE = 0.13) than that with *L'Itinéraire* (mean = 2.88, SE = 0.13). An ANOVA using *perceived commitment to the organization* and the same independent variables resulted in a statistically significant effect of *sponsorship implementation strategy* ($F(2, 177) = 8.42$, $p < .001$), with no other effect statistically significant. The perceived commitment of *L'Oréal* to the organization was lower in the sponsorship only conditions (mean = 3.58, SE = 0.19) than in the simultaneous philanthropy and sponsorship conditions (mean = 4.42, SE = 0.20; $p < .001$) as well as than in the sequential philanthropy and sponsorship conditions (mean = 4.65, SE = 0.20; $p < .001$). Perceived commitment was however not different in the latter two conditions ($p < .40$). These results confirm that the congruence and sponsorship strategy implementation manipulations were successful.

Test of the conceptual model

The theoretical model presented in Figure 1 first posits that while a firm's sponsorship implementation strategy has an impact on how sincere the sponsor is perceived to be, the degree of congruence between the firm and the sponsored organization should impact the extent to which the sponsorship is perceived as legitimate. These predictions were tested by conducting two ANOVAs using the experimental factors as independent variables and, in turn, *perceived sincerity* and *perceived legitimacy* as

Table 2. Impact of manipulated factors on mediating variables (ANOVA results).

	Dependent variable:			
	Perceived sincerity		Perceived legitimacy	
Source of variation	Mean squares	F statistic	Mean squares	F statistic
Sponsorship's implementation strategy (A)	18.47	4.84**	6.56	1.54
Sponsor-organization congruence (B)	0.78	0.41	19.88	9.31**
A × B	2.38	0.62	6.34	1.49

$**p < .01$.

dependent variables. The results of these analyses are displayed in Table 2. In agreement with the theoretical model, the firm's sponsorship strategy had a statistically significant effect on *perceived sincerity*, whereas sponsor-organization congruence had a statistically significant effect on *perceived legitimacy*. None of the other effects was statistically significant. As expected, the sponsor's perceived sincerity was the lowest in the sponsorship only conditions (mean = 3.71, SE = 0.17), intermediate in the simultaneous philanthropy-sponsorship conditions (mean = 4.24, SE = 0.18), and the highest in the sequential philanthropy-sponsorship conditions (mean = 4.45, SE = 0.18). Also, as expected, the perceived legitimacy of the sponsorship was greater in the congruent partnership conditions (mean = 5.02, SE = 0.15) than in the incongruent conditions (mean = 4.36, SE = 0.15). Therefore, H3 and H4 were supported.

In addition, the conceptual model posits that consumers' intention to choose a *L'Oréal* product when they need to buy a cosmetic item becomes more favorable as a result of an indirect effect of congruence through the perceived legitimacy of *L'Oréal* as a sponsor of the event and an indirect effect of *L'Oréal*'s sponsorship implementation strategy through the perceived sincerity of the sponsor (see Figure 1).

These predictions were tested using regression-based mediation analyses. More precisely, Hayes's (2018) PROCESS procedure (template 4 – allowing the estimation of models including a single mediator) was employed to perform the necessary statistical analyses. For these analyses, sponsorship strategy was coded as follows: sponsorship only (= 1), philanthropy and sponsorship combined (= 2), and philanthropy and sponsorship in sequence (= 3). As regards congruence, it was coded as incongruent (= 0) and congruent (= 1). Two mediation models were estimated, one based on the sequence involving sponsorship implementation strategy (Mediation sequence 1, i.e. H5a) and one based on the sequence involving congruence (Mediation sequence 2, i.e. H5b). These analyses were performed for both the 3-item and percentage purchase intention measures.

As shown in Table 3, the results are in line with the presumed mediation processes. In Mediation sequence 1, sponsorship implementation strategy has a positive and statistically significant impact on the sponsor's perceived sincerity, ($t(179) = 3.01$, $p < .01$), which has a positive impact on purchase intention (3-item: $t(178) = 5.94$, $p < .001$; percentage: $t(179) = 5.44$, $p < .001$). These latter results support H1. In Mediation sequence 2, the effect of congruence on perceived legitimacy is positive and statistically significant ($t(175 = 3.26$, $p < .01$) and, as expected, legitimacy impacts positively purchase intention (3-item: $t(174) = 4.42$, $p < .001$; percentage: $t(179) = 5.35$, $p < .001$). These latter results support H2. Since in the regression models only the mediating variables had a statistically significant effect

Table 3. Results of the mediating testing procedures.

Mediation sequence	Dependent variable	Independent variable(s)	Regression coefficient	Full model
1	Sincerity	Sponsorship strategy	0.37**	**
	Intention	Sincerity	0.43***	***
	(3 items)	Sponsorship strategy	0.20	
2	Legitimacy	Congruence	0.65**	**
	Intention	Legitimacy	0.32***	***
	(3 items)	Congruence	−0.16	
1	Sincerity	Sponsorship strategy	0.37**	**
	Intention	Sincerity	6.44***	***
	(percentage)	Sponsorship strategy	0.82	
2	Legitimacy	Congruence	0.65**	**
	Intention	Legitimacy	5.98***	***
	(percentage)	Congruence	−4.18	

$^*p < .05$, $^{**}p < .01$, $^{***}p < .001$.

on purchase intention, it can be concluded that all estimated effects of the manipulated variables are fully mediated in a manner that is consistent with the conceptual model. Therefore, in addition to supporting H1-H4, the results of the
mediation analysis support H5a and H5b.

Following the recommendations of Hayes (2018), the predictions that sincerity and
legitimacy act as mediators in mediation sequences 1 and 2, respectively, were further
tested by estimating the indirect effects of the manipulated variables on both purchase
intention measures. As can be seen in Table 4, 95% confidence intervals (constructed
via bootstrapping) (Hayes 2018) for both mediators do not include the zero value
regarding purchase intentions measured either with the 3-item additive scale (indirect
effect through sincerity: .06 to .29; indirect effect through legitimacy: .06 to .42) or with
the percentage scale (indirect effect through sincerity: .095 to 4.32; indirect effect
through legitimacy: 1.11 to 7.64). These results provide additional empirical evidence
that the effects of sponsorship implementation strategy and sponsor-organization congruence on consumers' intention to purchase *L'Oréal*'s products are mediated by perceived sincerity and perceived legitimacy, respectively (support of H5a and H5b).

Discussion

The results of this experimental study support the general proposition that consumers' intentions to buy products from a firm that sponsors a cause increase
when this firm is perceived as sincere in its involvement with the cause, and when
the social sponsorship is seen as legitimate. The results have also shown that these
two factors, that is, the sponsor's perceived sincerity and the sponsorship's legitimacy, can be enhanced by means of specific strategic moves. More precisely, a social
sponsorship should be perceived as more legitimate when the firm and the cause
are congruent than when they are not. Also, consumers' perceptions of the sponsor's sincerity are strengthened if the sponsor engages in simultaneous philanthropic activities with the cause, and even more if the philanthropic investments
occurred prior to the sponsorship.

It is relevant to note the analogy between the sincerity and legitimacy factors that
have been the object of this study and two dimensions that are often put forward to

Table 4. Estimated indirect effects.

Indirect effect	Coefficient	LLCI	ULCI
Purchase intention (3-item):			
Congruence → Legitimacy → Intention	.21	.06	.42
Strategy → Sincerity → Intention	.16	.06	.29
Purchase intention (percentage):			
Congruence → Legitimacy → Intention	3.92	1.11	7.64
Strategy → Sincerity → Intention	2.41	0.95	4.32

Note: Minimum $n = 181$; LLCI = lower limit confidence interval, ULCI = upper limit confidence interval; confidence level = .95; 1,000 bootstrap samples.

explain why a persuasive attempt is more or less effective, namely a source's expertise and trustworthiness (see Hovland, Janis, and Kelley 1953). Thus, a source's expertise as regards an object represents the extent to which it is perceived as making valid statements about that object. In the context of a social sponsorship, there is a logical correspondence with how much a sponsorship is seen as appropriate and valid, in other words, legitimate. A source's trustworthiness, for its part, represents how much the source is seen as honest and objective, two attributes that relates quite directly, in the context of a social sponsorship, to a firm's perceived sincerity. Therefore, the conceptual model that has guided this study appears to provide a coherent and generally agreed upon theoretical representation of some of the psychological processes that explain the effectiveness of social sponsorship.

Ohanian (1991) has also made a similar analogy in the context of celebrity endorsement where she examined the impact of three traits of celebrities on purchase intentions: expertise, trustworthiness, and attractiveness. In her study, Ohanian (1991) found that only expertise had a significant impact on purchase intentions. She explained these results by arguing that consumers expect celebrities to be attractive and generally grant them little trust because they know that they are being paid for their advocacy of the brand. This contrasts with sponsorship in general, and social sponsorship in particular, where consumers are likely to see the benefits that the sponsoring brand obtains as appropriate, given the financial investments that this relationship entails for the firm, and where it seems very possible for a sponsor to sincerely care for a cause, even though the partnership is commercially profitable. This probably explains why both legitimacy and sincerity had a statistically significant mediating impact in this study.

Another analogy relative to some socio-psychological mechanisms operating in persuasive attempts can be made with respect to the effects of the sponsorship implementation strategy observed in this research. As the results of the experiment have shown, consumers' intentions to purchase products from a social sponsor increase as the perceived sincerity of the sponsor is enhanced through its philanthropic involvement with the cause: sponsorship only (low sincerity, and weak intentions), philanthropy and sponsorship simultaneously (higher sincerity, and stronger intentions), and philanthropy followed by sponsorship (the highest sincerity, and the strongest intentions). This seems consistent with the research literature relative to the foot-in-the-door compliance technique where numerous studies have shown that people are more likely to agree to a large request (e.g. placing a conspicuous sign on one's yard) when they previously agreed to a smaller one (e.g. signing a petition) (see Burger

1999 for a review). In this context, the philanthropic involvement of a firm with a cause would be analogous to a small request (i.e. allowing the firm to become a partner of the cause with minimal commercial incidence) and the sponsorship as a larger one (i.e. allowing the firm to become a partner of the cause with significant commercial incidence).

Limitations

The research presented in this article suffers from some limitations that need to be taken into account when assessing its contribution to the scientific literature on social sponsorship. The first limitation relates to the perceived legitimacy of the sponsorship, a central construct in the theoretical framework of this research. Although the study results are consistent with the research hypotheses that concern this variable (i.e. positive relationships with sponsor-cause congruence and purchase intentions, mediating impact in the congruence-intention relationship), it remains to be demonstrated that consumers naturally produce legitimacy inferences when presented with social sponsorships. Prior research has shown that consumers may question the motivations behind companies' decision to support a cause (Bhattacharya and Sen 2004; Rifon et al. 2004; Simmons and Becker-Olsen 2006). However, in most studies these motivations are presumed and measured with the help of scales. Research should be conducted to verify that perceived legitimacy inferences are spontaneously made by consumers when they are exposed to social sponsorships (see Ellen, Webb, and Mohr 2006 for an example in the context of cause-related marketing). In addition to providing empirical evidence that the perceived legitimacy of a social sponsorship is a relevant construct, such research would potentially serve to provide directions for designing better measuring instruments to assess this construct.

A second limitation concerns the manipulation of sponsor-cause congruence in this study. While it certainly is appropriate to contrast conditions of low and high congruence, some researchers argue that the relationship between congruence and consumer responses may not be linear (see Fleck and Quester 2007; Jagre, Watson, and Watson 2001; Meyers-Levy and Tybout 1989), as moderate levels of incongruence may lead to more positive reactions than conditions of very low or very high incongruence (d'Astous and Bitz 1995). Although the extent to which two entities are perceived as being (in)congruent is likely to vary among consumers (Jagre, Watson, and Watson 2001) – which complicates the task of designing adequate manipulations –, evaluating the impact of this variable on consumer responses to social sponsorship would benefit from using progressive levels of intensity.

A third limitation of this research relates to the use of an after-only experimental design. The decision not to collect prior measures of intentions to purchase the sponsor's products or relevance of the cause to the study participants was based on the researchers' fear that prior testing could compromise the internal validity of the experiment by making the participants more sensitive to the experimental stimuli as well as the topic under study (Vargas, Duff, and Faber 2017). However, research indicates that consumers who have positive attitudes toward a sponsoring brand rate more favorably the sponsorship activities of that brand (Bhattacharya and Sen 2004;

Caemmerer and Descotes 2011). Also, Bhattacharya and Sen (2004) report that consumers who have developed a personal connection with a cause have a more favorable evaluation of the sponsorship. Although these results do not suggest that the pattern of effects observed in the present study would change as a function of these variables (i.e. interaction effects), the issue is sufficiently intriguing to be studied using appropriate experimental procedures (e.g. clearing the participants' short-term memory by incorporating a neutral task between the measures and the manipulations).

Managerial implications

The results of this experimental study suggest that sponsors of causes can stimulate positively consumers' intentions to purchase their products by enhancing the perceived legitimacy of their association with the sponsored cause, or causes, and also by demonstrating to consumers that their involvement is sincere.

As shown in this study, an effective way to increase perceived legitimacy is to select a cause that represents a good fit with the sponsor. However, this may not be possible, as congruent causes to sponsor are not always available. In addition, a firm could prefer to direct its sponsorship investments toward attractive causes (e.g. based on overall image, size of potential audience), although these causes might not be congruent. In such situations, it seems pertinent to consider the possibility of articulating the relationship between the firm and the incongruent cause (Carrillat and d'Astous 2015). As Cornwell, Weeks, and Roy (2005) have argued, a link between two entities (e.g. a firm and a cause) may exist because these two entities are seen as going well together on some dimensions (objectives, activities, image, place, etc.), but it can also be created and sustained by showing through appropriate communications that the relationship is meaningful. Marketers and advertisers appear to make little use of this communication strategy. For instance, The Royal Bank of Canada (RBC) sponsors Race for the Kids events worldwide to support the well-being of kids and youth.[2] Yet, despite the lack of natural fit between the company and the cause, communication campaigns do not explicitly show how the relationship between the two entities is meaningful. The results of this study indicate that this could potentially be a rewarding strategy, for instance by underlining that the bank *invests* in children who are the future of society.

A noteworthy contribution of this research is the demonstration that firms should benefit more from social sponsorship if they also show their commitment to causes by means of philanthropic actions. The results have indeed confirmed that when consumers are informed that the sponsor is also a philanthrope, their intentions to purchase its products increase significantly. Hence, investing in philanthropic activities with a cause appears as a profitable strategy when a sponsorship involving that cause is contemplated. Furthermore, the results have shown that the benefits that ensue are even greater when consumers learn that these philanthropic investments were made *before* the firm obtained the sponsorship rights. Interestingly, these effects were observed without mentioning to consumers how large the philanthropic investments were. Consequently, based on this study's results, firms that wish to sponsor a cause should seriously consider the option of getting into philanthropy as a first stage in building the relationship with that cause or, if it is not possible, as an additional support activity during the sponsorship. But importantly, consumers should be informed by means of appropriate marketing communication tools (e.g. advertising, signages on the sites of events, promotional items, press releases) of the sponsoring firm's philanthropic involvement with the cause and, when this is the case, that the firm-cause partnership was actually initiated through such charitable association. Unfortunately, firms do not always seem aware that they can leverage a great deal on their philanthropic activities. Still in reference to the above example of the Royal Bank of Canada and the Race for the Kids events, it is worth noting that absolutely no mention of the philanthropic activities of RBC, which are substantial,[3] can be found on the communication materials relative to the sponsorship of the cause. Here too, the results of this study suggest that cause sponsorship investments are likely to be more effective when consumers are informed of the sponsoring brand's philanthropic donations, especially when these were made prior to the sponsorship. Sponsors should be aware however of the possibility that communicating too forcefully this information could result in consumers surmising that the sponsoring brand exploits the partnership and does not have the interests of the cause at heart, hence compromising perceived sponsor's sincerity. In the context of sport sponsorship, Carrillat and d'Astous (2012) have shown that attitudes toward a sponsoring brand are negatively affected when sponsorship activities are too intense, presumably because consumers then question the sponsoring brand's altruism (this interpretation was not tested). These researchers argue that the negative impact for the sponsor of being perceived as overexploiting an event should even be more pronounced in less commercial contexts, such as the sponsorship of cultural events. Consequently, communication initiatives aimed at informing consumers of a sponsoring brand's philanthropic actions in the context of social sponsorship should be tested before their deployment as regards their impact on consumer inferences in general, and with respect to the perceived sincerity of the sponsor in particular.

Conclusion

To the authors' knowledge, this is the first study that has empirically assessed the impact on consumer responses of combining philanthropy with sponsorship in the context of a firm-cause partnership. The results should therefore be considered as preliminary, in need of being replicated using different stimuli (i.e. causes, sponsors, events) with the objective of generalizing the observed effects. Research should also be conducted in order to further explore and extend the conceptual framework that has guided this study. In particular, given the positive role played by congruence, further research could explore the impact of known antecedents of congruence in commercial sponsorships, such as image-based congruence and geographical origin (Carrillat, d'Astous, and Davoine 2013; Olson and Thjømøe 2011) in the context of social sponsorships where sincerity and legitimacy inferences are paramount. In the same vein, it would be pertinent to examine how the perceived legitimacy of a social sponsorship can be increased in situations where the sponsor and the cause are not congruent. Testing how messages in this case can successfully establish in consumers' minds a meaningful association between the sponsor and the cause (i.e. using articulation) and the impact of this change on perceived legitimacy certainly represents a research avenue of great relevance. In addition, research is needed to explore different means by which the leveraging impact of philanthropy in social sponsorship can be enhanced. This research focused on mentioning that the firm engages in philanthropic activities to support the cause. However, other cues, such as varying the magnitude of the philanthropic investments, the length of the philanthropic firm-cause collaboration (e.g. one year, five years), or the benefits to society that have already been achieved through donations, could be studied for their capacity to improve the effectiveness of social sponsorship. Finally, it would also be interesting to examine whether the commercial benefits associated with combining social sponsorship and philanthropy (in sequence or simultaneously) remain, and for how long, in the event of a philanthropic disengagement of the sponsor.

The research literature on social sponsorship is rather limited, in spite of the increasing importance that this type of investment takes among firms. It is hoped that the present study will contribute to stimulate further research in this area.

Notes

1. Although the majority of L'Oréal's products target women, gender did not moderate in a statistically significant way any of the relationships proposed in the conceptual model. The full results are available from the first author upon request.
2. http://rbcraceforthekids.com/.
3. http://www.rbc.com/community-sustainability/community/index.html.

Disclosure statement

No potential conflict of interest was reported by the authors.

ORCID

François Anthony Carrillat ⓘ http://orcid.org/0000-0001-6188-1372

References

Austin, J.E. 2000. Strategic collaboration between nonprofits and businesses. *Nonprofit and Voluntary Sector Quarterly* 29, no. 1_suppl: 69–97.

Austin, J.E., and M.M. Seitanidi. 2012. Collaborative value creation: A review of partnering between nonprofits and businesses: Part I. Value creation spectrum and collaboration stages. *Nonprofit and Voluntary Sector Quarterly* 41, no. 5: 726–58.

Becker-Olsen, K.L., and R.P. Hill. 2006. The impact of sponsor fit on Brand equity: The case of nonprofit service providers. *Journal of Service Research* 9, no. 1: 73–83.

Bhattacharya, C.B., and S. Sen. 2004. Doing better at doing good: When, why, and how consumers respond to corporate social initiatives. *California Management Review* 47, no. 1: 9–24.

Burger, J.M. 1999. The foot-in-the-door compliance procedure: A multiple-process analysis and review. *Personality and Social Psychology Review* 3, no. 4: 303–25.

Caemmerer, B., and R.M. Descotes. 2011. The effectiveness of sponsorship in legitimacy formation: The moderating role of pre-existing satisfaction. In *Advances in consumer research 39*, eds. R. Ahluwalia, T.L. Chartrand, and R.K. Ratner, 618–9. Ratner: Association for Consumer Research.

Carrillat, F.A., and A. d'Astous. 2012. The sponsorship-advertising interface: Is less better for sponsors? *European Journal of Marketing* 46, no. 3/4: 562–74.

Carrillat, F.A., and A. d'Astous. 2015. Sponsorship. In *Wiley encyclopedia of management (marketing) 9*. 3rd ed., eds. N. Lee and A. Farrell, 1–7. Hoboken: Wiley.

Carrillat, F.A., A. d'Astous, and V. Davoine. 2013. The sponsor-event geographical match as a dimension of event-sponsor fit: An investigation in Europe and North America. *Australasian Marketing Journal* 21, no. 4: 264–70.

Carrillat, F.A., B.A. Lafferty, and E.G. Harris. 2005. Investigating sponsorship effectiveness: Do less familiar brands have an advantage over more familiar brands in single and multiple sponsorship arrangements? *Journal of Brand Management* 13, no. 1: 50–64.

Collins, A.M., and E.F. Loftus. 1975. A spreading-activation theory of semantic processing. *Psychological Review* 82, no. 6: 407–28.

Cone. 2004. Cone Corporate Citizenship Study 2004. http://mycoachescorner.com/media/2004ConeCorporateCitizenshipStudy.pdf

Cornwell, T.B., C.S. Weeks, and D.P. Roy. 2005. Sponsorship-linked marketing: Opening the black box. *Journal of Advertising* 34, no. 2: 21–42.

Cuypers, I.R.P., P.-S. Koh, and H. Wang. 2016. Sincerity in corporate philanthropy: Stakeholder perceptions and firm value. *Organization Science* 27, no. 1: 173–88.

d'Astous, A., and P. Bitz. 1995. Consumer evaluations of sponsorship programmes. *European Journal of Marketing* 29, no. 12: 6–22.

Daw, J. 2011. Cause marketing vs. sponsorship – What' the difference? April 27. https://www.selfishgiving.com/blog/cause-marketing-101/cause-marketing-vs-sponsorship-whats-difference

Diehl, S., R. Terlutter, and B. Mueller. 2016. Doing good matters to consumers: The effectiveness of humane-oriented CSR appeals in cross-cultural standardized advertising campaigns. *International Journal of Advertising* 35, no. 4: 730–57.

Ellen, P.S., L.A. Mohr, and D.J. Webb. 2000. Charitable programs and the retailer: Do they mix? *Journal of Retailing* 76, no. 3: 393–406.

Ellen, P.S., D.J. Webb, and L.A. Mohr. 2006. Building Corporate Associations: Consumer attributions for corporate socially responsible programs. *Journal of the Academy of Marketing Science* 34, no. 2: 147–57.

Fleck, N.D., P. Quester. 2007. Birds of a feather flock together … Definition, role and measure of congruence: An application to sponsorship. *Psychology and Marketing* 24, no. 11: 975–1000.

Geue, M., and C. Plewa. 2010. Cause sponsorship: A study on congruence, attribution and corporate social responsibility. *Journal of Sponsorship* 3, no. 3: 228–41.

Gwinner, K.P., and J. Eaton. 1999. Building Brand image through event sponsorship: The role of image transfer. *Journal of Advertising* 28, no. 4: 47–57.

Hayes, A.F. 2018. *Introduction to mediation, moderation, and conditional process analysis*. 2nd ed. New York: The Guilford Press.

Hovland, C.I., I.L. Janis, and H.H. Kelley. 1953. *Communication and persuasion: Psychological studies of opinion change*. New Haven: Yale University Press.

IEG. 2015. Sponsorship spending report: Where the dollars are going and trends for 2015. https://www.sponsorship.com/IEG/files/4e/4e525456-b2b1-4049-bd51-03d9c35ac507.pdf.

IEG. 2019. Sponsorship spending report. http://www.sponsorship.com/Report.aspx#.

Jagre, E., J.J. Watson, and J.G. Watson. 2001. Sponsorship and congruity theory: A theoretical framework for explaining consumer attitude and recall of event sponsorship. In *Advances in consumer research 28*, eds. M.C. Gilly and J. Meyers-Levy, 439–45. Valdosta: Association for Consumer Research.

Kent, R.J., and C.T. Allen. 1994. Competitive interference effects in consumer memory for advertising: The role of Brand familiarity. *Journal of Marketing* 58, no. 3: 97–105.

Lacey, R., A.G. Close, and R.Z. Finney. 2010. The pivotal roles of product knowledge and corporate social responsibility in event sponsorship effectiveness. *Journal of Business Research* 63, no. 11: 1222–8.

Lafferty, B.A., and R.E. Goldsmith. 2005. Cause–Brand alliances: Does the cause help the Brand or does the Brand help the cause? *Journal of Business Research* 58, no. 4: 423–9.

Lii, Y.-S., and M. Lee. 2012. Doing right leads to doing well: When the type of CSR and reputation interact to affect consumer evaluations of the firm. *Journal of Business Ethics* 105, no. 1: 69–81.

MacKenzie, S.B., and R.J. Lutz. 1989. An empirical examination of the structural antecedents of attitude toward the ad in an advertising pretesting context. *Journal of Marketing* 53, no. 2: 48–65.

Matin, L., S. Ruiz, and A. Rubio. 2009. The role of identity salience in the effects of corporate social responsibility on consumer behavior. *Journal of Business Ethics* 84, no. 1: 65–78.

McDaniel, S.R. 1999. An investigation of match-up effects in sport sponsorship advertising: The implications of consumer advertising schemas. *Psychology and Marketing* 16, no. 2: 163–84.

Meyers-Levy, J., and A.M. Tybout. 1989. Schema congruity as a basis for product evaluation. *Journal of Consumer Research* 16, no. 1: 39–54.

Ohanian, R. 1991. The impact of celebrity spokespersons' perceived image on consumers' intention to purchase. *Journal of Advertising Research* 31, no. 1: 46–54.

Olson, E.L., and H.M. Thjømøe. 2011. Explaining and articulating the fit construct in sponsorship. *Journal of Advertising* 40, no. 1: 57–70.

Pappu, R., and T.B. Cornwell. 2014. Corporate sponsorship as an image platform: Understanding the roles of relationship fit *and* sponsor-sponsee similarity. *Journal of the Academy of Marketing Science* 42, no. 5: 490–510.

Rifon, N.J., S.M. Choi, C.S. Trimble, and H. Li. 2004. Congruence effects in sponsorship: The mediating role of sponsor credibility and consumer attributions of sponsor motive. *Journal of Advertising* 33, no. 1: 30–42.

Simmons, C.J., and K.L. Becker-Olsen. 2006. Achieving marketing objectives through social sponsorships. *Journal of Marketing* 70, no. 4: 154–69.

Speed, R., and P. Thompson. 2000. Determinants of sports sponsorship response. *Journal of the Academy of Marketing Science* 28, no. 2: 226–38.

Suchman, M.C. 1995. Managing legitimacy: Strategic and institutional approaches. *The Academy of Management Review* 20, no. 3: 571–610.

Taylor, C.R. 2018. Red alert: On the need for more research on corporate social responsibility appeals in advertising. *International Journal of Advertising* 37, no. 3: 337–9.

Uhrich, S., J. Koenigstorfer, and A. Groeppel-Klein. 2014. Leveraging sponsorship with corporate social responsibility. *Journal of Business Research* 67, no. 9: 2023–9.

Vargas, P.T., B.R.L. Duff, and R.J. Faber. 2017. A practical guide to experimental advertising research. *Journal of Advertising* 46, no. 1: 101–14.

Wakefield, K.L., and G. Bennett. 2010. Affective intensity and sponsor identification. *Journal of Advertising* 39, no. 3: 99–111.

Wyer, R.S., Jr., and D.E. Carlston. 1979. *Social cognition, inference, and attribution*. Hillsdale: Lawrence Erlbaum Associates.

Zajac, E.J., and J.D. Westphal. 1995. Accounting for the explanations of CEO compensation: Substance and symbolism. *Administrative Science Quarterly* 40, no. 2: 283–308.

Appendix

Experimental stimulus example: congruent sponsor-organization, philanthropy and sponsorship in sequence.

L'Oréal: an unfailing commitment to women's health

L'Oréal, a world leader in cosmetics, proves that it is committed to improving the conditions of women. The company has announced yesterday, during a press conference held in Montreal, that it has become the official sponsor of the **Run for the Cure** 2017 edition, organized by the *Canadian Breast Cancer Foundation*. To bring this partnership to people's attention, the L'Oréal logo will appear throughout the run path, on the sweaters, and on all printed materials.

Run for the Cure is an event organized by volunteers aimed at collecting funds that help the Foundation to fulfill each component of its mission; research and innovation, support for women suffering from breast cancer as well as their friends and family members, and promoting breast health as a priority through various awareness and education initiatives.

This sponsorship is not the first partnership between L'Oréal and the Canadian Breast Cancer Foundation. Indeed, during the previous year, L'Oréal has dedicated itself to the Foundation by means of financial contributions in the context of its philanthropic programme.

Communicating the fair trade message: the roles of reputation and fit

Jos Bartels, Machiel J. Reinders, Chrissie Broersen and Sarah Hendriks

ABSTRACT
This study examines the extent to which a company's fair trade reputation, and the fit between this reputation and the company's communicated fair trade message, influences consumer scepticism and positive electronic word-of-mouth. The results of two experiments show that a previous fair trade reputation has a direct and indirect effect, via consumer brand identification, on consumer scepticism. Moreover, the fit between the reputation and the communicated message seems to affect scepticism only when the communicated message is perceived as realistic. In industries with poor fair trade reputations (Study 1), the fit does not seem to have an effect on scepticism, while the fit influences scepticism in industries with a certain reputation history for fair trade (Study 2). Scepticism and consumer brand identification play an important mediating role in the relation among reputation, fit and consumers' electronic word-of-mouth intentions. Therefore, we conclude that communicating fair trade initiatives not only can be a rewarding effort but also seems to be a delicate matter.

Introduction

In recent decades, the literature on fair trade consumption has increased enormously (Andorfer and Liebe 2012; Castaldo et al. 2009; De Pelsmacker, Driesen, and Rayp 2005; Herédia-Colaço, do Vale, and Villas-Boas 2019). Consumers have become much more aware of the ethical consequences of their behaviour (Carrington, Neville, and Whitwell 2010; White, MacDonnell, and Ellard 2012), and although market shares of fair trade products, in general, are small, they are growing rapidly. For example, global retail sales of fair trade-certified products more than doubled between 2008 and 2015, reaching €7.3 billion (Fairtrade International 2017), and fair trade sales in the U.S. grew 33% in 2015.

Although these figures look promising, consumers' scepticism about firms that offer sustainable products is growing (Leonidou and Skarmeas 2017). For instance, a

2013 European Commission study reported that consumers may react cynically to sustainability initiatives, when they are perceived as being inconsistent with a company's other policies.

Moreover, a recent GfK research report in Germany found that 76% of the respondents had at least ambivalent thoughts about fair trade labels in a clothing context (Frank et al. 2016). In addition, disasters, such as the 2013 Rana Plaza collapse in Bangladesh, may lead to negative consumer attitudes towards the clothing industry's working conditions in developing countries. Thus, consumers are increasingly aware of fair trade initiatives, but also seem to be sceptical about these initiatives. Consumers' perceptions of a company's reputation might play an important role in explaining this scepticism.

Only a few studies focused on the impact of a company's reputation on consumers' evaluations of fair trade initiatives (Castaldo et al. 2009; Obermiller et al. 2009). Obermiller et al. (2009) investigated the effect of a general brand reputation on attitudes towards a fair trade advertisement. Castaldo et al. (2009) found a positive effect of a corporate social responsibility (CSR) reputation on consumers' trust in specific fair trade products.

Although literature often includes fair trade as a dimension of CSR (Inoue and Lee, 2011; Maloni and Brown, 2006; Öberseder et al., 2014; Pérez and Del Bosque 2013), one might expect a similar role for a company's fair trade reputation in consumers' evaluations of fair trade initiatives. However, none of the previous studies specifically examined this role of a company's fair trade reputation. Moreover, to our knowledge, no research focused on scepticism as a consequence of a previous fair trade reputation. Therefore, this study contributes to the literature, as we focus on (1) the role of a pre-existing fair trade reputation, instead of a general reputation, and (2) an important negative outcome for companies, namely, consumers' scepticism about a fair trade brand.

Castaldo et al. (2009) reasoned that companies with a high reputation for building positive relationships with society are eager to maintain this reputation. Therefore, consumers might think that these companies are more likely to act in line with their promises. To the best of our knowledge, no research in the fair trade context has investigated these assumptions. Given the rise of consumer scepticism about companies' sustainability initiatives and the negative consequences of this scepticism for companies (Leonidou and Skarmeas 2017), we investigate how consumers respond to a fair trade message about a company that does not fit (or fits) this company's previous fair trade reputation. According to Fombrun and Shanley (1990), consumers can use perceptions of an organization's reputation as cues with which to assess conflicting information about the company or organization. Therefore, consumers' responses to fair trade communication seem to be intertwined with a company's previous fair trade reputation.

In sum, this study aimed to investigate the role of a pre-existing fair trade reputation and the fit between this reputation and the communicated fair trade message in consumer evaluations of a company's brand. More specifically, in two experiments, we tested the effects of a company's fair trade reputation, as well as a (mis)fit in a communicated fair trade message by a third party, on consumer scepticism. We focus on fair trade communication about a brand by a third party to rule out consumers' perceptions of a company's self-interest, because previous studies have argued that, in general, non-corporate information sources are perceived as less biased than corporate sources (Du and Vieira 2012; Yoon et al. 2006). We further investigated the possible mediating role of consumer-brand identification in this relationship, as previous research has shown that consumer identification can play a crucial role in the effect of a company's CSR reputation on supportive and advocacy behaviours towards the company (Sen and Bhattacharya 2001).

Because consumer scepticism about a company's motives for CSR initiatives could result in a diminished intention to speak positively (Skarmeas and Leonidou 2013), or even to speak negatively about a brand (Leonidou and Skarmeas 2017), in Study 2, we focused on consumers' word-of-mouth intentions as behavioural outcome. Brands that implement socially responsible initiatives may count on consumers who will speak favourably about the brands to others (Stanaland et al. 2011). Recently, this consumer advocacy for brands has moved from an offline to an online environment (Eisingerich et al. 2015). This *electronic word-of-mouth* (eWOM) can be defined as 'any positive or negative statement made by potential, actual, or former customers about a product or company, which is made available to a multitude of people and institutions via the Internet' (Hennig-Thurau et al. 2004, 39). To date, no studies in the fair trade context have focused on eWOM. In the CSR context, Stanton et al. (2019) used eWOM as an independent variable to predict attitudes towards a company, while Vo et al. (2017) focused on the relation between CSR engagement and consumers' positive and negative responses on Twitter. Because eWOM has been proven to be an important influencer of consumers' decision making regarding companies and brands (Jin and Phua 2014; Laczniak et al. 2001; Rim and Song 2016), this study included eWOM intentions as a behavioural response to fair trade reputation and fit. In the next section, we elucidate the conceptual framework of this study.

Conceptual framework

Consumer scepticism

Consumer scepticism can be defined as a distrust or disbelief regarding advertising claims or public relations efforts (Forehand and Grier 2003; Obermiller and Spangenberg 1998). Consumers can use scepticism as a defence mechanism to protect themselves from possibly misleading marketing communications (Kim and Lee 2009). Sceptical consumers are unwilling to trust companies and their activities. Webb and Mohr (1998) found that higher levels of scepticism lead to negative attitudes towards socially responsible campaigns. A vast number of studies have investigated the effects of consumer scepticism. These studies found that the more sceptical consumers are, the less positive their attitudes, brand evaluations, and word-of-mouth intentions and the lower the consumers' purchase intentions (Becker-Olsen, Cudmore, and Hill 2006; de Vries et al. 2015; Leonidou and Skarmeas 2017; Skarmeas and Leonidou 2013; Yoon, Gürhan-Canli, and Schwarz 2006).

According to Forehand and Grier (2003), there are two types of consumer scepticism: dispositional scepticism and situational scepticism. Dispositional scepticism is defined as a personality trait or a general tendency to doubt companies' motives (Kim and Lee 2009). Situational scepticism, however, can be seen as a temporary state. Certain aspects of a marketing message can influence the level of one's scepticism. Under these conditions, one can argue that situational scepticism can be evoked independently of consumers' personality traits (Forehand and Grier 2003). As this study aimed to investigate the role of a company's previous fair trade reputation, and the fit between this reputation and the communicated fair trade message in consumer evaluations, in the remainder of this article, we focus on consumers' situational scepticism.

Reputation and scepticism

The reputation of a company can be defined as the result of all perceptions that individuals have of the company over time (Cornelissen 2017). Likewise, a company's fair trade reputation represents consumers' perceptions of a company's fair trade activities. Since the fair trade concept was developed, it has become increasingly integrated in CSR (Mohan 2009). Carrol (1991) previously introduced the ethical dimension in his pyramid of CSR as the '[o]bligation to do what is right, just and fair' (Carroll 1991, 42). As a result, a vast number of studies in the consumer context have integrated fair trade as one of the dimensions of CSR (Öberseder et al. 2014).

Several studies on CSR reputation showed that consumers have unfavourable attitudes about the CSR activities of companies with bad reputations. For example, Obermiller et al. (2009) found that when a well-known brand incorporates fair trade initiatives in its advertisements, this action leads to positive attitudes towards the brand than when an unknown brand incorporates fair trade initiatives. Bögel (2016) showed that when a company has a negative reputation, consumers are less likely to trust the company's CSR activities. More specifically, Vanhamme and Grobben (2009) found that companies that have built a longer CSR history, and thus, obtained a better CSR reputation, face less consumer scepticism than companies that only recently started CSR activities. These findings indicate that a company's previous CSR reputation influences consumer attitudes towards the company. In one of the few studies in the fair trade context, Castaldo et al. (2009) argued that consumers make decisions based on companies' fair trade positioning. The authors showed that if consumers believe a company is committed to its social and ethical initiatives, then consumers' trust in the company's fair trade products increases.

Based on these studies that related reputation to consumers' attitudes towards a company's CSR or fair trade initiatives, we expect that when a third party communicates about a brand with a high fair trade reputation, this communication will lead to less scepticism about the brand's fair trade initiatives compared to when a third party communicates about a brand with a low fair trade reputation. We hypothesized the following:

> H1: Fair trade communication about a brand with a high fair trade reputation leads to less scepticism than fair trade communication about a brand with a low fair trade reputation.

Fit and scepticism

In addition to the main effect of fair trade reputation, we expect that if this reputation is in line with the communicated fair trade message, consumers will experience less scepticism. This proposed effect can be explained by Osgood and Tannenbaum's (1955) principle of congruity. According to Osgood and Tannenbaum (1955, 43), 'changes in evaluation are always in the direction of increased congruity with the existing frame of reference'. In line with this definition, consumers prefer continuity in what they know or perceive about a product or a brand, and new information communicated about this brand.

To further elaborate on this assumption, we draw from associative network models, which imply that human memory is a network of interconnected nodes that activate each other in specific contexts (Hinton and Anderson 2014). According to Becker-Olsen et al. (2006), a good fit between a consumer's previous associations with a company and a company's current activities can be more easily integrated into the consumer's existing cognitive structure. Conversely, when a certain initiative does not fit consumers' expectations for a company, it is less likely that consumers automatically incorporate this new information into their memory (Becker-Olsen et al. (2006).

In the marketing context, we can draw from several streams of literature that have proven this fit leads to positive evaluations of companies or brands. First, literature on brand extensions showed that the fit between the parent brand and a new extension product is an important predictor of the success of the new product (Aaker and Keller 1990; Bottomley and Holden 2001; Völckner and Sattler 2006). Second, studies on cause-related marketing (CRM) provided evidence that the fit between a company and a cause leads to positive consumer evaluations (Gupta and Pirsch 2006; Polonsky and Speed 2001; Pracejus and Olsen 2004). For example, Nan and Heo (2007) found that a CRM message with a high fit between the brand and the cause leads to positive attitudes towards the advertisement and towards the brand. Elving (2013) tested the interaction effect of cause-company fit and reputation on scepticism, and found that consumers have the lowest levels of scepticism when a company has a good reputation, and a good fit between the company and the cause. Finally, in the CSR context, Du, Bhattacharya, and Sen (2007) showed that consumers' responses to CSR activities are dependent on the extent to which these CSR activities are consistent with the positioning of the brand or company. The authors found that when a brand had clearer CSR positioning, consumers' attributions of the company's motives for its CSR activities are less negative.

In sum, based on the principle of congruity and the associative network model approach, previous studies in several domains have found positive effects of fit on consumer evaluations of a brand. The fit between a communicated fair trade message and a company's fair trade reputation could have similar effects on consumer evaluations. For example, if consumers read a message about the new fair trade initiative of a brand with a strong fair trade reputation, such as Ben & Jerry's, this message could be perceived as more congruent with consumers' previous thoughts about the social responsibility of the brand than when consumers read a message about the new initiative of an oil company, such as ExxonMobil. In this study, we expected that the fit between a company's previous fair trade reputation and the company's communicated fair trade message diminishes consumer scepticism. Therefore, we proposed the following:

H2: A high fit between the communicated fair trade message and the company's fair trade reputation leads to less scepticism than a low fit between the communicated fair trade message and the company's fair trade reputation.

Mediating role of consumer-brand identification

Consumer identities can play an important role in consumer responses to brands (Reinders and Bartels 2017; Tian, Bearden, and Hunter 2001). Social identity theory is often used to explain the relation between consumer identities and these brands (Escalas and Bettman 2003; Stokburger-Sauer, Ratneshwar, and Sen 2012). Social identity can be defined as 'the individual's knowledge that he (or she) belongs to certain groups together with some emotional and value significance to him (or her) of the group membership' (Tajfel 1972, 31). Bhattacharya and Sen (2003) were among the first to introduce social identity into the consumer context, and suggested that consumers can identify with certain organizations to fulfil the consumers' self-definitional needs. In turn, Ahearne, Bhattacharya, and Gruen (2005) found that consumers' identification with a company leads to buying behaviour and positive word-of-mouth. More specifically, Bagozzi and Dholakia (2006) found that social identification can play an important role in brand communities. Researchers have found that consumers' identification with a brand can, for example, lead to stronger brand loyalty (Lam et al. 2010) and more positive word-of-mouth (Alberta, Merunkaa, and Valette-Florence 2013). Thus, brand identification is an important antecedent for brand-related behaviours.

Several studies have linked an organization's reputation to social identification. Sen and Bhattacharya (2001) found that consumers are more likely to identify with companies that have good CSR reputations than with companies that have bad reputations. More specifically, the authors found that customer-company identification mediates the effect of the company's CSR reputation on company evaluations. Hong and Yang (2009) also found benefits from a strong reputation regarding engendered customer-company identification. In their study, customer-company identification mediated the relation between reputation and positive word-of-mouth intentions. Recently, He, Li, and Harris (2012) focused on the role of brand identity in consumer loyalty. They argued that reputation is part of brand identity, and found that brand identification mediates the relation between brand identity and brand trust. Because scepticism is closely related to trust (Obermiller and Spangenberg 1998), we assume that consumers' identification with a brand can also play a mediating role in the relation between a company's fair trade reputation and consumers' scepticism. Therefore, we hypothesized the following:

H3a: Fair trade reputation has an indirect effect on scepticism via consumer-brand identification.

Several studies also indicated a mediating role of brand identification between fit and consumers' responses to a brand (Cha, Yi, and Bagozzi 2016; Li, Liu, and Huan 2019; Lii and Lee 2012). Although Lii and Lee (2012) did not directly investigate the mediating role of customer-company identification, their model implies that when different CSR initiatives fit the reputation of the company, this fit leads to different levels of identification. The authors also found that stronger customer-company identification

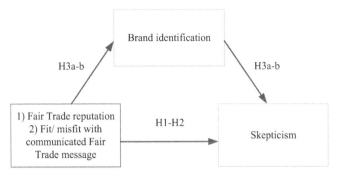

Figure 1. Conceptual model hypotheses H1–H3.

leads to positive in-role and extra-role behaviours. Moreover, Cha, Yi, and Bagozzi (2016) showed that CSR-brand fit strengthens brand identification, which, in turn, increases brand loyalty. Finally, Li, Liu, and Huan (2019) found that when a company introduces a new corporate social responsibility strategy, it leads to more customer-company identification only when the reputation of the company is high (ie when there is a fit between the company and the new corporate social responsibility strat-egy). Based on these findings, we also expect a mediating role for brand identification between fit and scepticism. Therefore, we hypothesized the following:

H3b: Fit has an indirect effect on scepticism via consumer-brand identification.

Figure 1 presents the conceptual model of hypotheses 1 through 3.

To test the hypotheses, we conducted two experimental studies. In both studies, 2×2 between-subject experimental designs were employed, including the following manipulations: communicated fair trade message (30% fair trade or 100% fair trade) and fair trade reputation (high versus low). By offering small percentages of fair trade ingredients in products, companies can bring suspicion on themselves, which would negatively influence brand purchase intention (Montoro Rios et al. 2006). Most of the studies in the fair trade context compared only consumer evaluations of products pre-sented as being 100% fair trade and consumer evaluations of products that are not fair trade at all (De Pelsmacker et al. 2005; Didier and Lucie 2008; Vanhamme and Grobben 2009). In the clothing context, Dickson (2001), for example, examined con-sumers' willingness to pay for clothing that either was labelled 'No Sweat' (ie pro-duced under fair circumstances) or had no label at all (ie regular brand), and found that consumers were positively influenced by a No Sweat label. However, to date, researchers have not investigated how consumers respond to messages in which a company is presented as *partly* fair trade, and how this presentation is related to the company's perceived fair trade reputation. In the present study, we expected a high fair trade reputation with a 30% fair trade message to present a low fit, and a 100% fair trade message to present a high fit. Conversely, a low fair trade reputation with a 100% fair trade message would present a low fit, while a low fair trade reputation with a 30% fair trade message would present a high fit. Although the percentage of 30% was chosen somewhat arbitrarily, in the fair trade context, certification organiza-tions (ie Rainforest Alliance) use this percentage as their minimum criterion for carry-ing the label. Table 1 shows the four conditions in both experiments.

Table 1. Fair trade reputation versus communicated fair trade message.

	Fair trade reputation	
Communicated fair trade message	Low	High
30%	Fit	Misfit
100%	Misfit	Fit

Study 1 method

Context

In Study 1, we used apparel brands. Recently, the apparel industry has faced many issues related to low contract prices and labour exploitation (Ma, Lee, and Goerlitz 2016). Therefore, fashion brands have received negative publicity (Goworek et al. 2012). The clothing sector responded to this negative publicity with the introduction of prosocial initiatives, such as fair trade production. For example, clothing brands, such as Nike, H&M, and Zara, began prosocial initiatives (Kozlowski, Bardecki, and Searcy 2012). Moreover, Government legislation, such as the California Transparency in Supply Chains Act, forced manufacturers and retailers to behave more ethically (Ma et al. 2016). These developments make it worthwhile to investigate consumers' fair trade perceptions of the apparel industry.

Pre-test Study 1

Study 1 included two clothing brands that were perceived as either high or low in fair trade. Therefore, a pre-test was conducted to determine which clothing brand was perceived as being the most fair trade and which brand was the least, to be able to represent a 100% versus a 30% fair trade brand. A within-subject design was used that included six clothing brands: H&M, Zara, Primark, Kuyichi, TOMS, and Nudie Jeans. A total of 29 Dutch respondents were asked whether they were familiar with the six brands, and to what extent they perceived the brand as being fair trade (ie having a fair trade reputation). Only respondents who indicated that they were familiar with the brand were included when the fair trade reputation was measured. To measure fair trade reputation, we used a three-item scale following Hsu (2012). We used only three of the five original items, because two items have the same meaning when they are translated into Dutch. The three items were measured on a 7-point Likert scale. For example, participants were asked to indicate to what extent they agreed with the following statement: 'Brand X is a well-respected brand considering its fair trade products' (1 = strongly disagree, 7 = strongly agree).

    We conducted paired sample t tests to choose the brand with the strongest fair trade associations and the brand with the weakest fair trade associations. Kuyichi and TOMS had the strongest reputations concerning fair trade ($M_{Kuyichi}$=4.81; SD = 1.16 and M_{TOMS}=4.76; SD = 1.43). A dependent t-test showed that the difference between these two brands was not statistically significant ($t(1, 10)$ = −.393, p=.70). Because more participants were familiar with the TOMS brand than with Kuyichi, we selected TOMS as the fair trade brand to include in the main study. We selected Primark as the low fair trade reputation brand, as this brand clearly had the weakest fair trade reputation (M = 1.60; SD = 1.10).

Main study

The data were collected with convenience sampling. The sample consisted of 198 Dutch participants; 152 of the participants were female, and 46 were male, with a mean age of 29.3 years ($SD = 11.67$). Participants from the pre-test were not invited to participate in the main study.

Participants were randomly assigned to one of the following four conditions, which Fairtrade Netherlands communicates: (1) TOMS is 100% fair trade, (2) TOMS is 30% fair trade, (3) Primark is 100% fair trade and (4) Primark is 30% fair trade. Due to the exclusion of participants based on their non-familiarity with the assigned brand, the final numbers of participants for the conditions were not equal. Specifically, for TOMS ($N = 70$), the 30% condition consisted of 31 participants, and the 100% condition consisted of 39 participants. Moreover, for Primark ($N = 128$), 68 participants for the 30% condition completed the survey, and 60 full responses were included for the 100% condition. Because the conditions were divided unevenly, we used Levene's test to assess homogeneity of variance (ie the variance was equal across groups).

Participants were first exposed to a Facebook page for Fairtrade Netherlands containing a message presenting a brand (TOMS or Primark) and the percentage of the brand that was fair trade (30% or 100%). Subsequently, the participants were asked to complete a self-administered survey containing the following measures.

Measures

First, for the manipulation check on fair trade reputation, the same Hsu (2012) scale was used as in the pre-test (Cronbach's α was .95 for TOMS and .92 for Primark).

Situational scepticism was measured with an adapted version of Obermiller and Spangenberg's (1998) advertising scepticism scale. We used three items on a 7-point Likert scale anchored by *totally disagree* and *totally agree*. A sample item included 'I am sceptical about the fair trade production of TOMS/Primark'. The reliability of the scale was adequate for TOMS and Primark (Cronbach's α was .83 and .69, respectively). *Consumer-brand identification* was measured with Leach et al.'s (2008) three-item 7-point Likert scale. The reliability of this scale was good (Cronbach's α was .94 for TOMS and .92 for Primark). Additionally, we incorporated the *credibility of the message* and the *credibility of the source* as control variables in the study. For the credibility of the message and the credibility of the source, we used a two-item 7-point Likert scales: 'The Facebook message that I just read is reliable' (Cronbach's α was .82 for TOMS and .84 for Primark), and 'Fairtrade Netherlands is a reliable source' (Cronbach's α was .90 for TOMS and .85 for Primark). We used confirmatory factor analysis to test whether the two dimensions of credibility were perceived as being distinct. The two-dimensional model in which both dimensions were correlated ($r=.67$) showed a much better fit ($\chi^2/df=.53$; CFI = 1.00; TLI = 1.00; RMSEA=.00) than the one-dimensional model ($\chi^2/df = 39.11$; CFI=.81; TLI=.43; RMSEA=.44). Finally, we included demographic variables (ie age, gender, income and education) as descriptive variables in the analyses. Multi-item scales were averaged across their scale items to create composite construct scores.

Study 1 results

Manipulation check and control variables

First, the manipulation check showed that participants in the TOMS condition provided statistically significantly higher scores for fair trade reputation ($M = 5.23$,
$SD = 1.16$) than participants in the Primark condition ($M = 1.57$, $SD = 95$;
$t(1, 196) = 22.60$, $p < .01$). Additionally, Fairtrade Netherlands was perceived as a credible
source ($M = 4.83$, $SD = 1.23$). An ANOVA showed that the difference between the
conditions was not statistically significant ($F(3, 194) = .54$, $p = .72$). Finally, participants
perceived the Facebook message to be credible ($M = 4.03$, $SD = 1.39$). However, an
ANOVA showed that the differences between the conditions were statistically significant ($F(3, 194) = 12.29$, $p < .01$). A post hoc analysis showed that the Primark 100% fair
trade condition was perceived as the least reliable ($M = 3.23$, $SD = 1.52$), whereas the
other three conditions did not differ statistically significantly.

Hypotheses testing

First, to test the main effect of a company's fair trade reputation on consumer scepticism (H1), one-way ANOVA showed a statistically significant difference in scepticism
between a high fair trade reputation ($M = 3.38$; $SD = 1.08$) and a low fair trade reputation ($M = 4.84$; $SD = 1.15$), $F(1, 196) = 76.15$, $p < .01$). Furthermore, because the group
sizes were unequal, Levene's test indicated equal variances ($F(3, 194) = .10$; $p = .96$). In
H2, we expected that a high fit between the communicated fair trade identity and the
fair trade reputation would lead to less scepticism than a low fit between the communicated fair trade identity and the fair trade reputation. One-way ANOVA revealed that
the effect of fit on scepticism was not statistically significant ($F(1, 196) = 1.71$, $p = . 19$).
A high fit did not lead to less scepticism ($M = 4.20$; $SD = 1.40$) than a low fit ($M = 4.44$;
$SD = 1.25$). Again, Levene's test indicated equal variances ($F(1, 196) = 1.96$; $p = .16$).

   To test H3a, in which we assumed that reputation had an indirect effect on scepticism via consumer-brand identification, we used the Hayes PROCESS (2012), model 4,
using 5000 bootstrap samples. The regression analysis showed that when reputation
and brand identification were simultaneously regressed on scepticism, the coefficient
of reputation was statistically significant ($\beta = 1.24$; $SE = .20$; $p < .01$), while the coefficient
of identification was also statistically significant ($\beta = -.18$; $SE = .09$; $p < .05$). In addition,
the indirect effect of reputation on scepticism through identification was statistically
significant (estimated effect $= .22$), with a 95% bias-corrected bootstrap confidence
interval excluding zero (.03 to .44). Thus, H3a was supported.

   To test H3b, in which we assumed that fit had an indirect effect on scepticism via
consumer-brand identification, we used the Hayes PROCESS (2012), model 4, using
5000 bootstrap samples. The regression analysis showed that when fit and brand identification were simultaneously regressed on scepticism, the coefficient of fit was, as
expected, not statistically significant ($\beta = .23$; $SE = .17$; $p = .19$), while the coefficient of
identification was statistically significant ($\beta = -.47$; $SE = .08$; $p < .01$). In addition, the indirect effect of fit on scepticism through identification was not statistically significant

(estimated effect=.02), with a 95% bias-corrected bootstrap confidence interval including zero (−.12 to .17). H3b was not supported.

Discussion

Hypothesis 1, in which we proposed that a previous fair trade reputation should have an impact on consumers' scepticism, was supported. This study extends previous research in the CSR context (Bögel 2016; Vanhamme and Grobben 2009), as in the fair trade context, we also found that companies with a bad fair trade reputation seem to suffer more in terms of the negative reactions of consumers to the brands than companies with a good fair trade reputation. In addition, hypothesis H3a, in which we expected that the relation between the previous fair trade reputation and scepticism is mediated by consumer brand identification, was supported. This result is consistent with previous studies, which found that social identification can play a role in explaining the relation between reputation and company-related outcomes (Hong and Yang 2009; Sen and Bhattacharya 2001).

In contrast to our expectation that the fit would influence consumer scepticism, H2 was not supported. Although previous research on the fit between a sponsor and its cause showed that a higher fit leads to less scepticism (Elving 2013), the present results imply that for the fit between a company's previous reputation and the company's communicated fair trade message, different processes might occur. In the context of fair trade apparel, there did not seem to be many sustainable brands that would fit a 100% communicated message, and therefore, even a 30% communicated message could have led to a lack of fit for less sustainable apparel brands. More specifically, the apparel brands that were perceived as mostly fair trade were still evaluated as being just above the midpoint of the scale, while the apparel brands that were perceived as the least fair trade were evaluated below the midpoint of the scale. These results could be explained by the fact that the number of ethical initiatives in the apparel industry has been low compared to other industries, such as the food industry. Di Benedetto (2017) recently argued that there is a lack of availability and visibility of ethical clothing products in retail stores. More specifically, few clothing brands use ethical labelling as a strategic positioning option (Connolly and Shaw 2006). In the food context, Du, Bhattacharya, and Sen (2007) compared the positioning of three sustainable food brands, where the brand that was the least sustainable still had some associations with environmental sustainability. In that study, the authors found that clear positioning on sustainabllity leads to several advantages, such as consumers' advocacy behaviours. Thus, in contrast to Study 1, in Study 2, we chose the cocoa industry as the context, because this industry seems to have more developed fair trade associations.

Study 2

Scepticism and eWOM

Study 2 served two main purposes: (1) to test hypotheses H1 through H3 in a different product category and (2) to extend the model with electronic word-of-mouth as the

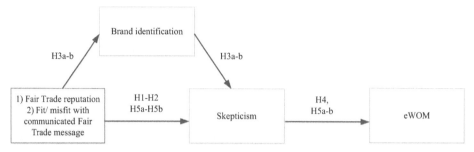

Figure 2. Conceptual model hypotheses H1–H5 (Study 2).

outcome variable. Previous studies showed that consumer scepticism is negatively related to word-of-mouth intentions (Leonidou and Skarmeas 2017; Skarmeas and Leonidou 2013). Moreover, Pérez and de los Salmones (2018) found that negative attitudes towards fair trade have a negative relation with positive WOM intentions. In line with the previous studies on the role of consumer scepticism in offline word-of-mouth, we expected consumer scepticism about the fair trade brand to lead to less positive online word-of-mouth, especially because social media have made it even more convenient to convey positive and negative opinions about a brand (Mangold and Faulds 2009). In addition, in the CSR context, these online WOM intentions have become more relevant (Oh and Ki 2019). Therefore, we proposed:

H4: Scepticism is negatively related to consumers' positive eWOM about a fair trade brand.

In Study 1, we hypothesized that the relations between a company's fair trade reputation and scepticism, and between fit and scepticism, are mediated by consumer brand identification. We expected that through this mechanism, a company's fair trade reputation and fit also indirectly affect eWOM intentions. In this respect, Skarmeas and Leonidou (2013) found that CSR scepticism mediates the relation between consumers' attitudes towards a company's CSR motives and word-of-mouth intentions. Chung and Lee (2019) recently found that attitudes towards the company mediate the relation between CSR history (ie reputation) and offline word-of-mouth intentions. The authors also found a mediating role for attitudes towards the company between the fit of the CSR topic and the company, and WOM intentions. Following these results, we expect the following:

H5a: Fair trade reputation has an indirect effect on eWOM via consumer-brand identification and scepticism.

H5b: Fit has an indirect effect on eWOM via consumer-brand identification and scepticism.

Figure 2 identifies the key constructs included in the second study.

Method Study 2

Context

Since the apparel industry only seemed to have some clearly positioned fair trade brands and a vast number of non-fair trade brands, in Study 2, we used a sector that has already achieved a larger market share of fair trade products. We used cocoa brands that are well known in the Netherlands, as the turnover for fair trade cocoa industry worldwide ($150 billion in 2014) is several times higher than the fair trade cotton industry ($51 billion in 2014) (Fairtrade International 2015). Moreover, the Netherlands is one of the biggest importers of cocoa in the world (CBI, Dutch Ministry of Foreign Affairs 2017).

Pre-test

We conducted a pre-test to investigate what brands in the Netherlands are perceived as fair trade brands. Respondents ($N = 28$) had to evaluate the fair trade reputation of the following six brands: Ben & Jerry's, Tony's Chocolonely and Starbucks, which communicate a greater fair trade reputation, versus three 'regular' brands, Hertog, Milka and Douwe Egberts. Respondents were first asked to indicate their familiarity with the brand. We removed one respondent that was not familiar with one or more brands. To measure fair trade reputation, we used a three-item scale based on Hsu (2012). We conducted paired sample t tests to choose the brand with the strongest fair trade associations and the brand with the weakest fair trade associations. Tony's Chocolonely had the strongest reputation concerning fair trade ($M = 6.45$; $SD = 0.98$) and Hertog ($M = 2.96$; $SD = .90$) and Milka ($M = 3.10$; $SD = 1.05$) had the weakest fair trade reputations. A paired sample t test showed that Tonýs Chocolonely had a significantly stronger fair trade reputation than Ben & Jerry's ($t(1, 27) = 3.26$; $p < .01$). Since the averages of Hertog and Milka did not differ significantly ($t(1, 27) = .81$; $p = .42$), we chose Milka as the brand with the lowest reputation in the main study. In the Netherlands, Hertog is also an ice cream brand (with or without chocolate), while Milka is much more clearly positioned as a chocolate brand.

Sample and procedure main study

To test the hypotheses, we conducted an online experiment with a 2 (high fair trade reputation − low fair trade reputation)×2 (30%−100% fair trade) between-subjects design. The data were collected by convenience sampling. In total, 205 Dutch participants were obtained. The sample comprised 56 males and 149 females with a mean age of 33.3 years ($SD = 14.9$). 47.5% of the participants had a high educational level (ie at least a bachelor's degree). Participants from the pre-test were not invited to participate in the main study.

Participants were randomly assigned to one of the following four conditions in which Fairtrade Netherlands communicates: (1) Tony's Chocolonely is 100% fair trade chocolate; (2) Tony's Chocolonely is 30% fair trade chocolate; (3) Milka is 100% fair trade chocolate; (4) Milka is 30% fair trade chocolate. The participants were first shown a Facebook page of Fairtrade Netherlands. Subsequently, the participants were asked to complete a self-administered survey containing the following measures.

Measures

First, for the *manipulation check on fair trade reputation*, the same Hsu (2012) scale was used as in the pre-test (Cronbach's α were .97 for Tony's Chocolonely and .95 for Milka). *Situational scepticism* was measured with an adapted version of the advertising scepticism scale of Obermiller and Spangenberg (1998). We used three items on a seven-point Likert scale anchored by 'totally disagree' and 'totally agree'. A sample item includes 'I am sceptical about whether Milka/Tony's Chocolonely is a fair trade product'. The reliability of the scale was adequate for both Milka and Tony's Chocolonely (Cronbach's α=.80 and .92 respectively). *Electronic word of mouth* towards the brand was measured with a 3-item 7-point Likert scale from Eisingerich et al. (2015). An example item is 'To what extent is it likely that you recommend Milka/ Tony's Chocolonely on social sites such as Facebook?' The reliability of the scale was adequate for both Milka and Tony's Chocolonely (Cronbach's α=.79 and .82 respectively). *Consumer-brand identification* was measured with a 3-item 7-point Likert scale by Leach et al. (2008). The reliability of this scale was good (Cronbach's α were .93 for Tony's Chocolonely and .94 for Milka). Additionally, we incorporated *brand awareness, credibility of the message* and *credibility of the source* as control variables in the study. We used a single item to measure brand awareness based on Yoo, Donthu, and Lee (2000): 'I am aware of Milka/Tony's Chocolonely'. For both credibility of the message and credibility of the source, 2-item 7-point Likert scales were used: 'The message that I just read is reliable' and 'Fairtrade Netherlands is a reliable source'. A confirmatory factor analysis was used to test whether the two dimensions of credibility were perceived as distinct. The two-dimensional model in which both dimensions were correlated (r=.82) showed a much better fit (χ^2/df=.90; CFI = 1.00; TLI = 1.00; RMSEA=.00) than the one-dimensional model (χ^2/df = 5.57; CFI=.97; TLI=.83; RMSEA=.15). The reliabilities of these scales were good (Cronbach's α were .83 for credibility of the message and .90 for credibility of the source). Finally, demographic variables (ie age, gender, income and education) were included as descriptive variables in the analyses. Multi-item scales were averaged across their scale items to create composite construct scores.

Results of Study 2

Manipulation check and control variables

The manipulation check showed that participants scored Tony's Chocolonely significantly higher for fair trade reputation (M = 5.24, SD = 1.27) than Milka (M = 3.22, SD = 1.11; F(1, 203)=146.46, p<.01). Additionally, fair trade Netherlands was perceived as a credible source (M = 5.09, SD = 1.20). An ANOVA showed that there was a non-significant difference between the conditions (F(3, 201)=1.33, p=.27). Finally, participants perceived the Facebook message as being fairly credible (M = 4.71, SD = 1.25). An ANOVA showed that the differences between the conditions were significant (F(3, 201)=3.73, p<.05). A post hoc analysis showed that the Milka 30% fair trade condition was perceived as less credible (M = 4.35, SD = 1.29) than Tony's Chocolonely 100% fair trade condition (M = 5.07, SD = 1.17).

Hypotheses tests

First, to test the main effect of fair trade reputation on consumer scepticism (H1), the one-way ANOVA showed a significant difference regarding scepticism between high fair trade reputation ($M = 3.69$; $SD = 1.36$) and low fair trade reputation ($M = 4.06$; $SD = 1.22$), F(1, 203)=4.19, $p<.05$). In H2, we expected that a high fit between the communicated fair trade identity and the fair trade reputation would lead to less scepticism than a low fit between communicated identity and reputation. A one-way ANOVA revealed a significant effect of fit on scepticism (F(1, 203)=14.42, $p<.01$). High fit led to less scepticism ($M = 3.55$; $SD = 1.29$) than low fit ($M = 4.21$; $SD = 1.22$).

To test H3–H5, we conducted the bootstrapping procedure following Preacher and Hayes (2008) in AMOS 23 (Arbuckle, 2014). H3a, in which we assumed that fair trade reputation had an indirect effect on scepticism via consumer-brand identification, was confirmed. The indirect effect of reputation on scepticism through identification was significant (estimated effect= $-.13$; $p<.01$). H3b, in which we assumed that fit had an indirect effect on scepticism via consumer-brand identification, was also confirmed. The indirect effect of fit on scepticism through identification was significant (estimated effect= $-.11$; $p<.05$). In H4, we proposed that scepticism is negatively related to the consumers' positive eWOM about a fair trade brand. The direct effect was significant (estimated effect= $-.18$; $p<.05$).

Finally, H5a,b, in which we assumed that fair trade reputation and fit had an indirect effect on eWOM via consumer-brand identification and scepticism, were confirmed. The indirect effects of reputation on eWOM through identification (estimated effect=.25; $p<.01$) and through scepticism (estimated effect=.05; $p<.01$) were significant. The indirect effects of fit on eWOM through identification (estimated effect= $-.22$; $p<.01$) and through scepticism (estimated effect= $-.10$; $p<.01$) were also significant.

General discussion

Summary of the findings and discussion

The aim of this study was to investigate the role of previous fair trade reputation and the fit between this reputation and the communicated fair trade message in consumer evaluations of a company's brand. This study contributes to knowledge of consumers' responses to the fair trade communication of organizations. More specifically, the results show that when a company with a strong fair trade reputation communicates fair trade initiatives there is less scepticism regarding these fair trade initiatives. In turn, lower scepticism leads to higher online positive consumer advocacy behaviours. Consumers' identification with the specific brand seemed to be an important mediating variable in this relationship. In contrast to previous reputation, the role of fit between previous reputation and the communicated fair trade initiative in consumers' scepticism was less clear. In Study 1, where the evaluation of the fair trade reputation of the industry in general seems to be rather low, we did not find an effect of fit on scepticism. In Study 2, where the previous fair trade reputation was evaluated much more positively, there was a direct and indirect effect of fit on scepticism.

This study extends the previous research in several ways. First, previous work on consumers' responses to fair trade mostly focused on comparing fair trade with non-fair brands and consumers' willingness to pay for fair trade products (Andorfer and Liebe 2012). These fair trade products are mainly signalled by fair trade labels with specific claims (Ingenbleek and Reinders 2013). Research has already shown that consumers can be sceptical about these sustainability claims (Mohr, Eroğlu, and Ellen 1998). The results of this study provide more insights into the underlying processes of consumers' situational scepticism (Forehand and Grier 2003; Skarmeas and Leonidou 2013). Since the results confirmed that previous fair trade reputation influences scepticism, we follow up on Elving's (2013) claim that more research is required regarding brands' reputation and brands' engagement with pro-social initiatives. We find that, dependent on previous fair trade reputation, consumers' can become more or less sceptical towards the fair trade messages of a company or brand.

Second, this study extends our knowledge of the role of fit in communicating sustainability initiatives. Previous studies have already found that a fit between a company and the social cause in general leads to more positive responses towards the company or brand (Nan and Heo 2007) and to greater belief in the credibility of the firm (Becker-Olsen et al. 2006). Our study seems to be the first to investigate the effect of fit between a company's previous fair trade reputation and its communicated fair trade message on consumer scepticism. More specifically, we found that communicating different levels of fair trade led to different consumer responses based on consumers' perceptions of the company's previous reputation. Although the results in Study 1 were inconclusive, Study 2 confirmed that a high fit between a company's previous reputation and its communicated fair trade message leads to less scepticism. These results are in line with Du, Bhattacharya, and Sen (2010); they argued that the way consumers respond to CSR communication messages is related to the way they perceive the company's previous reputation. An explanation for the inconclusive results in Study 1 could be that participants, given the low score they ascribed to the industry, consider the clothing industry to have a bad reputation and are therefore already sceptical about any fair trade message deriving from any clothing brand. In this context, Shaw et al. (2006) argued that consumers are increasingly aware of child labour and other pertinent issues and concerns in the clothing industry. Moreover, the media have also often reported on scandals about clothing brands that violate ethical norms (Islam and Deegan 2010), leading to possible negative perceptions of the ethical awareness of the clothing industry. Since Du, Bhattacharya, and Sen (2010) have claimed that consumers' perceptions of suspicious industries could influence the effectiveness of communication about socially responsible behaviour, perhaps the low overall scores for Fair Trade reputation in Study 1 could explain why fit did not influence consumer scepticism in the apparel context.

Third, we further elaborate on underlying processes that explain consumers' situational scepticism by investigating the mediating role of consumer-brand identification. Previous research has already found that identification plays an important role in consumer responses to CSR initiatives (Sen and Bhattacharya 2001). More specifically, CSR reputation has proven to lead to stronger consumer-brand identification (He, Li, and Harris 2012; Hong and Yang 2009). This study extends this work on the role of social identification since we show that strong identification can lead to lower levels of consumer scepticism. Moreover, our results imply that consumer-brand identification seems to at least partly mediate the relationship between a company's previous fair trade reputation and consumer scepticism regarding the communicated fair trade initiative of the company. Study 2 also showed that the relationship between the fit of a company's fair trade reputation and its communicated message and scepticism is partly determined by a consumer's identification with the company.

Finally, the results of our study contribute to a stream of research on consumers' positive online advocacy behaviours (Hennig-Thurau et al. 2004). More specifically, we found that in the fair trade context, consumers' scepticism has a negative spillover effect on positive eWOM. The more scepticism there is towards the communicated fair trade message the less consumers are willing to demonstrate positive eWOM. This result extends previous work in the offline context in which scepticism leads to lower positive WOM (Skarmeas and Leonidou 2013). A vast number of studies show that consumers are active online more than ever (Floyd et al. 2014; Moriuchi and Takahashi 2018; Liu and Park 2015). In addition, online word-of-mouth seems to have more social risks because it can reach a larger audience, and the communicated messages are less tailored (Eisingerich et al. 2015). Thus, investigating the factors that influence eWOM in response to organizations' fair trade initiatives can provide valuable insights into how online consumer advocacy can be explained. Our results show that both a company's previous fair trade reputation and the fit between this reputation and the communicated fair trade message have an indirect effect on eWOM via consumer-brand identification and scepticism.

Practical implications

This study has several implications for practice. First, and not surprisingly, reputation matters. Building a reputation on fair trade will have beneficial effects for the company. Managers should realize, however, that this seems to be a long-term investment. Ingenbleek and Reinders (2013) have already demonstrated this for fair trade in the coffee industry; it took more than a decade before the market shares of fair trade coffee rose substantially. Moreover, this rise in market shares was mainly initiated by the market leaders in the industry at that time. Thus, if an organization seeks short-term profit, communicating fair trade initiatives may be a risky endeavour. Moreover, it is important for managers to realize that the fair trade reputation of an industry can have a major effect on consumers' online responses to company initiatives. If you are in a specific industry that has a low fair trade reputation in general (eg the apparel industry), it will be much more difficult to reap the advantages of communicating a fair trade message. Thus, investing in fair trade initiatives in low reputation industries requires a long-term view.

Second, besides the reputation of the company or the industry the company is part of, the fit between reputation and the communicated fair trade message seems to be very important. One could wonder if communicating fair trade initiatives, however sincere the intentions, should be avoided if the fair trade concept is not currently incorporated into the company. In other words, if a fair trade strategy is not (yet) integrated into the core strategy of an organization, communicating fair trade initia-tives could backfire and lead to increasingly sceptical responses. Thus, in line with Du, Bhattacharya, and Sen (2007), we believe that reaping relational rewards from commu-nicating fair trade seems to be dependent on the clear positioning of the company.

Third, when a company is perceived as having a strong fair trade reputation, this will lead to stronger consumer brand-identification, which in turn leads to more online advocacy behaviours. Thus, for a company to manage its fair trade reputation, devel-oping an identity centred on a fair trade strategy is crucial. Fombrun and Rindova (2000) already suggested that companies who follow an identity-centred approach seem to have the strongest reputations. Managers could therefore invest in creating consumers' sense of belonging to strengthen the bond between the consumer and the brand. More specifically, if consumers perceive a fit between a company's fair trade reputation and its communicated message, using an identity-centred approach could further increase the status of the fair trade reputation and therefore lead to an enhancement of consumers' self-esteem.

Finally, managers should realize that scepticism leads to less positive eWOM. Since greater numbers of consumers are now online, positive online advocacy behaviours could be crucial to building a fair trade reputation. It seems to be important for organ-izations to keep scepticism as low as possible. Thus, carefully building a fair trade reputation is crucial for establishing consumers' identification with the brand and enhancing their trust in the company.

Limitations and future research

This study has some limitations. First, although most hypotheses were supported, we did not find an effect of fit in Study 1. We argued that this result could be due to the fact that the number of ethical initiatives in the apparel industry has been rather low compared to other industries, such as the food industry. Therefore, we tested the effect of fit on scepticism in another industry with more developed fair trade initia-tives. Although we did find this support for the role of fit in scepticism in Study 2, these results should be further confirmed by investigating other industries. Future research could focus on a clear distinction between industries based on the current state of their fair trade initiatives. Moreover, some industries are more complex in the sense that consumers will not always be able to distinguish the different degrees of sustainability of all of the company's products and services (eg financial service pro-viders). For example, a banking company can score high for labour conditions and low for environmental sustainability. Including consumers' awareness of these different forms of sustainability could be important for future research on the effect of fair trade reputation on consumers' responses to fair trade initiatives.

Second, we used a third-party message to communicate the company's fair trade initiatives. Although, in both studies, both the message and the third-party were per-ceived as credible, one could wonder what the effect on consumer scepticism is when the company communicates the initiatives itself. Research in the crisis communication context, for example, has found that consumers respond differently to a crisis when the crisis message is communicated by an organization versus a third-party (Jin, Liu,

and Austin 2014). Future research could therefore focus on the distinction of consumer responses to fair trade communications by a third-party versus the company itself.

Third, our study focused on positive online word-of-mouth. Although online consumer communication has increased over the past decade (Chen and Xie 2008; Sparks,
Perkins, and Buckley 2013), research had indicated that consumers with unfavourable
product judgments will more often engage in word-of-mouth than consumers with
favourable product associations (Anderson 1998). Consequently, Leonidou and
Skarmeas (2017) argue that it is therefore logical to link scepticism to negative word-
of-mouth intentions. Although we found a clear negative relationship between scepticism and positive online advocacy behaviours, the relationship between scepticism
and negative word-of-mouth could be included in future research.

Fourth, the way stakeholders perceive companies' fair trade initiatives may differ.
While some initiatives may be seen as genuine/intrinsic (eg fair trade is integrated into
the Dutch chocolate brand Tony's Chocolonely), others may be perceived as forms of
green washing/extrinsic (eg Shell is only supporting a local community in Nigeria to
gain a more positive reputation). A vast number of studies have emphasized the
importance of these so called intrinsic and extrinsic motive attributions in the CSR
context (Ellen et al. 2006; Schons, Scheidler, and Bartels 2017; Vlachos et al. 2009).
Future research could also include these motive attributions in consumers' responses
to communicated fair trade messages.

Finally, studies on CSR regularly focus on consumers' considerations concerning
product quality (corporate abilities, CA) and CSR (Brown and Dacin 1997; Marín,
Cuestas, and Román 2016). These CA and CSR associations can have an important
influence on consumer brand perceptions (Brown and Dacin 1997; Sen and
Bhattacharya 2001). Previous research has shown various effects of CA and CSR associations on consumer perceptions and behaviours (Chen 2001; Du, Bhattacharya, and
Sen 2007; Feldman and Vasquez-Parraga 2013). Future research could investigate the
possible mediating or moderating roles that these consumer CA and CSR associations
play in the relationship among fair trade reputation, reputation-message fit and consumer scepticism.

Conclusion

This study shows that previous fair trade reputation can play an important role in
positive and negative consumer responses towards a brand. Moreover, in low fair
trade reputation industries, the fit between a companies' previous reputation and
its communicated message seems to be less important than in industries that
have already developed a reputation for fair trade. Consumers will be sceptical
about fair trade initiatives in these bad reputation industries anyway. In sum, we
conclude that communicating fair trade initiatives can be rewarding. However,
whatever context a brand is in, fair trade communication still seems to be a delicate matter and companies should only communicate these initiatives when the
ethical shoe fits.

Disclosure statement

No potential conflict of interest was reported by the authors.

References

Aaker, D.A., and K.L. Keller. 1990. Consumer evaluations of brand extensions. *Journal of Marketing* 54, no. 1: 27–41.

Ahearne, M., C.B. Bhattacharya, and T. Gruen. 2005. Antecedents and consequences of customer-company identification: Expanding the role of relationship marketing. *Journal of Applied Psychology* 90, no. 3: 574–85.

Alberta, N., D. Merunka, and P. Valette-Florence. 2013. Brand passion: Antecedents and consequences. *Journal of Business Research* 66, no. 7: 904–9.

Anderson, E.W. 1998. Customer satisfaction and word of mouth. *Journal of Service Research* 1, no. 1: 5–17.

Andorfer, V.A., and U. Liebe. 2012. Research on fair trade consumption—a review. *Journal of Business Ethics* 106, no. 4: 415–35.

Arbuckle, J.L. 2014. *Amos 23.0 user's guide*. Chicago: IBM SPSS.

Bagozzi, R.P., and U.M. Dholakia. 2006. Antecedents and purchase consequences of customer participation in small group Brand communities. *International Journal of Research in Marketing* 23, no. 1: 45–61.

Becker-Olsen, K.L., B.A. Cudmore, and R.P. Hill. 2006. The impact of perceived corporate social responsibility on consumer behavior. *Journal of Business Research* 59, no. 1: 46–53.

Bhattacharya, C.B., and S. Sen. 2003. Consumer-company identification: a framework for understanding consumers' relationships with companies. *Journal of Marketing* 67, no. 2: 76–88.

Bögel, P.M. 2016. Company reputation and its influence on consumer trust in response to ongoing CSR communication. *Journal of Marketing Communications* 25, no. 2: 115–136.

Bottomley, P.A., and S.J. Holden. 2001. Do we really know how consumers evaluate brand extensions? Empirical generalizations based on secondary analysis of eight studies. *Journal of Marketing Research* 38, no. 4: 494–500.

Brown, T.J., and P.A. Dacin. 1997. The company and the product: Corporate associations and consumer product responses. *Journal of Marketing* 61, no. 1: 68–84.

Carrington, M.J., B.A. Neville, and G.J. Whitwell. 2010. Why ethical consumers don't walk their talk: Towards a framework for understanding the gap between the ethical purchase intentions and actual buying behaviour of ethically minded consumers. *Journal of Business Ethics* 97, no. 1: 139–58.

Carrol, A.B. 1991. The pyramid of corporate social responsibility: toward the moral management of organizational stakeholders. *Business Horizons* 34, no. 4: 39–48.

Castaldo, S., F. Perrini, N. Misani, and A. Tencati. 2009. The missing link between corporate social responsibility and consumer trust: The case of fair trade products. *Journal of Business Ethics* 84, no. 1: 1–15.

CBI, Dutch Ministry of Foreign Affairs 2017. https://www.cbi.eu/market-information/cocoa/netherlands/, retrieved November 2017.

Cha, M.K., Y. Yi, and R.P. Bagozzi. 2016. Effects of customer participation in corporate social responsibility (CSR) programs on the CSR-Brand fit and brand loyalty. *Cornell Hospitality Quarterly* 57, no. 3: 235–49.

Chen, A.C.-H. 2001. Using free association to examine the relationship between the characteristics of brand associations and brand equity. *Journal of Product & Brand Management* 10, no. 7: 439–51.

Chen, Y., and J. Xie. 2008. Online consumer review: Word-of-mouth as a new element of marketing communication mix. *Management Science* 54, no. 3: 477–91.

Chung, A., and K.B. Lee. 2019. Corporate apology after bad publicity: A dual-process model of CSR fit and CSR history on purchase intention and negative word of mouth. *International Journal of Business Communication*: 1–20. DOI:10.1177/2329488418819133.

Connolly, J., and D. Shaw. 2006. Identifying fair trade in consumption choice. *Journal of Strategic Marketing* 14, no. 4: 353–68.

Cornelissen, J.P. 2017. *Corporate communication: a guide to theory and practice*, 5th ed. London: Sage publications.

De Pelsmacker, P.,. L. Driesen, and G. Rayp. 2005. Do consumers care about ethics? willingness to pay for Fair-Trade coffee. *Journal of Consumer Affairs* 39, no. 2: 363–85.

De Vries, G., B.W. Terwel, N. Ellemers, and D.D. Daamen. 2015. Sustainability or profitability? How communicated motives for environmental policy affect public perceptions of corporate greenwashing. *Corporate Social Responsibility and Environmental Management* 22, no. 3: 142–54.

Di Benedetto, C.A. 2017. Corporate social responsibility as an emerging business model in fashion marketing. *Journal of Global Fashion Marketing* 84, no. 4: 251–65.

Dickson, M.A. 2001. Utility of no sweat labels for apparel consumers: Profiling label users and predicting their purchases. *Journal of Consumer Affairs* 35, no. 1: 96–119.

Didier, T., and S. Lucie. 2008. Measuring consumer's willingness to pay for organic and fair trade products. *International Journal of Consumer Studies* 32, no. 5: 479–90.

Du, S., C.B. Bhattacharya, and S. Sen. 2007. Reaping relational rewards from corporate social responsibility: The role of competitive positioning. *International Journal of Research in Marketing* 24, no. 3: 224–41.

Du, S., C.B. Bhattacharya, and S. Sen. 2010. Maximizing business returns to corporate social responsibility CSR: the role of CSR communication. *International Journal of Management Reviews* 12, no. 1: 8–19.

Du, S., and E.T. Vieira. 2012. Striving for legitimacy through corporate social responsibility: Insights from oil companies. *Journal of Business Ethics* 110, no. 4: 413–27.

Eisingerich, A.B., H.H. Chun, Y. Liu, H.(M.). Jia, and S.J. Bell. 2015. Why recommend a Brand face-to-face but not on Facebook? How word-of-mouth on online social sites differs from traditional word-of-mouth. *Journal of Consumer Psychology* 25, no. 1: 120–8.

Ellen, P.S., D.J. Webb, and L.A. Mohr. 2006. Building corporate associations: Consumer attributions for corporate socially responsible programs. *Journal of the Academy of Marketing Science*
34, no. 2: 147–57.

Elving, W.J. 2013. Scepticism and corporate social responsibility communications: the influence
of fit and reputation. *Journal of Marketing Communications* 19, no. 4: 277–92.

Escalas, J.E., and J.R. Bettman. 2003. You are what they eat: the influence of reference groups on
consumers' connections to brands. *Journal of Consumer Psychology* 13, no. 3: 339–48.

Fairtrade International, FLO 2015. *Scope and benefits of fairtrade.* 7th ed.

Fairtrade International, FLO 2017. https://monitoringreport2016.fairtrade.net/en/, retrieved
December 2017.

Feldman, M.P., and A.Z. Vasquez-Parraga. 2013. Consumer social responses to CSR initiatives versus corporate abilities. *Journal of Consumer Marketing* 30, no. 2: 100–11.

Floyd, K., R. Freling, S. Alhoqail, H.Y. Cho, and T. Freling. 2014. How online product reviews affect
retail sales: A meta-analysis. *Journal of Retailing* 90, no. 2: 217–32.

Fombrun, C.J., and V.P. Rindova. 2000. The road to transparency: Reputation management at
royal Dutch/shell. *The Expressive Organization* 7: 7–96.

Fombrun, C., and M. Shanley. 1990. What's in a name? Reputation building and corporate strategy. *Academy of Management Journal* 33, no. 2: 233–58.

Forehand, M.R., and S. Grier. 2003. When is honesty the best policy? The effect of stated company intent on consumer skepticism. *Journal of Consumer Psychology* 13, no. 3: 349–56.

Frank, R., M. Unfried, R. Schreder, and A. Dieckmann. 2016. Ethical textile consumption: Only a
question of selflessness? *GfK Research* 8, no. 1: 53–7.

Goworek, H., T. Fisher, T. Cooper, S. Woodward, and A. Hiller. 2012. The sustainable clothing
market: an evaluation of potential strategies for UK retailers. *International Journal of Retail &
Distribution Management* 40, no. 12: 935–55.

Gupta, S., and J. Pirsch. 2006. The company-cause-customer fit decision in cause-related marketing. *Journal of Consumer Marketing* 23, no. 6: 314–26.

Hayes, A.F. 2012. PROCESS: A versatile computational tool for observed variable mediation, moderation, and conditional process modeling [white paper]. Retrieved from http://www.afhayes.
com/public/process2012.pdf

He, H.,. Y. Li, and L. Harris. 2012. Social identity perspective on brand loyalty. *Journal of Business
Research* 65, no. 5: 648–57.

Hennig-Thurau, T.,. K.P. Gwinner, G. Walsh, and D.D. Gremler. 2004. Electronic word-of-mouth via
consumer-opinion platforms: What motivates consumers to articulate themselves on the internet? *Journal of Interactive Marketing* 18, no. 1: 38–52.

Herédia-Colaço, V., R.C. do Vale, and S.B. Villas-Boas. 2019. Does fair trade breed contempt? A
cross-country examination on the moderating role of brand familiarity and consumer expertise on product evaluation. *Journal of Business Ethics* 156, no. 3: 737–758.

Hinton, G.E., and J.A. Anderson, eds. 2014. *Parallel models of associative memory: Updated edition.*
New York and London: Taylor & Francis Group.

Hong, S.Y., and S.U. Yang. 2009. Effects of reputation, relational satisfaction, and customer–company identification on positive word-of-mouth intentions. *Journal of Public Relations Research*
21, no. 4: 381–403.

Hsu, K.-T. 2012. The advertising effects of corporate social responsibility on corporate reputation
and brand equity: Evidence from the life insurance industry in Taiwan. *Journal of Business
Ethics* 109, no. 2: 189–201.

Ingenbleek, P.T., and M.J. Reinders. 2013. The development of a market for sustainable coffee in
The Netherlands: Rethinking the contribution of fair trade. *Journal of Business Ethics* 113,
no. 3: 461–74.

Inoue, Y., and S. Lee. 2011. Effects of different dimensions of corporate social responsibility on
corporate financial performance in tourism-related industries. *Tourism Management* 32, no. 4:
790–804.

Islam, M.A., and C. Deegan. 2010. Media pressures and corporate disclosure of social responsibility performance information: a study of two global clothing and sports retail companies. *Accounting and Business Research* 40, no. 2: 131–48.

Jin, Y., B.F. Liu, and L.L. Austin. 2014. Examining the role of social media in effective crisis management: The effects of crisis origin, information form, and source on publics' crisis responses. *Communication Research* 41, no. 1: 74–94.

Jin, S.A.A., and J. Phua. 2014. Following celebrities' tweets about brands: The impact of twitter-based electronic word-of-mouth on consumers' source credibility perception, buying intention, and social identification with celebrities. *Journal of Advertising* 43, no. 2: 181–95.

Kim, Y.J., and W.N. Lee. 2009. Overcoming consumer skepticism in cause-related marketing: the effects of corporate social responsibility and donation size claim objectivity. *Journal of Promotion Management* 15, no. 4: 465–83.

Kozlowski, A., M. Bardecki, and C. Searcy. 2012. Environmental impacts in the fashion industry: A life-cycle and stakeholder framework. *Journal of Corporate Citizenship* 45: 17–36.

Laczniak, R.N., T.E. Decarlo, and S.N. Ramaswami. 2001. Consumers' response to negative word-of-mouth communication: An attribution theory perspective. *Journal of Consumer Psychology* 11, no. 1: 57–73.

Lam, S.K., M. Ahearne, Y. Hu, and N. Schillewaert. 2010. Resistance to brand switching when a radically new brand is introduced: A social identity theory perspective. *Journal of Marketing* 74, no. 6: 128–46.

Leach, C.W., M. van Zomeren, S. Zebel, M.L.W. Vliek, S.F. Pennekamp, B. Doosje, J.W. Ouwerkerk, and R. Spears. 2008. Group-level self-definition and self-investment: A hierarchical multicomponent model of in-group identification. *Journal of Personality and Social Psychology* 95, no. 1: 144–65.

Leonidou, C.N., and D. Skarmeas. 2017. Gray shades of green: Causes and consequences of green skepticism. *Journal of Business Ethics* 144, no. 2: 401–15.

Li, Y., B. Liu, and T.C.T. Huan. 2019. Renewal or not? Consumer response to a renewed corporate social responsibility strategy: Evidence from the coffee shop industry. *Tourism Management* 72: 170–9.

Lii, Y.S., and M. Lee. 2012. Doing right leads to doing well: When the type of CSR and reputation interact to affect consumer evaluations of the firm. *Journal of Business Ethics* 105, no. 1: 69–81.

Liu, Z., and S. Park. 2015. What makes a useful online review? Implication for travel product websites. *Tourism Management* 47: 140–51.

Ma, Y.J., H.H. Lee, and K. Goerlitz. 2016. Transparency of global apparel supply chains: Quantitative analysis of corporate disclosures. *Corporate Social Responsibility and Environmental Management* 23, no. 5: 308–18.

Maloni, M.J., and M.E. Brown. 2006. Corporate social responsibility in the supply chain: An application in the food industry. *Journal of Business Ethics* 68, no. 1: 35–52.

Mangold, W.G., and D.J. Faulds. 2009. Social media: The new hybrid element of the promotion mix. *Business Horizons* 52, no. 4: 357–65.

Marín, L., P.J. Cuestas, and S. Román. 2016. Determinants of consumer attributions of corporate social responsibility. *Journal of Business Ethics* 138, no. 2: 247–60.

Mohan, S. 2009. Fair trade and corporate social responsibility. *Economic Affairs* 29, no. 4: 22–8.

Mohr, L.A., D. Eroğlu, and P.S. Ellen. 1998. The development and testing of a measure of skepticism toward environmental claims in marketers' communication. *Journal of Consumer Affairs* 32, no. 1: 30–55.

Montoro Rios, F.J., T. Luque Martinez, F. Fuentes Moreno, and P. Cañadas Soriano. 2006. Improving attitudes toward brands with environmental associations: An experimental approach. *Journal of Consumer Marketing* 23, no. 1: 26–33.

Moriuchi, E., and I. Takahashi. 2018. An empirical investigation of the factors motivating Japanese repeat consumers to review their shopping experiences. *Journal of Business Research* 82: 381–90.

Nan, X., and K. Heo. 2007. Consumer responses to corporate social responsibility CSR initiatives: Examining the role of brand-cause fit in cause-related marketing. *Journal of Advertising* 36, no. 2: 63–74.

Obermiller, C., and E.R. Spangenberg. 1998. Development of a scale to measure consumer skepticism toward advertising. *Journal of Consumer Psychology* 7, no. 2: 159–86.

Obermiller, C., C. Burke, E. Talbott, and G.P. Green. 2009. Taste great or more fulfilling': The effect of brand reputation on consumer social responsibility advertising for fair trade coffee. *Corporate Reputation Review* 12, no. 2: 159–76.

Öberseder, M., B.B. Schlegelmilch, P.E. Murphy, and V. Gruber. 2014. Consumers' perceptions of corporate social responsibility: Scale development and validation. *Journal of Business Ethics* 124, no. 1: 101–15.

Oh, J., and E.J. Ki. 2019. Factors affecting social presence and word-of-mouth in corporate social responsibility communication: Tone of voice, message framing, and online medium type. *Public Relations Review* 45, no. 2: 319.

Osgood, C.E., and P.H. Tannenbaum. 1955. The principle of congruity in the prediction of attitude change. *Psychological Review* 62, no. 1: 42–55.

Pérez, A., and I.R. Del Bosque. 2013. Measuring CSR image: Three studies to develop and to validate a reliable measurement tool. *Journal of Business Ethics* 118, no. 2: 265–86.

Pérez, A., and M.D.M.G. de los Salmones. 2018. Information and knowledge as antecedents of consumer attitudes and intentions to buy and recommend Fair-Trade products. *Journal of Nonprofit & Public Sector Marketing* 30, no. 2: 111–33.

Polonsky, M.J., and R. Speed. 2001. Linking sponsorship and cause related marketing: Complementarities and conflicts. *European Journal of Marketing* 35, no. 11/12: 1361–89.

Pracejus, J.W., and G.D. Olsen. 2004. The role of brand/cause fit in the effectiveness of cause-related marketing campaigns. *Journal of Business Research* 57, no. 6: 635–40.

Preacher, K.J., and A.F. Hayes. 2008. Asymptotic and resampling strategies for assessing and comparing indirect effects in multiple mediator models. *Behavior Research Methods* 40, no. 3: 879–91.

Reinders, M.J., and J. Bartels. 2017. The roles of identity and brand equity in organic consumption behavior: Private label brands versus national brands. *Journal of Brand Management* 24, no. 1: 68–85.

Rim, H., and D. Song. 2016. How negative becomes less negative": Understanding the effects of comment valence and response sidedness in social media. *Journal of Communication* 66, no. 3: 475–95.

Schons, L.M., S. Scheidler, and J. Bartels. 2017. Tell me how your treat your employees! *Journal of Marketing Behavior* 3, no. 1: 1–37.

Sen, S., and C.B. Bhattacharya. 2001. Does doing good always lead to doing better? Consumer reactions to corporate social responsibility. *Journal of Marketing Research* 38, no. 2: 225–43.

Shaw, D.S., G. Hogg, E. Wilson, E. Shiu, and L. Hassan. 2006. Fashion victim: The impact of fair trade concerns on clothing choice. *Journal of Strategic Marketing* 14, no. 4: 427–40.

Skarmeas, D., and C.N. Leonidou. 2013. When consumers doubt, watch out! The role of CSR skepticism. *Journal of Business Research* 66, no. 10: 1831–8.

Sparks, B.A., H.E. Perkins, and R. Buckley. 2013. Online travel reviews as persuasive communication: The effects of content type, source, and certification logos on consumer behavior. *Tourism Management* 39: 1–9.

Stanaland, A.J., M.O. Lwin, and P.E. Murphy. 2011. Consumer perceptions of the antecedents and consequences of corporate social responsibility. *Journal of Business Ethics* 102, no. 1: 47–55.

Stanton, S.J., J. Kim, J.C. Thor, and X. Deng. 2019. Incentivized methods to generate electronic word-of-mouth: Implications for the resort industry. *International Journal of Hospitality Management* 78: 142–9.

Stokburger-Sauer, N., S. Ratneshwar, and S. Sen. 2012. Drivers of consumer-brand identification. *International Journal of Research in Marketing* 29, no. 4: 406–18.

Tajfel, H. 1972. Experiments in a vacuum. In *The context of social psychology*, ed. J. Isreal and H. Tajfel. London: Academic Press.

Tian, K.T., W.O. Bearden, and G.L. Hunter. 2001. Consumers' need for uniqueness: Scale development and validation. *Journal of Consumer Research* 28, no. 1: 50–66.

Vanhamme, J., and B. Grobben. 2009. "Too good to be true!" The effectiveness of CSR history in countering negative publicity. *Journal of Business Ethics* 85, no. S2: 273–83.

Vlachos, P.A., A. Tsamakos, A.P. Vrechopoulos, and P.K. Avramidis. 2009. Corporate social responsibility: Attributions, loyalty, and the mediating role of trust. *Journal of the Academy of Marketing Science* 37, no. 2: 170–80.

Vo, T.T., X. Xiao, and S.Y. Ho. 2017. How does corporate social responsibility engagement influence word of mouth on twitter? Evidence from the airline industry. *Journal of Business Ethics* 157, no. 2: 525–42.

Völckner, F., and H. Sattler. 2006. Drivers of brand extension success. *Journal of Marketing* 70, no. 2: 18–34.

Webb, D.J., and L.A. Mohr. 1998. A typology of consumer responses to cause-related marketing: From skeptics to socially concerned. *Journal of Public Policy & Marketing* 17: 226–38.

White, K., R. MacDonnell, and J.H. Ellard. 2012. Belief in a just world: Consumer intentions and behaviors toward ethical products. *Journal of Marketing* 76, no. 1: 103–18.

Yoo, B., N. Donthu, and S. Lee. 2000. An examination of selected marketing mix elements and brand equity. *Journal of the Academy of Marketing Science* 28, no. 2: 195–211.

Yoon, Y., Z. Gürhan-Canli, and N. Schwarz. 2006. The effect of corporate social responsibility CSR activities on companies with bad reputation. *Journal of Consumer Psychology* 16, no. 4: 377–90.

When partners divorce: understanding consumers' reactions to partnership termination in cause-related marketing programs

H. Aghakhani, S. W. Carvalho and P. H. Cunningham

ABSTRACT

Cause-related marketing (CRM) is a pervasive, global marketing tactic used to aid consumer persuasion. While considerable academic research has been directed to understanding this practice and its impact on consumers, virtually nothing is known about the effect on consumers' attitudes and purchase intentions when a sponsoring firm terminates a CRM partnership. To address this knowledge gap, two experiments with samples of adult North American consumers were conducted. Study 1's findings suggest that the termination of a CRM partnership has a negative, direct effect on both brand perceptions and purchase intentions. Results also suggest that the impact is lessened (but not overcome) if the sponsoring firm switches its support to a new cause, regardless of the levels of fit between the brand and cause. In Study 2, when an altruistic reason was used to motivate the termination, consumers responded more positively when the decision was made solely by the sponsoring firm than when it was made mutually by the sponsoring firm and the cause. However, when the decision to terminate the partnership was motivated by an operational reason, consumers responded better when the decision was made mutually.

Introduction and purpose of the study

For many years, companies have engaged in mutually beneficial partnerships with social causes as a persuasive communication tool. This marketing strategy has been termed cause-related marketing (CRM). CRM is defined as 'the process of formulating and implementing marketing activities that are characterized by an offer from the firm to contribute a specified amount to a designated cause when customers engage in revenue-providing exchanges' (Varadarajan and Menon 1988, p. 60).

The effectiveness of CRM as a tool to persuade consumers has been extensively studied by marketing academics for more than thirty years. As a consequence, a significant but fragmented body of knowledge about the practice has accumulated.

Despite the extensive research that has been directed to understanding this practice and its impact on consumers, one aspect of CRM has received little attention. Almost nothing is known about the impact on consumers' brand perceptions and purchase intentions when a firm terminates a partnership with a cause.

Some programmes are long-lived and well known by many consumers. Such programmes include General Mill's long-running Boxtops for Education or the Susan G. Komen Run for the Cure (Rozensher 2013). Other programmes have more limited lives. Yoplait's Save Lids to Save Lives, for example, was born in 1998 and terminated in 2016 (Hessekiel 2017). Of the ten most influential CRM programmes listed in *AdAge* in 2010, only one (the Dove Campaign for Real Beauty) remained active in 2017 (Hessekiel 2010, 2017). Thus, terminating a CRM partnership or making a change in the use of sponsorship dollars is not unusual. Some sponsorships end quietly, but others are announced publicly. For example, Nike's nine-year sponsorship of the Livestrong Foundation (formerly the Lance Armstrong Foundation) was widely publicized after Armstrong confessed to doping (Manfred 2013).

Some programmes are quickly forgotten, but others remain in consumers' memories. Many people today still remember the famous American Express Statue of Liberty Restoration campaign even though it only ran during 1983. Whirlpool's Habitat for Humanity lasted three years from 2004 to 2007, and it is still recalled.

Most CRM programmes have a finite life, and sponsors may terminate their partnership with a cause or switch it to another cause for a number of reasons, either positive or negative (Berger, Cunningham, and Drumwright 1999). These include no longer achieving the goals of the CRM programme, or partnering with a cause that no longer resonates with major stakeholders such as consumers, retailers or employees. The firm could also face financial constraints limiting the resources it can devote to the programme. The cause does not have national or international reach desired by its business partner, or the cause partner does not share equitably in the work associated with undertaking the programme. One of the earliest documented CRM partnerships was American Express's CRM programme aimed at raising money to support the restoration of the Statue of Liberty. Once the goal of the programme was achieved, the firm moved its sponsorship to other activities.

To address the knowledge gap in the literature with regard to the effects of terminating a CRM partnership, we took the approach of most CRM persuasion researchers and conducted two on-line experiments. Unlike the majority of the previous work, however, we used samples of adult North American consumers instead of students. Using adult consumers is a more realistic and managerially relevant way to understand the impact of a termination of a partnership on consumers' brand perceptions and purchase intentions.

In the first experiment, we manipulated brand-cause fit (high versus low) and three CRM partnership decisions (terminate the partnership, switch from one cause to another cause, and a control condition – continue the sponsorship). In the second experiment, we varied the sponsor's motivation underpinning the decision to terminate the partnership. We used (1) operational reasons related to a lack of fit between the firm and cause, or (2) an altruistic reason stating that the firm was switching from its initial charity to a new one because the initial charity had multiple sponsors and the new charity had few sponsors and needed more support. We also manipulated the source of the decision. In the first case, the sponsoring firm made the decision on its own. In the second case, the decision was a mutual one made jointly by the sponsoring firm and the charity.

Our findings reveal that consumers, in general, view a divorce between a firm and its charity partner negatively. When compared to the control condition in Study 1, termination of a partnership negatively affected consumers' brand perceptions. This effect was lessened when the sponsoring firm switched its sponsorship to an alternate charity. Our findings from Study 2 demonstrate that the sponsor's reason for the termination (operational or altruistic) and the source of the decision (sponsoring firm alone or a mutual decision by the sponsoring firm and the charity) interact in predicting both brand perceptions and purchase intentions.

Our research makes a number of theoretical and managerial contributions. First, it addresses a major gap in the literature – consumers' response to a termination of an existing CRM partnership. Second, it provides a bridge between two major streams within the literature. Bergkvist and Zhou (2019) divide the CRM research into two major streams: persuasion research and CRM programme management. The current research bridges these two streams. It demonstrates how the decision to terminate a CRM partnership can negatively affect persuasion, and it also provides insights as to what CRM programme managers can do to mitigate these negative effects. Finally, our research introduces and tests the concept that consumers with high communal norms have more favourable responses to CRM programmes.

In the next section, we review the relevant literature followed by an explanation of our research methodology and findings. A discussion of the findings, study limitations, and directions for future research conclude the paper.

Literature review and hypotheses

There is a long history of research on CRM. Varadarajan and Menon (1988) defined and drew academic attention to the practice. A more recent definition, particularly relevant to the current research, classifies CRM as a form of 'leveraged marketing communications (LCM), that is, marketing communications that aim for the brand to benefit from consumers' positive associations to another object (e.g. a charity and the cause)' (Bergkvist and Taylor 2016, p. 2). Today's use of CRM seems to combine aspects of both definitions and in doing so has become a pervasive, global marketing tactic whose use grew by 18.5% between 2011 and 2016 (IEG 2017).

Use of CRM continues to expand globally. It is estimated that 85% of the corporate members of the Promotion Marketing Association (PMA) use CRM (PMA and Gable Group 2000). Research has shown that CRM programmes are generally viewed positively by consumers (Webb and Mohr 1998) particularly when donations to the cause are sizeable and have a significant impact (Harvey and Strahilevitz 2009; Moosmayer and Fuljahn 2010). There is a considerable body of research on how CRM impacts consumer recall, attitudes, and persuasion (e.g. Ross, Patterson, and Stutts 1992; Dahl and Lavack 1995; Berger, Cunningham, and Kozinets 1998; Brønn and Vrioni 2001; Gupta and Pirsch 2006).

Brand-cause fit has been an important area of research, but one that has produced equivocal results (Hibbert et al. 2007; Kim, Cheong, and Lim 2015; Guerreiro, Rita, and Trigueiros 2016). The impact on consumer perceptions has been assessed by comparing high-alignment programmes (i.e. when a firm and a cause are significantly related such as a grocery store giving products to a food bank) with low-alignment programmes (i.e. when a car company supports the arts) (Ellen, Mohr, and Webb 2000). This body of research has shown that the degree of fit may induce favourable attitudes towards the brand under some conditions but not others (Nan and Heo 2007).

The emotional impact of CRM programmes has also been explored. In particular, Chang (2011) and Strahilevitz (1995) examined the effects of guilt appeals on consumers' purchase intentions. Strahilevitz and Myers (1998) used a variation of brand-cause fit and compared the effects on consumer persuasion, emotion and willingness to purchase when a cause was linked with either a utilitarian or a hedonic product.

There has been some research related to whether the length of the CRM programme (its temporal duration) influences consumers' perceptions and behaviour, but it has also produced equivocal results. Youn and Kim (2018), for example, found that long-term programmes were more influential in the case of high-involvement products. Their findings did not hold for low involvement products, however. The authors found that altruistic attributions made by consumers mediated the effect of temporal duration on purchase intentions only in the low involvement condition. In contrast, van den Brink, Odekerken-Schröder, and Pauwels (2006) discovered that strategic (long-term) CRM programmes enhanced brand loyalty for low involvement products. Tactical (short-term) programmes did not affect brand loyalty for either high or low involvement products.

Despite these equivocal findings, and the fact that many CRM programmes are relatively short-lived, we found little research addressing the issue of CRM partnership termination and the impact of this decision on consumers' brand perceptions and purchase intentions. The only relevant piece of research we found was part of a symposium presented at the North American Association for Consumer Research conference in 2008. In a series of experiments, Strahilevitz (2008) presented the 'take-aversion' phenomenon in which she argued that donors react more negatively when taking away from a charity (undoing a donation) than not giving to it in the first place (not making a donation). She found that even when participants were given the option of switching their donation to another cause, their preference was to continue to donate to the original cause. Her findings may provide insight into consumers' reactions to the termination of a sponsorship. Consumers may be averse to 'taking away' a sponsorship commitment from a cause and may react negatively to a CRM partnership termination. This 'take away' phenomenon might persist even when the sponsorship of one cause is terminated but switched to another cause.

The field of sports and sponsorship marketing may also provide some insight into the effects of partnership termination. Farrelly (2010), for example, studied the termination of sports sponsorships. His qualitative study examined the factors leading to the termination. Jensen and Cornwell (2017) built on Farrelly's work but examined termination of sports sponsorships from the perspective of both partners (the sponsoring firm and the sports organization). However, they did not assess the impact of partnership termination on fans or other stakeholders.

Given the scarcity of extant research, we believe that there is an important knowledge gap in the literature. We began to address it using two on-line experiments. In the first Study, we address the questions of whether or not a termination of a sponsorship would result in a significant decline in brand perceptions and purchase intentions. We also asked whether or not the firm could take mitigating actions to reduce the negative impacts, such as switching its sponsorship support to a different cause. We expected that a process similar to the 'take away' phenomenon presented by Strahilevitz (2008) may predict consumers' response to a CRM partnership termination. Thus, we tested the following hypotheses:

H1: Termination of a CRM partnership will result in lower brand perceptions and consequently, lower intentions to purchase the brand on the part of consumers.

H2: Termination of a CRM partnership, followed by a subsequent move of the sponsorship to a different cause, will be viewed less negatively and will have a lower impact on brand perceptions and purchase intention than termination alone.

Since we found strong evidence in support of the above two hypotheses in Study 1, we extended our work and conducted a second study. In Study 2, we used attribution theory as a guide (Fiske and Taylor 1991). Attribution theory helps explain what information consumers use and combine to form causal judgments or explanations of events. The importance of consumer attributions about a firm's motives for undertaking a CRM programme has been shown to act as an important explanatory variable impacting brand perceptions and purchase intentions. The Corporate Social Responsibility (CSR) literature as well as the CRM literature has explored the impact of consumer attributions about firms' motivations (e.g. Carvalho, Muralidharan, and Bapuji 2015). While CSR has been defined in many ways, it usually refers to how a company views its voluntary obligations to its stakeholders to create economic, social, and environmental well-being (Dahlsrud 2008; Carvalho et al. 2010). Bolton and Mattila (2015), for example, found that the effectiveness of CSR varies as a function of the company's motives. In a series of experiments, they demonstrated that CSR improves consumer satisfaction and loyalty when the company's motives to engage in CSR are perceived as altruistic (i.e. showing a selfless concern for the well-being of others or society), versus being self-serving (i.e. an operational decision made by the firm to increase the profitability arising from the programme).

Recommendations arising from Gupta and Pirsch's (2006) study of CRM programmes also suggest a relationship between type of motivation underpinning its reasons for undertaking a CRM programme and consumer perceptions. They state, 'marketing managers should select a cause that makes sense to the consumer to be a partner in the alliance, build a general positive feeling toward their brand, and *limit any self-serving promotion of the cause-related marketing alliance to the target consumer population*' [italics added] (p.314). While the literature has not examined termination decisions, it suggests that consumers will have higher brand perceptions and purchase intentions when the firm's motives underpinning a termination decision or sponsorship switching decision are motivated by an altruistic reason rather than an operational reason.

Previous research has also suggested that consumer scepticism or suspicion about the motives of firms using CRM programmes to promote their brands and increase sales undermines the effectiveness of these initiatives (Barone, Miyazaki and Taylor 2000; Brønn and Vrioni 2001; Szykman, Bloom, and Blazing 2004; Anuar and Mohamad 2012; Bae 2018). Consumers are particularly skeptical in cases where the sponsoring firm acts in an opportunistic way and exploits the cause for its own purposes or gain (Gurin 1987). Those who value and respond to CRM programmes regard them as partnerships designed to benefit both the sponsoring firm and society (through a social cause). In other words, they expect them to have an element of altruism. Consumers and causes alike fear that a sponsoring firm may misuse its greater power and resources and undertake CRM campaigns only to increase profits (i.e. operational motivation) (Baylin, Cunningham, and Cushing 1994).

Research on the persuasiveness of communications aimed at consumers has long used the source of the message as an important variable that interacts with other variables like message framing, and content type in its impact on choice (e.g. Karmarkar and Tormala 2010; Sparks, Perkins and Buckley 2013). Given the importance of the information source in consumer persuasion, and the presence of consumer scepticism with regard to a firm's motivation for undertaking a CRM initiative, it seems likely that decisions made mutually by the sponsoring firm and the cause will be viewed less suspiciously than those made by the sponsoring firm alone.

In light of the above noted literature, we propose that these two factors (1) the motivation for the firm's decision and (2) the source of the decision will interact to moderate the impact of the termination decision on consumers' brand perceptions and their subsequent purchase intentions.

In light of the findings related to consumer scepticism, we manipulated the firm's motivation for the change in sponsorship in two different ways. If the firm makes the decision to move its sponsorship from one cause to another for altruistic reasons – that is, it would lead to a higher social benefit, the literature suggests that scepticism will be lower and thus brand perceptions and purchase intentions should be higher. For example, if the sponsoring firm explained its motive for switching to an alternative cause because the charity had greater need and fewer sponsors than the charity currently being sponsored (an altruistic reason), it will be viewed more favourably. Alternatively, the firm could switch its sponsorship for operational reasons such as improved fit between the company's products and the cause represented by the charity (i.e. a decision that would increase the effectiveness of the programme to benefit the company). Under the latter circumstance, scepticism about the decision should be higher.

Since attribution theory suggests that consumers combine information to form summary judgments, we propose an interaction between these two factors (i.e. decision motivation: altruistic vs operational), and decision source (i.e. a sponsoring firm decision vs a mutual decision made jointly by the sponsoring firm and cause). The literature led us to the following hypotheses:

H3a: Altruistic Motivation - When the decision to terminate a CRM partnership is motivated by an altruistic reason, consumers will report more positive brand perceptions and purchase intentions when the decision is made solely by the sponsoring firm than when it is made mutually by the sponsoring firm and the charity.

H3b: Operational Motivation - When the decision to terminate a CRM partnership is motivated by an operational reason, consumers will report more positive brand perceptions and purchase intentions when the decision is made mutually by the sponsoring firm and the charity than when it is made solely by the sponsoring firm.

In designing Study 2, we included what we also believe to be an important potential covariate – communal norms. Social psychologists classify relationships as being either exchange relationships or communal relationships (Mills and Clark 1982). When consumers evaluate information and assess others' decisions, they use different norms depending on the type of relationship (either exchange or communal norms) (Bolton and Mattila 2015). The norm in exchange relationships is that there is a balance of giving and receiving between the parties. If one person gives another a benefit, he/she will expect to receive a comparable benefit (Mills and Clark 1982; Clark, 1984). In communal relationships, people create benefits for others without expecting a benefit in return. These relationships are guided by the norm that people 'help each other on the basis of needs or to demonstrate general concern for each other's welfare' (Bolton and Mattila 2015, p.141).

We contend that communal norms are a critical characteristic that will help to classify participants most attracted to CRM programmes. Differences in communal norms may potentially affect the results of the study. Since communal norms increase people's feelings of responsibility for the misfortune of others (Winterich and Zhang 2014), they are proposed to have an impact on how consumers respond to CRM decisions such as the termination of a CRM partnership.

Building on earlier work by Aggarwal (2004) and others, Bolton and Mattila (2015) found that CSR programmes (measured as either philanthropy or sustainability) are more effective in creating positive consumer responses when consumers hold communal norms than when they hold exchange norms. These authors made the point that communal norms are paramount when consumers engage in welfare-oriented behaviours such as donating money to charity, or volunteering time. Since CRM is a social welfare-oriented practice as well as a persuasive practice, we propose that consumers holding communal norms will have more positive views of, and be more likely to support, brands associated with causes (i.e. CRM programmes).

Bolton and Mattila (2015) also found that people use relationship norms as standards to evaluate appropriate behaviour – in our study whether to terminate a sponsorship or switch support to another cause. Those who have communal norms also felt grateful toward those organizations or people who helped and resentful towards those who refused to help (Bar-Tal et al. 1977). Finally, individuals in communal (vs exchange) relationships expect partners to be more responsive to their needs and provide more help (Bolton and Mattila 2015). This literature, therefore, suggests that consumer response to CRM programmes is a function of communal norms versus exchange norms (Bolton and Mattila 2015). Due to the importance of communal norms in affecting consumers' responses to social welfare-oriented practices such as CRM programmes, we include communal norms as a covariate variable in Study 2.

Study 1

Study 1 had three main objectives. The first objective was to evaluate the effects of a termination of a CRM partnership. We proposed that it would lower brand perceptions

and purchase intentions on the part of consumers. Second, we wanted to explore possible mitigating actions a firm might take to lessen the negative impact of the decision to terminate a CRM partnership. We hypothesized, therefore, that if the firm
terminates an existing partnership, but switches its support to another cause, consumers would perceive the termination of the partnership less negatively. Third, since previous CRM research has demonstrated the importance of brand-cause fit, we tested its
potential impact on consumers' response to a CRM partnership termination.

Similar to what was done in previous studies (e.g. Nan and Heo 2007; Aghakhani,
Akhgari, and Main 2019), we tested our hypotheses using a fictitious brand and fictitious charities. We did this to rule out the possibility that consumers' prior beliefs and
attitudes about existing brands and/or causes would influence their reactions to sponsorship decisions. Further, in this and the subsequent study, for operationalization purposes, we used the brand and not the firm as the sponsor. We did this because firms
(e.g. General Mills) make sponsorship decisions but they usually tie the CRM programmes to a specific brand (e.g. Yoplait's Save Lids to Save Lives). As a consequence,
consumers tend to see the brand (Yoplait) and not the firm (General Mills) as the
sponsor behind the CRM programme. Similarly, we used the charity as the beneficiary
of the sponsorship and not the cause behind the charity. It should be noted that, in
most CRM programmes, sponsoring firms provide funds to charities and not directly
to causes. In other words, the charity is the main institution behind the cause and the
decision maker unit in the CRM partnership decision. Although we did not focus on
the cause in our operationalization, the name of the fictitious charity (e.g. Healthy Diet
Research Association) reflected the cause (e.g. obesity prevention). In addition, in
Study 2, we also explicitly mentioned to participants the cause behind the charity (e.g.
'… Healthy Diet Research Association to reduce the impact of obesity, which is mostly
caused by sugar consumption.') (see Appendix 1).

Method

Our sample consisted of 292 adults residing in the United States (48.6% female,
$M_{age} = 35.6$, SD $= 10.39$) who were recruited using Amazon Mturk. Participants were
given a small monetary incentive to encourage them to participate. They were randomly assigned to one of six conditions in a 2 (brand-cause fit: high vs low) × 3
(sponsorship decision: terminate the sponsorship, switch the sponsorship to a different
cause, and a control condition – continue with the sponsorship) factorial design.

Each participant was presented with a print advertisement for a fictitious brand of
orange juice with the tagline 'Sunshine Orange Juice. Naturally rich in vitamin C.'
Previous research has demonstrated that orange juice is considered a low-involvement
(Harris 1987; Yang 2014) and utilitarian product (Mort and Rose 2004; Shavitt and
Nelson 2009). We chose to use a utilitarian product in this and the subsequent study
to avoid the variance in results caused by the differences in consumers attributions
with regard to hedonic versus utilitarian products. The ad featured the following statement: 'Sunshine Orange Juice has been a sponsor of [name of sponsored charity]. For
every bottle of juice sold, we donate 5 cents to this worthy cause' (see Appendix 1 for
a sample of the study materials). Brand-cause fit was manipulated by varying the

name of the sponsored charity. The Traffic Safety Research Association (TSRA) was used for the low brand-cause fit condition, and the Healthy Diet Research Association (HDRA) was used for the high brand-cause fit condition.

To manipulate the sponsorship decision, all participants were randomly assigned to one of three conditions. For the termination condition, participants were told, 'In its most recent board meeting, *Sunshine Orange Juice* decided NOT to continue this sponsorship.' In the condition where the sponsoring brand switched to another charity, participants were told, 'In its most recent board meeting, *Sunshine Orange Juice* decided to end its support of HDRA (TSRA) and instead sponsor TSRA (HDRA).' Further, in the switch condition, the company's decision was either to switch from a charity with high brand-cause fit (HDRA) to a charity with low brand-cause fit (TSRA) or vice versa. Finally, in the sponsorship continuation condition, participants were told, 'In its most recent board meeting, *Sunshine Orange Juice* decided to continue this sponsorship for one more year.'

Measures

After viewing the fictitious ad, participants were asked to indicate their perception of and their future intentions to purchase the advertised brand. Brand perception was measured on a 5-item, 9-point semantic differential scale: 'not socially responsible – socially responsible', 'unreliable – reliable', 'bad corporate citizen – good corporate citizen', 'untrustworthy – trustworthy', and 'not giving back to the community - giving back to the community.' The five items loaded on a single distinct factor; therefore, they were averaged to form a brand perception index ($\alpha = .95$). Purchase intention was measured by asking participants two questions: 'if you were looking for an orange juice, how likely are you to consider buying *Sunshine Orange Juice*?' and 'I would definitely buy *Sunshine Orange Juice*' (1 = very unlikely; 9 = very likely) ($r = .89$, $p < .001$). We also measured the following demographic factors: gender, age, education, and income. Since none of the demographic variables significantly influenced the hypothesized relationships, they were dropped from further analysis.

Results and discussion

Brand perceptions: Results of an ANOVA with brand-cause fit and the sponsorship decision as independent variables, and brand perceptions as the dependent variable, revealed a main effect of the sponsorship decision on brand perceptions. As expected, termination of the CRM partnership resulted in lower brand perceptions. That is, brand perceptions were lowest when the decision was to terminate the sponsorship and highest when the decision was to continue the current sponsorship. Further, when the decision was to switch the sponsorship to another charity, the impact on brand perceptions was lower than in the continue condition, but higher than the decision to terminate the partnership ($M_{terminate} = 3.99$ vs $M_{switch} = 5.00$ vs $M_{continue} = 5.49$; $F(2,286) = 32.28$, $p < .001$, $\eta^2 = .18$).

These latter findings were independent of whether the company was switching from a low to high brand-cause fit situation or high to low brand-cause fit situation. Further, the main effect of brand-cause fit and the interaction between fit and the sponsorship decision were not significant ($p > .13$ and $p > .77$ respectively). Brand-cause fit has been an important aspect of CRM research, but studies to date have produced equivocal results (Hibbert et al. 2007; Guerreiro, Rita, and Trigueiros 2016). In this study, results align with the findings that brand-cause fit had a null effect (Lafferty 2007, 2009).

Purchase Intentions: An ANOVA with brand-cause fit and the sponsorship decision as independent variables and purchase intention as the dependent variable also revealed a main effect of the sponsorship decision. More specifically, purchase intention was lowest when the decision was to terminate the sponsorship. Purchase intention was not as low when the decision was to switch to another charity, and purchase intention was the highest when the decision was to continue with the current sponsorship ($M_{terminate} = 3.51$ vs $M_{switch} = 4.37$ vs $M_{continue} = 4.83$; $F(2,286) = 17.79$, $p < .001$, $\eta2 = .1$). Again, consistent with the findings related to brand perceptions, the results also showed that switching to a different charity reduces consumers' intention to purchase the brand when compared with the decision to continue the sponsorship ($p < .05$). There was no significant difference in purchase intention between the two fit conditions ($p = .37$). In addition, both the main effect of brand-cause fit and the interaction effect between band-cause fit and the sponsorship decision were not significant ($p > .51$ and $p > .81$ respectively). This suggests that the decision made by the company to switch to another charity had a significant negative impact on consumers' intention to purchase the product independent of whether the company was switching from a low to high or a high to low brand-cause fit case.

Taken together, the findings of this experiment confirm that consumers respond negatively to the termination of a CRM partnership (H1) regardless of whether or not brand-cause fit is high or low. Further, results also demonstrated that switching to another charity does indeed reduce consumers' negative response to the termination but does not completely eliminate it (H2). That is, consumers still respond negatively to a switching decision when compared to continuing with the current CRM partnership. It seems that consumers object to a 'divorce' or change in the firm's commitment even though there may be a subsequent 're-marriage'.

Study 2

Study 2 was designed to build on and extend the findings from Study 1. It tests Hypotheses 3a and 3b regarding the interactive effects of decision source (sponsoring brand or a mutual decision) and decision motivation (altruistic or operational reason) on how consumers respond to the termination of a CRM partnership. It also examines the effects of a potentially important covariate – communal norms held by some consumers. More specifically, we expect consumers with higher communal norms to find CRM programmes more persuasive. We also expect that when the decision to terminate the partnership is motivated by an altruistic reason, consumers will respond more positively if the decision is solely made by the sponsoring brand. However, when the decision to terminate the partnership is motivated by an operational reason, we propose that consumers will respond more positively when the decision is made mutually by the sponsoring brand and the charity.

Method

One hundred and sixty-seven adults residing in the United States (59.3% female, $M_{age} = 35.25$, SD $= 11.74$) were recruited using Amazon Mturk to participate in an online experiment in exchange for a small monetary incentive. Participants were randomly assigned to one of four conditions in a 2 (decision motivation: operational vs altruistic) $\times$ 2 (decision source: sponsoring brand decision (Sunshine Orange Juice) vs a mutual decision made jointly by the sponsoring brand and charity) between-subjects factorial design.

Each participant was presented with a fictitious press release from the same fictitious company used in Study 1, Sunshine Orange Juice (see Appendix I for a sample of the Study 2 materials). In all of the four conditions, the press release stated, 'Sunshine Orange Juice has been a sponsor of Traffic Safety Research Association (TSRA). For many years, it has donated 5% of its sales to TSRA to support its ongoing effort to provide help to those affected by traffic accidents, which is not related to Sunshine's core business.' To manipulate the decision motivation variable, we gave information to participants to create two conditions: (1) for the operational condition – it was noted that 'there is a lack of fit between Sunshine and TSRA.' It was also stated that this brand-cause partnership should be replaced 'with a charity that fits better with Sunshine's social responsibilities,' (2) for the altruistic condition – it was noted that 'TSRA is already sponsored by many other major corporations.' It was also stated that this brand-cause partnership should be replaced 'with a charity that receives less support from other companies and firms.'

To manipulate the decision source variable, participants in the sponsoring brand decision condition were told that the decision to terminate Sunshine's partnership with TSRA was made solely by Sunshine, while participants in the mutual decision condition were told that the decision was a mutual one made jointly by Sunshine and TSRA. It should be noted that we decided not to have a condition in which the charity drove the decision since it is rare for the charity partner to terminate a partnership unless there is a powerful ethical reason for the termination. Finally, in all of the conditions, the press release also stated that Sunshine would end its support of TSRA and instead sponsor the Healthy Diet Research Association (HDRA).

As was the case in Study 1, participants were asked to read the press release, and then were asked to indicate their perception of the brand and their future intentions to purchase the brand. In addition, we added a measure that evaluates participants' perceptions of communal norms to this study. Finally, participants were asked some demographical questions, were thanked, and were debriefed on the purpose of the research. Since none of the demographic variables significantly influenced the hypothesized relationships, they were dropped from further analysis.

Dependent measures

Brand perceptions and purchase intentions were measured using the same measures as were used in Study 1 ($\alpha = .95$ and $r = .94$ respectively). We measured communal norms and added it to the model as a covariate. This measure included two seven-point Likert scale items that asked participants to indicate how much they agreed with the following statements: 'Sunshine helps people in time of need' and 'Sunshine would help people even if it is not good for business.' These items were adapted from Hon and Grunig (1999). The average of these two items comprised the communal norms measure ($r = .80$).

Manipulation checks

The decision motivation manipulation was checked by asking respondents to indicate if 'a lack of fit between Sunshine and TSRA' was the main reason for ending the brand-cause partnership. Participants rated this question on a seven-point Likert scale ranging from 1 = strongly disagree to 7 = strongly agree. To check the manipulation of the decision source, participants were asked, 'Who made the decision to end the relationship between TSRA and Sunshine?' There were three possible answers: Sunshine, TSRA, or a mutual decision.

Results and discussion

Manipulation checks: An ANOVA using decision motivation and decision source as independent variables and the decision motivation manipulation check as the dependent variable revealed a main effect of decision motivation. Participants reading the operational motivation condition agreed more that the decision to terminate the partnership was due to a lack of fit between the two organizations than those in the altruistic motivation condition ($M_{operational} = 6.36$ vs $M_{altruistic} = 3.10$, $F(1, 163) = 151.29$, $p < .001$). No other main or interactive effects were found to be significant ($p > .5$).

To test the accuracy of the decision source manipulation, a chi-square test was conducted. Results show a significant difference between those who were told that the decision to terminate the partnership was made solely by Sunshine and those who were told that the decision was made mutually by Sunshine and TSRA (Pearson $\chi^2 = 114.94$, $p < .001$). In particular, 96% of those in the sponsoring brand decision condition reported Sunshine as the decision source, and over 84% of those in the mutual condition reported that the decision was made mutually by Sunshine and TSRA.

Brand perceptions: We did an ANCOVA analysis with decision motivation and decision source as the independent variables, perceptions of communal norms as a covariate, and brand perceptions as the dependent variable. Results showed a significant crossover interaction between decision motivation and decision source in predicting brand perceptions ($F(1, 162) = 7.47$, $p < .01$) providing support for H3a and b. There were no main effects of either decision motivation or decision source ($p > .80$). As expected, perceptions of communal norms were also significant. An increase in perceptions of communal norms was associated with higher brand perceptions ($F(1, 162) = 126.18$, $p < .001$, $\beta = .80$).

As can be seen in Figure 1, simple contrast analysis revealed a marginally significant effect of decision source on brand perceptions when the decision was motivated by an altruistic reason. Brand perceptions were marginally higher when the decision was made by Sunshine alone (the sponsoring brand's decision) than when it was made mutually by Sunshine and TSRA (a mutual decision) ($M_{Sunshine} = 7.30$

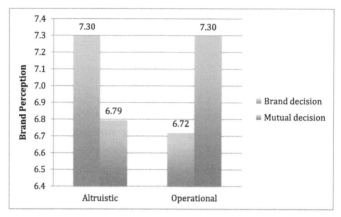

Figure 1. Interaction between decision motivation and decision source on brand perception.

vs $M_{mutual} = 6.79$; $F(1, 162) = 3.28$, $p = .07$). However, when the decision was based on an operational motivation, brand perceptions were significantly lower when the decision was made by Sunshine (the sponsoring brand's decision) than when it was made mutually by Sunshine and TSRA (mutual decision) ($M_{Sunshine} = 6.72$ vs $M_{mutual} = 7.30$; $F(1, 162) = 4.25$, $p < .05$). This finding again supports H3a and H3b. When the termination decision was motivated by altruistic reasons, consumers responded more positively when the decision to terminate the partnership was made solely by the sponsoring brand than when it was a mutual decision. However, when the termination of the partnership was motivated by operational reasons, consumers responded more positively when the decision was made mutually by the sponsoring brand and the charity than when it was made solely by the sponsoring brand.

The results also revealed a significant effect of decision motivation on brand perceptions when the decision was made solely by the sponsoring brand (Sunshine). Brand perceptions were also significantly higher when the decision was motivated by altruistic reasoning than when an operational reason was used to motivate the decision ($M_{altruistic} = 7.30$ vs $M_{operational} = 6.72$; $F(1, 162) = 4.08$, $p < .05$). However, when the decision was made mutually by the sponsoring brand and the charity (a mutual decision), brand perceptions were marginally higher when the decision had an operational motive than when it had an altruistic motive ($M_{operational} = 7.30$ vs $M_{altruistic} = 6.79$; $F(1, 162) = 3.45$, $p = .07$). These results suggest that when making a decision to terminate a CRM partnership, the sponsoring brand will be much better off if the decision is motivated by altruistic rather than operational reasons. However, when the decision to terminate a CRM partnership arises from a mutual decision, it is better for the sponsoring brand if the decision is motivated by operational rather than altruistic reasons.

Purchase intentions: An ANCOVA was performed using decision motivation and decision source as the independent variables, perceptions of communal norms as a covariate, and purchase intentions as the dependent variable. Results showed a main effect of decision motivation. Purchase intentions were significantly higher when the decision to terminate the CRM partnership was based on altruistic motives than when it was based on an operational motives ($M_{altruistic} = 5.00$ vs $M_{operational} = 4.52$; $F(1,$

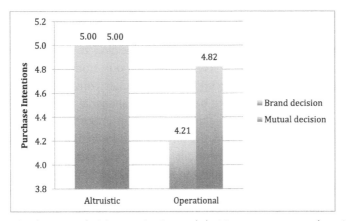

Figure 2. Interaction between decision motivation and decision source on purchase intention.

$162) = 7.37$, $p < .01$). Results also revealed a marginally significant effect of decision source. Purchase intentions were marginally higher when the decision to terminate the partnership was made by both the sponsoring brand and the charity (a mutual decision,) than when it was made solely by the sponsoring brand (a sponsoring brand decision) ($M_{mutual} = 4.91$ vs $M_{brand} = 4.60$; $F(1, 162) = 2.96$, $p < .09$). These main effects were qualified by a marginally significant interaction between decision motivation and decision source in predicting purchase intentions ($F(1, 162) = 3.02$, $p = .08$) giving further support for H3a and b.

Perceptions of communal norms were also significant. An increase in perceptions of communal norms was associated with higher purchase intentions ($F(1, 162) = 102.37$, $p < .001$, $\beta = .82$).

As can be seen in Figure 2, simple contrast analysis revealed a significant simple effect of decision source on purchase intention when the decision was based on an operational motive. Purchase intention was significantly higher when the decision was a mutual one made by the sponsoring brand and the charity than when it was made solely by the sponsoring brand ($M_{mutual} = 4.82$ vs $M_{brand} = 4.21$; $F(1, 162) = 5.92$, $p < .05$). When the decision to terminate the partnership was motivated by altruistic reasons, there was no significant difference in purchase intentions in either of the sponsoring brand alone or mutual decision scenarios.

Results also revealed a significant simple effect of decision motivation on purchase intention when the decision was made by the sponsoring brand. Purchase intentions were significantly higher when the decision was based on an altruistic motive than when it was based on an operational motive ($M_{altruistic} = 5.00$ vs $M_{operational} = 4.21$; $F(1, 162) = 9.38$, $p < .01$). There was no significant difference in purchase intention between altruistic and operational motivation when the decision to terminate the partnership was a mutual decision made by both the sponsoring brand and the charity.

Discussion

Despite the fact that most CRM partnerships are terminated at some point in time, there is virtually no literature to which academics or managers can turn to better understand the consequences of terminating a CRM partnership. In fact, after a thorough search, we were able to find only one article in the public press that talked about the importance of having an exit strategy when deciding to terminate a CRM partnership (Klein 2014). Thus, the major contribution of our study is that we address this important gap in the literature. Second, we used adult consumers (instead of student participants) to give our results more general and managerial relevance. Third, we measured, tested and demonstrated the significance of an important covariate – communal norms. Fourth, we showed the negative impact of terminating a CRM partnership on brand perceptions and purchase intentions. This finding adds to the body of literature on the effects of cause duration. While van den Brink, Odekerken-Schröder, and Pauwels (2006) found that short-term (tactical) programmes had no effect on brand loyalty, our study suggests that any termination has an impact on purchase intentions of low involvement, utilitarian products. Finally, we tested and demonstrated the effect of two variables (decision source and motivation for the termination) as factors that may mitigate the negative impact of a CRM partnership termination.

We conducted two on-line experiments using a between-subjects factorial design. In our first study, we found that consumers' brand perceptions and purchase intentions are negatively affected when a sponsoring brand makes the decision to terminate its support of a charity. We also explored the question of whether or not the sponsoring brand could take action to mitigate the negative impact of a termination. We found that the negative impact is mitigated when the sponsoring brand switches its support to another charity. While this action lessened the negative impact on brand perceptions and purchase intentions resulting from the CRM partnership termination, it did not completely overcome the negative effect.

We undertook a second study in order to extend our investigation of the termination of a CRM partnership. We varied two factors: the decision source (whether the decision was made by the sponsoring brand alone or jointly by the sponsoring brand and the charity), and the motivation of the decision (whether it was for operational reasons related to fit, or whether the termination was motivated by altruistic reasons).

With regard to brand perceptions, we found no main effect of the two independent variables, but we did find an important crossover interaction. When partners divorce, brand perceptions were higher when the sponsoring brand alone made the decision and motivated by an altruistic reason. When the decision to terminate the partnership was motivated by an operational reason, brand perceptions were higher when both the sponsoring brand and the charity made the decision mutually.

When purchase intentions were the dependent variable, we did find a main effect related to how the decision was motivated. It is better to use altruistic reasons to justify the decision to terminate a CRM partnership. We also found that the negative impact of the divorce on consumers' perceptions was mitigated when a mutual decision to terminate a CRM partnership was made (rather than the sponsoring brand making the decision alone). There was also a marginally significant interaction between the two variables. Given the literature on consumer scepticism, it is likely that these results arise because they lessen scepticism (i.e. altruistic motives and joint decision making by the charity and the sponsoring brand result in lower scepticism on the part of consumers).

In the second study, we also tested the importance of communal norms as a poten-tial covariate. We found that consumers who had such norms were more likely to have stronger brand perceptions and purchase intentions as a result of a CRM pro-gramme. Consumers who have a higher level of communal norms may particularly resent changes in CRM partnerships believing that brands are no longer addressing an important societal need, even when the sponsoring brand switches its support to another charity. Replacing one charity with an alternative charity may also affect con-sumers' (with high communal norms) assessments of authenticity of the corporation's commitment to making a positive social change (Berglind and Nakata, 2005). Previous studies have rarely included communal norms as a covariate in CRM persuasion stud-ies, and our work suggests that this may be an important oversight.

Limitations and directions for future research

All research is subject to some limitations. We used two experiments to study the impact of the termination of a CRM partnership on consumers' brand perceptions and purchase intentions. While experiments allow researchers to control key variables and make strong inferences about cause and effect, future research should be undertaken to validate our findings in a more natural setting. It should also be noted that our samples were drawn from online panels of adult Americans. Such samples may be overly homogeneous since some other CRM researchers have shown that culture (Lavack and Kropp 2003) and self-construal (Kim and Johnson 2013; Youn and Kim 2018) may have an impact on consumers' response to CRM partnerships. Future research, therefore, could strive for more variance in sample design to study the impact of these factors on our findings.

Directions for future research abound despite the extensive body of literature that has explored CRM programmes. Brand-cause fit, for example, has been extensively studied in the context of CRM programmes, but the extant research has produced equivocal results (Hibbert et al. 2007; Guerreiro, Rita, and Trigueiros 2016). Our work also produced mixed results. Brand-cause fit showed a null effect in Study 1, but when used as the basis of the operational motivation, it did have an impact on con-sumer perceptions. Thus, more research is required to better explain the equivocal findings such as ours with regard to this important variable.

In our experiments, we kept the temporal duration of the sponsor's support consist-ent across our studies. Extending our research to examine the potential effects of tem-poral duration could be an important area for future studies.

While we used attribution theory to guide our studies, future research could explore additional theoretical frameworks to shed even more light on these findings and more deeply understand the consequences of the termination of CRM partner-ships. Strahilevitz (2008) study of the impact of withdrawing donations to a cause uncovered a 'take-away' effect, and this could be explored as another theory to explain the negative effect on brand perceptions and purchase intentions when CRM partnerships are terminated.

Authenticity theory may prove to be an especially fruitful route. Consumers have been shown to be highly sceptical about the genuineness or authenticity of a firm's desire to help a cause. The termination of a CRM partnership may further validate this scepticism in consumers' eyes (Brønn and Vrioni 2001). Authenticity may be especially relevant since Chang (2012b) argued that there are potentially more negative associations with CRM programmes than there are with other sponsorship programmes. Alhouti, Johnson and Holloway (2016) study of corporate social responsibility programmes (programmes similar in many aspects to CRM programmes), suggested that consumers' perceptions of authenticity of a firm's programmes impact their attitudes. In a similar vein, Bolton and Mattila's (2015), study of corporate social responsibility strategies demonstrated that they are ineffective if consumers perceive a company's motivations to be self-serving. Thus, deeper application of authenticity theory to CRM partnership termination may prove to be fruitful.

Termination of a CRM partnership may also signal to consumers that the firm is less trustworthy and sincere in its sponsorship of a social cause. Indeed, Rozensher (2013) has already pointed out the importance of consumer trust if a partnership is to stand out in the minds of consumers. Thus, future research could investigate the role of consumer trust and its impact in magnifying or mitigating the negative consequences associated with CRM partnership terminations.

The impact of visual executions in advertisements related to a CRM partnership termination is another route that could be explored by researchers in the future. For example, in the situation where a firm switches its support to a new cause, making the cause more prominent than the brand in the visuals in an advertisement or news release may lead to a more a positive response (Small and Verrochi 2009; Chang 2012a; Chang and Chen 2017). Future research could also investigate whether levels of involvement with the sponsored social cause would impact consumers' response to a CRM partnership termination. We speculate that the higher the involvement with the social cause, the higher the negative response of consumers to a CRM partnership termination.

Furthermore, in this research, we used a non-existent brand (Sunshine) and participants were only given information about a single product (orange juice). In other words, in our study the brand, organization and product all have the same name. In the real world, however, companies may use different names for each of their products and create different branding messages for different brand categories. Thus, another avenue for future research is to examine how terminating a CRM sponsorship impacts product, family and corporate brands.

Finally, Robinson, Irmak, and Jayachandran (2012) examined the effect of consumer choice when selecting causes for a firm to sponsor. Future research could extend this research to see if giving consumers the choice of a new cause to sponsor would mitigate the negative effects of termination.

Disclosure statement

No potential conflict of interest was reported by the authors.

Funding

The research was supported by the Social Sciences and Humanities Research Council of Canada (SSHRC) grant #430-2016-00798.

References

Aggarwal, P. 2004. The effects of brand relationship norms on consumer attitudes and behavior. *Journal of Consumer Research* 31, no. 1: 87–101.

Aghakhani, H., M. Akhgari, and K. Main. 2019. When does money priming affect helping behavior? *Australasian Marketing Journal* 27, no. 1: 32–40.

Alhouti, S., C.M. Johnson, and B.B. Holloway. 2016. Corporate social responsibility authenticity: Investigating its antecedents and outcomes. *Journal of Business Research* 69, no. 3: 1242–9.

Anuar, M.M., and O. Mohamad. 2012. Effects of skepticism on consumer response toward cause-related marketing in Malaysia. *International Business Research* 5, no. 9: 98–105.

Bae, M. 2018. Overcoming skepticism toward cause-related marketing claims: the role of consumers' attributions and a temporary state of skepticism. *Journal of Consumer Marketing* 35, no. 2: 194–207.

Barone, M.J., A.D. Miyazaki, and K.A. Taylor. 2000. The influence of cause-related marketing on consumer choice: Does one good turn deserve another? *Journal of the Academy of Marketing Science* 28, no. 2: 248–62.

Bar-Tal, D., Y. Bar-Zohar, M.S. Greenberg, and M. Hermon. 1977. Reciprocity behavior in the relationship between donor and recipient and between harm-doer and victim. *Sociometry* 40, no. 3: 293–8.

Baylin, G., P.H. Cunningham, and P. Cushing. 1994. Cause-related marketing: Ethical practice or exploitive procedure? *The Philanthropist* 12, no. 2: 15–33.

Berger, I.E., P.H. Cunningham, and M.E. Drumwright. 1999. Social alliances: Company/nonprofit collaboration. *Social Marketing Quarterly* 3: 49–53.

Berger, I.E., P.H. Cunningham, and R.V. Kozinets. 1998. Consumer persuasion through cause-related advertising. *Advances in consumer research*, eds. Eric J. Arnould and Linda M. Scott, 26, 491–497. Provo, UT: Association for Consumer Research.

Bergkvist, L., and C.R. Taylor. 2016. Leveraged marketing communications: a framework for explaining the effects of secondary Brand associations. *AMS Review* 6: 157–75.

Bergkvist, L., and K.Q. Zhou. 2019. Cause-related marketing persuasion research: an integrated framework and directions for further research. *International Journal of Advertising* 38, no. 1: 5–25.

Berglind, M., and C. Nakata. 2005. Cause-related marketing: More buck than bang? *Business Horizons* 48, no. 5: 443–53.

Bolton, L.E., and A.S. Mattila. 2015. How does corporate social responsibility affect consumer response to service failure in buyer–seller relationships? *Journal of Retailing* 91, no. 1: 140–53.

Brønn, P., and A.B. Vrioni. 2001. Corporate social responsibility and cause-related marketing: An overview. *International Journal of Advertising* 20, no. 2: 207–22.

Carvalho, S.W., E. Muralidharan, and H. Bapuji. 2015. Corporate social 'irresponsibility': Are consumers' biases in attribution of blame helping companies in product–harm crises involving hybrid products? *Journal of Business Ethics* 130, no. 3: 651–63.

Carvalho, S.W., S. Sen, M. de Oliveira Mota, and R.C. de Lima. 2010. Consumer reactions to CSR: a brazilian perspective. *Journal of Business Ethics* 91, no. S2: 291–310.

Chang, C.T. 2011. Guilt appeals in cause-related marketing: the subversive roles of product type and donation magnitude. *International Journal of Advertising* 30, no. 4: 587–616.

Chang, C.T. 2012a. Missing ingredients in cause-related advertising: the right formula of execution style and cause framing. *International Journal of Advertising* 31, no. 2: 231–56.

Chang, C.T. 2012b. The effectiveness of advertising that leverages sponsorship and cause-related marketing: A contingency model. *International Journal of Advertising* 31, no. 2: 317–37.

Chang, C.T., and P.C. Chen. 2017. Cause-related marketing ads in the eye tracker: it depends on how you present, who sees the ad, and what you promote. *International Journal of Advertising* 36, no. 2: 336–55.

Clark, M.S. 1984. Record keeping in two types of relationships. *Journal of Personality and Social Psychology* 47, no. 3: 549–57.

Dahl, W.D., and A.M. Lavack. 1995. Cause-related marketing: Impact of size of corporate donation and size of cause-related promotion on consumer perceptions and participation. *AMA Winter Educators' Conference*, Chicago 477–481.

Dahlsrud, A. 2008. How corporate social responsibility is defined: An analysis of 37 definitions. *Corporate Social Responsibility and Environmental Management* 15, no. 1: 1–13.

Ellen, P.M., L.A. Mohr, and D. Webb. 2000. Charitable programs and the retailer: Do they mix? *Journal of Retailing* 76, no. 3: 393–406.

Farrelly, F. 2010. Not playing the game: Why sport sponsorship relationships break down. *Journal of Sport Management* 24, no. 3: 319–37.

Fiske, S.T., and S.E. Taylor. 1991. *Social cognition.* 2nd ed. New York: McGraw-Hill.

Guerreiro, J., P. Rita, and D. Trigueiros. 2016. A text mining-based review of cause-related marketing literature. *Journal of Business Ethics* 139, no.1: 111–28.

Gupta, S., and J. Pirsch. 2006. The company-cause-customer fit decision in cause-related marketing. *Journal of Consumer Marketing* 23, no. 6: 314–26.

Gurin, M.G. 1987. Cause-related marketing in question. *Advertising Age* Special Report, July 27: S-16.

Harris, G. 1987. The implications of low-involvement theory for advertising effectiveness. *International Journal of Advertising* 6, no. 3: 207–21.

Harvey, J.A., and M.A. Strahilevitz. 2009. The power of pink: Cause-related marketing and the impact on breast cancer. *Journal of the American College of Radiology* 6, no. 1: 26–32.

Hessekiel, D. 2010. The most influential cause marketing campaigns. *AdAge.* February 10, https://adage.com/article/goodworks/influential-marketing-campaigns/142037/.

Hessekiel, D. 2017. four cause marketing classics passed last year – and a new era began. *Forbes.* April 18, https://www.forbes.com/sites/davidhessekiel/2017/04/18/four-cause-marketing-classics-passed-last-year-and-a-new-era-began/#55e5f8907e8d.

Hibbert, S., A. Smith, A. Davies, and F. Ireland. 2007. Guilt appeals: Persuasion knowledge and charitable giving. *Psychology and Marketing* 24, no. 8: 723–42.

Hon, L.C., and J.E. Grunig. 1999. *Guidelines for measuring relationships in public relations.* Gainesville, FL: Institute for Public Relations, Commission on PR Measurement and Evaluation.

IEG 2017. Sponsorship spending forecast: Continued growth around the world. http://www.sponsorship.com/IEGSR/2017/01/04/Sponsorship-Spending-Forecast–Continued-Growth-Ar.aspx.

Jensen, J.A., and B.T. Cornwell. 2017. Why do marketing relationships end? findings from an integrated model of sport sponsorship decision-making. Journal of Sport Management 31, no. 4: 401–18.

Karmarkar, U.R., and Z.L. Tormala. 2010. Believe me, I have no idea what I'm talking about: the effects of source certainty on consumer involvement and persuasion. *Journal of Consumer Research* 36, no. 6: 1033–49.

Kim, J.E., and K.K.P. Johnson. 2013. The impact of moral emotions on cause-related marketing campaigns: a cross-cultural examination. *Journal of Business Ethics* 112, no. 1: 79–90.

Kim, K., Y. Cheong, and J.S. Lim. 2015. Choosing the right message for the right cause in social cause advertising: type of social cause message, perceived company-cause fit and the persuasiveness of communication. *International Journal of Advertising* 34, no. 3: 473–94.

Klein, P. 2014. The coming end of corporate charity, and how companies should prepare. Forbes Post July 9: https://www.forbes.com/sites/forbesleadershipforum/2014/07/09/the-coming-end-of-corporate-charity-and-how-companies-should-prepare/#41c1a3dd1071.

Lafferty, B.A. 2007. The relevance of fit in a cause-Brand alliance when consumers evaluate corporate credibility. *Journal of Business Research* 60, no. 5: 447–53.

Lafferty, B.A. 2009. Selecting the right cause partners for the right reasons: The role of importance and fit in cause–Brand alliances. *Psychology and Marketing* 26: 359–82.

Lavack, A.M., and F. Kropp. 2003. A cross-cultural comparison of consumer attitudes toward cause-related marketing. *Social Marketing Quarterly* 9, no. 2: 3–16.

Manfred, T. 2013. Nike cuts ties with the livestrong foundation. *Business Insider* May 28, https://www.businessinsider.com/nike-cuts-ties-with-livestrong-2013-5.

Mills, J., and M.S. Clark. 1982. Exchange and communal relationships. *Review of Personality and Social Psychology* 3: 121–44.

Moosmayer, D.C., and A. Fuljahn. 2010. Consumer perceptions of cause related marketing campaigns. *Journal of Consumer Marketing* 27, no. 6: 543–9.

Mort, G.S., and T. Rose. 2004. The effect of product type on value linkages in the means-end chain: implications for theory and method. *Journal of Consumer Behaviour* 3, no. 3: 221–34.

Mort, G.S., and T. Rose. 2004. The effect of product type on value linkages in the means-end chain: implications for theory and method. *Journal of Consumer Behaviour* 3, no. 3: 221–34.

Nan, X., and K. Heo. 2007. Consumer responses to corporate social responsibility (CSR) initiatives: Examining the role of brand-cause fit in cause-related marketing. *Journal of Advertising* 36, no. 2: 63–74.

PMA and Gable Group 2000. *Survey of Cause Marketing*. Available at www.pmalink.org/members/causemarketing2000/default.asp.

Robinson, S.R., C. Irmak, and S. Jayachandran. 2012. Choice of cause in cause-related marketing. *Journal of Marketing* 76, no. 4: 126–39.

Ross, J.K., L.T. Patterson, and M.A. Stutts. 1992. Consumer perceptions of organizations that use cause-related marketing. *Journal of the Academy of Marketing Science* 20, no. 1: 93–7.

Rozensher, S. 2013. The growth of cause marketing: past, current, and future trends. *Journal of Business & Economics Research* 11, no. 4: 181–6.

Shavitt, S., and M.R. Nelson. 2009. The social identity function in person perception: Communicated meanings of product preferences. In *Why we evaluate: Function of attitudes*. Eds. G.R. Maio and J.M. Olson, 37–57. Mahwah, NJ: Erlbaum.

Small, D.A., and N.M. Verrochi. 2009. The face of need: Facial emotion expression on charity advertisements. *Journal of Marketing Research* 46, no. 6: 777–87.

Sparks, B.A., H.E. Perkins, and R. Buckley. 2013. Online travel reviews as persuasive communication: The effects of content type, source, and certification logos on consumer behavior. *Tourism Management* 39: 1–9.

Strahilevitz, M. 1995. Why cause-related marketing may be especially advantageous for marketers of 'decadent' products: The roles of consumption joy and indulgence guilt. *Association for Consumer Research Annual Conference*, Minneapolis, MN.

Strahilevitz, M. 2008. Why might one feel guilty for giving a homeless guy a dollar? The effects of endowment, peer awareness and guilt on charitable giving. *ACR North American Advances*

Strahilevitz, M., and J. Myers. 1998. Donations to charity as purchase incentives: How well they work may depend on what you are trying to sell. *Journal of Consumer Research* 24, no. 4: 434–46.

Szykman, L.R., P.N. Bloom, and J. Blazing. 2004. Does corporate sponsorship of a socially-oriented message make a difference? An investigation of the effects of sponsorship identity on responses to an anti-drinking and driving message. *Journal of Consumer Psychology* 14, no. 1–2: 13–20.

van den Brink, D., G. Odekerken-Schröder, and P. Pauwels. 2006. The effect of strategic and tactical cause-related marketing on consumers' brand loyalty. *Journal of Consumer Marketing* 23, no. 1: 15.

Varadarajan, P.R., and A. Menon. 1988. Cause-related marketing: A coalignment of marketing strategy and corporate philanthropy. *Journal of Marketing* 52, no. 3: 58–74.

Webb, D.J., and L.A. Mohr. 1998. A typology of consumer responses to cause-related marketing: from skeptics to socially concerned. *Journal of Public Policy & Marketing* 17, no. 2: 226–238.

Winterich, K.P., and Y. Zhang. 2014. Accepting inequality deters responsibility: How power distance decreases charitable behavior. *Journal of Consumer Research* 41: 274–293.

Yang, S. 2014. How packaging of juice products influence customer experience. MSc thesis. Wageningen, Netherlands.

Youn, S., and H. Kim. 2018. Temporal duration and attribution process of cause-related marketing: Moderating roles of self-construal and product involvement. *International Journal of Advertising* 37, no. 2: 217–35.

Appendix 1

Sample study materials: study 1

Sunshine Orange Jui

Naturally rich in vitamin C

Sunshine Orange Juice is naturally rich in the antioxidant vitamin C, an ingredient known for preventing some heart diseases.

Sunshine Orange Juice has been a sponsor of the Healthy Diet Research Association (HDRA). For Every bottle of juice sold, we donate 5 cents to this worthy cause.

In its most recent board meeting, Sunshine Orange Juice decided to continue this sponsorship for one more year.

Visit www.sunshine.com for more information about our product

Sample study materials: study 2

Naturally rich in vitamin C

Sunshine Orange Juice is naturally rich in the antioxidant
vitamin C, an ingredient known for preventing some heart diseases.

Nov 4, 2018

Sunshine Orange Juice has been a sponsor of Traffic Safety Research Association (TSRA). For many years it has donated 5% of its sales to TSRA to support its ongoing effort to provide help to those affected by traffic accidents, which is not related to Sunshine's core business.

Recently, the Board of Directors of Sunshine orange juice decided to re-evaluate the partnership between Sunshine and TSRA. It discussed the fact that TSRA is already sponsored by many other major corporations. The Board decided to recommend that Sunshine ends its partnership with TSRA and replace it with a charity that receives less support from other companies and brands. Sunshine wants to make it clear that this decision was solely made by its Board of Directors and had no participation of members of TSRA.

Following its Board of Director's recommendation, Sunshine recently announced that it will end its support of TSRA and instead sponsor Healthy Diet Research Association (HDRA) to reduce the impact of obesity, which is mostly caused by sugar consumption. Sunshine believes that HDRA is underfunded and, for that reason, is a better partner for Sunshine. The phase out of the sponsorship of TSRA and the start of the sponsorship of HDRA will take place simultaneously at the beginning of 2019. Sunshine will promote this new initiative through its 2019 Super Bowl ads and other marketing activities over the next few months.

When good becomes bad: the role of corporate crisis and issue congruence

Yoojung Kim and Sejung Marina Choi

ABSTRACT
This study investigates how different types of corporate crises and issue congruence interplay in determining the effects of a previous corporate social responsibility (CSR) initiative in a company facing a crisis. The findings suggest that a previous CSR initiative can more effectively protect a company's image when the company has a competence-related rather than a morality-related crisis. In addition, when the social cause of the CSR initiative is congruent with the issue of the negative event, consumers will respond more negatively than when there is no issue congruence between CSR and the negative event. Moreover, there is an interaction effect between issue congruence and the type of crisis. That is, when a firm has a moral crisis that is associated with the social cause supported in a previous CSR initiative, consumers perceive the firm's CSR initiative to have been less sincere than if the firm were facing a competence-related crisis.

Introduction

As corporate social responsibility (CSR) has become an increasingly indispensable part of corporate landscape, consumers are more likely to purchase a product that supports a particular cause such as environmental improvement or breast cancer support (Cone 2017). A large body of research supports the positive effects of CSR on consumer behavior. For example, CSR initiatives have a positive effect on consumers' brand and product evaluations, over and above economic or rational considerations (Klein and Dawar 2004), as well as an impact on their brand choices and brand recommendations (Brown and Dacin 1997; Drumwright 1994; Sen and Bhattacharya 2001).

While CSR initiatives are generally viewed in a positive light, companies are also accused of socially irresponsible activities. Incidents of irresponsible behaviors have become increasingly common in the business world. Such issues range from product quality issues, such as BMW recalls for fire risk or the exploding Samsung Galaxy Note's battery explosion, to ethical concerns, such as United Airline's violent removal of a passenger from an overbooked flight or Apple's labor issues in Chinese factories. As social media and diverse communication channels have made negative information on firms more readily available, negative coverage often results in serious damage to the firm's image. Considering the growing interest in and importance of CSR initiatives in terms of firms' reputation and image, CSR initiatives may have significant implications for firms' confronting crises.

In a corporate crisis, on one hand, previous research suggests that CSR activities serve as insurance (Becker-Olsen, Cudmore, and Hill 2006; Klein and Dawar 2004). That is, previous CSR activities may sustain consumers' positive impressions of a company, and thus, prompt consumers to maintain a positive or neutral attitude toward the company, despite a negative event. On the other hand, CSR initiatives may backfire in the event of a crisis. In this case, previous CSR initiatives may not protect against crises and may even worsen consumer attitudes toward the company caused by due to allegations of social irresponsibility (Eabrasu 2012; Vanhamme et al. 2015; Wagner, Lutz, and Weitz 2009).

Considering the mixed results as to whether previous CSR initiatives have buffering or aggravating effects, exploring the role of CSR in consumer-firm relationships under a crisis would be a significant contribution to both academia and the business world. Regarding this issue, previous research has examined the effects of the source of CSR (a third party or company) (Vanhamme et al. 2015), timing of CSR (proactive and reactive CSR), the abstractness of the CSR statement (Wagner, Lutz, and Weitz 2009), crisis type (accident vs. transgression) (Kim, Kim, and Cameron 2009), and negative publicity type (customer orientation vs. service quality orientation) (Eisingerich et al. 2011). In contrast to previous studies, we first categorize the nature of corporate crisis (competence vs. morality). We then investigate which type of crisis has a larger impact on consumer perception when the company has previously participated in a CSR activity.

Another important aim of this study is to investigate the effect of congruence or perceived fit between the issue of corporate crisis and the cause of CSR programs (Lafferty, Goldsmith, and Hult 2004; Lunenberg, Gosselt, and De Jong 2016; Pracejus and Olsen 2004). A significant body of research has documented the overall positive effects of company-cause congruence in CSR activities on consumers' attitudes toward a company. However, when the corporate crisis is directly relevant to the cause that the company previously supported via a CSR campaign, companies may have a different response than that observed in the existing literature for companies not experiencing crises. Therefore, we examine the moderating role of perceived fit between the negative information and the cause of CSR activities in the context of a corporate crisis.

Consequently, the primary research questions addressed by this study are: (1) How does a previous CSR initiative affect consumers' responses to a company affected by a crisis and how does that differ given the type of negative information associated with the crisis, that is, competence vs. morality? (2) How does the perceived fit between the negative information and the cause of CSR moderate the effects of a previous CSR initiative on consumers' responses to a company's crisis?

Theoretical framework and hypothesis development

Negative information and CSR initiatives

How consumers process negative information is crucial to understanding its impact on consumer-corporate associations, which include all the information and beliefs that a person holds regarding a particular company (Brown and Dacin 1997). For information processing, previous research suggested that negative information is likely to exert a stronger and more powerful impact on formation of corporate associations than equally positive information (Baumeister et al. 2001; Herr, Kardes, and Kim 1990; Rozin and Royzman 2001; Skowronski and Carlston 1989). Therefore, negative information about a company or its products likely results in negative corporate associations, which in turn, are likely to influence, negatively, consumers' behavior toward a company, its products, and eventually negatively affect sales and profits (Einwiller et al. 2006).

Competence and morality are two important dimensions of negative information processing regarding a company (Folkes and Kamins 1999; Skowronski and Carlston 1989; Votola and Unnava 2006). Negative information related to competence concerns a company's failure to meet quality standards, as perceived by consumers (Wojciszke, Brycz, and Borkenau 1993). Morality-related information, on the other hand, concerns corporate behavior that conflicts with consumers' established ethical standards (Shim, Chung, and Kim 2017; Wojciszke, Brycz, and Borkenau 1993). Research on negative information suggests that consumers tend to react differently to negative information about a firm's moral behavior versus its competence (Brown and Dacin 1997; Folkes and Kamins 1999). While competence-related failure is more tolerable and acceptable than moral failure in individuals (Kanouse and Hanson 1972; Votola and Unnava 2006; Wojciszke, Brycz, and Borkenau 1993), the reverse may be true when the target of the negative information is a company. This is because consumers expect companies to produce goods competently due to the purchase costs (Brown and Dacin 1997). Therefore, consumers tend to be more critical when companies are unable to produce quality products than when companies behave unethically (Ahluwalia, Burnkrant, and Unnava 2000; Brown and Dacin 1997; Gurhan-Canli and Batra 2004).

While consumers' expectations of a firm's morality seem to be lower than for its competence, consumers have higher expectations regarding a firm's ethics when the firm is actively involved in a CSR activity. A company's CSR initiative is closely associated with morality in the sense that they contribute to the development of good will in the community and society. Thus, firms with active CSR initiatives can generally establish positive reputations for doing something socially desirable. It is possible, however, for a corporate positive reputation to have a negative effect. According to the contrast effect theory (Anderson 1973; Sherif and Hovland 1961), one's initial attitude serves as a reference point for judging new information; when this new information conflicts with the established reference, the unexpected nature of such information can significantly affect the final evaluation. Applying this contrast effect, when a company that previously engaged in CSR efforts confronts a moral crisis, consumers' positive impressions of the company that were created by the CSR activity may trigger a contrasting effect. Accordingly, the previous CSR involvement makes a company's current moral misdeeds more salient to consumers' information processing.

In addition, based on attribution theory (Kelley 1972), a company's moral crisis is likely to lead consumers to be more skeptical of the company's previous CSR engagement, and attribute the engagement to less altruistic motives. Although CSR activities unquestionably contain a moral aspect, consumers' attributions to corporate CSR activities remain mixed: the activities are believed to be driven by intrinsic, extrinsic motives, or both (Ellen, Webb, and Mohr 2006). When consumers view corporate CSR motives as more profit-oriented than altruistic, their evaluations of the firm are likely to deteriorate. Thus, negative information in the morality-related domain can be a signal to consumers that a firm with previous CSR activities may have been insincere and did not truly care about its supported cause. This inconsistency makes consumers suspicious of the firm's motives and may lead to even less favorable perceptions of the company during a moral crisis.

Previous literature on attribution theory also suggests a relationship between attribution and subsequent attitudes and behaviors (Kelley and Michela 1980). If consumers develop attributions for corporate motives for a CSR initiative, these attributions influence later attitudes and behaviors. When a company that previously engaged in a CSR activity faces a crisis, consumers' attributions may become negative, eventually leading to decreased corporate credibility, negative attitudes toward the company, and lower purchase intentions (Becker-Olsen, Cudmore, and Hill 2006; Ellen, Mohr, and Webb 2000; Inoue and Kent 2014; Menon and Kahn 2003; Rifon et al. 2004; Sen and Bhattacharya 2001). Therefore, we first formulate the following hypothesis:

H1: A previous CSR initiative by a company will generate less favorable consumer responses toward the company ((a) motive attributions, (b) credibility, (c) attitude toward the company, (d) purchase intention) when the company faces a moral crisis than when it faces a competence crisis.

Issue congruence between CSR initiatives and negative information

Previous research has emphasized the effects of congruence in CSR initiatives (Lafferty, Goldsmith, and Hult 2004; Menon and Kahn 2003; Pracejus and Olsen 2004), and existing literature documents the mixed results regarding company-cause congruence of CSR activities in terms of consumers' attitudes toward a company. Some researchers suggest that relationships between organizations that fit together well are viewed as stronger and more favorable than relationships between organizations that do not fit together well (Basil and Herr 2006; Zdravkovic, Magnusson, and Stanley 2010). In contrast, other researchers suggest highly fitting relationships may increase consumers' skepticism about company motives and lead consumers to respond more positively to non-fitting relationships between cause and company (Ellen, Mohr, and Webb 2000). Despite assertions that fit is important, there are numerous determinants of fit between a cause and a company and fit is derived from numerous dimensions such as mission, products, markets, technologies, attributes, brand concepts, or any other key association (Simmons and Becker-Olsen 2006; Zdravkovic, Magnusson, and Stanley 2010).

While most of the literature focuses on the effects of congruence between company and cause, in this paper, we examine the congruence between the issue of CSR initiatives and negative information. For example, a company has previously been involved in CSR activity to improve child nutrition, but this company faces a crisis involving a nutrition quality problem in its products. Another example is that a company's previous CSR initiative is to help child welfare, but becomes involved in a crisis regarding child labor. These examples are based on the fit between the cause of CSR initiatives and negative information as a result of the issue.

For a company that has previously been involved in CSR activity, negative information may reflect the company's violation of its core or protected values (Baron and Spranca 1997). Protected values are key values that should not be sacrificed for any compensating benefits, no matter how small the sacrifice or how large the benefit (Baron and Spranca 1997). In the case of a company's CSR initiative, the cause represents the company's protected value, with its CSR activity serving as a public announcement of the company's willingness to endorse that particular value. In this regard, when a company that previously supported a particular value (i.e. the CSR cause) becomes involved in a negative event closely related with the social cause, consumers may react with strong skepticism toward the company since the company's transgression seems even more salient. When there is a congruence between the issue of negative information and the CSR cause, a company's previous CSR initiative may lead to even more unfavorable perceptions of the company by drawing greater attention to the negative event (Bhattacharya et al. 2006; Szykman, Bloom, and Jennifer 2004). We, therefore, formulate the following hypothesis:

H2: A previous CSR initiative will generate a less positive response toward the company ((a) motives, (b) credibility, (c) attitude toward the company, (d) purchase intention) when there is congruence between the CSR cause and the negative information than when there is no congruence.

Moreover, the congruence between the issue of negative information and the CSR cause varies depending on the type of negative information (i.e. competence vs. morality). As CSR initiatives, by nature, belong to the moral domain, a firm's previous CSR engagement helps to support its moral image. However, when a firm, initially perceived as ethical because of its CSR initiative, becomes involved in a moral crisis, stronger negative attributions are generated by consumers toward the firm. Moreover, when a firm's moral crisis is directly related to its previously supported CSR cause, consumers may perceive its CSR initiative as having been less appropriate and more self-serving. In contrast, when a firm faces a competence-related crisis, the congruence may not engender as great an impact as a moral crisis because such negative issue indirectly relates to the moral aspect of CSR. Thus, congruence between the issue of negative information and the CSR cause may generate greater negative reaction to the company when such information is related to morality rather than competence. We, therefore, formulate the following hypothesis:

H3: When negative information concerns a company's morality, the effect of congruence between the issue of negative information and the CSR cause on consumers' responses to the company ((a) motives, (b) credibility, (c) attitude toward the company, (d) purchase intention) will be more negative than when the negative information concerns competence.

Method

Overview and design

This study examined consumer evaluations of a company faced with a negative event and its congruence with a previous CSR initiative using a 2x2 between-subjects design (negative information: competence, morality); (issue congruence: congruence, incongruence). The stimuli consisted of four different versions of a scenario describing the company's negative event, as well as its previous CSR activity. The type of negative information and issue congruence were manipulated based on pretesting. In addition, the intensity of the negative information related to competence and morality, the plausibility of the negative information, and the importance of the CSR activity were pretested.

Stimuli

Two short news articles about a fictitious tire company, Company X, were created. A fictitious company was used in order to minimize any potential confounding effects of participants' prior brand exposure. For the first factor, the type of negative information, the competence-related negative information condition was an uneven tire wear problem caused by a design flaw in the manufacturing process. In the morality-related negative information condition, Company X had improperly disposed of tires in developing countries. For the second main effect of issue-congruence, in the condition of congruent CSR social cause and negative information in the competence domain, a fictitious CSR campaign described the company's support of a safe-driving program. In the condition of congruent CSR social cause and negative information in the morality domain, a fictitious CSR campaign depicted the company as supporting an environmental protection program. In the condition of incongruent CSR social cause and negative information for both competence and morality domains, a fictitious CSR campaign supporting cancer-fighting initiatives was created. All the stimuli used in the main study appear in Appendix 1.

Pretests

A series of pretests determined the execution of the experimental manipulations aligned with the independent variables. The first pretest was to develop two types and equivalent degree of negative information related to competence and morality. Participants ($n = 15$) received four versions of scenarios regarding the company's negative information related to competence and morality: (1) a slow leak tire problem (2) an uneven tire wear problem and morality ($M_{competence\ 2} = 4.93$) (3) tire dumping practices ($M_{morality\ 1} = 1.87$), and (4) workers health problem ($M_{morality\ 2} = 2.53$). A six-item, seven-point, Likert-type scale, ranging from 1 (strongly disagree) to 7 (strongly agree) measured the perceived negative information of competence and morality. The statements included six items: 'This company has product quality issues'. 'This company has some problems with its ethical practices'. 'This company has some problems with its performance'. 'This company's negative information relates to its technical problems'. 'The negative information about this company relates to its deceitfulness'. 'This company does not care about moral issues'. The results show that perceptions of negative information type about Company X in four scenarios significantly differed from one another ($M_{competence\ 1}$ vs. $M_{morality\ 1}$, $t\ (14) = 5.84$; $p < .001$; $M_{competence\ 1}$ vs. $M_{morality\ 2}$; $t\ (14) = 4.02$; $p < .01$, $M_{competence\ 2}$ vs. $M_{morality\ 1}$, $t\ (14) = 5.60$; $p < .001$, $M_{competence\ 2}$ vs. $M_{morality\ 2}$; $t\ (14) = 3.29$; $p < .01$). In terms of equivalent degree of negative information related to competence and morality, the pretest used a four-item seven-point semantic differential scale anchored by serious/trivial, significant/insignificant, important/unimportant, and negative/positive. Based on paired samples t test results, an uneven tire wear situation ($M = 2.02$) used for the competence-related negative condition, and tire dumping practices ($M = 1.76$) used for the morality-related negative condition because no significant difference with these versions of scenarios, $t\ (14) = .96$; $p > .05$.

In the second pretest, another group of subjects ($n = 102$) responded to determine if the social cause of CSR initiatives related to participants' knowledge and interests. Measurement of the perceived importance of the cause of CSR used a five-item seven-point semantic differential scale anchored by unimportant to me/important to me, means nothing to me/means a lot to me, is personally relevant/is personally irrelevant (Reversed), doesn't matter a great deal to me/does matter a great deal to me, is of no concern to me/is of great concern to me (Menon and Kahn 2003). A one way ANOVA test confirmed no significant difference of consumers' perceived importance of cause among 'safe driving' ($M = 5.82$), 'environment protection' ($M = 5.29$), and 'fight cancer' ($M = 5.45$), $F\ (2, 99) = 2.2$; $p > .05$. In addition, the Bonferroni post hoc test determined the relationship among these three issues, and the results indicated no significant difference for each pair of issues, safe-driving vs. environment ($p > .05$), safe-driving vs. fight cancer ($p > .05$), and environment vs. fight cancer ($p > .05$).

The third pretest developed the issue-congruence condition of whether or not the cause of a company's prior CSR efforts relates to the issue of the company's negative event. Accordingly, a set of issues with negative information along with selected causes from the second pretest constituted the third pretest. A small group of participants ($n = 43$) judged perceptions of issue-congruence with a five-item, seven-point, Likert-type scale ranging from 1 (strongly disagree) to 7 (strongly agree). Adjustment of the measures, adopted from Menon and Kahn (2003), created fit for the study's context. The statements included: 'The issue of this company's scandal is logically related to this social issue'. 'This social issue is a fit with this company's scandalous issue'. 'It is strange to see this scandalous company in this situation sponsoring this social issue (Reversed)'. 'This social issue is similar with this company's scandal'. and 'The social issue and this company's scandal match'. The pretest results showed a significant difference between congruent and incongruent pairs in both the competence and morality domains. In the domain of competence-related negative information, $M_{congruence} = 4.98$; $M_{incongruence} = 3.81$; $t\ (23) = 2.14$; $p < .05$. In addition, in the morality domain, $M_{congruence} = 4.72$; $M_{incongruence} = 3.23$; $t\ (16) = -2.18$; $p < .05$. In this pretest, the plausibility of the news article was measured with a three-item, seven point semantic differential scale anchored by not plausible/plausible, not credible/credible, and didn't make sense/did make sense. No significant difference appeared between competence- ($M = 5.85$) and morality- ($M = 5.41$) based negative news information, $t\ (41) = 1.84$; $p > .05$.

Participants and procedure

A total of 122 undergraduate students (mean age = 21; 50% male) from a large southwestern university in the United States participated in this experiment in exchange for extra credit. Ninety-five percent of the participants reported driving a car and 83% owned a car. The experiment was administered online. Prospective participants who were enrolled in campus-wide elective or introductory communication courses received an informed consent form. Upon agreeing to participate, participants were directed to a study website where they were randomly assigned to one of the four experimental conditions. After reading a newspaper article about the company's CSR campaign, its negative information was provided. They then answered a series of questions on their evaluation of the company and demographic factors.

Dependent variables

Four dependent variables were used for the evaluation of the company. The variable 'Altruistic Motive Attributions' ($\alpha = .99$) was measured using a seven-item, seven-point Likert scale to identify perceptions of the level of altruism behind the company's CSR initiative (Rifon et al. 2004). Corporate Credibility (1 = dishonest, not dependable, not trustworthy, not credible, unconvincing, unbelievable, biased; 7 = honest, dependable, trustworthy, credible, convincing, believable, unbiased; $\alpha = .89$) (MacKenzie and Lutz 1989) and Attitude toward the Company (1 = unfavorable, negative, bad, not likeable, unpleasant; 7 = favorable, positive, good, likable, pleasant; $\alpha = .94$) (MacKenzie and Lutz 1989; Yoon, Gurhan-Canli, and Schwarz 2006) were also measured. Finally, Purchase Intention ($\alpha = .87$) was assessed using a three-item, seven-point Likert scale for questions such as 'How likely would you be to buy a product from Company X?' (Aaker, Vohs, and Mogilner 2010; Einwiller et al. 2006).

Covariates

'Congruence between the Cause and the Company' ($\alpha = .83$) was measured on a five-item, seven-point Likert-type scale to assess the congruence of the pairings of the social cause and the company (Menon and Kahn 2003). Specifically, participants reacted to five statements: 'Company X is logically related to the cause,' 'The cause is a fit with consumers of Company X,' 'It is strange to see the company sponsoring this cause' (reversed item), 'This cause is similar to Company X,' and 'Overall, the cause and Company X closely match.' A second set of statements to assess 'Perceived Role of CSR' ($\alpha = .81$) were also measured on a five-item, seven-point Likert-type scale (Singhapakdi et al. 1996). The five items included: 'Being ethical and socially responsible is the most important thing a company can do,' 'The ethics and social responsibility of a company are essential to its long term profitability,' 'A company's first priority should be employee morale,' 'Good ethics are often good business,' and 'Social responsibility and profitability can exist together.'

Results

Manipulation checks

To assess the different types of negative information, participants were asked to rate the extent to which the news article included evidence of competence or morality. As expected, participants in the competence condition indicated that the negative information is more related to competence ($M = 5.06$) than morality ($M = 3.92$, t (120) = 6.92; $p < .001$), and participants in the morality condition believed that the information is more related to morality ($M = 5.01$) than competence ($M = 3.53$, t (120) = −7.61; $p < .001$). In terms of issue congruence, a t-test confirmed that there is a significant difference (t (120) = 4.13; $p < .001$) between issue congruence ($M = 4.40$) and issue incongruence ($M = 3.55$). In addition, the degree and believability of negative information were examined to ensure that both negative information were perceived as plausible without notable differences between the two manipulation conditions. There was no significant difference between competence ($M = 2.32$) and morality-related negative information ($M = 2.02$), (t (120) = 1.73; $p > .05$) in terms of the level of negative information. A t-test also confirmed that the news articles regarding competence ($M = 5.30$) and morality-related negative information ($M = 5.34$) were both highly believable, with no difference in their plausibility (t (120) = −.21; $p > .05$).

Hypothesis testing

Two-way analyses of covariance (ANCOVA) examined the hypotheses with two covariates, cause-company congruence and perceived role of CSR. For the type of negative information factor, the ANCOVA results indicated significant main effects on consumers' corporate motive attribution (F (1, 116) = 26.84; $p < .001$). It suggests that a previous CSR program leads to more altruistic corporate motives being assigned for competence-related ($M = 4.41$) than for morality-related negative information ($M = 3.26$), confirming Hypothesis 1a. However, a company's previous CSR activity did not significantly affect corporate credibility depending on type of negative information ($M_{competence} = 3.15$, $M_{morality} = 2.95$, F (1, 116) = .98; $p > .05$), thus not supporting Hypothesis 1 b. In addition, after controlling the covariate of the perceived role of CSR ($p < .05$), a company's previous CSR initiative led to more positive attitudes toward the company when it is in a competence-related rather than a morality-related crisis ($M_{competence} = 3.25$, $M_{morality} = 2.69$, F (1, 116) = 6.61; $p < .01$), thus supporting Hypothesis 1c. Finally, there was no significant impact from CSR initiatives on participants' purchase intentions based on the type of negative information ($M_{competence} = 2.63$, $M_{morality} = 2.86$, F (1, 116) = 1.06; $p > .05$), thus not supporting Hypothesis 1d.

For the issue congruence factor, the ANCOVA results showed significant main effects on consumers' corporate motive attribution (F (1, 116) = 6.79; $p < .05$). The results suggest that the issue-congruence condition ($M = 3.51$) generates less altruistic motive attribution than the issue-incongruent condition does ($M = 4.16$). In addition, after controlling the covariate of the perceived role of CSR ($p < .05$), the results revealed a significant main effect on credibility, attitude toward the company, and purchase intention. The issue-congruence ($M = 2.80$) created lower credibility than the

Table 1. Cell means (standard deviations).

	Issue congruence	Altruistic motive	Credibility	Attitude	Purchase intention
NI: Competence	Congruence	4.38 (1.36)	2.86 (1.00)	2.92 (1.00)	2.60 (1.01)
	Incongruence	4.44 (1.11)	3.40 (.92)	3.61 (1.37)	2.70 (1.19)
NI: Morality	Congruence	2.76 (1.20)	2.74 (1.11)	2.39 (1.01)	2.53 (1.29)
	Incongruence	3.76 (1.25)	3.20 (1.24)	2.95 (1.29)	3.13 (1.42)

NI, negative information.

Table 2. Summary of the results of hypothesis testing.

IVs		DVs	Result
Negative Information (NI)	H1a	Altruistic Motive	Supported
	H1b	Credibility	Not Supported
	H1c	Attitude	Supported
	H1d	Purchase Intention	Not Supported
Issue Congruence (IC)	H2a	Altruistic Motive	Supported
	H2b	Credibility	Supported
	H2c	Attitude	Supported
	H2d	Purchase Intention	Supported
NI x IC	H3a	Altruistic Motive	Supported
	H3b	Credibility	Not Supported
	H3c	Attitude	Not Supported
	H3d	Purchase Intention	Not Supported

Table 3. Univarite F-values for altruistic motive, credibility, attitude, and purchase intention.

	Altruistic motive	Credibility	Attitude	Purchase intention
Negative information (NI)	26.84***	.98	6.61*	1.06
Issue congruence (IC)	6.79*	5.81*	11.15**	5.06*
Cause-company congruence	1.44	.17	1.25	1.96
Attitude toward CSR	.44	4.87*	5.96*	11.33**
IC x NI	5.37*	.01	.17	1.03

$^{*}p < .05;$ $^{**}p < .01;$ $^{***}p < .001.$

issue-incongruence $(M = 3.30)$, $F (1, 116) = 5.81; p < .05$. The issue-congruence $(M = 2.39)$ generated less positive attitude toward the company than the issue-incongruence $(M = 3.18)$, $(F (1, 116) = 11.15; p < .01)$. Finally, The issue-congruence $(M = 2.48)$ led to lower purchase intention than the issue-incongruence $(M = 3.01)$, $(F (1, 116) = 5.06; p < .05)$. Thus, the finding supports hypotheses 2a, 2b, 2c and 2d.

In terms of the issue congruence x negativity type interaction, there was significant interaction effects on corporate motive attribution $(F (1, 116) = 5.37; p < .05)$. When issue congruence exists, morality-related negative information $(M = 2.67)$ generated less altruistic motive attribution than competence-related negative information $(M = 4.35, F (1, 116) = 5.37; p < .05)$. Similarly, participants attributed more altruistic motives for a competence-related crisis $(M = 4.21)$ than a morality-related crisis $(M = 3.59, F (1, 175) = 5.97; p < .05)$ in issue-incongruence condition, thus supporting Hypothesis 3a. However, no interaction effects of issue-congruence and the type of negative information appeared on consumers' perceptions of corporate credibility, attitudes toward the company and purchase intentions, leaving hypotheses 3b, 3c, and 3d unsupported. All means and standard deviations are reported in Table 1, summary of hypotheses testing is reported in Table 2, and Univariate F-values for dependent variables are reported in Table 3.

Discussion

The primary aim of this study was to examine the role of the type of negative information in the effect of CSR initiatives in the context of a corporate crisis. The findings of the study indicate that a firm's previous CSR efforts are less likely to prevent negative responses toward the company when the company is experiencing a morality-related crisis than competence-related crisis. The results imply that if a firm with a previous participation in CSR initiatives encounters a moral crisis, the morality-related negative information provides more diagnostic cues to consumers than a firm's competence-related crisis does due to the salient contradiction between a firm's previous CSR initiatives and its transgression in a moral domain. Consequently, these findings provide a new perspective on CSR effects during corporate crises. While many firms participate in CSR initiatives because of a desire to enhance perceptions of their altruism, these efforts may not always have the desired effect, especially when a firm is facing a morality-related crisis.

This study also examined the effects of issue congruence between the negative information and the social causes of CSR initiatives. The results indicate that when the issue of negative information is congruent with a firm's previous involvement in a social cause, consumers ascribe less altruistic motives to the firm's CSR involvement, have a lower perception of corporate credibility, less favorable attitudes toward the company, and lower purchase intention. Moreover, interaction effects between the issue congruence and type of negative information on consumer's motive attribution were found. The most negative impact can be expected when a negative issue in the moral domain is congruent with a firm's CSR cause. In the moral domain, a company's transgression is viewed as an obvious violation of the company's protected values (i.e. the cause of the company's CSR initiative), causing consumers to view the company as pursuing other benefits at the cost of a core value. Ultimately, when the crisis issue is congruent with a firm's previous CSR initiatives, it is more difficult for the firm to protect itself or to avoid damage to its reputation when the crisis is a moral one than when it is related to product harm.

Theoretically, this study extends attribution theory by suggesting that consumers' attribution of a firm's CSR motives may be the primary underlying cause of the effect of CSR initiatives during a corporate crisis. By applying attribution theory to different types of corporate crisis settings, the findings of this study suggest that consumers' judgment of a firm's motives for previous CSR initiatives play an important role in their perceptions of the firm when it is in a crisis situation, and consumers tend to doubt the firm's motives more in a moral crisis than in a product-harm crisis.

Another significant implication of this study is the exploration of a new dimension of congruence (i.e. congruence between the issue of negative information and the CSR cause). Previous research has mainly focused on company-cause congruence, overlooking the multidimensionality of congruence (Menon and Kahn 2003; Lichtenstein, Drumwright, and Braig 2004; Rifon et al. 2004; Zdravkovic, Magnusson, and Stanley 2010). In this regard, this study extends understanding of the role of congruence on consumers' attributions by examining the relationship between the issue of the firm's negative information and the cause sponsored by the firm through a CSR campaign. The findings of this research demonstrate the importance of congruence in this new dimension by showing how the issue congruence between the social cause and negative information influences consumer perceptions of the company and its CSR initiative.

From a managerial perspective, this study has important implications for companies in today's business world. The findings of the study confirm that CSR initiatives may help to protect corporate reputations from the impact of negative information, especially when a company's negative event relates to competence, rather than morality. More interestingly, however, is the significant diminishment, and even reversal, of this buffering effect when there is congruence between the negative event and a CSR initiative supported by the company. Given the issue congruence effect on consumer attribution of a firm's motives for its CSR initiatives, it is important for companies to support social causes, since failure to do so may significantly damage their reputations and images. Therefore, when companies embrace social causes, they must demonstrate their genuine and sincere commitment by avoiding any potential negative events in the domain that their CSR initiative supports. The potential effects of issue congruence and negativity type presented in this report also provide some insights into ways in which companies can respond to various types of crises.

Although the present study contributes to the emerging body of literature on CSR, this study is not without limitations. The use of a fictitious company restricts the external validity while allowing the study to control the manipulation of negativity type and issue congruence effects. In addition, although CSR campaign and corporate crisis are manipulated as highly believable news article, it still lacks realism because the study doesn't include the actual CSR campaign with a long-term commitment as well as time-order separation between the CSR and the company's crisis. Furthermore, using one type of product/company (i.e. a tire company) and employing a student sample highlights the opportunity for more work to be done on this issue. Further research concerning with actual CSR campaign, other product categories and a sample of general consumers is suggested to better identify the degree of generalizability of the findings.

This study explores the effect of previous CSR initiatives on a company in the context of a corporate crisis. An interesting topic for future research may involve examining the effects of CSR on nonprofit organizations that collaborate with a company experiencing a crisis. By partnering with companies that support CSR, nonprofit organizations could benefit from positive consumer attitudes toward the company resulting from its CSR initiatives (Lichtenstein, Drumwright, and Braig 2004). However, when these partner companies become embroiled in negative events, nonprofits can also have their reputations negatively impacted by their association with the company. Thus, studying this potential negative effect on associated organizations is also an important and interesting research area. Another fruitful area of research would be examining consumers' emotional responses to the effects of CSR initiatives in the context of a corporate crisis. The focus of the current study was on the cognitive processes of attribution influenced by perceptions of CSR in corporate crisis situations. However, it is also important to know whether or not consumers have emotional responses, such as anger or betrayal, and/or the perception of being owed an apology by the company. Moreover, these feelings could manifest themselves in other behaviors, such as complaining, negative word-of-mouth and price sensitivity (Bloemer, Ruyter, and Wetzels 1998; Folkes 1984). All of these issues present promising avenues for future research.

Disclosure statement

No potential conflict of interest was reported by the authors.

Funding

This research was supported by Konkuk University in 2016.

References

Aaker, J., K. Vohs, and C. Mogilner. 2010. Nonprofits are seen as warm and for-profits as competent: Firm stereotypes matter. *Journal of Consumer Research* 37, no. 2: 224–37.

Ahluwalia, R., R.E. Burnkrant, and H.R. Unnava. 2000. Consumer response to negative publicity: The moderating role of commitment. *Journal of Marketing Research* 37, no. 2: 203–14.

Anderson, R. 1973. Consumer dissatisfaction: The effect of disconfirmed expectancy on perceived product performance. *Journal of Marketing Research* 10, no. 1: 38–44.

Baron, J., and M. Spranca. 1997. Protected values. *Organizational Behavior and Human Decision Processes* 70, no. 1: 1–16.

Basil, D. Z., and P. M. Herr. 2006. Attitudinal balance and cause-related marketing: an empirical application of balance theory, *Journal of Consumer Psychology* 16, no. 4, 391–403

Baumeister, R.F., E. Bratslavsky, C. Finkenauer, and K.D. Vohs. 2001. Bad is stronger than good. *Review of General Psychology* 5, no. 4: 323–370

Becker-Olsen, K.L., B.A. Cudmore, and R.P. Hill. 2006. The impact of perceived corporate social responsibility on consumer behavior. *Journal of Business Research* 59, no. 1: 46–53.

Bhattacharya, S., C.S. Trimble, S.M. Choi, and N.J. Rifon. 2006. *Advice for industries: The case for stigmatized products in cause brand alliances*, ed. J.I. Richards, 253–85. Reno: American Academy of Advertising.

Bloemer, J., K. Ruyter, and M. Wetzels. 1998. Customer loyalty in a service setting. In *European advances in consumer research*, eds. B.G. Englis, and A. Olofsson, 162–9. Provo: Association for Consumer Research.

Brown, T.J., and P.A. Dacin. 1997. The company and the product: Corporate associations and consumer product responses. *Journal of Marketing* 61, no. 1: 68–84.

Cone. 2017. Cone Communications CSR Study. http://www.conecomm.com/research-blog/2017-csr-study.

Diehl, S., R. Terlutter, and B. Mueller. 2016. Doing good matters to consumers: The effectiveness of humane-oriented CSR appeals in cross-cultural standardized advertising campaigns. *International Journal of Advertising* 35, no. 4: 730–57.

Drumwright, M.E. 1994. Socially responsible organizational buying: Environmental concern as a noneconomic buying criterion. *Journal of Marketing* 58, no. 3: 1–19.

Eabrasu, M. 2012. A moral pluralist perspective on corporate social responsibility: From good to controversial practices. *Journal of Business Ethics* 110, no. 4: 429–39.

Einwiller, S.A., A. Fedorikhin, A.R. Johnson, and M.A. Kamins. 2006. Enough is enough! When identification no longer prevents negative corporate associations. *Journal of the Academy of Marketing Science* 34, no. 2: 185–94.

Eisingerich, A.B., G. Rubera, M. Seifert, and G. Bhardwaj. 2011. Doing good and doing better despite negative information?: The role of corporate social responsibility in consumer resistance to negative information. *Journal of Service Research* 14, no. 1: 60–75

Ellen, P.S., L.A. Mohr, and D.J. Webb. 2000. Charitable programs and the retailer: Do they mix? *Journal of Retailing* 76, no. 3: 393–406.

Ellen, P. S., D. J. Webb, and L. A. Mohr. 2006. Building corporate associations: Consumer attributions for corporate socially responsible programs, *Journal of the Academy of Marketing Science* 34, no. 2, 147–157

Folkes, V.S. 1984. Consumer reaction to product failure: An attributional approach. *Journal of Consumer Research* 10, no. 4: 398–409.

Folkes, V.S., and M.A. Kamins. 1999. Effects of information about firm's ethical and unethical actions on consumers attitudes. *Journal of Consumer Psychology* 8, no. 3: 243–59.

Gurhan-Canli, Z., and R. Batra. 2004. When corporate image affects product evaluations: The moderating role of perceived risk. *Journal of Marketing Research* 41, no. 2: 197–205.

Herr, P., F.R. Kardes, and J.Kim. 1990. Effects of word-of-mouth and product-attribute information on persuasion: An accessibility-diagnosticity perspective, *Journal of Consumer Research* 17, no. 4, 454–462

Inoue, Y., and A. Kent. 2014. A conceptual framework for understanding effects of corporate social marketing on consumer behavior. *Journal of Business Ethics* 121, no. 4: 621–33.

Kanouse, D.E., and L.R. Hanson. Jr. 1972. Negativity in evaluations. In *Attribution: Perceiving the causes of behavior*, eds. E.E. Jones, D.E. Kanouse, S. Valins, H.H. Kelley, R.E. Nisbett, and B. Weiner, 47–62. Morristown: General Learning Press.

Kelley, H.H. 1972. Attribution in social interaction. In *Attribution: Perceiving the cause of behavior*, eds. E.E. Jones, D.E. Kanouse, S. Valins, H.H. Kelley, R.E. Nisbett, and B. Weiner, 126. Morristown: General Learning Press.

Kelley, H.H., and J.L. Michela. 1980. Attribution theory and research. *Annual Review of Psychology* 31: 457–501.

Kim, J., H.J. Kim, and G.T. Cameron. 2009. Making nice may not matter: The interplay of crisis type, response type and crisis issue on perceived organizational responsibility. *Public Relations Review* 35, no. 1: 86–88

Klein, J., and N. Dawar. 2004. Corporate social responsibility and consumers' attributions and Brand evaluations in a product-harm crisis. *International Journal of Research in Marketing* 21, no. 3: 203–17.

Lafferty, B.A., R.E. Goldsmith, and G.T.M. Hult. 2004. The impact of the alliance on the partners: A look at cause-Brand alliances. *Psychology and Marketing* 21, no. 7: 509–31.

Lichtenstein, D.R., M.E. Drumwright, and B.M. Braig. 2004. The effect of corporate social responsibility on customer donations to corporate-supported nonprofits. *Journal of Marketing* 64: 16–32.

Lunenberg, K., J.F. Gosselt, and M.D.T. De Jong. 2016. Framing CSR fit: How corporate social responsibility activities are covered by news media. *Public Relations Review* 42, no. 5: 943–51.

MacKenzie, S.B., and R.L. Lutz. 1989. An empirical examination of the structural antecedents of attitude toward the ad in an advertising pretesting context. *Journal of Marketing* 53, no. 2: 48–65.

Menon, S., and B.E. Kahn. 2003. Corporate sponsorships of philanthropic activities: When do they impact perception of sponsor brand? *Journal of Consumer Psychology* 13, no. 3: 316–27.

Pracejus, J.W., and G.D. Olsen. 2004. The role of cause/brand fit in the effectiveness of cause-related marketing campaigns. *Journal of Business Research* 57, no. 6: 635–40.

Rifon, N.J., S.M. Choi, C.S. Trimble, and H. Li. 2004. Congruence effects in sponsorship: The mediating role of sponsor credibility and consumer attributions of sponsor motive. *Journal of Advertising* 33, no. 1: 30–42.

Rozin, P., and E. B. Royzman. 2001. Negativity bias, negativity dominance, and contagion, *Personality and Social Psychology Review* 5, no. 4, 296–320

Sen, S., and C.B. Bhattacharya. 2001. Does doing good always lead to doing better? Consumer reaction to corporate social responsibility. *Journal of Marketing Research* 38, no. 2: 225–44.

Sherif, M., and C.I. Hovland. 1961. *Social judgment: Assimilation and contrast effects in communication and attitude change.* New Haven: Yale University Press.

Shim, K., M. Chung, and Y. Kim. 2017. Does ethical orientation matter? Determinants of public reaction to CSR communication. *Public Relations Review* 43, no. 4: 817–28.

Simmons, C. J., and K. L. Becker-Olsen. 2006. Achieving marketing objectives through social sponsorships, *Journal of Marketing* 70, no. 4, 154–169

Singhapakdi, A., S. Vitell, K.C. Rallapalli, and K.L. Kraft. 1996. The perceived role of ethics and social responsibility: A scale development. *Journal of Business Ethics* 15, no. 11: 1131–40.

Skowronski, J.J., and D.E. Carlston. 1989. Negative and extremity biases in impression formation: A review of explanations. *Psychological Bulletin* 105, no. 1: 131–42.

Szykman, L.R., P.N. Bloom, and B. Jennifer. 2004. Does corporate sponsorship of socially-oriented message make a difference? An investigation of the effects of sponsorship identity on responses to an anti-drinking and driving message. *Journal of Consumer Psychology* 14, no. 1–2: 13–20.

Vanhamme, J., V. Swaen, G. Berens, and C. Janssen. 2015. Playing with fire: Aggravating and buffering effects of ex ante CSR communication campaigns for companies facing allegations of social responsibility. *Marketing Letters* 26, no. 4: 565–78.

Votola, N.L., and H.R. Unnava. 2006. Spillover of negative information on brand alliances. *Journal of Consumer Psychology* 16, no. 2: 196–202.

Wojciszke, B., H. Brycz, and P. Borkenau. 1993. Effects of information content and evaluative extremity on positivity and negativity biases. *Journal of Personality and Social Psychology* 64, no. 3: 327–35.

Yoon, Y., Z. Gurhan-Canli, and N. Schwarz. 2006. The effect of corporate social responsibility (CSR) activities on companies with bad reputations. *Journal of Consumer Psychology* 16, no. 4: 377–90.

Zdravkovic, S., P. Magnusson, and M. S. Stanley. 2010. Dimensions of fit between a brand and a social cause and their influence on attitudes, *International Journal of Research in Marketing* 27, no. 2, 151–160

Appendix 1: Experimental stimuli

<Company Information>

The following information is about a real, well-known tire company that has been in business for many decades. For the purposes of this study, we will call it Company X.

1.. *Safe driving program*

Company X is one of the world's largest tire companies. Last year, the company attained the highest revenues and market share among its competitors. Its employees range from world-class development engineers, technicians, and researchers to highly trained specialists in sales,

marketing, finance, communications, and human resources. In addition, Company X is committed to reducing the rate of fatalities and accidents among young drivers. To promote responsible driving for young people, Company X launched its national safe driving program. The
program includes informing young drivers about a variety of critical defensive driving skills and
accident avoidance techniques, and helping them understand vehicle dynamics and tire safety
and protection.

2.. *Environmental protection*

Company X is one of the world's largest tire companies. Last year, the company attained the highest
revenues and market share among its competitors. Its employees range from world-class development engineers, technicians, and researchers to highly trained specialists in sales, marketing, finance,
communications, and human resources. In addition, Company X is committed to socially responsible
activities related to environmental protection. Environmental activities include minimizing waste and
emissions, reusing and recycling materials, and responsibly managing energy use.

3.. *Fighting cancer*

Company X is one of the world's largest tire companies. Last year, the company attained the
highest revenues and market share among its competitors. Its employees range from world-class
development engineers, technicians, and researchers to highly trained specialists in sales, marketing, finance, communications, and human resources. In addition, Company X is committed to
socially responsible activities related to fighting cancer. Cancer support initiatives include educational programs promoting cancer prevention and a healthy lifestyle, funding for a cancer
research center, and sponsorship of cancer awareness events.

<Newspaper Article>

   The following newspaper article is about an incident that Company X was recently involved
in. Please read this carefully and answer the following questions about your reaction to the
news article.

1.. *Competence*

Recently, Company X confronted government scrutiny for its uneven tire wear problem. According
to Consumer Reports, since last fall, more than one thousand cases of uneven tire wear have
been reported regarding Company X. Due to a design flaw in the manufacturing process, a particular model of tires, K117 OEM, had a rear wheel geometry and alignment problem, leading to
uneven tire wear. Research conducted by the National Engineering Laboratory showed that
uneven tire wear wastes gas and can create deadly driving situations. Currently, state and federal
investigators have joined in the investigation of the uneven tire wear problem of Company X.

2.. *Morality*

Recently, Company X confronted government scrutiny for dumping used tires in some developing countries. According to Consumer Reports, since last fall, thousands of discarded tires that
were found in some developing countries were reported to be products of Company X. While
company executives were aware of the tire dumping, in order to reduce costs, they did not
take any action to resolve the problem. Research conducted by the National Chemical
Laboratory shows that tires will not decompose into the soil even after 100 years and discarded
tires can have hazardous effects on the environment. Currently, state and federal investigators
have joined in the investigation of the problem of improperly disposed tires by Company X.

Celebrity endorsements: a literature review and research agenda

Lars Bergkvist ⓘ and Kris Qiang Zhou

(*Received 12 December 2014; accepted 26 December 2015*)

This paper presents a narrative review of celebrity endorsement research. The review identifies six areas of research on celebrity endorsements (celebrity prevalence, campaign management, financial effects, celebrity persuasion, non-evaluative meaning transfer, and brand-to-celebrity transfer). A review of the research in each area identifies key findings, conflicting results, and research gaps. In addition, this paper reviews the celebrity endorsement literature with a focus on the psychological processes underlying celebrity endorsement effects that has been put forward in the literature. Based on the review an agenda for future research is offered.

Introduction

Celebrity endorsements enjoy enduring popularity as a means to enhance marketing communications. A global study of TV advertising found that featuring celebrities in TV advertising is common on every continent, although there are large differences in the prevalence between countries (Praet 2008). Lately, celebrities are increasingly promoting brands in different online environments (Wood and Burkhalter 2014). Celebrity endorsements are equally popular among marketing academics and there is a steady flow of celebrity endorsement articles in marketing and advertising journals.

In spite of the interest among academics and the large number of studies there is no recent review of the celebrity endorsement literature. It appears that no review has been published since the meta-analysis by Amos, Holmes, and Strutton (2008) and the narrative review by Erdogan (1999). Since celebrity endorsement research is continually developing both in terms of breadth, going into new directions such as studies of sales effects and stock market reactions, and depth, more studies on well-known topics such as source effects, an updated review of the literature seems timely. In fact, more than 60 articles on celebrity endorsements have been published in marketing and advertising journals since 1999 and more than half of these were published after 2008, strongly suggesting that the field has developed considerably since the previous reviews.

The review by Erdogan (1999) focused almost exclusively on the persuasive effects of celebrity endorsements, particularly the source credibility and attractiveness models, and paid limited or no attention to other areas of celebrity endorsement research. Moreover, Erdogan (1999) did not rely on a survey of marketing and advertising journals; the reviewed literature is a mix of academic journals, marketing and advertising textbooks, and anecdotal evidence reported in trade magazines.

The meta-analysis by Amos, Holmes, and Strutton (2008), on the other hand, did carry out a comprehensive survey of articles published in academic journals. However, the focus of their analysis was exclusively on the effect of source factors such as expertise and attractiveness on brand evaluations. Their analysis did not include any other dependent variables such as brand personality traits or sales, or independent variables such as endorsement announcements or celebrity personality traits.

The purpose of this review is to provide an overview of celebrity endorsement research, with an aim to identify distinct research areas, key results, conflicting findings, psychological process theories, and to identify research gaps. This purpose was addressed in a narrative review based on literature searches of 10 leading general marketing journals and 5 advertising journals. Thus, the present review contributes to the advertising literature by providing an up-to-date review of a dynamic and growing field and also by having a broader scope than previous reviews including not only studies of the persuasive effects of celebrity endorsements but also other types of studies.

Literature search

In order to identify a comprehensive set of articles on celebrity endorsements, 10 key general marketing journals (European Journal of Marketing, International Journal of Research in Marketing, Journal of the Academy of Marketing Science, Journal of Consumer Psychology, Journal of Consumer Research, Journal of Marketing, Journal of Marketing Research, Marketing Letters, Marketing Science, Psychology & Marketing) and 5 advertising journals (International Journal of Advertising, Journal of Advertising, Journal of Advertising Research, Journal of Current Issues & Research in Advertising, Journal of Marketing Communications) were initially searched. The search included all articles available in the journal databases published until December 2013. Each journal was searched separately without limits on the time period. Keyword searches on article titles were made using the most common ways to identify the celebrity endorsements (e.g., 'celebrity endorsement,' 'celebrity,' 'celebrities,' 'endorsement,' or 'endorsements'). Following the first search, additional articles were identified from the reference lists in the initial articles. In addition, articles published after 2013 but before the manuscript was finalized were added to the review. Finally, to ensure that all important articles were identified, an additional step was to conduct a comprehensive search of the *Web of Science* for articles citing influential articles such as McCracken's (1989) article. In total, 126 articles were included in this review.

What are celebrity endorsements?

A large majority of the reviewed articles do not define what they mean by celebrity endorsement. Of those that do, almost all refer to McCracken's (1989, 310) definition, according to which a celebrity endorser is 'any individual who enjoys public recognition and who uses this recognition on behalf of a consumer good by appearing with it in an advertisement.' This definition seems somewhat dated in today's world of advertising. Celebrity endorsements appear in many other modes of communication than advertising. For example, celebrities include brand names or pictures of brands in their Twitter postings (Wood and Burkhalter 2014) and there is a plethora of celebrity branded products (Keel and Nataraajan 2012). It also seems limiting to only include consumer goods: celebrities endorse business-to-business products and services (e.g., Tiger Woods endorsement of Accenture), consumer services (e.g., Kobe Bryant and Lionel Messi for

Turkish Airlines), and non-commercial entities such as political parties (see Veer, Becir-ovic, and Martin 2010) and non-profit organizations (see Garcia de los Salmones, Domi-nguez, and Herrero 2013). It is also important to note that celebrity endorsements are based on an agreement in which the celebrity gives the brand (or other entity) permission to use her/his name and/or physical appearance in certain ways. Therefore, the following updated definition is proposed: *a celebrity endorsement is an agreement between an individual who enjoys public recognition (a celebrity) and an entity (e.g., a brand) to use the celebrity for the purpose of promoting the entity.*

An overview of celebrity endorsement research

One of the aims of the present study is to identify distinct areas of celebrity endorsement research. This was approached by analyzing the research problems and methodology of the reviewed articles. The research problem was analyzed in terms of the overall research question addressed and the dependent and independent variables of the study, while the methodology was analyzed in terms of method of data collection, unit of observation, and unit of analysis. The analysis identified six areas that were distinctly different with respect to the typical research problem addressed and the dependent and independent variables, and that were in most cases also different with respect to the data collection method and the units of observation and analysis. The six areas are celebrity prevalence, campaign management, financial effects, celebrity persuasion, non-evaluative meaning transfer, and brand-to-celebrity transfer. The six research areas, their characteristics, and key results are summarized in Table 1. The following sections review the research carried out in each of these areas.

Celebrity prevalence

The goals of celebrity prevalence studies are mainly descriptive with a focus on ascertaining the frequency of celebrities in advertising, often in cross-national comparisons. Additional objectives include finding out whether celebrity endorsements are more commonly used for certain types of products and whether there are differences depending on the type of media. The method typically employed in these studies is content analysis.

Celebrity endorsements are considerably more prevalent in Asian countries compared to Europe and the US: a cross-national comparison of 6359 TV ads from 25 countries found celebrities in less than 15% of the ads in a number of European countries and the US, while the share in Asia ranged from 25% (China) to 61% (South Korea) (Praet 2008). Similar results were obtained in an earlier study that compared the US and South Korea and found that 60% of the TV ads in Korea featured a celebrity while less than 10% of ads in the US did (Choi, Lee, and Kim 2005). Recently, a celebrity prevalence study of US magazine ads found that celebrities were used in 10% of all ads (Belch and Belch 2013).

In addition to the frequency of celebrities in advertising, celebrity prevalence studies have investigated differences in portrayal and the type of product endorsed between female and male celebrities in the US (Stafford, Spears, and Hsu 2003), differences between South Korean and US celebrity advertising with respect to celebrity characteristics (e.g., age, gender, profession), the type of product endorsed, and the information content of the ad (Choi, Lee, and Kim 2005), and the prevalence of celebrity endorsements in different types of magazines (e.g., sports, entertainment) and in different product categories (e.g., cosmetics, fashion) (Belch and Belch 2013).

Table 1.   Research areas in celebrity endorsement research.

Research area	Research problem	Dependent variables	Independent variables	Method	Unit of observation	Unit of analysis	Main results
Celebrity prevalence	What is the frequency of celebrity endorsements?	Frequency of celebrity endorsement	Country, product category, type of media vehicle	Content analysis	Ad	Ad	There are large cross-national variations in the prevalence of celebrity endorsements, ranging from less than 15% in Europe and the US up towards 60% in some Asian countries.
Campaign management	How should celebrity endorsement campaigns be managed?	n.a.	n.a.	Personal interviews, surveys	Manager	Manager	Descriptive research shows the steps in celebrity endorsement planning and the factors marketing practitioners consider to be most important when selecting celebrities. Prescriptive research analyzes how to optimally select celebrities for endorsements.
Financial effects	What is the financial impact on firms or SBUs of celebrity endorsements?	Sales, share price	Endorsement announcement, celebrity performance	Modeling/ econometrics	Celebrity-related event	Firm/SBU	Celebrity endorsements have positive effects on sales. There are mixed results concerning the effect of celebrity endorsements on share prices, some studies found positive effects and other studies no effects.
Celebrity persuasion	What is the effect on consumer brand evaluations of celebrity endorsements?	Brand attitude, purchase intention	Source variables, fit, celebrity transgressions	Experiments	Consumer	Brand/ad	These studies show that persuasion is greater when celebrity expertise and attractiveness are high, that trustworthiness has no effect on persuasion, and that celebrity transgressions have a negative effect on brand evaluations. Results are mixed with respect to celebrity liking, multiple endorsements by the same celebrity, and the role of celebrity—brand fit.
Non-evaluative meaning transfer	If and how do celebrity characteristics and traits transfer to brands?	Perceived brand characteristics	Celebrity personality traits and characteristics	Experiments	Consumer	Brand/ad	Both positive and negative characteristics and personality traits transfer from celebrities to brands.
Brand-to-celebrity transfer	Do brand associations transfer to celebrities?	Perceived celebrity traits and characteristics	Brand characteristics	Experiments	Consumer	Celebrity	There are a limited number of studies but results suggest brand associations could transfer to celebrities.

A challenge for celebrity prevalence research is to take this research area beyond pure descriptive research. While it is interesting for advertising academics and practitioners to know the extent of celebrity endorsement in different countries, media, and for different products, this type of study often struggles to make a contribution to the advertising literature. Future research in this area could aim to test theories of what factors lead to increased use of celebrity endorsers (e.g., intensity of product category competition, product price) or to aim for increased theoretical depth by using interpretive qualitative research to unearth broad themes or narratives, or to probe deeper into the role of the celebrity endorser in different contexts.

Campaign management

Studies in campaign management have focused on how advertising practitioners select celebrities, either describing this process or prescribing how it should be done. Some studies have investigated the process and criteria of selecting a celebrity from the perspective of practitioners. Based on interviews and a survey of UK advertising agencies, Erdogan and associates (Erdogan and Baker 2000; Erdogan and Drollinger 2008) identified several discrete steps in the (most often informal) process advertising agencies employ to select celebrity endorsers. This information was then used to propose a normative seven-step model of celebrity selection: (1) account meeting, (2) creative brief, (3) creative proposal, (4) research, (5) initial contact, (6) campaign proposal, and (7) final negotiations. Erdogan and Drollinger (2008) suggest that advertising agencies can improve their celebrity endorsement decision making by following this model. However, it should be noted that the model is based on descriptive research of actual practices in the UK and that no compelling arguments are presented supporting that this would be the optimal approach to celebrity selection.

A study by Erdogan, Baker, and Tagg (2001) investigated what factors UK advertising agencies take into account when selecting celebrities. The three factors rated as most important were (1) celebrity–target audience match, (2) celebrity–product/brand match, and (3) overall image of the celebrity. It is of some interest to note that there appears to be only one study of the factor rated as most important by marketing practitioners, that is, celebrity–target audience match, which is the study by Choi and Rifon (2012).

A different approach was taken by Zwilling and Fruchter (2013) who applied a genetic algorithm to an optimal product design model to select the optimal celebrity for a given brand. The model takes into account both product attributes and celebrity traits based on the assumption that consumers construct a brand based on both of these. Based on an empirical test of their model Zwilling and Fruchter (2013) claim that it outperformed alternative ways of selecting celebrities. However, given the mathematical complexities of their model it seems less than likely that it would gain widespread usage among marketing practitioners and academics.

In all, there is limited research to date on how marketing practitioners relate to the selection of celebrity endorsers and, perhaps, more importantly how celebrity endorsers should be chosen and there is much room for further research in this area.

Financial effects

Two types of studies focus on the financial effects of celebrity endorsements either by looking at the effect of celebrity endorsements on sales or share prices.

The effect of celebrity endorsers on sales

Despite recent marketer interest in the return on investment on advertising expenditure (Taylor 2010), there are only a few studies of the sales effects of celebrity endorsements. In a recent study Elberse and Verleun (2012) used data from 51 athlete endorsements to analyze the impact of endorsements on sales. Using intervention model analysis Elberse and Verleun (2012) found a significant increase in sales for 43 of the 51 endorsements and an average 4% increase in sales over the endorsement period. Elberse and Verleun (2012) also found that a major achievement by a celebrity (e.g., winning a championship) led to a further significant increase in sales. A study of golf player endorsements, with a particular focus on Tiger Woods, found a significant effect of celebrity endorsements on sales and a significant effect of long-term player performance (Chung, Derdenger, and Srinivasan 2013). However, unlike the study by Elberse and Verleun (2012) the study by Chung, Derdenger, and Srinivasan (2013) failed to find a short-term effect of major achievements in the form of tournament wins.

There is also a study of the sales effects on the books endorsed by Oprah Winfrey in Oprah's Book Club (Garthwaite 2014). These endorsements are different from traditional celebrity endorsements in that it is a book title, in many cases available from several publishers, rather than a brand that is endorsed, and that Oprah Winfrey is not paid for the endorsement. Not unexpectedly given the popularity of the Oprah show, Garthwaite (2014) found a large significant sales effect immediately following and up to six months after the endorsement. However, the results showed that the sales increase came from cannibalization of the sales of other book titles and there was no increase in the total book market as a result of the endorsement.

Thus, extant research strongly suggests that celebrity endorsements have positive effects on sales. However, the limited number of studies and the almost exclusive focus on athlete endorsers warrant more research on the relationship between celebrity endorsements and sales.

The effect of celebrity endorsers on share prices

Another approach, in addition to sales effects, to studying the financial effects of celebrity endorsements is to look at the effect of celebrity endorsements on the market value of the firm. These studies tend to focus on the stock market response to three types of celebrity endorsement variables: (1) the announcement of the endorsement, (2) celebrity performance (e.g., sports results), and (3) negative celebrity events. Studies of both celebrities in general (Agrawal and Kamakura 1995) and athletes (Elberse and Verleun 2012; Farrell et al. 2000) have found a significant effect, or abnormal return, on share prices on the day the celebrity endorsement is announced, with average excess returns ranging between a quarter and a half percent. However, a study by Ding, Molchanov, and Stork (2011) failed to find abnormal returns for celebrity endorsement announcements, with the exception of technology firms, and Fizel, McNeil, and Smaby (2008) failed to find support for abnormal returns for athlete endorsements, with the exception of endorsements by golf players. Thus, the evidence for firm valuation effects of celebrity endorsement announcements is mixed (except for celebrity golf players).

With respect to celebrity performance in the form of athletes' sports results, the effects on firm valuation are consistent, although the number of studies is limited. The available studies show that major achievements by athletes (e.g., winning a tournament) lead to abnormal positive returns on the stock exchange (Elberse and Verleun 2012; Farrell et al. 2000; Mathur, Mathur, and Rangan 1997; Nicolau and Santa-María 2013).

Naturally, the effect on firm valuation of celebrity transgressions is expected to be negative. However, a study by Louie, Kulik, and Jacobson (2001) found that negative events only have a negative effect on firm value if the celebrity is culpable for the event. If the celebrity was not seen as deserving blame for the event the effect on firm valuation was positive. Two more recent studies focused exclusively on celebrity transgressions and either found weak evidence for a negative effect on firm valuation of celebrity misbehavior (Bartz, Molchanov, and Stork 2013) or, in the case of the Tiger Woods scandal, a substantive negative effect on the market value of the main sponsors (Knittel and Stango 2014).

Thus, although it seems clear that celebrity endorsements and celebrity behavior can have both positive and negative effects on firm valuation, the exact nature of this relationship seems unclear and there is ample room for more research. For example, the mixed results suggest that there may be additional factors moderating the relationship.

Celebrity persuasion

The majority of celebrity endorsement studies fall within the category of celebrity persuasion research. These studies investigate the effect of celebrities on post-endorsement brand attitude (A_{Brand}), quality perceptions, brand purchase intention (PI_{Brand}), or other evaluations of the brand (for simplicity these will all be referred to as brand evaluations in the following, unless there is reason to specify the exact dependent variable used in a certain context). Ever since early studies established that celebrity endorsements tend to have a positive effect on brand evaluations (e.g., Atkin and Block 1983; Friedman and Friedman 1979; Petty, Cacioppo, and Schumann 1983) the focus of celebrity persuasion research has been on identifying factors that either contribute to the persuasive effect via a main effect or moderate it. Studies in this category of research have looked at factors relating to the celebrity (e.g., celebrity attractiveness, celebrity transgressions), the endorsement situation (e.g., celebrity expertise, celebrity–brand fit), and the target audience. Most of these studies have focused mainly on testing certain effects on brand evaluations and there are few studies of the underlying psychological processes. Celebrity persuasion studies tend to be carried out in the same manner as advertising experiments: participants are exposed to a print ad with the celebrity endorsement followed by immediate measurement of the dependent variables. The data are normally cross-sectional and there appears to be no study analyzing longitudinal data.

Source effects

There is a fair amount of research on celebrity source effects drawing on the work of Hovland and associates (e.g., Hovland and Weiss 1951–52; Hovland, Janis, and Kelley 1953) and McGuire (1985). This research focuses on source factors such as credibility, attractiveness, and liking. Generally, it is assumed that celebrities who are perceived as credible, attractive, and who are well liked will have positive effects on brand evaluations.

Some celebrity endorsement studies have treated credibility as one bi-dimensional variable, while other studies have treated expertise and trustworthiness as separate variables. Studies by Lafferty and Goldsmith (1998) and Spry, Pappu, and Cornwell (2011) found a positive effect of celebrity credibility, analyzed as one variable, on brand evaluations. There are also several studies showing a positive effect of celebrity expertise on brand evaluations (e.g., Eisend and Langner 2010; Ohanian 1991; Rossiter and Smidts 2012). However, there appears to be no support for a positive effect of trustworthiness, analyzed as a separate variable, on brand evaluations: studies by Rossiter and Smidts (2012) and Ohanian (1991) found a significant positive effect on brand evaluations of expertise but there was no positive effect of trustworthiness. In relation to this, Rossiter and Smidts (2012) argue that perceived trustworthiness will not lead to a positive celebrity endorsement effect as consumers are well aware that celebrities have been paid for their endorsement. With respect to moderating variables, results in a study by Lord and Putrevu (2009) suggest that expertise has greater effects for informational than transformational communication strategies (see Rossiter and Percy 1997) and Till and Busler (2000) found that fit between the celebrity and the brand moderated the effect of expertise such that better fit entailed greater effects of expertise.

Several studies have demonstrated a positive effect of celebrity attractiveness on brand evaluations (e.g., Eisend and Langner 2010; Kahle and Homer 1985; Liu and Brock 2011; Lord and Putrevu 2009; Till and Busler 2000). However, while most studies have found a positive relationship between celebrity attractiveness and brand evaluations it should be noted that there are studies that have failed to support this relationship (e.g., Kamins 1990; Ohanian 1991). This suggests that there are factors moderating the relationship. However, to date the only moderating variable supported by research results is communication strategy: Lord and Putrevu (2009) found a significant effect of celebrity attractiveness for a transformational communication strategy but not for an informational strategy. Other studies have failed to find support for moderating effects. For example, results in the study by Till and Busler (2000) did not support a moderating effect of fit on the relationship between celebrity attractiveness and brand evaluations.

An interesting source factor is celebrity liking, which has also been labeled attitude toward the celebrity, celebrity likability, or celebrity affect. There are surprisingly few studies that have included celebrity liking as an independent variable in celebrity endorsement research. A likely reason for this limited interest is that it is implicitly assumed that celebrities are selected because they are well liked and that few brands would choose a less liked celebrity as endorser. In the few studies that exist, research results in terms of effects on brand evaluations are mixed: some studies have found a positive effect of celebrity liking on brand evaluations (Bergkvist, Hjalmarson, and Mägi, in press; Kahle and Homer 1985; Misra and Beatty 1990; Silvera and Austad 2004), some studies no effect (Fleck, Korchia, and Le Roy 2012; Miller and Allen 2012), and one study even found a negative effect (Rossiter and Smidts 2012). Thus, the role of celebrity liking is far from clear.

The source effects research in celebrity endorsements has made relatively little progress over the years. The theoretical frameworks are based on the work of Hovland (Hovland and Weiss 1951–52; Hovland, Janis, and Kelley 1953) and McGuire (McGuire 1985), and there are few attempts, if any, to address the contradictory results for source effects. A recent source effects model that could be useful in explaining the contradictory results was developed by Kang and Herr (2006). This model incorporates features from dual-process models such as the elaboration likelihood model (ELM) (Petty, Cacioppo, and Schumann 1983) and the heuristic-systematic model (Chaiken 1980) and the flexible correction model (Wegener and Petty 1995). Depending on consumers' ability and motivation to process information, whether the source could be a central argument in favor of the product, and whether source biases are detected or corrected for the model predicts three different outcomes: (1) source effects are generally positive if consumers' ability and/or motivation to process information is low; (2) source effects are positive if consumers' ability and/or motivation to process information is high and the source is relevant for the product; or (3) source effects can be negative if consumers' ability and/or motivation to process information is high and they correct for source bias to such an extent that it offsets other effects. Thus, the integrative model developed by Kang and Herr (2006) could potentially be used to explain the conflicting source effects results in celebrity endorsement research.

Fit between the celebrity and the brand or product category

A number of studies have investigated the role of fit between the celebrity and the brand or the product category. Fit, which has also been referred to as congruency, similarity, and relevance in different studies, generally refers to the degree of similarity or consistency between the celebrity and the brand (or product category). It follows that fit, just like celebrity expertise, is specific to a particular endorsement situation (unlike celebrity attractiveness and liking which are independent of the situation). Fit has been operationalized variously as a main effect on brand evaluations or as a moderator of other main effects such as attractiveness and expertise (the matchup hypothesis).

Several studies have found support for a positive main effect of fit on brand evaluations in the sense that better fit between the celebrity and brand leads to more positive brand evaluations (e.g., Choi and Rifon 2012; Kamins and Gupta 1994; Kirmani and Shiv 1998). There is also one study that found a more positive effect on PI_{Brand} (but not A_{Brand}) of moderate fit compared to both poor and good fit (Lee and Thorson 2008). Similar results were obtained in a study by Törn (2012) who found that an endorsement with less fit (vs. more fit) had larger positive effects on PI_{Brand}. Moreover, a recent study by Bergkvist, Hjalmarson, and Mägi (in press) found that the main effect of fit on A_{Brand} is mediated by attitude toward the endorsement alliance between the celebrity and the brand ($A_{Endorsement}$). This result is consistent with the results in studies in related areas such as cause-related marketing and sponsorships which also have found that attitude toward the alliance mediates the effects of fit on brand evaluations (e.g., Basil and Herr 2006; Mazodier and Merunka 2012). It is noteworthy that two studies have found the main effect of fit to be moderated by involvement such that fit only has a positive effect on brand evaluations under conditions of high involvement (Kirmani and Shiv 1998; Lee and Thorson 2008).

There is mixed support for the matchup hypothesis that celebrity endorsement effects are stronger under conditions of high fit rather than low fit. Misra and Beatty (1990) found that fit moderated the relationship between celebrity liking and A_{Brand}, with higher correlations under conditions of high fit than low fit, Till, Stanley, and Priluck (2008) found more positive conditioning effects on A_{Brand} under conditions of high fit (vs. low fit), and Rice, Kelting, and Lutz (2012) found that fit moderated the negative effects of multiple endorsements and the positive effects of multiple endorsers on brand evaluations (but only under conditions of high involvement). On the other hand, Kamins and Gupta (1994) and Lynch and Schuler (1994) failed to find support for a matchup effect on brand evaluations, and Till and Busler (2000) found no support for a matchup effect on the effect of attractiveness on brand evaluations and only partial support for expertise.

It is noteworthy that there are no studies of factors mitigating the negative effects of low celebrity–brand fit. This is the case in other areas where fit plays an important role. For example, sponsorship research shows that both articulation (i.e., explaining the relationship between the sponsor and the event) (Cornwell et al. 2006) and message repetition (Dardis 2009) mitigate the negative effects of low fit.

Multiple endorsements by the same celebrity

The results in the research on multiple endorsements by the same celebrity are mixed. An early study by Mowen and Brown (1981) reports significant negative effects on brand evaluations when the number of brands endorsed by one celebrity increased from one to five. Tripp, Jensen, and Carlson (1994) found no significant effects of increasing the number of brands endorsed from one to two but they report significant negative effects on celebrity source perceptions (liking, expertise, trustworthiness) and attitude toward the ad when the number of endorsements increase from two to four. However, there were no significant effects on brand evaluations. Rice, Kelting, and Lutz (2012) report interactions between the number of brands a celebrity endorses and involvement and celebrity–brand fit. Under conditions of low involvement, there is a negative effect on brand evaluations of increasing the number of brands endorsed. However, under high involvement, there is only a negative effect of a higher number of endorsed brands if celebrity–brand fit is low. Results in Chen et al. (2013) suggest that there may be an interaction effect between the different brands endorsed by the same celebrity, with no negative effects if a celebrity endorses two similar brands and negative effects if the two brands are dissimilar. However, Chen et al. (2013) did not test different levels of number of brands endorsed. Moreover, a survey of Chinese consumers carried out by Hung, Chan, and Tse (2011) suggests that celebrity endorsements will be less effective if celebrities are perceived by consumers as having too many endorsements (a situation that is common in China where celebrities tend to endorse a multitude of brands).

Thus, there seems to be negative effects of multiple endorsements of the same celebrity but these negative effects are qualified by moderating variables. However, given the limited number of studies and the mixed results there is scope for further research on the effects of multiple celebrity endorsements.

Celebrity transgressions

An inherent risk in all celebrity endorsements is misbehavior by the celebrity that spills over to brands endorsed by the celebrity. Several studies of celebrity transgressions have demonstrated that these have a negative effect on consumer evaluations of brands endorsed by the celebrity (e.g., Bailey 2007; Edwards and La Ferle 2009; Fong and Wyer 2012; Till and Shimp 1998; Um 2013; White, Goddard, and Wilbur 2009), although there are studies that have failed to demonstrate a negative effect (e.g., Money, Shimp, and Sakano 2006).

The negative effect of celebrity transgression is moderated by some factors. Results in studies by Louie and Obermiller (2002) and Um (2013) show that attribution of responsibility moderates the negative effect of transgressions: if the celebrity is blamed for the transgression there is a negative effect on the brand. If other factors are blamed there is less or no negative effect. Similar results were obtained in a study by Votolato and Unnava (2006) who found negative brand effects when the celebrity was seen as immoral but not when the celebrity was seen as incompetent.

In addition, results in the study by Um (2013) suggest that the negative effects of transgressions are mitigated if consumers have a high level of identification with the celebrity or if consumers have a high level of brand commitment. The negative effects of transgressions are also mitigated when celebrities admit their guilt instead of denying it (Carrillat, d'Astous, and Lazure 2013).

Thus, there is strong evidence in favor of negative effects on the brand from celebrity transgressions. However, this relationship is subject to moderating effects of a number of different variables.

Target audience factors

There is limited research on the effect of target audience factors on celebrity persuasion. With respect to target audience age differences, a study by Atkin and Block (1983) found greater celebrity endorsement effects on younger (13−17 years) than older (18−77 years) consumers. However, both Freiden (1984) and Ohanian (1991) failed to find age-related differences in response to celebrity endorsements. A few studies have looked at gender differences in response to celebrity advertising. Bush, Martin, and Bush (2004) found a stronger celebrity role model influence for female teenagers than male and Liu and Brock (2011) found that male consumers were more responsive to female celebrity attractiveness than female consumers. However, Ohanian (1991) did not find any significant gender differences in either celebrity source factors or brand evaluations.

There appears to be only one study that has examined cross-cultural differences in consumer response to celebrity endorsements. However, Money, Shimp, and Sakano (2006) failed to uncover any cultural differences in response to celebrity transgressions between Japanese and American consumers.

Thus, there have been few studies of target audience differences in response to celebrity endorsements and results are mixed with respect to both age and gender. The limited interest in cross-cultural differences is surprising as there should be much scope for studies of cross-cultural differences in this area given the large differences between Asian and Western countries in the prevalence of celebrity endorsements, which was noted in the section on celebrity prevalence studies.

Other factors

There appears to be only one study of the effects on brand evaluations of the gender of the celebrity: Freiden (1984) found no differences depending on whether the celebrity endorser was a man or a woman. The dearth of research on endorser gender effects is somewhat surprising as persuasion research shows that men and women respond differently to male and female communicators (e.g., Reid et al. 2009) and there could be interesting interactions between the gender of the celebrity and the gender of the target audience.

There are two studies that support the notion that celebrity endorsements lead to positive brand effects as a result of role model influence (Bush, Martin, and Bush 2004; Rossiter and Smidts 2012) and it has also been shown that low visibility (i.e., the celebrity is not well known) has a negative effect on brand evaluations (Rossiter and Smidts 2012). Also, a recent study by Bergkvist, Hjalmarson, and Mägi (in press) found that the perceived motive for the celebrity's endorsement of a brand is important for brand evaluations. Their results showed a positive effect on brand evaluations if the celebrity was perceived as being motivated not only by money but also by the quality of the brand.

Non-evaluative meaning transfer

A relatively recent area in celebrity endorsement research is non-evaluative meaning transfer. This line of research draws on the ideas presented in the influential article by

McCracken (1989) and the aim is to demonstrate the transfer of non-evaluative characteristics (e.g., character traits) from the celebrity to the brand. In addition, there is some
research on the psychological process underlying non-evaluative meaning transfer.

The idea that the effects on the brand of celebrity endorsements go beyond brand evaluations was introduced in a conceptual article by McCracken (1989). His meaning transfer model suggests that celebrities transfer a wide range of associations, evaluative and
non-evaluative, to the brand. However, despite McCracken's (1989) article being one of
the most cited on celebrity endorsements there are surprisingly few empirical studies of
non-evaluative meaning transfer. Two early studies by Langmeyer and Walker (1991a,
1991b) provided some support for the notion of non-evaluative meaning transfer. However, neither of these studies had an experimental research design that permitted causal
conclusions and the results are only tentatively supportive of meaning transfer. To date,
there appear to be only three studies that have found empirical support for the transfer of
non-evaluative celebrity associations using an experimental design that permits causal
conclusions: Batra and Homer (2004) found transfer of positively valenced personality
traits from the celebrity to the brand, Miller and Allen (2012) found transfer of negatively
valenced personality traits, and Campbell and Warren (2012) found transfer of both positively and negatively valenced traits. Moreover, Campbell and Warren (2012) found that
fit moderated the transfer of traits from celebrity to brand: their results show that positive
traits only transfer under conditions of high fit whereas negative traits transferred to the
brand also under conditions of low fit. Although these studies are concordant in demonstrating non-evaluative meaning transfer this area seems under-researched.

The limited interest in doing research on non-evaluative meaning transfer is somewhat surprising. McCracken's (1989) article is one of the most cited articles on celebrity
endorsement yet it appears to have had limited influence beyond supplying a frequently
used definition of celebrity endorsements. In his article McCracken takes a critical view
of the source models and argues that the academic and professional literature on celebrity
endorsements is 'littered with data that cannot be explained by the source models'
(McCracken 1989, 311). Instead of only relying on source models, McCracken argues,
celebrity endorsement models also need to take into account the various meanings with
which celebrities are imbued. Overall, this is an under-researched area of celebrity
endorsement and more research is warranted.

Brand-to-celebrity transfer

A nascent stream of research is brand-to-celebrity transfer. This research looks into
whether associations transfer from the brand to the celebrity. The focus has been on both
evaluative and non-evaluative associations.

For celebrities it could be damaging to their career and reputation if the brands they
endorse are in the wrong industry (e.g., tobacco or alcohol), have a poor image, or commit
some kind of transgression if the negative associations in these cases spill over on the
celebrity. Conversely, transfer of positive associations from the brand to the celebrity
could have positive effects on both reputation and career. This issue is of interest not only
to the celebrities themselves but also to the brands they endorse as one endorsement may
have indirect negative or positive effects on other endorsements.

To date, there are only two studies of transfer from brand to celebrity. An experimental study by White, Goddard, and Wilbur (2009) manipulated the behavior of the endorsed
brand but found no negative effects on global attitude toward the celebrity as a result of a
brand transgression. However, Arsena, Silvera, and Pandelaere (2014) demonstrated in

three experiments that personality traits associated with brands transfer to celebrities. This transfer is subject to the boundary condition that pre-existing traits of the celebrity that conflict with the brand traits negate the transfer. Arsena, Silvera, and Pandelaere (2014) attribute the transfer to the psychological process of spontaneous trait transference (Skowronski et al. 1998). Thus, there is plenty of room for future research on brand-to-celebrity transfer. For example, it would be of interest to study what factors regulate whether there is transfer from the brand to the celebrity, from the celebrity to the brand, or no transfer at all.

What are the psychological processes underlying celebrity endorsement effects?

Early celebrity endorsement persuasion research often relied on the ELM to account for celebrity endorsement persuasion effects (e.g., Heath, McCarthy, and Mothersbaugh 1994; Petty, Cacioppo, and Schumann 1983). In this theoretical framework celebrities were seen as peripheral cues which had a positive effect on brand evaluations under conditions of low-effort processing. However, a limitation of the ELM is that it does not specify the mechanism through which the peripheral cue operates (Eagly and Chaiken 1993), so if there is a positive effect on brand evaluations it is not clear why it happened.

A specific mechanism that has been tested in celebrity endorsement research is evaluative conditioning, which is defined as 'changes in the liking of a stimulus that result from pairing that stimulus with other positive or negative stimuli' (De Houwer, Thomas, and Baeyens 2001, 853). A study by Till, Stanley, and Priluck (2008) demonstrated that an evaluative conditioning procedure which repeatedly paired a celebrity with a brand led to increased liking of the brand. Existing theory and empirical evidence provide a strong case in favor of evaluative conditioning effects for celebrity endorsements. Celebrities are chosen because they are well liked or have other desirable properties and they are often paired with the brand in a manner that should promote evaluative conditioning (e.g., spatio-temporal contiguity and repetition). However, outside the laboratory it is close to impossible to differentiate evaluative conditioning effects from other types of persuasive effects (De Houwer 2007, 234) and it seems likely that also other psychological processes such as inferences should apply to celebrity endorsements. In fact, a study by Kirmani and Wright (1989) found that celebrity endorsers trigger inferences of high campaign costs which, in turn, lead to more positive brand evaluations.

Evaluative conditioning has also been used to account for non-evaluative meaning transfer in celebrity endorsements. Miller and Allen (2012) demonstrated the transfer of negative character traits from celebrities to brands within an evaluative conditioning framework. However, whether the underlying mechanism for the transfer of non-evaluative associations really is evaluative conditioning is controversial among psychologists (Meersmans et al. 2005).

Apart from the studies reviewed in this section, there appear to be few studies that investigate the processes underlying celebrity endorsement effects by analyzing the mediating effects of process variables or testing hypotheses that rule out alternative process accounts. Thus, there is plenty of scope for further research on the mechanisms that cause celebrity endorsement effects.

Research agenda

The literature review identified several instances of conflicting results and points to several gaps in celebrity endorsement knowledge which offer promising avenues for further research. Some brief suggestions for further research were noted in the reviews of celebrity prevalence and financial effects studies. It was also noted that non-evaluative meaning transfer and brand-to-celebrity transfer are under-researched areas with plenty of room for further studies. The greatest challenge for future research can be found in the area of celebrity persuasion. This is the area where the bulk of celebrity endorsement research has been carried out to date and where future advertising research is most likely to be focused since the ultimate goal of celebrity endorsement is to persuade consumers to buy brands. However, there are signs of stagnation within celebrity persuasion research with respect to both research problems and methodology. The following sections outline a broad research agenda that aims to revitalize celebrity persuasion research and to integrate it with campaign management research. The research agenda is organized into three areas that come across as the most important areas to develop in future research on celebrity persuasion. These areas are practical relevance, theoretical depth, and methodological innovation.

Practical relevance

A number of prominent academics have criticized research in marketing (Lehmann, McAllister, and Staelin 2011), consumer behavior (Pham 2013), and advertising (Armstrong 2011; Rossiter and Percy 2013) for not being relevant to marketing practitioners. The same criticism can be directed towards celebrity endorsement research. Research has little to say about how to select celebrity endorsers, how to manage celebrity campaigns, and other practical matters. It is telling that there are only a handful of studies on campaign management and that only one study, by Choi and Rifon (2012), has addressed celebrity–target audience match, the factor rated as most important when selecting celebrity endorsers by practitioners (Erdogan, Baker, and Tagg 2001). This points to the need for an increased focus on practical relevance in celebrity endorsement research.

A first step towards making normative recommendations on how to select celebrities is to understand how practitioners currently do this. This requires research investigating and describing the managerial processes involved. However, extant research on how advertisers select celebrities for their campaigns is limited to two qualitative studies of the UK market (Erdogan and Baker 2000; Erdogan and Drollinger 2008). This leaves considerable room for studies of practitioners in other markets, cross-national comparisons (e.g., Asian vs. Western markets), and for studies using more quantitative approaches. Of particular interest would be to study both the process and what factors are considered when selecting celebrities. It would also be of interest to investigate whether celebrity endorsements are pitted against other alternatives such as sponsorships, product placements, and non-celebrity advertising campaigns. Studies in this area should also consider to what extent factors such as brand familiarity (new vs. established brands), type of product (utilitarian, experiential, symbolic), communication objectives, and the campaign's target audience influence celebrity selection.

Interesting research opportunities lie in tackling research problems related to the management of ongoing endorsement campaigns. Given the research showing that fit influences the persuasive effects of celebrity endorsements (e.g., Choi and Rifon 2012; Kirmani and Shiv 1998) it would be of interest to investigate campaign management tactics that mitigate the negative effects of low fit. This research could draw on sponsorship research and test tactics such as articulation (Cornwell et al. 2006) and message repetition (Dardis 2009), which both could be addressed in experimental research designs. Another campaign tactic where celebrity endorsement research could draw on sponsorship research is activation, that is, campaign tactics that encourage interaction with the brand, a tactic which has been found to have positive effects on brand evaluations (Weeks, Cornwell, and Drennan 2008). In a celebrity endorsement context this could mean giving the target audience the opportunity to experience the brand at concerts or other performances by a celebrity endorsing the brand or online activities where the celebrity is used to promote interaction with the brand. Moreover, research shows that the perceived motive of the celebrity for doing the endorsement influences brand evaluations (Bergkvist, Hjalmarson, and Mägi, in press), which suggests that tactics that promote quality-related motives could have positive effects on brand evaluations. These tactics could come in the form of advertising copy that suggests or states that the celebrity has other motives, in addition to money, for endorsing the product.

Practitioners regard target audience factors as very important for celebrity endorsement campaigns (Erdogan, Baker, and Tagg 2001). However, research on how different target audiences respond to celebrity endorsement is limited and results have been mixed in the few existing studies of differences in response for different age and gender groups. Thus, it would be of value to investigate age and gender differences in response to celebrity endorsements. It would also be of value to make cross-national or cross-cultural comparisons in response to celebrity endorsements.

Theoretical depth

There are few studies on the psychological mechanisms underlying celebrity persuasion and non-evaluative meaning transfer. Instead the focus has been on demonstrating effects and identifying moderating variables. However, if celebrity endorsement research is going to contribute to a more complete understanding of how celebrity endorsements work there is a need for work with greater theoretical depth. This involves identifying applicable processes and testing their relevance to celebrity endorsements. This can be done in studies whose research design and/or hypotheses rule out alternative explanations, or by analyzing mediating variables indicative of the underlying process. An elegant way to investigate process theories is to run studies with competing hypotheses (Armstrong, Brodie, and Parsons 2001; see Rindfleisch and Inman 1998 for an example of how this can be done).

There is a wide range of theories from psychology that could be applicable to celebrity endorsements. Cognitive response theory (e.g., Wright 1973) could be employed to investigate information processing under conditions of high involvement and shed light on issues such as why fit is more important under conditions of high involvement than low involvement (Kirmani and Shiv 1998). The heuristic–systematic model (e.g., Chaiken 1980) could be used to study low-effort processing to shed light on how celebrities function as peripheral cues. For example, it could be the case that a well-chosen celebrity triggers the use of heuristics such as 'experts' statements can be trusted' (Ratneshwar and Chaiken 1991). Another potentially fruitful approach would be to study the role of inferences in a celebrity endorsement context (see Kardes, Posavac, and Cronley 2004 for a review of inference), as suggested by the results in the study by Kirmani and Wright (1989). In addition, given the limited number of studies using an evaluative conditioning framework (e.g., Till, Stanley, and Priluck 2008) there should be room for more work. Also, the spontaneous trait transference theory used by Arsena, Silvera, and Pandelaere (2014) could offer a useful theoretical framework to explicate non-evaluative meaning transfer.

Methodological innovation

There is plenty of room for innovative thinking when it comes to research methodology in celebrity endorsement research. In particular celebrity persuasion research has almost exclusively been carried out with traditional ad experiments using print ad stimuli, forced exposure, and immediate measurement. The same applies to non-evaluative meaning transfer and brand-to-celebrity transfer, although much fewer studies have been carried out. This methodological standardization has led to efficiency in terms of number of studies but it has also hampered creativity with respect to the research problems addressed. Therefore, openness to alternative research methodologies should function as a springboard for renewing celebrity endorsement research, particularly celebrity persuasion research.

Using print ads to expose experiment participants to celebrity endorsements is convenient. However, globally newspaper and magazine advertising make up 23% of advertising media spending, while TV and the Internet make up 40% and 24%, respectively (Advertising Age 2014). In addition, celebrity endorsements increasingly come in non-advertising forms such as Twitter postings (Wood and Burkhalter 2014) and stealth marketing during interviews on TV talk shows (Kaikati and Kaikati 2004). Thus, there is reason to use other formats than print ads in celebrity endorsement research. Moreover, the often surreptitious nature of celebrity endorsements in social media and stealth marketing techniques is interesting not only from an information processing perspective but also from an ethical point of view. A useful approach to non-advertising celebrity endorsements would be to use a persuasion knowledge framework (Friestad and Wright 1994) which could incorporate recent research on consumers' naïve persuasion theories (Briñol, Rucker, and Petty 2015).

Forced exposure is an appropriate methodology for studying information processing. However, forced exposure cannot be used to study issues such as attention and the effects of competitive advertising. As a consequence consumer attention to celebrity endorsements has been largely ignored in academic research (but not marketing practitioner research, see Rossiter and Percy 1997). This is noteworthy as advertising textbooks tend to argue that celebrities attract attention (e.g., Belch and Belch 2009) and 'breaking through the clutter' is often heard as a primary concern for advertising practitioners. More knowledge about if, when, and how celebrities attract attention to advertising would be of value to practitioners and further understanding of how celebrity endorsements work for academics. This research problem could be addressed in laboratory experiments using clutter reels, which expose participants to a series of ads or other stimuli, or in survey research studying real-life campaigns. Attention could be measured using ad recall, ad recognition, and open-ended measures of message take-out (see overview of measures in Rossiter and Percy 1997, 565–567).

In most laboratory experiments measurement is done immediately following exposure to the stimuli. This is also the case in celebrity endorsement research. However, studies in advertising show that the relationship between constructs such as attitude toward the ad and brand attitude is different depending on whether measurement is done immediately following exposure or with a delay (Bergkvist and Rossiter 2008; Chattopadhyay and Nedungadi 1992). In celebrity endorsement research results in Eisend and Langner (2010) show that consumer response to celebrity attractiveness and expertise is different in direct and delayed measurement. Celebrity attractiveness is relatively more important for brand evaluations in immediate measurement and celebrity expertise is relatively more important in delayed measurement. As delayed measurement more closely resembles the situation in real-life campaigns, particularly if the study participants have multiple exposures to the celebrity endorsement, delayed measurement would add mundane realism to experimental studies. It would also make it possible to study if the role of frequently studied variables is different with delayed measurement. For example, the results in the sponsorship study by Dardis (2009) suggest that the role of fit could change if measurement is delayed and the number of exposures to the endorsement is increased. Moreover, delayed measurement would allow for investigation of the sleeper effect (i.e., that the negative effect of low source credibility diminishes over time, see Hovland and Weiss 1951–52). Thus, experiments with delayed measurement or longitudinal studies could shed new light on the operation of factors currently considered to be well understood.

Discussion

This paper identified six categories of celebrity endorsement research and reviewed extant research within each category. Overall, research on celebrity endorsements has established that these have a positive effect on sales, that persuasion is greater when celebrity expertise and attractiveness are high, that non-evaluative characteristics can transfer from celebrities to brands, and that celebrity transgressions have a negative effect on the evaluations of endorsed brands. However, there are mixed results when it comes to the effect of celebrity endorsements on share prices, the effect of celebrity liking and multiple endorsements by the same celebrity on celebrity persuasion, and the role of celebrity–brand fit. In addition there are too few studies on target audience factors and brand-to-celebrity transfer to draw any firm conclusions, and many areas that are unexplored.

In the area of celebrity persuasion there are signs of stagnation with respect to both research problems and methodology. It was suggested that this stagnation could be addressed by paying more attention to the practical relevance of the research problems addressed, by increasing the theoretical depth of studies, and by a more innovative approach to research methodology. In the other research areas the problem is not stagnation but rather that the areas are under-researched and there is a general need for more research. Overall, much more work remains to be done on the fascinating research topic of celebrity endorsements.

Disclosure statement

No potential conflict of interest was reported by the authors.

ORCID

Lars Bergkvist ⓘ http://orcid.org/0000-0002-4271-9182

References

Advertising Age. 2014. *Marketing fact pack 2015*. New York: Crain Communications.
Agrawal, Jagdish, and Wagner A. Kamakura. 1995. The economic worth of celebrity endorsers: An event study analysis. *Journal of Marketing* 59 (July): 56–62.
Amos, Clinton, Gary Holmes, and David Strutton. 2008. Exploring the relationship between celebrity endorser effects and advertising effectiveness: A quantitative synthesis of effect size. *International Journal of Advertising* 27, no. 2: 209–34.

Armstrong, J. Scott. 2011. Evidence-based advertising: An application to persuasion. *International Journal of Advertising* 30, no. 5: 743–67.

Armstrong, J. Scott, Roderick J. Brodie, and Andrew G. Parsons. 2001. Hypotheses in marketing science: Literature review and publication audit. *Marketing Letters* 12 (May): 171–87.

Arsena, Ashley, David H. Silvera, and Mario Pandelaere. 2014. Brand trait transference: When celebrity endorsers acquire brand personality traits. *Journal of Business Research* 67 (July): 1537–43.

Atkin, Charles, and Martin Block. 1983. Effectiveness of celebrity endorsers. *Journal of Advertising Research* 23 (February/March): 57–61.

Bailey, Ainsworth Anthony. 2007. Public information and consumer skepticism effects on celebrity endorsements: Studies among young consumers. *Journal of Marketing Communications* 13 (June): 85–107.

Bartz, Sherry, Alexander Molchanov, and Philip A. Stork. 2013. When a celebrity endorser is disgraced: A twenty-five-year event study. *Marketing Letters* 24 (June): 131–41.

Basil, Debra Z., and Paul M. Herr. 2006. Attitudinal balance and cause-related marketing: An empirical application of balance theory. *Journal of Consumer Psychology* 16, no. 4: 391–403.

Batra, Rajeev, and Pamela M. Homer. 2004. The situational impact of brand image beliefs. *Journal of Consumer Psychology* 14, no. 3: 318–30.

Belch, George E., and Michael A. Belch. 2009. *Advertising and promotion: An integrated marketing communications perspective*. 8th ed. New York: McGraw-Hill/Irwin.

Belch, George E., and Michael A. Belch. 2013. A content analysis study of the use of celebrity endorsers in magazine advertising. *International Journal of Advertising* 32, no. 3: 369–89.

Bergkvist, Lars, Hanna Hjalmarson, and Anne Mägi. In press. A new model of how celebrity endorsements work: Attitude toward the endorsement as a mediator of celebrity source and endorsement effects. *International Journal of Advertising*. http://dx.doi.org/10.1080/02650487.2015.1024384

Bergkvist, Lars, and John R. Rossiter. 2008. The role of ad likability in predicting an ad's campaign performance. *Journal of Advertising* 37 (Summer): 85–97.

Briñol, Pablo, Derek Rucker, and Richard E. Petty. 2015. Naïve theories about persuasion: Implications for information processing and consumer attitude change. *International Journal of Advertising* 34, no. 1: 85–106.

Bush, Alan J., Craig A. Martin, and Victoria D. Bush. 2004. Sports celebrity influence on the behavioral intentions of generation Y. *Journal of Advertising Research* 44 (March): 108–18.

Campbell, Margaret C., and Caleb Warren. 2012. A risk of meaning transfer: Are negative associations more likely to transfer than positive associations? *Social Influence* 7, no. 3: 172–92.

Carrillat, François A., Alain d'Astous, and Josianne Lazure. 2013. For better, for worse?: What to do when celebrity endorsements go bad. *Journal of Advertising Research* 53 (March): 15–30.

Chaiken, Shelly. 1980. Heuristic versus systematic information processing and the use of source versus message cues in persuasion. *Journal of Personality and Social Psychology* 39, no. 5: 752–66.

Chattopadhyay, Amitava, and Prakash Nedungadi. 1992. Does attitude toward the ad endure? The moderating effects of attention and delay. *Journal of Consumer Research* 19 (June): 26–33.

Chen, Arthur Cheng-Hsui, Rita Ya-Hui Chang, Ali Besherat, and Daniel W. Baack. 2013. Who benefits from multiple brand celebrity endorsements? An experimental investigation. *Psychology & Marketing* 30 (October): 850–60.

Choi, Sejung Marina, Wei-Na Lee, and Hee-Jung Kim. 2005. Lessons from the rich and famous: A cross-cultural comparison of celebrity endorsement in advertising. *Journal of Advertising* 34 (Summer): 85–98.

Choi, Sejung Marina, and Nora J. Rifon. 2012. It is a match: The impact of congruence between celebrity image and consumer ideal self on endorsement effectiveness. *Psychology & Marketing* 29 (September): 639–50.

Chung, Kevin Y.C., Timothy P. Derdenger, and Kannan Srinivasan. 2013. Economic value of celebrity endorsements: Tiger Woods' impact on sales of Nike golf balls. *Marketing Science* 32 (March/April): 271–93.

Cornwell, T. Bettina, Michael S. Humphreys, Angela M. Maguire, Clinton S. Weeks, and Cassandra L. Tellegen. 2006. Sponsorship-linked marketing: The role of articulation in memory. *Journal of Consumer Research* 33 (December): 312–21.

Dardis, Frank E. 2009. Attenuating the negative effects of perceived incongruence in sponsorship: How message repetition can enhance evaluations of an "incongruent" sponsor. *Journal of Promotion Management* 15, no. 1–2: 36–56.

De Houwer, Jan. 2007. A conceptual and theoretical analysis of evaluative conditioning. *The Spanish Journal of Psychology* 10, no. 2: 230–41.

De Houwer, Jan, Sara Thomas, and Frank Baeyens. 2001. Associative learning of likes and dislikes: A review of 25 years of research on human evaluative conditioning. *Psychological Bulletin* 127 (November): 853–69.

Ding, Haina, Alexander E. Molchanov, and Philip A. Stork. 2011. The value of celebrity endorsements: A stock market perspective. *Marketing Letters* 22 (June): 147–63.

Eagly, Alice H., and Shelly Chaiken. 1993. *The psychology of attitudes.* Belmont, CA: Wadsworth CENGAGE Learning.

Edwards, Steven M., and Carrie La Ferle. 2009. Does gender impact the perception of negative information related to celebrity endorsers? *Journal of Promotion Management* 15, no. 1–2: 22–35.

Eisend, Martin, and Tobias Langner. 2010. Immediate and delayed advertising effects of celebrity endorsers' attractiveness and expertise. *International Journal of Advertising* 29, no. 4: 527–46.

Elberse, Anita, and Jeroen Verleun. 2012. The economic value of celebrity endorsements. *Journal of Advertising Research* 52 (June): 149–65.

Erdogan, B. Zafer. 1999. Celebrity endorsements: A literature review. *Journal of Marketing Management* 14 (May): 291–314.

Erdogan, B. Zafer, and Michael J. Baker. 2000. Towards a practitioner-based model of selecting celebrity endorsers. *International Journal of Advertising* 19, no. 1: 25–43.

Erdogan, B. Zafer, Michael J. Baker, and Stephen Tagg. 2001. Selecting celebrity endorsers: The practitioner's perspective. *Journal of Advertising Research* 41 (May/June): 39–48.

Erdogan, B. Zafer, and Tanya Drollinger. 2008. Endorsement practice: How agencies select spokespeople. *Journal of Advertising Research* 48 (December): 573–82.

Farrell, Kathleen A., Gordon V. Karels, Kenneth W. Monfort, and Christine A. McClatchey. 2000. Celebrity performance and endorsement value: The case of Tiger Woods. *Managerial Finance* 26, no. 7: 1–15.

Fizel, John, Chris R. McNeil, and Timothy Smaby. 2008. Athlete endorsement contracts: The impact of conventional stars. *International Advances in Economic Research* 14 (May): 247–56.

Fleck, Nathalie, Michael Korchia, and Isabelle Le Roy. 2012. Celebrities in advertising: Looking for congruence or likability? *Psychology & Marketing* 29 (September): 651–62.

Fong, Candy P.S., and Robert S. Wyer, Jr. 2012. Consumers' reactions to a celebrity endorser scandal. *Psychology & Marketing* 29 (November): 885–96.

Freiden, Jon B. 1984. Advertising spokesperson effects: An examination of endorser type and gender on two audiences. *Journal of Advertising Research* 24 (October/November): 33–41.

Friedman, Hershey H., and Linda Friedman. 1979. Endorser effectiveness by product type. *Journal of Advertising Research* 19 (October): 63–71.

Friestad, Marian, and Peter Wright. 1994. The persuasion knowledge model: How people cope with persuasion attempts. *Journal of Consumer Research* 21 (June): 1–31.

Garcia de los Salmones, Maria del Mar, Rafael Dominguez, and Angel Herrero. 2013. Communication using celebrities in the non-profit sector: Determinants of its effectiveness. *International Journal of Advertising* 32, no. 1: 101–19.

Garthwaite, Craig L. 2014. Demand spillovers, combative advertising, and celebrity endorsements. *American Economic Journal: Applied Economics* 6 (April): 76–104.

Heath, Timothy B., Michael S. McCarthy, and David L. Mothersbaugh. 1994. Spokesperson fame and vividness effects in the context of issue-relevant thinking: The moderating role of competitive setting. *Journal of Consumer Research* 20 (March): 520–34.

Hovland, Carl I., Irving L. Janis, and Harold H. Kelley. 1953. *Communication and persuasion: Psychological studies of opinion change.* New Haven, CT: Yale University Press.

Hovland, Carl I., and Walter Weiss. 1951-52. The influence of source credibility on communication effectiveness. *Public Opinion Quarterly* 15 (Winter): 635–50.

Hung, Kineta, Kimmy W. Chan, and Caleb H. Tse. 2011. Assessing celebrity endorsement effects in China: A consumer-celebrity relational approach. *Journal of Advertising Research* 51 (December): 608–23.

Kahle, Lynn R., and Pamela M. Homer. 1985. Physical attractiveness of the celebrity endorser: A social adaptation perspective. *Journal of Consumer Research* 11 (March): 954–61.

Kaikati, Andrew M., and Jack G. Kaikati. 2004. Stealth marketing: How to reach consumers surreptitiously. *California Management Review* 46 (Summer): 6–22.

Kamins, Michael A. 1990. An investigation into the "match-up" hypothesis in celebrity advertising: When beauty may be only skin deep. *Journal of Advertising* 19 (March): 4–13.

Kamins, Michael A., and Kamal Gupta. 1994. Congruence between spokesperson and product type: A matchup hypothesis perspective. *Psychology & Marketing* 11 (November/December): 569–86.

Kang, Yong-Soon, and Paul M. Herr. 2006. Beauty and the beholder: Toward an integrative model of communication source effects. *Journal of Consumer Research* 33 (June): 123–30.

Kardes, Frank R., Steven S. Posavac, and Maria L. Cronley. 2004. Consumer inference: A review of processes, bases, and judgment contexts. *Journal of Consumer Psychology* 14, no. 3: 230–56.

Keel, Astrid, and Rajan Nataraajan. 2012. Celebrity endorsements and beyond: New avenues for celebrity branding. *Psychology & Marketing* 29 (September): 690–703.

Kirmani, Amna, and Baba Shiv. 1998. Effects of source congruity on brand attitudes and beliefs: The moderating role of issue-relevant elaboration. *Journal of Consumer Psychology* 7, no. 1: 25–47.

Kirmani, Amna, and Peter Wright. 1989. Money talks: Perceived advertising expense and expected product quality. *Journal of Consumer Research* 16 (December): 344–53.

Knittel, Christopher R., and Victor Stango. 2014. Celebrity endorsements, firm value, and reputation risk: Evidence from the tiger woods scandal. *Management Science* 60 (January): 21–37.

Lafferty, Barbara A., and Ronald E. Goldsmith. 1998. Corporate credibility's role in consumers' attitudes and purchase intentions when a high versus a low credibility endorser is used in the ad. *Journal of Business Research* 44 (February): 109–16.

Langmeyer, Lynn, and Mary Walker. 1991a. A first step to identify the meaning in celebrity endorsers. In *Advances in consumer research*, vol. 18, ed. R.H. Holman and M.R. Solomon, 364–71. Provo, UT: Association for Consumer Research.

Langmeyer, Lynn, and Mary Walker. 1991b. Assessing the effects of celebrity endorsers: Preliminary findings. In *Proceedings of the 1991 Conference of the American Academy of Advertising*, ed. R.H. Holman, 32–42. New York: American Academy of Advertising.

Lee, Jung-Gyo, and Esther Thorson. 2008. The impact of celebrity-product incongruence on the effectiveness of product endorsement. *Journal of Advertising Research* 48 (September): 433–49.

Lehmann, Donald R., Leigh McAllister, and Richard Staelin. 2011. Sophistication in research in marketing. *Journal of Marketing* 75 (July): 155–65.

Liu, Matthew Tingchi, and James L. Brock. 2011. Selecting a female athlete endorser in China: The effect of attractiveness, match-up, and consumer gender difference. *European Journal of Marketing* 45, no. 7/8: 1214–35.

Lord, Kenneth R., and Sanjay Putrevu. 2009. Informational and transformational responses to celebrity endorsements. *Journal of Current Issues & Research in Advertising* 31 (Spring): 1–13.

Louie, Therese A., Robert L. Kulik, and Robert Jacobson. 2001. When bad things happen to the endorsers of good products. *Marketing Letters* 12 (February): 13–23.

Louie, Therese A., and Carl Obermiller. 2002. Consumer response to a firm's endorser (dis)association decisions. *Journal of Advertising* 31 (Winter): 41–52.

Lynch, James, and Drue Schuler. 1994. The matchup effect of spokesperson and product congruency: A schema theory interpretation. *Psychology & Marketing* 11 (September/October): 417–45.

Mathur, Lynette Knowles, Ike Mathur, and Nanda Rangan. 1997. The wealth effects associated with a celebrity endorser: The Michael Jordan phenomenon. *Journal of Advertising Research* 37 (May/June): 67–73.

Mazodier, Marc, and Dwight Merunka. 2012. Achieving brand loyalty through sponsorship: The role of fit and self-congruity. *Journal of the Academy of Marketing Science* 40 (November): 807–20.

McCracken, Grant. 1989. Who is the celebrity endorser? Cultural foundations of the endorsement process. *Journal of Consumer Research* 16 (December): 310–21.

McGuire, William J. 1985. Attitudes and attitude change. In *Handbook of social psychology*, 3rd ed., ed. G. Lindzey and E. Aronson, 233–346. Hillsdale, NJ: Lawrence Erlbaum Associates.

Meersmans, Tom, Jan De Houwer, Frank Baeyens, Tom Randell, and Paul Eelen. 2005. Beyond evaluative conditioning? Searching for associative transfer of nonevaluative stimulus properties. *Cognition and Emotion* 19, no. 2: 283–306.

Miller, Felicia M., and Chris T. Allen. 2012. How does celebrity meaning transfer? Investigating the process of meaning transfer with celebrity affiliates and mature brands. *Journal of Consumer Psychology* 22 (July): 443–52.

Misra, Shekhar, and Sharon E. Beatty. 1990. Celebrity spokesperson and brand congruence. *Journal of Business Research* 21 (September): 159–73.

Money, R. Bruce, Terence A. Shimp, and Tomoaki Sakano. 2006. Celebrity endorsements in Japan and the United States: Is negative information all that harmful? *Journal of Advertising Research* 46 (March): 113–23.

Mowen, John C., and Stephen W. Brown. 1981. On explaining and predicting the effectiveness of celebrity endorsers. In *Advances in consumer research*, vol. 8, ed. K.B. Monroe, 437–41. Ann Arbor, MI: Association for Consumer Research.

Nicolau, Juan L., and María J. Santa-María. 2013. Celebrity endorsers' performance on the "ground" and on the "floor". *Marketing Letters* 24 (June): 143–49.

Ohanian, Roobina. 1991. The impact of celebrity spokespersons' perceived image on consumers' intention to purchase. *Journal of Advertising Research* 31 (February/March): 46–54.

Petty, Richard E., John T. Cacioppo, and David Schumann. 1983. Central and peripheral routes to advertising effectiveness: The moderating role of involvement. *Journal of Consumer Research* 10 (September): 135–46.

Pham, Michel Tuan. 2013. The seven sins of consumer psychology. *Journal of Consumer Psychology* 23 (October): 411–23.

Praet, Carolus. 2008. The influence of national culture on the use of celebrity endorsement in television advertising: A multi-country study. Paper presented at the International Conference on Research in Advertising (ICORIA), Antwerp, Belgium.

Ratneshwar, S., and Shelly Chaiken. 1991. Comprehension's role in persuasion: The case of its moderating effect on the persuasive impact of source cues. *Journal of Consumer Research* 18 (June): 52–62.

Reid, Scott A., Nicholas A. Palomares, Grace L. Anderson, and Beverly Bondad-Brown. 2009. Gender, language, and social influence: A test of expectation states, role congruity, and self-categorization theories. *Human Communication Research* 35 (October): 465–90.

Rice, Dan Hamilton, Katie Kelting, and Richard J. Lutz. 2012. Multiple endorsers and multiple endorsements: The influence of message repetition, source congruence and involvement on brand attitudes. *Journal of Consumer Psychology* 22 (April): 249–59.

Rindfleisch, Aric, and Jeffrey J. Inman. 1998. Explaining the familiarity-liking relationship: Mere exposure, information availability, or social desirability? *Marketing Letters* 9 (February): 5–19.

Rossiter, John R., and Larry Percy. 1997. *Advertising communications & promotion management*. 2nd ed. New York: McGraw-Hill.

Rossiter, John R., and Ale Smidts. 2012. Print advertising: Celebrity presenters. *Journal of Business Research* 65 (June): 874–9.

Rossiter, John R., and Larry Percy. 2013. How the roles of advertising merely appear to have changed. *International Journal of Advertising* 32, no. 3: 391–8.

Silvera, David H., and Benedikte Austad. 2004. Factors predicting the effectiveness of celebrity endorsement advertisements. *European Journal of Marketing* 38, no. 11/12: 1509–26.

Skowronski, John J., Donal E. Carlston, Lynda Mae, and Matthew T. Crawford. 1998. Spontaneous trait transference: Communicators take on the qualities they describe in others. *Journal of Personality and Social Psychology* 74 (April): 837–48.

Spry, Amanda, Ravi Pappu, and T. Bettina Cornwell. 2011. Celebrity endorsement, brand credibility and brand equity. *European Journal of Marketing* 45, no. 6: 882–909.

Stafford, Marla Royne, Nancy E. Spears, and Chung-kue Hsu. 2003. Celebrity images in magazine advertisements: An application of the visual rhetoric model. *Journal of Current Issues & Research in Advertising* 25 (Fall): 13–20.

Taylor, Charles R. 2010. Measuring return on investment from advertising: 'Holy grail' or necessary tool?. *International Journal of Advertising* 29, no. 3: 345–8.

Till, Brian D., and Michael Busler. 2000. The match-up hypothesis: Physical attractiveness, expertise, and the role of fit on brand attitude, purchase intent and brand beliefs. *Journal of Advertising* 29 (Autumn): 1–13.

Till, Brian D., and Terence A. Shimp. 1998. Endorsers in advertising: The case of negative celebrity information. *Journal of Advertising* 27 (Spring): 67−82.

Till, Brian D., Sarah M. Stanley, and Randi Priluck. 2008. Classical conditioning and celebrity endorsers: An examination of belongingness and resistance to extinction. *Psychology & Marketing* 25 (February): 179−96.

Törn, Fredrik. 2012. Revisiting the match-up hypothesis: Effects of brand-incongruent celebrity endorsements. *Journal of Current Issues & Research in Advertising* 33 (May): 20−36.

Tripp, Carolyn, Thomas D. Jensen, and Les Carlson. 1994. The effects of multiple product endorsements by celebrities on consumers' attitudes and intentions. *Journal of Consumer Research* 20 (March): 535−47.

Um, Nam-Hyun. 2013. Celebrity scandal fallout: How attribution style can protect the sponsor. *Psychology & Marketing* 30 (June): 529−41.

Veer, Ekant, Ilda Becirovic, and Brett A.S. Martin. 2010. If Kate voted conservative, would you? The role of celebrity endorsements in political party advertising. *European Journal of Marketing* 44, no. 3/4: 436−50.

Votolato, Nicole L., and H. Rao Unnava. 2006. Spillover of negative information on brand alliances. *Journal of Consumer Psychology* 16, no. 2: 196−202.

Weeks, Clinton S., T. Bettina Cornwell, and Judy C. Drennan. 2008. Leveraging sponsorships on the internet: Activation, congruence, and articulation. *Psychology & Marketing* 25 (July): 637−54.

Wegener, Duane T., and Richard E. Petty. 1995. Flexible correction processes in social judgment: The role of naïve theories in correction for perceived bias. *Journal of Personality and Social Psychology* 68 (January): 36−51.

White, Darin W., Lucretia Goddard, and Nick Wilbur. 2009. The effects of negative information transference in the celebrity endorsement relationship. *International Journal of Retail & Distribution Management* 37, no. 4: 322−35.

Wood, Natalie T., and Janée N. Burkhalter. 2014. Tweet this, not that: A comparison between brand promotions in microblogging environments using celebrity and company-generated tweets. *Journal of Marketing Communications* 20, no. 1−2: 129−46.

Wright, Peter L. 1973. The cognitive processes mediating acceptance of advertising. *Journal of Marketing Research* 10 (February): 53−62.

Zwilling, Moti, and Gila E. Fruchter. 2013. Matching product attributes to celebrities who reinforce the brand: An innovative algorithmic selection model. *Journal of Advertising Research* 53 (December): 391−410.

Cause-related marketing persuasion research: an integrated framework and directions for further research

Lars Bergkvist 🆔 and Kris Qiang Zhou 🆔

ABSTRACT

This paper presents an integrative review of the literature on cause-related marketing (CRM) persuasion research (i.e. studies of how CRM influences evaluations of the partner brand). The aim of the study was to review CRM persuasion research and to integrate the findings into a theoretical framework that could direct future research efforts in the area. Drawing on Bergkvist and Taylor's model of Leveraged Marketing Communications (LMC), a dual-path model of CRM persuasion effects was developed. According to the model, CRM affects brand evaluations along two paths: the indirect transfer path which is mediated by attribution of motives and the direct transfer path in which attitude towards the cause is transferred to the brand. The model incorporates results from extant research and provides guidance for future studies.

Introduction

Cause-related marketing (CRM) has been part of the marketing manager's toolbox for more than three decades. After a relatively modest start in the late 1970s, the number of CRM campaigns has increased steadily over the years and there are several examples of successful collaborations between brands and causes that have yielded benefits for both parties. One such example is the cause (RED), which was founded by the rock star Bono and the lawyer Bobby Shriver in 2006, and has since raised more than $350 million from a number of different CRM projects (Garrahan 2016). The list of brands that has partnered with (RED) to support their fight against the transmission of HIV/AIDS from mother to child during pregnancy includes a wide variety of brands such as Starbucks, Apple, Nike, Le Creuset, and Alessi (see also https://red.org/). The (RED) projects are typical CRM campaigns in that they tie donations from the brand to the cause to consumers' purchases of the brand.

CRM has received ample research attention and there is a substantial and growing marketing literature on CRM. Varadarajan and Menon (1988, 60) formally define CRM as 'the process of formulating and implementing marketing activities that are characterized by an offer from the firm to contribute a specified amount to a designated cause when customers engage in revenue-providing exchanges that satisfy organizational and individual objectives.' This is by far the most widely cited definition in the CRM literature and there appears to have been no attempt to criticize and replace it. In a broader context, Bergkvist and Taylor (2016) classify CRM as a form of leveraged marketing communications (LMC), that is, marketing communications that aim for the brand to benefit from consumers' positive associations to another object (e.g. a cause).

The present study focuses on CRM persuasion research, that is, research aimed at understanding the effect of CRM on consumer evaluations of the partner brand. Similar to other types of LMC, this is where most CRM research efforts are invested (Bergkvist and Taylor 2016). The reason for this research focus is that it corresponds to one of the main objectives of marketers for doing CRM campaigns, that is, to persuade more consumers to like and buy the brand. In addition, attitude change and persuasion research take a prominent place in advertising research more broadly (Kim et al. 2014; Norris and Colman 1992). CRM persuasion research tends to focus on factors that influence how consumers respond to and process advertising with a CRM component. Although CRM persuasion research is the area where the bulk of CRM research has been carried out, there is no systematic review of the literature within this area. There are reviews that have taken a broader approach by placing CRM within a corporate social responsibility context (Peloza and Shang 2011) or taking a macro view, including both brand and cause managerial perspectives, of CRM (Lafferty, Lueth, and McCafferty 2016), or that have taken a narrow approach by applying a quantitative text-mining approach to map and analyse the topics addressed in academic CRM research (Guerreiro, Rita, and Trigueiros 2016) or focusing on a few managerially relevant aspects of CRM research (Hemat and Yuksel 2014). None of these reviews have focused on consumer response to CRM and its effects on brand evaluations, and there has been no attempt to synthesize extant CRM persuasion research into an integrative theoretical framework or model. The present study fills this gap by reviewing the CRM persuasion literature with the aim to develop an integrative theoretical framework that summarizes extant research and provides guidance for future studies.

Thus, the purpose of the present study is to critically review the CRM persuasion literature in order to provide an overview and synthesis of the literature, and to integrate the findings into a theoretical framework. In addition, the study identifies research gaps and presents an agenda for further research. This purpose was addressed by means of a narrative literature review based on articles published in a broad range of general marketing and advertising journals. The present study thus contributes to the advertising literature by providing a state-of-the-art of overview of a large and growing field of research, proposing an integrative theoretical framework, and identifying directions for further research.

Literature search

The first step towards identifying relevant articles for the review was to search 10 general marketing journals (*European Journal of Marketing, International Journal of Research in Marketing, Journal of the Academy of Marketing Science, Journal of Consumer Psychology, Journal of Consumer Research, Journal of Marketing, Journal of Marketing Research, Marketing Letters, Marketing Science, Psychology & Marketing*) and five advertising journals (*International Journal of Advertising, Journal of Advertising, Journal of Advertising Research, Journal of Current Issues & Research in Advertising, Journal of Marketing Communications*). The end date for the search was 31 December 2016, with no limit on how far back the search could go. Each journal was searched using the most common ways to identify CRM (e.g. 'cause-related marketing,' 'cause-related,' 'CRM'). Once the first set of articles was identified, their reference lists were searched for additional relevant articles. The selection of articles was screened to make sure that it only comprised articles published in peer-reviewed journals listed in the Australian Business Deans Council journal ranking (http://www.abdc.edu.au/pages/abdc-journal-quality-list-2013.html) to ensure a minimum level of journal quality. In the end, the initial selection of articles for the review was made up of 123 articles.

Overview of CRM research

The focus of the present research is CRM persuasion research, which will be discussed at length in the remainder of the paper, starting in the next section. However, there is also CRM research with a different focus. In addition to CRM persuasion research, the review identified two broad areas of CRM research which will be briefly discussed in this section.

Studies of *feedback effects on the cause* focus on whether CRM has positive or negative effects on the cause partner in the CRM alliance. Although there are studies that exclusively focus on effects of CRM on the cause (e.g. Basil and Herr 2003), most studies in this area are CRM persuasion studies that also study effects on the cause (e.g. Lafferty, Goldsmith, and Hult 2004; Samu and Wymer 2009). Several of these studies have found that CRM can have positive feedback effects on the cause (e.g. Lafferty and Goldsmith 2005; Lafferty and Edmondson 2009; Lafferty, Goldsmith, and Hult 2004; Samu and Wymer 2009, 2014). However, there appears to be only one study demonstrating not only positive but also negative feedback effects on the cause: Basil and Herr (2003) found negative effects on attitude towards the cause (A_{Cause}) when consumers held negative A_{Brand} towards the partner brand, or when cause–brand fit was low. Studies have also found that feedback effects are moderated by fit (Lafferty, Goldsmith, and Hult 2004; Samu and Wymer 2009, 2014), although neither of these studies have found that low fit leads to negative effects on A_{Cause}. In addition, studies have found that feedback effects were stronger for unfamiliar than familiar causes (Lafferty and Goldsmith 2005), and for cause-related than brand-related messages (Samu and Wymer 2009, 2014).

The second broad CRM research area is *CRM campaign management*. This category includes studies of how brands and causes manage CRM campaigns and why they undertake them (e.g. Bennett 2002; Liston-Heyes and Liu 2013; Liu 2013; Liu and Ko 2011; Liu, Liston-Heyes, and Ko 2010; Runté, Basil, and Deshpande 2009), and normative articles that prescribe how CRM campaigns should be managed to achieve the best outcomes for the brand (e.g. Andreasen 1996; Gourville and Rangan 2004). In a marketing context, studies of CRM management are mainly of interest because they point to practical issues that could be addressed in CRM persuasion research. Some of these will be discussed in connection with the research agenda presented later in this paper.

CRM persuasion research

CRM persuasion research is by far the largest area of CRM research. Studies in this area investigate the effects of different CRM factors on brand evaluations (for simplicity, this paper will refer to brand attitude [A_{Brand}], brand purchase intentions, and similar overall evaluations as brand evaluations). In addition, there are a few studies of the effects of CRM on consumers' willingness to pay for brands (Koschate-Fischer, Stefan, and Hoyer 2012), and brand choice (e.g. Strahilevitz 1999; Yechiam et al. 2006). CRM persuasion research shares the same intellectual roots as advertising research building on theories and methods originally developed by psychologists such as Hovland (e.g. Hovland, Janis, and Kelley 1953) and McGuire (e.g. McGuire 1969). Typical CRM persuasion studies are based on laboratory experiments, often with student participants, and they tend to use advertising stimuli, although there has been an increase in the use of scenario descriptions as experimental stimuli (e.g. Barone, Norman, and Miyazaki 2007; Ellen, Webb, and Mohr 2006; Kim and Johnson 2013; Vanhamme et al. 2012). Moreover, CRM persuasion studies focus on outcomes in terms of attitude change and overlook outcomes in terms of change in brand awareness, an outcome which is highly relevant for advertising practitioners (Rossiter and Percy 2017; Rossiter, Percy, and Bergkvist 2018).

The effect of CRM on brand-related outcomes

A number of studies have compared the effects of CRM on brand evaluations to a control condition with no CRM or to other forms of marketing communications (Table 1). These comparisons have found that CRM, in almost all cases, had a positive effect on brand-related outcomes in comparison to a control condition or a discount of an equivalent size as the CRM contribution. However, it should be kept in mind that there is likely to be a publication bias favouring positive results over null results (Borenstein et al. 2009, 277–91) and that there most likely are unpublished studies with null results. Research has also found that CRM tends to have less positive effects on brand-related outcomes than unconditional donations, although the number of studies is limited. For comparisons with sponsorships, results are mixed and the number of studies is limited.

Factors influencing the effectiveness of CRM persuasion

CRM persuasion research has mostly focused on factors influencing the effects of CRM on brand evaluations (or similar outcome variables). These factors fall into one of six

Table 1. Studies that have investigated the relative effectiveness of CRM.

CRM compared to	CRM more effective	No significant difference	CRM less effective
Control group	Arora and Henderson (2007)[a]; Koschate-Fischer, Stefan, and Hoyer (2012)[c]; Lafferty (2009)[a]; van den Brink, Odekerken-Schröder, and Pauwels (2006)[a]; Yechiam et al. (2006)[b]; Zemack-Rugar et al. (2016)[a]	Nan and Heo (2007)[a]; Vilela and Nelson (2016)[a]	
Discount	Arora and Henderson (2007)[a]; Henderson and Arora (2010)[a]; Strahilevitz (1999)[b]; Westberg and Pope (2014)[a]; Yechiam et al. (2006)[b]	Winterich and Barone (2011)[b, d]	
Sponsorship	Westberg and Pope (2014)[a]	Chang (2012a)[a, d]	Lii and Lee (2012)[a]
Unconditional donation		Chen and Huang (2016)[a]; Dean (2003)[a]	Cui et al. (2003)[a]; Lii and Lee (2012)[a]

[a]Dependent variable: Brand evaluations.
[b]Dependent variable: Brand choice.
[c]Dependent variable: Willingness to pay.
[d]These studies were not designed to compare the relative effectiveness of CRM compared to discounts/sponsorships but rather to investigate what factors influence consumers' preferences for either promotion type and the results show differential effects for different groups of consumers (see Table 2).

categories: cause–brand fit, brand factors, cause factors, donation factors, campaign factors, and individual factors (Table 2).

Cause–brand fit

The factor that has received most research attention in CRM persuasion research is consumers' perceived fit between the cause and the brand. Fit in CRM studies is usually defined as consumers' overall perceived fit, or congruity, between the cause and the brand (e.g. Koschate-Fischer, Stefan, and Hoyer 2012; Vock, Dolen, and Kolk 2013), which is similar to the way fit is defined for celebrity endorsements (Bergkvist and Zhou 2016) and sponsorships (Cornwell, Weeks, and Roy 2005). Fit is variously operationalized on the product category level (also referred to as functional fit), by measuring fit between the cause and the product type (e.g. Ellen, Webb, and Mohr 2006; Lafferty 2007), or on the brand level (image fit), by measuring fit between the cause and the brand (e.g. Gorton et al. 2013; Samu and Wymer 2014). In some cases, fit is operationalized both on the product-category and brand level by using various types of combined measures (e.g. Barone, Norman, and Miyazaki 2007; Lafferty, Goldsmith, and Hult 2004). Cause–brand fit is usually assumed to have a positive main effect on brand evaluations and results in CRM persuasion research tend to be in line with this (Table 2). However, the review found two studies that report a null effect of cause–brand fit on brand evaluations (Lafferty 2007, 2009). A likely explanation for these divergent results is that the manipulation of fit was only partly successful. The manipulation checks in both studies show that the mean perceived fit in the low-fit group was on or above the mid-point of the response scale (11.87 and 14.25, respectively, on a 3 to 21 scale with mid-point 12), which means that the fit, although it was statistically significantly lower than in the high-fit group (mean fit scores 14.31 and 15.76, respectively), was perceived as neutral or moderately high, and that there was no comparison between low fit and high fit in the studies. Studies that have found a significant effect of cause–brand fit tend to have perceived fit mean scores below the mid-point of the response scale in the low-fit group and mean scores above the mid-point in the high-fit group. For example, recent studies have reported mean cause–brand fit scores of 3.11 vs. 5.52 (Das et al. 2016), 2.90 vs. 4.93 (Elving 2013), and 2.78 vs. 4.98 (Gupta and Pirsch 2006) (measured on 7-point response scales with mid-point 4). Moreover, there was one study with a null effect of cause–brand fit on brand choice (Hoek and Gendall 2008). In this study, there was no quantitative pre-test or manipulation check, only a qualitative pre-test, and it is not possible to assess whether the fit manipulation was successful or not.

Brand factors

The results in CRM persuasion studies for brand familiarity and pre-existing A_{Brand} are consistent and in line with the results in studies of other types of LMC (Bergkvist and Taylor 2016): there are more pronounced positive effects for unfamiliar (vs. familiar) brands and a positive pre-existing A_{Brand} leads to positive (post-CRM) brand evaluations (Table 2). A number of studies have compared hedonic (frivolous) and utilitarian (practical) products. Hedonic products are those whose 'consumption is motivated mainly by the desire for sensual pleasure, fantasy and fun,' while the consumption of utilitarian products 'is motivated mainly by the desire to fill a basic need or accomplish a functional task' (Strahilevitz and Myers 1998, 436). The empirical evidence shows that the effects of CRM on brand evaluations tend to be more positive for hedonic than utilitarian products.

Table 2. Factors influencing the effectiveness of CRM found in CRM persuasion research.

CRM Factor	Dependent variable	Nature of effect	Studies	Relationship qualified by
Cause–brand fit				
Cause–brand fit	Brand evaluations	Positive effect of increased cause–brand fit on brand evaluations.	Das et al. (2016); Elving (2013); Folse et al. (2014); Gorton et al. (2013); Gupta and Pirsch (2006); see also overview in Peloza and Shang (2011)	Interaction with target audience–cause fit (Gupta and Pirsch 2006), and with type of product (hedonic vs. utilitarian), donation framing (specific vs. unspecific amount), and type of purchase (planned vs. unplanned) (Das et al. 2016).
Cause–brand fit	Brand evaluations	Null effect of cause–brand fit on brand evaluations.	Lafferty (2007, 2009)	
Cause–brand fit	Brand choice	Null effect of cause–brand fit on brand choice.	Hoek and Gendall (2008)	
Brand factors				
Brand familiarity	Brand evaluations	Positive effect of unfamiliar (vs. familiar) brand on brand evaluations.	Arora and Henderson (2007); Lafferty (2009)	
Type of product	Brand evaluations	Positive effect of hedonic (vs. utilitarian) product on brand evaluations.	Chang (2008, 2011, 2012b); Das et al. (2016); Guerreiro, Rita, and Trigueiros (2015); Strahilevitz (1999); Strahilevitz and Myers (1998)	Interaction with size of donation amount (Strahilevitz 1999), donation framing (percentage vs. absolute amount) (Chang 2008), message appeal (guilt appeal vs. no guilt appeal) (Chang 2011), and message focus (brand-centred vs. cause-centred ad message) (Chang 2012b), and with cause-brand fit, and donation framing (specific vs. unspecific amount) (Das et al. 2016).
Corporate credibility	Brand evaluations	Positive effect of increased corporate credibility on brand evaluations.	Lafferty (2007)	
Pre-existing A_{Brand}	Brand evaluations	Positive effect of increased pre-existing A_{Brand} on post-CRM brand evaluations.	Basil and Herr (2006); Dean (2003); Lafferty, Goldsmith, and Hult (2004)	Interaction with A_{Cause} (Basil and Herr 2006) and company reputation (Dean 2003).
Cause factors				
Consumer–cause fit	Brand evaluations	Positive effect of increased target audience–cause fit on brand evaluations.	Chowdhury and Khare (2011); Vanhamme et al. (2012)	Three-way interaction between target audience–cause fit, brand involvement, and type of product (Chowdhury and Khare 2011).
Cause involvement	Brand evaluations	Positive effect of increased consumer cause involvement on brand evaluations.	Gorton et al. (2013); Grau and Folse (2007)	
Perceived importance of the cause	Brand evaluations	Positive effect of increased perceived importance of the cause on brand evaluations.	Gorton et al. (2013); Lafferty (2009)	Interaction with brand familiarity (Lafferty 2009).
Attitude towards the cause (A_{Cause})	Brand evaluations	Positive effect of increased A_{Cause} on brand evaluations.	Basil and Herr (2006); Lafferty, Goldsmith, and Hult (2004)	Interactions with pre-existing A_{Brand} (Basil and Herr 2006) and cause familiarity (Lafferty, Goldsmith, and Hult 2004).
Cause-proximity	Brand evaluations	Positive effect of local (vs. national) cause on brand evaluations.	Grau and Folse (2007)	Results held only for participants with low (vs. high) cause involvement.
Cause-proximity	Brand evaluations	Null effect of local (vs. national) cause on brand evaluations.	Ross, Patterson, and Stutts (1992)	
Cause-proximity	Brand evaluations	Positive effect of international (vs. national) cause on brand evaluations.	Vanhamme et al. (2012)	
Cause-proximity	Brand evaluations	Null effect of international (vs. national) cause on brand evaluations.	La Ferle, Kuber, and Edwards (2013)	

(continued)

Table 2. (*Continued*)

CRM Factor	Dependent variable	Nature of effect	Studies	Relationship qualified by
Cause-proximity	Brand evaluations	Positive effect of temporally close (vs. distant) cause on brand evaluations.	Tangari et al. (2010)	Results held only for present-oriented (vs. future-oriented) participants.
Type of need supported by the cause	Brand evaluations	Positive effect of primary (vs. secondary) needs on brand evaluations.	Vanhamme et al. (2012)	
Donation factors				
Donation amount	Brand evaluations	Positive effect of increased donation amount on brand evaluations.	Folse, Niedrich, and Grau (2010); Koschate-Fischer, Huber, and Hoyer (2016); Müller, Fries, and Gedenk (2014); Olsen, Pracejus, and Brown (2003)	Interactions with timing of price increase (Koschate-Fischer, Huber, and Hoyer 2016) and type of donation (money, goods, or both) (Müller, Fries, and Gedenk 2014).
Donation amount	Brand choice	Positive effect of increased donation amount on brand choice.	Müller, Fries, and Gedenk (2014); Pracejus, Olsen, and Brown (2003)	Interaction with whether there is a financial trade-off in terms of a higher purchasing cost for the brand (Müller, Fries, and Gedenk 2014).
Donation amount	Willingness to pay	Positive effect of increased donation amount on willingness to pay.	Koschate-Fischer, Stefan, and Hoyer (2012)	Interaction with consumers' attitude towards helping others, A_{Cause}, cause–brand fit, cause involvement, and cause affinity.
Donation amount	Brand evaluations	Negative effect of increased donation amount on brand evaluations.	Chang (2008, 2011)	Interaction with product price (Chang 2008)
Donation amount	Brand evaluations	Null effect of increased donation amount on brand evaluations.	Holmes and Kilbane (1993); Human and Terblanche (2012)	
Donation framing	Brand evaluations	A specific donation amount ('20% of profits') had more positive effects on brand evaluations than an unspecific amount ('a portion of profits').	Das et al. (2016); Hyllegard et al. (2011)	Interaction with cause–brand fit, type of product (hedonic vs. utilitarian), and type of purchase (planned vs. unplanned) (Das et al. 2016).
Donation framing	Brand evaluations	Donations expressed in absolute dollar terms had more positive effects on brand evaluations than donations expressed in percentage of sales price.	Chang (2008); Kleber, Florack, and Chladek (2016)	Interaction with donation amount and product price (Chang 2008) and consumer numeracy (Kleber, Florack, and Chladek 2016).
Donation form	Brand evaluations	Positive effect of donation in cash (vs. goods) on brand evaluations.	Folse et al. (2014)	The negative effect of donating goods is mitigated if the donated goods are congruent with the cause.
Choice of cause	Brand evaluations	Allowing consumers to choose what cause the money will be donated to had a positive effect on brand evaluations compared to a donation to a cause selected by the brand.	Kull and Heath (2016); Robinson, Irmak, and Jayachandran (2012)	Interaction with restricted (vs. unrestricted) choice of cause and pre-existing brand image (Kull and Heath 2016), and consumer self-construal (collectivist vs. non-collectivist) and cause–brand fit (Robinson, Irmak, and Jayachandran 2012).
Campaign and message factors				
Campaign duration	Brand evaluations	Positive effect of long (vs. short) campaign duration on brand evaluations.	Youn and Kim (2018)	Interaction with self-construal and product category involvement.
Campaign duration	Brand loyalty	Positive effect of long (vs. short) campaign duration on brand loyalty.	van den Brink, Odekerken-Schröder, and Pauwels (2006)	Interaction with product involvement.
Advertising message focus	Brand evaluations	Positive effect of cause-dominated (vs. brand-dominated) advertising message on brand evaluations.	Samu and Wymer (2009, 2014)	Interaction with cause–brand fit (Samu and Wymer 2014).

(*continued*)

Table 2. (*Continued*)

CRM Factor	Dependent variable	Nature of effect	Studies	Relationship qualified by
Advertising message focus	Brand evaluations	Positive effect of brand-dominated (vs. cause-dominated) picture in the advertising message on brand evaluations.	Lafferty and Edmondson (2009)	
Advertising message focus	Brand evaluations	Mixed results in which brand-dominated ads had positive brand evaluation effects for utilitarian products but not hedonic products, and cause-dominated ads had positive brand evaluation effects for hedonic products but not utilitarian products.	Chang (2012b)	Interaction with type of product (hedonic vs. utilitarian).
Message appeal	Brand evaluations	Positive effect of guilt (vs. no guilt) message appeal on brand evaluations.	Chang (2011)	Interactions with product type (hedonic vs. utilitarian) and donation amount.
Cause description vividness	Brand choice; willingness to pay	Positive effect of vivid (vs. pallid) cause description in the advertising message on brand evaluations.	Baghi, Rubaltelli, and Tedeschi (2009)	
Individual factors				
Gender	Brand evaluations	Women's brand evaluations were more positive than men's brand evaluations.	Ross, Patterson, and Stutts (1992); Chéron, Kohlbacher, and Kusuma (2012)	
Gender	Brand evaluations	No difference between men's and women's brand evaluations.	Vilela and Nelson (2016)	
Product usage	Brand evaluations	Positive effect of heavy (vs. light) product usage on brand evaluations.	Chang (2012a)	
Self-construal	Promotion evaluation; promotion preference; promotion choice	Positive effect of interdependent (vs. independent) self-construal on evaluation, preference, and choice of CRM compared to a discount.	Winterich and Barone (2011)	Interactions with target audience-cause fit, charity efficiency, and product type (indulgent vs. healthy).
Self-construal	Brand evaluations	Positive effect of interdependent (vs. independent) self-construal on brand evaluations.	Chen and Huang (2016); Youn and Kim (2018)	Interactions with campaign duration and product category involvement (Youn and Kim 2018).
Social value orientation	Brand evaluations	Positive effect of pro-social (vs. pro-self) value orientation on brand evaluations.	Vock, Dolen, and Kolk (2013)	Interaction with cause-brand fit.
Guilt sensitivity	Product choice; product preference	Positive effect of high (vs. low) guilt sensitivity on product choice and preference.	Zemack-Rugar et al. (2016)	Interaction with product type (utilitarian vs. hedonic).
Consumer moral identity centrality	Brand evaluations	Positive effect of high (vs. low) centrality of moral identity on brand evaluations.	He et al. (2016)	Interaction with brand social responsibility image and emotional brand attachment.

Cause factors

Three cause-related factors studied in CRM persuasion research share a common theme: consumer–cause fit, cause involvement, and the perceived importance of the cause, all relate to the consumer's perceived personal relevance of the cause. All three factors have been found to be positively related to brand evaluations (Table 2). Similar results in studies of other LMC lend further credence to the results in CRM studies. There are, for example, studies showing positive effects on brand evaluations of target audience-sponsored object fit for sponsorships (e.g. Close, Krishen, and Latour 2009; Mazodier and Merunka 2012) and target audience–celebrity fit for celebrity endorsements (Choi and Rifon 2012), and of event involvement for sponsorships (e.g. Ko et al. 2008; Neijens, Smit, and Moorman 2009). A fourth factor with positive effect on brand evaluations is A_{Cause}, a relationship with direct parallels in celebrity endorsements where it has been shown that attitude towards the celebrity has a positive effect on brand evaluations (e.g. Bergkvist, Hjalmarson, and Mägi 2016; Kahle and Homer 1985).

Studies of cause physical and temporal proximity have yielded weak and mixed results (Table 2). Across studies there were null results (La Ferle, Kuber, and Edwards 2013; Ross, Patterson, and Stutts 1992), significant main effects that held only in a subset of the population under study (Grau and Folse 2007; Tangari et al. 2010), and one instance of a significant main effect contrary to the hypothesized relationship (Vanhamme et al. 2012). The theoretical expectation across studies is that proximal causes should have a more positive effect on brand evaluations than distant causes, although the theoretical account varies. The positive effect of proximal causes has been accounted for by relying on a combination of signalling theory and social impact theory (Grau and Folse 2007, 21), or social exchange theory (Vanhamme et al. 2012, 264). The weak and conflicting results in combination with rather vague theoretical accounts together suggest that the proximity of the cause may be of limited importance for consumers' brand evaluations.

Donation factors

There are single studies of donation factors such as donation form (goods vs. money) and choice of cause (i.e. allowing consumers to choose the donation recipient) and multiple studies of the effects of the size of donation amount and the way the donation amount is framed (Table 2). The results for donation framing consistently show a consumer preference for specific donation amounts and donations expressed in dollar terms. The results for donation amount, however, are mixed. There are studies showing positive, null, and negative effects of increasing the donation amount. A possible explanation for the null results lies in the relatively small difference between the low and high CRM donation amounts in those studies: The highest donation amount was two or six times higher than the lowest donation amount (Holmes and Kilbane 1993; Human and Terblanche 2012). In contrast, in the studies with a positive donation-amount effect, the difference between low and high donation amounts ranged between 8 and 64 times (Folse, Niedrich, and Grau 2010; Koschate-Fischer, Stefan, and Hoyer 2012; Müller, Fries, and Gedenk 2014; Olsen, Pracejus, and Brown 2003). Thus, it could be the case that a large increase in donation amount is required for there to be a noticeable effect on brand evaluations.

The negative effects of increasing the donation amount found in two studies by Chang (2008, 2011) are harder to explain. Chang (2008, 2011) did not hypothesize the main effects of donation amount, only various interaction effects, and there is neither a formal

theoretical account of the effect nor a test of mediation effects. Chang (2011, 607) specu-
lates that the negative effects could have been caused by consumers' attribution of negative motives. However, mediation analyses in the study by Koschate-Fischer, Stefan, and
Hoyer (2012) show that consumers attribute negative motives to low, not high, donation
amounts. Another possible explanation could lie in cultural differences but the two studies
with negative effects were carried out in Taiwan (Chang 2008) and the United States
(Chang 2011), respectively, while the studies with positive effects were carried out in the
United States and Germany (Folse, Niedrich, and Grau 2010; Koschate-Fischer, Stefan, and
Hoyer 2012; Müller, Fries, and Gedenk 2014; Olsen, Pracejus, and Brown 2003), which suggests that the negative effect cannot be accounted for by cultural differences. Moreover,
the studies by Chang (2008, 2011) manipulated donation amount framing (absolute vs.
relative), type of product (hedonic vs. utilitarian), and advertising message appeal (guilt
vs. non-guilt appeal) as independent variables which rule out that any of these factors
could have caused the reversal of the donation amount effects. Thus, there appears to
have been idiosyncratic factors in the studies by Chang (2008, 2011) causing the donation
effects to be reversed compared to the other studies.

Campaign and message factors
Consistent results in two studies show positive effects of longer (vs. shorter) campaign
duration on brand evaluations and brand loyalty (Table 2). In addition, there are single
studies of message factors such as message appeal and cause description. There are a
larger number of studies of message focus (brand-dominated vs. cause-dominated), but
the results appear to be conflicting. Two studies report positive effects on brand evaluations of a cause-dominated message (Samu and Wymer 2009, 2014), while another study
reports positive effects of a brand-dominated message (Lafferty and Edmondson 2014). A
third study reports mixed results with positive effects of brand-dominated messages for
utilitarian products and positive effects of cause-dominated messages for hedonic products (Chang 2012b). The results in the latter study could explain the conflicting findings in
the previous studies, if the products in the studies by Samu and Wymer (2009, 2014) were
hedonic and the product in the study by Lafferty and Edmondson (2014) was utilitarian.
However, while the product in the study by Lafferty and Edmondson (2014), granola bars,
is likely perceived as a utilitarian product, the products in Samu and Wymer's (2009, 2014)
studies, baby clothes and a book retailer, are not likely to be perceived as hedonic by consumers. Thus, there is a need for additional research to resolve the conflicting findings for
message focus.

Individual factors
The only individual factors that have received repeated research attention are gender and
self-construal (Table 2). For gender, results are weak and mixed, at best suggesting that
women are more responsive to CRM than men, while the results for self-construal consistently show more positive brand evaluations for people with interdependent self-
construal compared to those with independent self-construal. For other individual factors,
there are single studies of factors related to product usage, moral orientation, and various
other factors. The relatively limited interest in individual CRM persuasion factors is similar
to the situation in celebrity endorsement research (Bergkvist and Zhou 2016).

Integrating CRM persuasion research into a theoretical framework

The review of CRM persuasion research shows that the extant body of research is some-what fragmented and that studies tend to focus on one or a few factors of potential inter-est, often without placing them in a broader context. This points to the need for a theoretical framework that could aid the systematic organization of findings from extant research and guide future research efforts. Such a framework was created by using parts of the model of LMC in Bergkvist and Taylor (2016) and extending these to fit in a specific CRM context. The resulting model has two paths accounting for main effects of LMC on brand evaluations, *indirect affect transfer* and *direct affect transfer*, which were adapted and used as an integrative theoretical framework for CRM persuasion research (Figure 1). The development of the model was guided by the results in CRM persuasion research reviewed in this paper.

Indirect affect transfer

Persuasion in the indirect transfer path occurs when different levels of cause–brand fit and donation amount, and different types of donation and message factors trigger attributions of firm motives. Positive motive attributions are consumer perceptions that the brand genuinely wants to help the cause regardless of self-interest and negative motive attribu-tions are consumer perceptions that the brand is primarily acting out of self-interest (Folse, Niedrich, and Grau 2010). If the attributed motives are positive (negative), this will lead to a positive (negative) attitude towards the CRM alliance which, in turn, leads to pos-itive (negative) brand evaluation effects. Thus, indirect affect transfer takes place as the result of a cognitive process in which brand motives are inferred from one or several cam-paign factors (Figure 1).

Extant CRM research supports that CRM affects brand evaluations according to the indi-rect affect transfer path. Several studies have found that consumers' motive attributions mediate the effects of cause–brand fit on brand evaluations in such a way that low fit leads to attribution of negative motives and high fit leads to attribution of positive motives

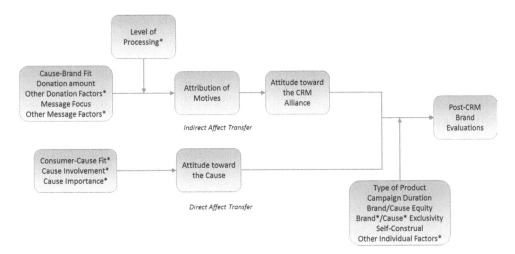

Figure 1. The indirect and direct affect transfer paths of CRM persuasion effects.
Note: *The effect of these factors has not yet been confirmed in CRM research.

(e.g. Barone, Miyazaki, and Taylor 2000; Bigné, Currás-Pérez, and Aldás-Manzano 2012; Ellen, Webb, and Mohr 2006; Elving 2013; Gorton et al. 2013; Samu and Wymer 2014). Studies also show that increasing the donation amount (Koschate-Fischer, Stefan, and Hoyer 2012) and using a cause-focused message (Samu and Wymer 2014) lead to attribution of positive motives, and there is evidence that attitude towards the alliance mediates the effect of other variables on brand evaluations (Lafferty, Goldsmith, and Hult 2004). However, there are some relationships that remain to be tested in empirical research. These will be discussed in the agenda for further research presented later in the paper.

Direct affect transfer

Persuasion in the direct transfer path occurs when consumers' liking of a cause (A_{Cause}) transfers to the brand (Figure 1), a process that can be accounted for, depending on the situation, by balance theory, evaluative conditioning, or adaptive learning (see overview in Bergkvist and Taylor [2016]). This means that the affect transfer could be the result of a either a cognitive process, associative learning, or both. The direct transfer from A_{Cause} to the brand has been supported in CRM persuasion research (e.g. Basil and Herr 2006; Lafferty, Goldsmith, and Hult 2004). Research in other studies suggest that factors such as consumer–cause fit, cause involvement, and cause importance are positively related to A_{Cause}, as it has been demonstrated that an increase in these factors has a positive effect on brand evaluations (Gorton et al. 2013; Lafferty and Edmondson 2009; Vanhamme et al. 2012), an effect which likely is mediated by A_{Cause}.

Moderating factors

CRM persuasion research has shown that the effects of CRM on brand evaluations are moderated by several factors. Studies have found that CRM has more positive effects on brand evaluations if the campaign duration is long rather than short (e.g. van den Brink, Odekerken-Schröder, and Pauwels 2006; Youn and Kim 2018), the product is hedonic rather than utilitarian (e.g. Das et al. 2016; Guerreiro, Rita, and Trigueiros 2015; Strahilevitz and Myers 1998), if the brand is unfamiliar rather than familiar (e.g. Arora and Henderson 2007; Lafferty 2009), and if the cause is familiar rather than unfamiliar (e.g. Lafferty, Goldsmith, and Hult 2004). Studies have also found that CRM has more positive effects on brand evaluations for consumers with an interdependent (vs. independent) self-construal (e.g. Chen and Huang 2016; Winterich and Barone 2011; Youn and Kim 2018). These factors are included as moderators of both indirect and direct affect transfer in the framework in Figure 1 (brand/cause familiarity is subsumed under brand/cause equity), which also includes moderating factors from the original framework in Bergkvist and Taylor (2016) not yet verified in CRM persuasion research.

Research agenda

The review of the CRM literature points to several opportunities for future research.

Confirming and refining the CRM persuasion model

The proposed framework for CRM persuasion effects (Figure 1) points to several interesting opportunities for further research. First of all, there are a number of factors proposed in the model that have not yet been empirically verified in a CRM context. Thus, there are opportunities for experimental research testing whether the effect of other donation factors (e.g. donation framing, donation form, choice of cause) and other message factors (e.g. message appeal, cause description) on brand evaluations is mediated by attribution of motives and attitude towards the CRM alliance. Similarly, empirical studies could determine whether consumer–cause fit, cause involvement, and cause importance are positively related to A_{Cause}.

Studies of the proposed moderating variables in the theoretical framework could be modelled on studies of factors moderating celebrity endorsements. For example, studies of celebrity endorsements have shown that the effect of celebrity–brand fit, which is analogous to cause–brand fit, is more pronounced under conditions of high-effort processing than low-effort processing (Kirmani and Shiv 1998; Lee and Thorson 2008), that is, when more time and effort are invested in processing a message (Petty, Cacioppo, and Schumann 1983). Similarly, there is research showing that decreasing celebrity exclusivity (i.e. if celebrities endorse an increasing number of brands) will, under certain conditions, have negative effects on brand evaluations (Rice, Kelting, and Lutz 2012). Celebrity endorsements are similar to CRM in many ways and running similar studies with CRM stimuli should be relatively straightforward.

An important development of the model would be to try to establish the relative importance of the different factors influencing brand evaluations. For example, is cause–brand fit more important for brand evaluations than donation amount? Or is donation framing more important than message focus? Answering research questions like these would both increase academics understanding of how CRM works and offer useful guidance to managers planning CRM campaigns. However, answering research questions like this may pose a challenge from methodological point of view. Laboratory experiments tend to rely on a limited number of campaign stimuli (usually one that is varied with respect to the independent variables) and the relative importance of CRM factors may vary depending on idiosyncrasies of the material being used (cf. Wells 2001). If an experimental approach is used, this needs to be counteracted by using multiple campaign stimuli, at the same time as steps are taken to avoid order effects and other disadvantages of the use of multiple stimuli. Alternatively, research on these issues could use survey research to capture consumers' response to multiple real-world CRM campaigns. This approach would require that the measured campaigns were either precoded with respect to the independent variables of interest (e.g. cause–brand fit, donation amount) or that survey participants' perceptions of the independent variables were captured in questions included in the survey instrument. The relative impact of independent variables could then be estimated using statistical analysis methods such as regression analysis.

Studying the relative importance of different CRM factors rests on the assumption that several CRM factors simultaneously influence brand evaluations, both in the indirect and direct affect transfer paths, in a process similar to the expectancy-value models that are commonly assumed to account for attitude formation (e.g. Ajzen 2001). However, an intriguing possibility for the indirect transfer path is that consumers' motive attributions are the result of a disconfirmation process, which would mean that motive attributions could be the result of a single CRM factor. Such a process could be studied and understood using a selective hypothesis testing framework (Sanbonmatsu et al. 1998). According to this theoretical framework, in many situations people hold a preliminary hypothesis which they try to confirm or disconfirm. If the initial hypothesis is confirmed, it is accepted as true; if it is disconfirmed, a new hypothesis replaces the initial hypothesis in a second round of hypothesis testing; and so on, until a hypothesis is accepted. For example, in a CRM setting, it is likely that many consumers hold the view that a company's primary motive is to make profits and that their actions are primarily motivated by profit considerations. When exposed to a CRM campaign, consumers will look for evidence supporting their initial profit-motive hypothesis. If the initial information confirms the hypothesis, the attributed motives will be negative, and the effect on brand evaluations will be negative. This means that the order in which information is processed decides the outcome, rather than what weight is given to different types of information. This alternative theoretical account could be tested in an experiment in which varies the order that information that either confirms or disconfirms the profit-motive hypothesis is introduced (for examples of studies using a selective-hypothesis framework, see Posavac et al. [2004, 2005]). For example, high cause–brand fit would likely disconfirm the hypothesis while a low donation amount would confirm it. If the attribution of motives is the result of selective hypothesis testing, presenting the information about the low donation amount before the information about the high cause–brand fit would lead to attribution of negative motives and a negative effect on brand evaluations. Conversely, presenting the information about the high cause–brand fit before the information about the low donation amount should lead to attribution of positive motives.

Studying a broader range of outcome variables

CRM persuasion research has focused mainly on A_{Brand} as outcome variable and to some extent on related variables such as brand purchase intention, brand choice, and willingness to pay. However, studies of managers undertaking CRM show that they are also interested in other outcome variables. For example, Liu (2013, 255) reports that important goals for managers responsible for CRM campaigns are to attract attention, build brand awareness, and create a consistent brand image. This suggests that CRM persuasion research can increase its practical relevance by broadening the range of outcome variables included in CRM research. It is also important from a theoretical perspective to get a fuller understanding of how CRM works.

An important part currently missing in CRM research is how CRM campaigns influence learning of brand benefit beliefs. Brand benefit beliefs are of central importance for the formation of brand attitude and brand choice (Rossiter, Percy, and Bergkvist 2018) and the extent to which CRM could influence benefit beliefs should be investigated in future studies. It would also be of value to investigate if and how CRM influences corporate and brand image factors. For studies of image factors, CRM research could draw on research on sponsorships (e.g. Gwinner and Eaton 1999) or celebrity endorsements (see overview in Bergkvist and Zhou [2016]).

There is a dearth of research on the effect on attention to advertising and brand awareness learning in CRM research, same as for all types of LMC (Bergkvist and Taylor 2016) and for advertising research in general (Rossiter and Percy 2017). A particular challenge with research on attention and brand awareness learning is that this will require that the standard advertising experiment procedure used in CRM persuasion research is changed. Specifically, this would mean that research studying CRM effects on attention would have to abandon forced exposure to the CRM stimuli and expose experiment participants to multiple stimuli without focusing their attention on the target stimuli (e.g. by using clutter reels). Studies of the effects on brand awareness learning would also have to abandon forced exposure and make sure that they use valid measures of brand awareness (Rossiter and Percy 2017).

Methodology development

Almost all CRM persuasion studies are based on experiments that compare different levels of the independent variables (e.g. high vs. low cause–brand fit, hedonic vs. utilitarian product type) in order to ascertain the effect of these independent variables. However, most studies do not include a no-CRM control condition or at least one condition with some other form of marketing activity (e.g. discount, sponsorship, celebrity endorsement). This means that these studies compare the effectiveness of different levels of cause–brand fit, brand-, cause-, donation-, and campaign factors without knowing whether any level of the factor is more effective than not using CRM at all. An important step towards improvement of this unsatisfactory situation would be that CRM persuasion studies routinely include a no-CRM control condition. A further step would be to develop and test hypotheses of whether there are CRM factors or levels of CRM factors that would make CRM less effective than a no-CRM option. And from a managerial view, it is desirable to systematically compare CRM to other forms of LMC.

The literature review pointed to a need to improve the use of manipulation checks (or pre-tests) to make sure that experimental treatments work as intended. As mentioned previously, it appears that conflicting results for cause–brand fit in different studies are the result of varying success in manipulating perceived cause–brand fit. While the studies that found a significant effect of cause–brand fit reported manipulation check scores below the mid-point of the response scale for the low-fit condition (e.g. Das et al. 2016; Elving 2013; Gupta and Pirsch 2006), the two studies with null results reported manipulation check scores on or above the mid-point of the response scale for the low-fit condition manipulation checks (Lafferty 2007, 2009), which shows that the low-fit conditions were not perceived as low fit by experiment participants in the latter studies. Naturally, it is a concern if experimental manipulations result in varying levels of the independent variable under study as results will not be comparable between studies and the accumulation of knowledge will be hampered. This situation would be avoided if manipulation checks of binary, low-high, independent variables were tested for statistical significance against the mid-point of the response scale rather than the two groups against each other (i.e. the mean score in the low condition should be significantly lower than the mid-point of the response scale and the mean score in the high condition should be significantly higher than the mid-point of the response scale). Following this procedure may not ensure complete comparability between studies but it will greatly improve comparability between studies and reduce the risk of unexplained conflicting results.

The literature review also showed that almost all CRM persuasion studies are based on laboratory experiments. These experiments typically employ a single forced exposure to advertising stimuli and measure the outcome more or less immediately following exposure. However, real-world CRM campaigns often run over an extended time period and its effects are the result of repeated exposures over a long time. Research on, for example, the effects of advertising (Bergkvist and Rossiter 2008; Chattopadhyay and Nedungadi 1992) and celebrity endorsements (Eisend and Langner 2010) shows that the long-term effects are different from the short-term effects. Thus, it would be of value to either change the methodology of experiments and use multiple exposures over time (see Bergkvist and Rossiter [2008] for an example of how this can be done) and measure the outcome with a delay, or to rely on other methods than experiments (e.g. survey-based studies of real-world campaigns).

Conclusion

This study reviewed extant research in the field of CRM persuasion research and fitted previous research into an integrative framework based on Bergkvist and Taylor's (2016) model of LMC. The framework provides context for existing research and guidance for future studies. The review showed that results in extant research are consistent with respect to the effect of some factors on brand evaluations (e.g. positive effect of increased cause–brand fit; positive effect of specific donation amounts), mixed for some factors (e.g. donation amount; message focus), and that some variables seem to have limited or no effect on brand evaluations (e.g. donation proximity). The agenda for future research suggests a number of potentially fruitful avenues for further research based on gaps and conflicting findings in previous research, and implications drawn from the integrative framework.

The review found some methodological limitations in previous studies, particularly with respect to the use of manipulation checks. It is mainly the responsibility of researchers to make sure that experimental manipulations work as intended. However, journal reviewers and editors play an important role in promoting sound research methodology and review teams should be observant when it comes to the use of manipulation checks and whether manipulations were successful.

The review of the CRM persuasion literature shows that research in this field is relatively uniform with respect to research problems, methodology, and outcome variables. New studies tend to add one or two new independent and/or moderating variables but stay safely within the established paradigm. Over time, this will have the effect that the contributions made by new studies will be increasingly marginal and it would be beneficial for the field if some researchers were willing to take a less safe approach and explore new theories, approaches, and methodologies.

Disclosure statement

No potential conflict of interest was reported by the authors.

ORCID

Lars Bergkvist (iD) http://orcid.org/0000-0002-4271-9182
Kris Qiang Zhou (iD) http://orcid.org/0000-0003-2230-514X

References

Ajzen, I. 2001. Nature and operation of attitudes. *Annual Review of Psychology* 52: 27–58.

Andreasen, A.R. 1996. Profits for nonprofits: Find a corporate partner. *Harvard Business Review* 74 (Nov/Dec): 47–59.

Arora, N., and T. Henderson. 2007. Embedded premium promotions: Why it works and how to make it more effective. *Marketing Science* 26, no. 4: 514–31.

Baghi, I., E. Rubaltelli, and M. Tedeschi. 2009. A strategy to communicate corporate social responsibility: Cause related marketing and its dark side. *Corporate Social Responsibility and Environmental Management* 16 (Jan/Feb): 15–26.

Barone, M.J., A.D. Miyazaki, and K.A. Taylor. 2000. The influence of cause-related marketing on consumer choice: Does one good turn deserve another? *Journal of the Academy of Marketing Science* 28 (Spring): 248–62.

Barone, M.J., A.T. Norman, and A.D. Miyazaki. 2007. Consumer response to retailer use of cause-related marketing: Is more fit better? *Journal of Retailing* 83, no. 4: 437–45.

Basil, D.Z., and P.M. Herr. 2003. Dangerous donations? The effects of cause-related marketing on charity attitude. *Journal of Nonprofit & Public Sector Marketing* 11, no. 1: 59–76.

Basil, D.Z., and P.M. Herr. 2006. Attitudinal balance and cause-related marketing: An empirical application of balance theory. *Journal of Consumer Psychology* 16, no. 4: 391–403.

Bennett, R. 2002. Corporate perspectives on cause related marketing. *Journal of Nonprofit & Public Sector Marketing* 10, no. 1: 41–59.

Bergkvist, L., H. Hjalmarson, and A. Mägi. 2016. A new model of how celebrity endorsements work: Attitude toward the endorsement as a mediator of celebrity source and endorsement effects. *International Journal of Advertising* 35, no. 2: 171–84.

Bergkvist, L., and J.R. Rossiter. 2008. The role of ad likability in predicting an ad's campaign performance. *Journal of Advertising* 37 (Summer): 85–97.

Bergkvist, L., and C.R. Taylor. 2016. Leveraged marketing communications: A framework for explaining the effects of secondary brand associations. *AMS Review* 6 (Dec): 157–75.

Bergkvist, L., and K.Q. Zhou. 2016. Celebrity endorsements: A literature review and research agenda. *International Journal of Advertising* 35, no. 4: 642–63.

Bigné, E., R. Currás-Pérez, and J. Aldás-Manzano. 2012. Dual nature of cause-brand fit: Influence on corporate social responsibility consumer perception. *European Journal of Marketing* 46, no. 3/4: 575–94.

Borenstein, M., L.V. Hedges, J.P.T. Higgins, and H.R. Rothstein. 2009. *Introduction to meta-analysis*. Chichester: John Wiley & Sons.

Chang, C. 2012a. The effectiveness of advertising that leverages sponsorship and cause-related marketing: A contingency model. *International Journal of Advertising* 31, no. 2: 317–37.

Chang, C.-T. 2008. To donate or not to donate? Product characteristics and framing effects of cause-related marketing on consumer purchase behavior. *Psychology & Marketing* 25 (Dec): 1089–110.

Chang, C.-T. 2011. Guilt appeals in cause-related marketing: The subversive roles of product type and donation magnitude. *International Journal of Advertising* 30, no. 4: 587–16.

Chang, C.-T. 2012b. Missing ingredients in cause-related advertising: The right formula of execution style and cause framing. *International Journal of Advertising* 31, no. 2: 231–56.

Chattopadhyay, A., and P. Nedungadi. 1992. Does attitude toward the Ad endure? The moderating effects of attention and delay. *Journal of Consumer Research* 19 (June): 26–33.

Chen, Z., and Y. Huang. 2016. Cause-related marketing is not always less favorable than corporate philanthropy: The moderating role of self-construal. *International Journal of Research in Marketing* 33 (Dec): 868–80.

Chéron, E., F. Kohlbacher, and K. Kusuma. 2012. The effects of brand-cause fit and campaign duration on consumer perception of cause-related marketing in Japan. *Journal of Consumer Marketing* 29, no. 5: 357–68.

Choi, S.M., and N.J. Rifon. 2012. It is a match: The impact of congruence between celebrity image and consumer ideal self on endorsement effectiveness. *Psychology and Marketing* 29 (Sep): 639–50.

Chowdhury, T.G., and A. Khare. 2011. Matching a cause with self-schema: The moderating effect on brand preferences. *Psychology & Marketing* 28 (Aug): 825–42.

Close, A.G., A.S. Krishen, and M.S. Latour. 2009. This event is me! How consumer event self-congruity leverages sponsorship. *Journal of Advertising Research* 49 (Sep): 271–84.

Cornwell, T.B., C.S. Weeks, and D.P. Roy. 2005. Sponsorship-linked marketing: Opening the black box. *Journal of Advertising* 34 (Summer): 21–42.

Cui, Y., E.S. Trent, P.M. Sullivan, and G.N. Matiru. 2003. Cause-related marketing: How generation Y responds. *International Journal of Retail & Distribution Management* 31, no. 6: 310–20.

Das, N., A. Guha, A. Biswas, and B. Krishnan. 2016. How product–cause fit and donation quantifier interact in cause-related marketing (CRM) settings: Evidence of the cue congruency effect. *Marketing Letters* 27 (June): 295–308.

Dean, D.H. 2003. Consumer perception of corporate donations: Effects of company reputation for social responsibility and type of donation. *Journal of Advertising* 32 (Winter): 91–102.

Eisend, M., and T. Langner. 2010. Immediate and delayed advertising effects of celebrity endorsers' attractiveness and expertise. *International Journal of Advertising* 29, no. 4: 527–46.

Ellen, P.S., D.J. Webb, and L.A. Mohr. 2006. Building corporate associations: Consumer attributions for corporate socially responsible programs. *Journal of the Academy of Marketing Science* 34 (Mar): 147–57.

Elving, W.J.L. 2013. Scepticism and corporate social responsibility communications: The influence of fit and reputation. *Journal of Marketing Communication* 19, no. 4: 277–92.

Folse, J.A.G., S.L. Grau, J.G. Moulard, and K. Pounders. 2014. Cause-related marketing: Factors promoting campaign evaluations. *Journal of Current Issues & Research in Advertising* 35, no. 1: 50–70.

Folse, J.A.G., R.W. Niedrich, and S.L. Grau. 2010. Cause-relating marketing: The effects of purchase quantity and firm donation amount on consumer inferences and participation intentions. *Journal of Retailing* 86, no. 4: 295–09.

Garrahan, M. 2016. Bono surveys a Red decade of 'conscious consumerism'. *Financial Times*, January 20.

Gorton, M., R. Angell, J. White, and Y.-S. Tseng. 2013. Understanding consumer responses to retailers' cause related voucher schemes. *European Journal of Marketing* 47, no. 11/12: 1931–53.

Gourville, J.T., and K.V. Rangan. 2004. Valuing the cause marketing relationship. *California Management Review* 47 (Fall): 38–57.

Grau, S.L., and J.A.G. Folse. 2007. Cause-related marketing (CRM):The influence of donation proximity and message-framing cues on the less-involved consumer. *Journal of Advertising* 36 (Winter): 19–33.

Guerreiro, J., P. Rita, and D. Trigueiros. 2015. Attention, emotions and cause-related marketing effectiveness. *European Journal of Marketing* 49, no. 11/12: 1728–50.

Guerreiro, J., P. Rita, and D. Trigueiros. 2016. A text mining-based review of cause-related marketing literature. *Journal of Business Ethics* 139 (Nov): 111–28.

Gupta, S., and J. Pirsch. 2006. The company-cause-customer fit decision in cause-related marketing. *Journal of Consumer Marketing* 23, no. 6: 314–26.

Gwinner, K.P., and J. Eaton. 1999. Building brand image through event sponsorship: The role of image transfer. *Journal of Advertising* 28 (Winter): 47–57.

He, H., W. Zhu, D. Gouran, and O. Kolo. 2016. Moral identity centrality and cause-related marketing: The moderating effects of brand social responsibility image and emotional brand attachment. *European Journal of Marketing* 50, no. 1/2: 236–59.

Hemat, H., and U. Yuksel. 2014. A critical review of corporate social responsibility practices from a marketing perspective: Is cause-related marketing really a 'Win-Win-Win' situation? In *Corporate social responsibility in the global business world*, eds. A.Y. Mermod and S.O. Idowu, 3–26. Berlin: Springer-Verlag.

Henderson, T., and N. Arora. 2010. Promoting brands across categories with a social cause: Implementing effective embedded premium programs. *Journal of Marketing* 74 (Nov): 41–60.

Hoek, J., and P. Gendall. 2008. An analysis of consumers' responses to cause related marketing. *Journal of Nonprofit & Public Sector Marketing* 20, no. 2: 283–97.

Holmes, J.H., and C.J. Kilbane. 1993. Cause-related marketing: Selected effects of price and charitable donations. *Journal of Nonprofit & Public Sector Marketing* 1, no. 4: 67–84.

Hovland, C.I., I.L. Janis, and H.H. Kelley. 1953. *Communication and persuasion: Psychological studies of opinion change*. New Haven: Yale University Press.

Human, D., and N.S. Terblanche. 2012. Who receives what? The influence of the donation magnitude and donation recipient in cause-related marketing. *Journal of Nonprofit & Public Sector Marketing* 24, no. 2: 141–60.

Hyllegard, K.H., R-N. Yan, J.P. Ogle, and J. Attmann. 2011. The influence of gender, social cause, charitable support, and message appeal on Gen Y's responses to cause-related marketing. *Journal of Marketing Management* 27 (Feb): 100–23.

Kahle, L.R., and P.M. Homer. 1985. Physical attractiveness of the celebrity endorser: A social adaptation perspective. *Journal of Consumer Research* 11 (Mar): 954–61.

Kim, J.-E., and K.K.P. Johnson. 2013. The impact of moral emotions on cause-related marketing campaigns: A cross-cultural examination. *Journal of Business Ethics* 112 (Jan): 79–90.

Kim, K., J.L. Hayes, J.A. Avant, and L.N. Reid. 2014. Trends in advertising research: A longitudinal analysis of leading advertising, marketing, and communication journals, 1980 to 2010. *Journal of Advertising* 43 (Fall): 296–16.

Kirmani, A., and B. Shiv. 1998. Effects of source congruity on brand attitudes and beliefs: The moderating role of issue-relevant elaboration. *Journal of Consumer Psychology* 7, no. 1: 25–47.

Kleber, J., A. Florack, and A. Chladek. 2016. How to present donations: The moderating role of numeracy in cause-related marketing. *Journal of Consumer Marketing* 33, no. 3: 153–61.

Ko, Y.J., K. Kim, C.L. Claussen, and T.H. Kim. 2008. The effects of sport involvement, sponsor awareness and corporate image on intention to purchase sponsors' products. *International Journal of Sports Marketing & Sponsorship* 9 (Jan): 79–94.

Koschate-Fischer, N., I.V. Huber, and W.D. Hoyer. 2016. When will price increases associated with company donations to charity be perceived as fair? *International Journal of Research in Marketing* 44 (Sep): 608–26.

Koschate-Fischer, N., I.V. Stefan, and W.D. Hoyer. 2012. Willingness to pay for cause-related marketing: The impact of donation amount and moderating effects. *Journal of Marketing Research* 49 (Dec): 910–27.

Kull, A.J., and T.B. Heath. 2016. You decide, we donate: Strengthening consumer–brand relationships through digitally co-created social responsibility. *International Journal of Research in Marketing* 33 (Mar): 78–92.

La Ferle, C., G. Kuber, and S.M. Edwards. 2013. Factors impacting responses to cause-related marketing in India and the United States: Novelty, altruistic motives, and company origin. *Journal of Business Research* 66 (Mar): 364–73.

Lafferty, B.A. 2007. The relevance of fit in a cause-brand alliance when consumers evaluate corporate credibility. *Journal of Business Research* 60, no. 5: 447–53.

Lafferty, B.A. 2009. Selecting the right cause partners for the right reasons: The role of importance and fit in cause–brand alliances. *Psychology & Marketing* 26 (Apr): 359–82.

Lafferty, B.A., and D.R. Edmondson. 2009. Portraying the cause instead of the brand in cause-related marketing Ads: Does it Really Matter? *Journal of Marketing Theory and Practice* 17 (Spring): 129–44.

Lafferty, B.A., and D.R. Edmondson. 2014. A note of the role of cause type in cause-related marketing. *Journal of Business Research* 67 (July): 1455–60.

Lafferty, B.A., and R.E. Goldsmith. 2005. Cause–brand alliances: Does the cause help the brand or does the brand help the cause? *Journal of Business Research* 58 (Apr): 423–29.

Lafferty, B.A., R.E. Goldsmith, G. Thomas, and M. Hult. 2004. The impact of the alliance on the partners: A look at cause-brand alliances. *Psychology & Marketing* 21 (July): 509–31.

Lafferty, B.A., A.K. Lueth, and R. McCafferty. 2016. An evolutionary process model of cause-related marketing and systematic review of the empirical literature. *Psychology & Marketing* 33 (Nov): 951–70.

Lee, J.-G., and E. Thorson. 2008. The impact of celebrity-product incongruence on the effectiveness of product endorsement. *Journal of Advertising Research* 48 (Sep): 433–49.

Lii, Y-S., and M. Lee. 2012. Doing right leads to doing well: When the type of CSR and reputation interact to affect consumer evaluations of the firm. *Journal of Business Ethics* 105 (Jan): 69–81.

Liston-Heyes, C., and G. Liu. 2013. A study of non-profit organisations in cause-related marketing: Stakeholder concerns and safeguarding strategies. *European Journal of Marketing* 47, no. 11/12: 1954–74.

Liu, G. 2013. Impacts of instrumental versus relational centered logic on cause-related marketing decision making. *Journal of Business Ethics* 113 (Mar): 243–63.

Liu, G., and W.-W. Ko. 2011. An analysis of cause-related marketing implementation strategies through social alliance: Partnership conditions and strategies objectives. *Journal of Business Ethics* 100 (May): 253–81.

Liu, G., C. Liston-Heyes, and W-W. Ko. 2010. Employee participation in cause-related marketing strategies: A study of management perceptions from British consumer service industries. *Journal of Business Ethics* 92 (Mar): 195–210.

Mazodier, M., and D. Merunka. 2012. Achieving brand loyalty through sponsorship: The role of fit and self-congruity. *Journal of the Academy of Marketing Science* 40 (Nov): 807–20.

McGuire, W.J. 1969. The nature of attitudes and attitude change. In *Handbook of Social Psychology*, 2nd ed., eds. G. Lindzey and E. Aronson, 136–314. Reading, MA: Addison-Wesley.

Müller, S.S., A.J. Fries, and K. Gedenk. 2014. How much to give? The effect of donation size on tactical and strategic success in cause-related marketing. *International Journal of Research in Marketing* 31 (June): 178–91.

Nan, X., and K. Heo. 2007. Consumer responses to corporate social responsibility (CSR) initiatives. *Journal of Advertising* 36 (Summer): 63–74.

Neijens, P., E. Smit, and M. Moorman. 2009. Taking up an event: Brand image transfer during the FIFA world cup. *International Journal of Market Research* 51, no. 5: 579–91.

Norris, C.E., and A.M. Colman. 1992. Context effects on recall and recognition of magazine advertisements. *Journal of Advertising* 21 (Sep): 37–46.

Olsen, G.D., J.W. Pracejus, and N.R. Brown. 2003. When profit equals price: Consumer confusion about donation amounts in cause-related marketing. *Journal of Public Policy & Marketing* 22 (Fall): 170–80.

Peloza, J., and J. Shang. 2011. How can corporate social responsibility activities create value for stakeholders? A systematic review. *Journal of the Academy of Marketing Science* 39 (Feb): 117–35.

Petty, R.E., J.T. Cacioppo, and D. Schumann. 1983. Central and peripheral routes to advertising effectiveness: The moderating role of involvement. *Journal of Consumer Research* 10 (Sep): 135–46.

Posavac, S.S., F.R. Kardes, D.M. Sanbonmatsu, and G.J. Fitzsimons. 2005. Blissful insularity: When brands are judged in isolation from competitors. *Marketing Letters* 16 (Apr): 87–97.

Posavac, S.S., D.M. Sanbonmatsu, F.R. Kardes, and G.J. Fitzsimons. 2004. The brand positivity effect: When evaluation confers preference. *Journal of Consumer Research* 31 (Dec): 643–51.

Pracejus, J.W., G. Douglas Olsen, and N.R. Brown. 2003. On the prevalence and impact of vague quantifiers in the advertising of cause-related marketing (CRM). *Journal of Advertising* 32 (Winter): 19–28.

Rice, D.H., K. Kelting, and R.J. Lutz. 2012. Multiple endorsers and multiple endorsements: The influence of message repetition, source congruence and involvement on brand attitudes. *Journal of Consumer Psychology* 22 (Apr): 249–59.

Robinson, S.R., C. Irmak, and S. Jayachandran. 2012. Choice of cause in cause-related marketing. *Journal of Marketing* 76 (July): 126–39.

Ross, J.K., III, L.T. Patterson, and M.A. Stutts. 1992. Consumer perceptions of organizations that use cause-related marketing. *Journal of the Academy of Marketing Science* 20 (Winter): 93–7.

Rossiter, J.R., and L. Percy. 2017. Methodological guidelines for advertising research. *Journal of Advertising* 46, no. 1: 71–82.

Rossiter, J.R., L. Percy, and L. Bergkvist. 2018. *Marketing communications: Objectives, strategy, tactics.* London: SAGE.

Runté, M., D.Z. Basil, and S. Deshpande. 2009. Cause–related marketing from the nonprofit's perspective: Classifying goals and experienced outcomes. *Journal of Nonprofit & Public Sector Marketing* 21, no. 3: 255–70.

Samu, S., and W. Wymer. 2009. The effect of fit and dominance in cause marketing communications. *Journal of Business Research* 62 (Apr): 432–40.

Samu, S., and W. Wymer. 2014. Cause marketing communications: Consumer inference on attitudes towards brand and cause. *European Journal of Marketing* 48, no. 7/8: 1333–53.

Sanbonmatsu, D.M., S.S. Posavac, F.R. Kardes, and S.P. Mantel. 1998. Selective hypothesis testing. *Psychonomic Bulletin & Review* 5 (June): 197–20.

Strahilevitz, M. 1999. The effects of product type and donation magnitude on willingness to pay more for a charity-linked brand. *Journal of Consumer Psychology* 8, no. 3: 215–41.

Strahilevitz, M., and J.G. Myers. 1998. Donations to charity as purchase incentives: How well they work may depend on what you are trying to sell. *Journal of Consumer Research* 24 (Mar): 434–46.

Tangari, A.H., J.A.G. Folse, S. Burton, and J. Kees. 2010. The moderating influence of consumers' temporal orientation on the framing of societal needs and corporate responses in cause-related marketing campaigns. *Journal of Advertising* 39 (Summer): 35–50.

van den Brink, D., G. Odekerken-Schröder, and P. Pauwels. 2006. The effect of strategic and tactical cause-related marketing on consumers' brand loyalty. *Journal of Consumer Marketing* 23, no. 1: 15–25.

Vanhamme, J., A. Lindgreen, J. Reast, and Nv. Popering. 2012. To do well by doing good: Improving corporate image through cause-related marketing. *Journal of Business Ethics* 109 (Sep): 259–74.

Varadarajan, P.R., and A. Menon. 1988. Cause-related marketing: A coalignment of marketing strategy and corporate philanthropy. *Journal of Marketing* 52 (July): 58–74.

Vilela, A.M., and M.R. Nelson. 2016. Testing the selectivity hypothesis in cause-related marketing among generation Y: [When] Does gender matter for short- and long-term persuasion? *Journal of Marketing Communications* 22(Feb): 18–35.

Vock, M., W. van Dolen, and A. Kolk. 2013. Changing behaviour through business-nonprofit collaboration? Consumer responses to social alliances. *European Journal of Marketing* 47, no. 9: 1476–503.

Wells, W.D. 2001. The perils of $N = 1$. *Journal of Consumer Research* 28 (Dec): 494–98.

Westberg, K., and N. Pope. 2014. Building brand equity with cause-related marketing: A comparison with sponsorship and sales promotion. *Journal of Marketing Communications* 20, no. 6: 419–37.

Winterich, K.P., and M.J. Barone. 2011. Warm glow or cold, hard cash? Social identity effects on consumer choice for donation versus discount promotions. *Journal of Marketing Research* 48 (Oct): 855–68.

Yechiam, E., G. Barron, I. Erev, and M. Erez. 2006. On the robustness and the direction of the effect of cause-related marketing. *Journal of Consumer Behaviour* 2 (June): 320–32.

Youn, S., and H. Kim. 2018. Temporal duration and attribution process of cause-related marketing: Moderating roles of self-construal and product involvement. *International Journal of Advertising* 37, no. 2: 217–35.

Zemack-Rugar, Y., R. Rabino, L.A. Cavanaugh, and G.J. Fitzsimons. 2016. When donating is liberating: The role of product and consumer characteristics in the appeal of cause-related products. *Journal of Consumer Psychology* 26 (Apr): 213–30.

Talking about CSR matters: employees' perception of and reaction to their company's CSR communication in four different CSR domains

Sarah Desirée Schaefer ⓘ, Ralf Terlutter ⓘ and Sandra Diehl ⓘ

ABSTRACT

Drawing on signaling and social identity theories, we analyze how liking of the company's CSR advertisements, message credibility, and cause-company fit influence employees' evaluation of their organization's CSR engagement and how this relates to employees' job satisfaction, organizational pride, and word-of-mouth about CSR. CSR is analyzed in four different domains: customer-oriented, employee-oriented, environment-oriented, and philanthropy-oriented CSR. Results of a study with the employees ($n = 432$) of a large European energy provider reveal that the cause-company fit of CSR engagement has the highest impact on evaluation of the CSR engagement in all CSR domains. Message credibility is important for the evaluation of CSR in the customer-oriented, environment-oriented, and philanthropy-oriented domains, while, noticeably, ad liking only shows an impact in the employee-oriented domain. CSR evaluation influences job satisfaction, organizational pride, and word-of-mouth in all four CSR domains, with some domain-related differences. Implications for CSR advertising, directions for future research and limitations are discussed.

Introduction

Corporate social responsibility (CSR), understood as companies' policies and practices that go beyond legal requirements and impact different stakeholder groups, has evolved into a business imperative worldwide (Du, Bhattacharya, and Sen 2015; Hopkins 2016). A basic belief underlying this sea change in corporate action and thinking is that if done well, CSR policies and practices can generate several benefits to companies (Dhanesh 2014; Carvalho et al. 2010). Some scholars even argue that CSR policies and practices can be considered as a key stakeholder relationship management instrument (Bhattacharya, Korschun, and Sen 2009).

While previous research has mainly focussed on CSR in relation to external stakeholders, especially customers (Du, Bhattacharya, and Sen 2010; Suh 2016), there has been an increasing interest in CSR related to internal stakeholders such as incumbent employees. Research on CSR and its impact on employees includes issues such as employee performance and cost (Sun and Yu 2015), employee engagement (May, Gilson, and Harter 2004, Chaudhary 2017, Rupp et al. 2018), CSR as an internal marketing strategy (Bhattacharya, Sen, and Korschun 2007) and also employees' reactions to CSR from an organizational justice perspective (Rupp et al. 2006). Previous research has also shown that positive effects on job-related outcomes such as job satisfaction, organizational pride, or positive word-of-mouth (WOM) about the organizational CSR engagement, can be expected when employees recognize their employer's engagement regarding CSR (Collier and Esteban 2007; Jones 2010; Suh 2016). However, an area which is clearly under-researched is the role played by a company's CSR communication and advertising in employees' evaluation of company CSR and how this impacts employees' work-related behaviours. Companies often actively communicate their CSR activities to their external and internal stakeholders. For instance, many companies include CSR activities in their annual reports and in newsletters, or refer to CSR activities in their advertising, for example in TV and radio advertising, and on the company website (Brunton, Eweje, and Taskin 2017). Many of these advertising activities also reach employees, even when other stakeholders may be the primary target groups of the company's advertising engagement. Employees are not only an internal stakeholder target group of CSR communication, they are also the face of their respective company and play a crucial role in shaping external stakeholders' perception and evaluation of the company's CSR (Collier and Esteban 2007; McShane and Cunningham 2012). Hence, knowing how employees evaluate the company's CSR advertising is important for any company (Vlachos, Panagopoulos, and Rapp 2014). Answering to recent calls for more research in this field (e.g., Dhanesh 2014; Crane and Glozer 2016; Suh 2016; Duthler and Dhanesh 2018; Taylor 2018), we address this important topic and investigate how a company's CSR advertising affects employees' evaluation of organizational CSR engagement and in turn how this impacts employee reactions.

CSR policies and practices can focus on many different aspects, which can be structured into four core domains: (1) *customer-oriented*, (2) *employee-oriented*, (3) *environment-oriented*, and (4) *philanthropy-oriented* activities (Farooq, Farooq, and Jasimuddin 2014). Research that examines the impact of different CSR domains on the relationship between CSR and employees' attitudes and behavioural intentions is scarce. There are numerous calls for a finer-grained understanding of the effects of different CSR practices (Ailawadi et al. 2014; Roeck et al. 2014; Rupp et al. 2015; Taylor 2018; Schaefer, Terlutter, and Diehl 2019).

This article contributes to the literature in several ways: Drawing from signaling theory and social identity theory, we develop and empirically test a model which explains the influence of a company's CSR advertising on favourable employee reactions. Unlike most previous research, which has primarily focussed on external stakeholders (in particular customers), we focus on employees. In this way, we address the need for

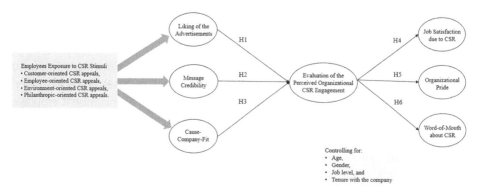

Figure 1. Conceptual model of the effects of CSR communication on employees.

enhanced research that sheds light on how this particular stakeholder group evaluates and subsequently responds to instances of CSR engagement (Aguinis and Glavas 2012; McShane and Cunningham 2012; Roeck et al. 2014; Rupp et al. 2015). By including the four domains of CSR engagement according to Farooq, Farooq, and Jasimuddin (2014) as moderators of the model relationships, we respond to the above-mentioned research gap in an attempt to gain a better understanding of the antecedents and effects of different CSR practices (Ailawadi et al. 2014; Roeck et al. 2014; Rupp et al. 2015; Taylor 2018). Thus, the study addresses recent calls for more research on CSR advertising, especially research into which types of CSR appeals work and whether there are differences in the effectiveness of these appeals (Taylor 2018; Schaefer et al. 2019).

Theoretical background: conceptual framework and hypotheses development

Figure 1 depicts our conceptual model. It investigates how employees' liking of company CSR advertisements, message credibility, and cause-company fit relate to employees' evaluation of the perceived organizational CSR engagement and how this relates to employees' attitudes and behavior at the workplace (specifically job satisfaction, organizational pride, and WOM). The four CSR domains according to Farooq, Farooq, and Jasimuddin (2014) are integrated as moderators in the model. Gender, age, tenure with the company, and job level are included as control variables.

We build our conceptual framework on insights from two theoretical domains: Signaling theory (Rynes 1991) and social identity theory (Ashforth and Mael 1989).

Signaling theory is especially useful for describing evaluation-making processes when two parties (e.g., employees and companies) have access to different information and thus face information asymmetry (Connelly et al. 2011). Drawing from signaling theory, there might be information asymmetry between the company itself and its employees regarding the company's CSR activities. The sender (e.g., the company) chooses whether and how to communicate information (e.g., about its CSR engagement) and the receiver (e.g., the employee) has to interpret the signal. Organizational CSR communication conveys signals about the company's organizational CSR engagement, for example, about the causes selected for or resources devoted to CSR. The signals are interpreted by the employee (the receiver), but not every employee has access to the same quality and quantity of CSR-related information, for instance because employees operate at different management levels or simply because they differ in their willingness to engage in CSR information or in their initiative in collecting firsthand information. Organizational communication material about company CSR engagement includes annual CSR reports or CSR advertisements. These are available to the general public and also to every employee. Hence, we suppose that CSR communication plays an important role as a signal in the employees' CSR evaluation-making process.

Social identity theory (Ashforth and Mael 1989) suggests that people classify themselves into social categories based on various factors, such as the company they work for, and that membership in these social categories influences an individual's self-concept. Applied to the CSR-evaluation-outcome context, employees seek to identify with the company they are working for. This implies that they are likely to experience the company's successes and failures as their own and will adopt attitudes and engage in behaviours that may help the company achieve its goals. Hence, social identity theory suggests that employees' evaluation of the perceived organizational CSR engagement can positively influence important job outcomes, such as employees' job satisfaction due to their company's CSR, their organizational pride, and their WOM about CSR. In the following, the model relationships will be discussed in more detail.

Company's CSR communication as a basis for employees' CSR evaluation

As stated in previous research (Du, Bhattacharya, and Sen 2010; Suh 2016), communication is critical in influencing employees' evaluations and responses to CSR efforts. The reason for this is that communication provides information about what was done and the aims behind organizational CSR efforts (Suh 2016).

Companies usually communicate their CSR efforts actively to their shareholders, stakeholders and the public (Brunton, Eweje, and Taskin 2017), for instance by issuing annual reports, or through conventional advertising, for example, on their website, on TV, or in print media (Dawkins 2005; Du, Bhattacharya, and Sen 2010). Since not every employee is involved in and/or aware of ongoing CSR initiatives, communication about these initiatives is important.

As outlined above, according to signaling theory (Connelly et al. 2011), employees might face information asymmetry when they have to evaluate the perceived organizational CSR engagement on the basis of the company's CSR communication advertisements. Hence, they may interpret the company's CSR advertisements as signals and may evaluate them (i) affectively (liking of the advertising stimuli) and (ii) cognitively (perceived message credibility). In addition, (iii) the perceived fit between the advertised CSR initiatives and the company (cause-company fit) has also been demonstrated to play an important role in CSR evaluation (Seok Sohn, Han, and Lee 2012; Zasuwa 2017).

The affective liking of CSR advertisements is one important driver for employees to evaluate the perceived organizational CSR engagement. For consumers, Diehl, Terlutter, and Mueller (2016) showed that the affective evaluation of advertising incorporating a CSR appeal led to more positive evaluations of the product as well as to a higher perceived social responsibility of the company. Another study conducted by del Mar García-De los Salmones and Perez (2018), which analyzed the effectiveness of

CSR advertising in the financial sector, also suggested that the more favourable the affective evaluation of CSR advertisements, the more favourable was the evaluation of the company. Thus, we assume:

> **Hypothesis H1:** The more a company's employees like their company's CSR advertisements, the more favourably will the employees evaluate their company's CSR engagement.

Message credibility, which can be considered as a primarily cognitive evaluation, can be defined as the degree to which a receiver perceives a message to be accurate, believable, trustworthy, and unbiased (Flanagin and Metzger 2000, 2007). The importance of perceived trustworthiness in order to legitimate the company as a socially responsible organization and to strengthen the company's reputation for doing good has been emphasized in several studies (Du, Bhattacharya, and Sen 2010; Pérez and Rodríguez del Bosque 2015). Additionally, the meta-analysis conducted by Eisend and Tarrahi (2016) corroborates the importance of message credibility with regard to the effectiveness of advertising/persuasion attempts. Thus, the perception of the message as believable and trustworthy can be considered as a crucial antecedent influencing employees' evaluation of their companýs CSR engagement. Therefore, we hypothesize:

> **Hypothesis H2:** Higher perceived message credibility will positively influence employees´ evaluation of their company's CSR engagement.

A further aspect of CSR communication that is likely to influence employees' evaluation of the organizational CSR engagement is cause-company fit (Kim, Cheong, and Lim 2015). Cause-company fit refers to the perceived congruence between the company's core business and the specific CSR issues which are being communicated (Du, Bhattacharya, and Sen 2010). Previous research on consumers revealed that a better cause-company fit led to improved consumer evaluations of the company associated with the funding (e.g. Becker-Olsen, Cudmore, and Hill 2006). Especially for employees, the perceived cause-company fit might be a crucial antecedent and signal for the evaluation of their company's CSR engagement since they are familiar with the prevailing business practices and how they align with environmental, organizational, or societal needs. Consequently, perceived cause-company fit might be an important factor in ensuring employees' positive perception of their company's CSR engagement (Lee, Park, and Lee 2013). Accordingly, we posit:

> **Hypothesis H3:** A higher perceived cause-company fit of the CSR engagement will positively influence employees´ evaluation of their company's CSR engagement.

Impact of employees' CSR evaluations on job satisfaction, pride, and WOM

Social identity theory suggests that employees have a desire to identify with their company due to its respectable image (Ashforth and Mael 1989) and that the company's CSR activities contribute to such an image. Hence, it is very likely that the positive evaluations of their company that result from its CSR engagement prompt employees to feel good and proud to belong to a socially well-regarded company (Collier and Esteban 2007; Jones 2010; Suh 2016).

Various studies have been conducted which reveal that CSR indeed has a positive influence on employees' attitudes and behavior at the workplace, such as job satisfaction (e.g. Valentine and Fleischman 2007; Lee, Park, and Lee 2013; Dhanesh 2014; Roeck et al. 2014; Du, Bhattacharya, and Sen 2015; Suh 2016; Aguinis and Glavas 2017) and organizational pride (e.g., Jones 2010). Job satisfaction can be defined as "a pleasurable or positive emotional state resulting from the appraisal of one's job or job experience" (Locke 1991, 1300). Moreover, job satisfaction is a focal construct in research because it can be considered as a strong predictor of employee-relevant behavior, such as absenteeism and job performance (Roeck et al. 2014). Previous research suggests that employees experienced greater job satisfaction when they considered their employer to be ethical (Roeck et al. 2014). It can be expected that organizational CSR engagement reflects desired ethical standards and business practices, which in turn stimulates employees to feel good and satisfied to be able to work for the company. Therefore, we hypothesize:

Hypothesis H4: A more favourable evaluation of the company's CSR engagement leads to greater employee job satisfaction due to the organizational CSR engagement.

Organizational pride can be defined as the extent to which employees experience a sense of pleasure and self-respect resulting from their organizational membership (Jones 2010). Positive perceptions of their company's CSR engagement are likely to lead not only to higher job satisfaction, but also to prompt employees to feel greater organizational pride in being a member of the company (Ashforth and Mael 1989). If the company takes social responsibility, the employees as members of the company are expected to be prouder of the organization they are working for and they identify with. Hence, and according to social identity theory, we posit:

Hypothesis H5: A more favourable evaluation of their company's CSR engagement leads to greater organizational pride on the part of the employees.

Another favourable employee behavior on which we focus in this study is WOM. Favourable WOM can be considered as a key behavioural outcome of positive organizational CSR engagement (Bhattacharya and Sen 2004). WOM is related to employees' willingness (intentions or behavior) to talk positively about their socially responsible company (e.g. to family, colleagues, and friends). We thus hypothesize:

Hypothesis H6: A more favourable evaluation of their company's CSR engagement leads to greater expressions of positive word-of-mouth about the organizational CSR engagement by employees.

Effects of different CSR domains

In this research, four core domains of CSR are investigated (Farooq, Farooq, and Jasimuddin 2014):

1. *Customer-oriented CSR* is the responsibility of a company towards its customers, for example, through ensuring product safety beyond the legal stipulations and customer care.

2. *Employee-oriented CSR* corresponds to a company's initiatives that ensure the wel-
    fare of its employees, for example, through organizational justice as well as career
    opportunities.
3. *Environment-oriented CSR* represents a company's responsibilities towards the nat-
    ural environment, for example, through protection of natural resources
    and animals.
4. *Philanthropy-oriented CSR* signifies the responsibility demonstrated by a company
    towards society, for example, through contributions to education or sports.

Research on the effects of different CSR domains is still scarce. Studies on customers (Du, Bhattacharya, and Sen 2007; Ailawadi et al. 2014) demonstrated that CSR
engagement in the different domains affected consumers' CSR attitudes and behavior
differently. We would like to contribute to this important research stream by investigating the effects of the four CSR domains on employees. Hence, we formulate the
following research question:

> **RQ1:** Do the effects of CSR communication on employees differ depending on the CSR
> domain (customer-oriented, employee-oriented, environment-oriented, philanthropy-
> oriented CSR)?

Research design and method

A cross-departmental investigation was carried out with the employees of a large
Western European energy provider in order to test the assumptions on which the
model is based. The energy industry was chosen because it represents a major sector
of the European economy. This sector is currently facing several challenges due to the
EU 2020 climate and energy package (Jellinek 2015) and CSR activities are very common in the energy sector.

Stimulus development

We developed four collages, one collage for each CSR domain. (See the Appendix for
an example (Figure A1) and Figure A2 for the translation of Figure A1.) In an attempt
to illustrate the company's CSR engagement in each domain in a more comprehensive
way, each collage comprised three CSR advertisements that were taken from the
company's current annual CSR report. The annual CSR report is available for employees on the intranet as well as on the company's website and it is widely distributed
by the company to various stakeholders. The collages were in colour and in the
German language.

CSR advertisements which incorporated customer-oriented CSR appeals included
clean energy as well as energy-saving issues, and also electro mobility. CSR advertisements which incorporated employee-oriented CSR appeals spotlighted family-friendly
human resources management, occupational health, and on-the-job training initiatives
which go beyond legal requirements. CSR advertisements which incorporated environment-oriented CSR appeals addressed an alternative energy source, an animal welfare
action, and an energy efficiency campaign. CSR advertisements which incorporated

philanthropy-oriented CSR appeals focussed on a charity project for people with low incomes regarding power saving, student grants, and employment in the region.

Pretest and manipulation check

The four collages underwent comprehensive pretesting. The objectives of the pretest were to determine (i) the suitability of the visual and textual advertisements' material, (ii) the advertisements' clarity, (iii) the advertisements' comprehensibility, (iv) the association of the employed advertisements with the corresponding CSR domain, (v) whether subjects had a clear understanding of the four CSR domains, and (vi) the processing time needed to grasp the idea of the collages. A total of 15 master students' (male/female: 5/10, average age: 24.2 years) participated in the pretest. Results indicated that both the visual and the textual material featured in the advertisements were regarded as appropriate and suitable. Moreover, neither picture quality nor information quality differed notably between the four appeals. Further, the wordings employed in the advertisements were clear and unambiguous, and the four collages were perceived as realistic. Additionally, message comprehension for all four collages was high. None of the students mentioned any difficulties with understanding the collages and their messages. The manipulation check of the four ad appeals was successful: Participants classified all four appeals correctly in the intended domain and perceived the four CSR domains as clearly different.

Data collection and sample

The main investigation employed a sample comprising 432 employees of a large Western European energy provider. The investigation was announced to all company employees by the CEO and an invitation containing a link to the survey website was sent out via email. Subjects took part during working hours, participation was voluntary, and no additional incentives to encourage participation were offered. Participants were assured of anonymity in order to reduce evaluation anxiety as well as social desirability bias. In addition, it was emphasized that data would be stored on an external server with no access by the company itself. Subjects were randomly assigned to one of the four collages and asked to complete the online survey. Of the 1,434 employees with online access, a total of 467 employees filled out the online questionnaire (response rate of 32.6%). After eliminating individual responses which had too many missing values, we arrived at the final sample of 432 employees (customer-oriented CSR collage: 110; employee-oriented CSR collage: 110; environment-oriented CSR collage: 107; and philanthropy-oriented CSR collage: 105).

The sample is comprised of 74.3% males and 25.7% females, which represents the distribution between the sexes at the company. 42.4% of the subjects are younger than 35, 48.4% are between 35 and 55 years, and 9.2% are older than 55, which is also representative of the age distribution within the company. 53.9% of the employees have been working for the energy provider for more than 10 years. In accordance with anonymity guidelines, we had to cluster the professions into engineering (31.9%), sales/marketing (8.6%), supporting services (accounting, human resources, IT etc.: 40.7%), and others (18.8%).

Operationalization and measurement model

We used items from established measures, which were adapted to the context at hand (Table 1). All items are measured on seven-point Likert-type scales. In addition, gender, age, tenure with the company, and job level were included as control variables in order to rule out other possible explanations for significant relationships. Recent research has shown that sociodemographic characteristics are likely to impact the value employees place on CSR (Ashforth, Harrison, and Corley 2008; Rupp et al. 2013; 2018) and for this reason may affect employees' perception and evaluation of the organizational CSR engagement. The survey was designed in English, later translated into German, and subsequently translated back into English by two professional translators. The questionnaire was also pretested for comprehensibility and adequate length ($n = 4$, two persons working in academia and two persons from outside academia), and no concerns were raised by the subjects. In addition, the questionnaire was also pretested by representatives of the top management and the communication department of the company.

In order to assess the measurement model, we conducted a confirmatory factor analysis (CFA) for the whole dataset and a multi-group CFA for the four CSR domains using IBM SPSS AMOS Version 25. Results reveal that our measurement models show an acceptable model fit (single-group: $\chi^2/df = 3.172$; CFI $= .955$; RMSEA $= .071$; multi-group model: $\chi^2/df = 1.784$; CFI $= .939$; RMSEA $= .043$). We assessed convergent validity of the measurement models by the average variance extracted (AVE). All indicators load significantly on their hypothesized latent construct and AVE for each construct exceeds the suggested threshold of .50. Moreover, AVE for each construct is greater than the square of any inter-construct correlation, demonstrating discriminant validity of the measurement model (Fornell and Larcker 1981). Results for the composite reliability and the indicator reliability exceed the suggested threshold of 0.6 (composite reliability) and 0.4 (indicator reliability). Overall, our measurement models fulfill the psychometric property requirements (Table 2).

In order to test whether our findings might be susceptible to common method variance (Chang, van Witteloostuijn, and Eden 2010), we applied the CFA marker variable technique, with employees' educational background as the marker variable. Employees' educational background was chosen since, as required by the literature, it is extraneous to our conceptual model. The common-method-adjusted correlations between the key variables of this study were not significantly different from the unadjusted correlations ($p < 0.05$), suggesting that common method variance did not present a problem in our study. Additionally, common method variance is less likely to occur for the complex relationships that we have in the current study (Williams, Hartman, and Cavazotte 2010). Moreover, we assured subjects of anonymity and confidentiality and stressed that there were no right or wrong answers to the questions.

We also evaluated the degree of multicollinearity among independent variables following the recommendations from Grewal, Cote, and Baumgartner (2004). Since all

Table 1. Key construct items and α.

Construct	Items	α
Liking of the Ads (Diehl, Terlutter, and Mueller 2016)	The ads of the organizational CSR engagement are likeable. The ads of the organizational CSR engagement are pleasant.	0.91
Message Credibility (Flanagin and Metzger 2000, 2007)	The messages of the organizational CSR engagement are believable. The messages of the organizational CSR engagement are not biased.	0.76
Cause-Company Fit (Berens, van Riel, and van Bruggen 2005; Nan and Heo 2007)	I think that the initiatives described in the messages represent a good match between (company) and cause. I think that the engagement described in the messages is appropriate for (company).	0.85
Evaluation of Perc. Organizational CSR Engagement (Valentine and Fleischman 2007)	I work for a socially responsible (company) that services the greater community. (Company) gives time, money, and other resources to socially responsible causes. Overall, I evaluate the organizational CSR engagement of (company) as … *	0.88
Job Satisfaction due to CSR (Valentine and Fleischman 2007)	I am satisfied with my job due to the organizational CSR engagement. I like working at (company) due to the organizational CSR engagement.	0.86
Organizational Pride (Jones 2010)	I am proud to work for (company). I am proud to be associated with (company).	0.91
Word-of-Mouth about CSR (Arnett, German, and Hunt 2003)	I bring up the organizational CSR engagement of (company) in a positive way in conversations I have with friends and acquaintances. I often speak favourably about the organizational CSR engagement of (company) in social situations.	0.75

Note. (company) = replaced by the name of the energy provider. α = Cronbach's Alpha. All scales ranged from 1 = "Strongly disagree" to 7 = "Strongly agree".
*Scale ranged from 1 = "Not good at all" to 7 = "Very good".

bivariate correlations are smaller than 0.9, variance inflation factors are smaller than 10 (in this study between 1.82 and 1.85), the Fornell and Larcker (1981) criterion indicates discriminant validity, and tolerance values are greater than 0.1 (in this study between .54 and .55), the existence of any severe multicollinearity is thus unlikely.

Results

Hypotheses were tested simultaneously with a structural equation model with IBM SPSS AMOS Version 25. In a next step, we calculated multi-group structural equation models to assess the impact of the four CSR domains on the outlined model, while controlling for gender, age, tenure with the company, and job level (for details see Table A1 in the Appendix). In order to test whether the strengths of the relationships between the variables in the outlined model varied significantly between the four CSR domains, structural invariance models were carried out and compared using pairwise (CSR domain by CSR domain) χ^2-difference tests.

Table 3 reveals the results of the structural equation models tested in the total sample and on the multi-group level. The proposed models could be largely confirmed by the data. Global fit indices indicate that the base and the multi-group

Table 2. Descriptives, CR, AVE, and Squared Inter-Construct Correlations.

Construct	M	SD	CR	AVE	1	2	3	4	5	6	7
1. Liking of the ads	5.44	1.28	.91	.83	1						
2. Message credibility	5.24	1.12	.86	.75	.36	1					
3. Cause-Company Fit	5.71	1.07	.85	.75	.32	.38	1				
4. Evaluation of perceived CSR	5.20	1.06	.81	.69	.21	.33	38	1			
5. Job satisfaction	4.60	1.39	.87	.76	.04	.20	.15	.23	1		
6. Organizational pride	6.06	1.12	.91	.83	.10	.09	.18	.29	.07	1	
7. Word-of-Mouth	5.74	1.16	.76	.61	.14	.08	.15	.18	.09	.40	1

Note. M = Mean. SD = Standard Deviation. CR = Composite Reliability. AVE = Average Variance Extracted. N = 432.

model have an acceptable fit (total sample: $\chi^2/df = 3.611$; CFI = .938; RMSEA = .078; multi-group model: $\chi^2/df = 1.873$; CFI = .921; RMSEA = .045).

Hypothesis H1 predicted that the more the employees liked the CSR advertisements, the more positive their evaluation of the perceived CSR engagement would be. The standardized path coefficient (γ) was .089 ($p > 0.10$), thus H1 was not confirmed for the whole dataset. On the multi-group level, γ ranked between $-.189$ and $+.250$ and, noticeably, for the employee-oriented CSR domain the relationship was significant, at least at $p < 0.10$. Pairwise χ^2-difference tests revealed that the γ in the employee-oriented CSR domain was different from the philanthropy-oriented CSR domain ($\Delta \chi^2 = 3.8$, $\Delta df = 1$, $p < 0.10$). On the multi-group level, H1 was rejected for the customer-oriented, the environment-oriented and the philanthropy-oriented CSR domains, while it was largely confirmed for the employee-oriented CSR domain.

Hypothesis H2 postulated that a higher perceived message credibility would positively influence employees' evaluation of the perceived CSR engagement of their company. Results confirmed this hypothesis in the whole dataset ($\gamma = .273$, $p < 0.01$). On the multi-group level, γ ranked between .089 and .345, and, apart from the employee-oriented CSR domain, all path coefficients were significant. In this relationship, pairwise χ^2-difference tests showed that the γ in the employee-oriented CSR domain was significantly lower than in the customer-oriented CSR domain ($\Delta\chi^2 = 3.5$, $\Delta df = 1$, $p < 0.10$) and in the philanthropy-oriented CSR domain ($\Delta\chi^2 = 4.8$, $\Delta df = 1$, $p < 0.05$). In addition, in the philanthropy-oriented CSR domain, γ was significantly stronger than in the environment-oriented CSR domain ($\Delta\chi^2 = 3.3$, $\Delta df = 1$, $p < 0.10$). On the multi-group level, H2 was rejected for the employee-oriented CSR domain, while it was confirmed for the customer-oriented, the environment-oriented and the philanthropy-oriented CSR domains.

Hypothesis H3, which predicted that a higher cause-company fit of the CSR engagement would positively influence employees' evaluation of the perceived CSR engagement of their company, was also confirmed by the data ($\gamma = .580$ in the whole dataset, $p < 0.01$). On the multi-group level, γ was significant for all domains and ranked between .442 and .878. χ^2 –difference tests indicated that the γ in the philanthropy-oriented CSR domain was significantly stronger than in the employee-oriented CSR domain ($\Delta\chi^2 = 4.7$, $\Delta df = 1$, $p < 0.05$), and also stronger than in the customer-oriented CSR domain ($\Delta\chi^2 = 3.5$, $\Delta df = 1$, $p < 0.10$), and in the environment-oriented domain ($\Delta\chi^2 = 6.0$, $\Delta df = 1$, $p < 0.05$). H3 was confirmed for all CSR domains.

Hypothesis H4, which assumed that a more favourable evaluation of the perceived CSR engagement of the company would positively influence employees' job

Table 3. Results from the structural equation models.

Path	Hypothesis	CSR (Domain)				
		Customer-oriented	Employee-oriented	Environ.-oriented	Philant.-oriented	Total Sample
Liking of the ads → Evaluation of perceived CSR	H1	.090	.250*	−.043	−.189	.089
Message credibility → Evaluation of perceived CSR	H2	.345***	.089	.259**	.333***	.273***
Cause-Company Fit → Evaluation of perceived CSR	H3	.442***	.568***	.579***	.878***	.580***
Evaluation of perceived CSR → Job satisfaction due to CSR	H4	.606***	.555***	.620***	.796***	.632***
Evaluation of perceived CSR → Organizational pride	H5	.441***	.613***	.672***	.419***	.541***
Evaluation of perceived CSR → Word-of-Mouth about CSR	H6	.499***	.576***	.611***	.559***	.593***
Model fit		χ^2 / df	CFI			RMSEA
Base model		3.611	.938			.078
Multi-group model		1.873	.921			.045

***$p < 0.01$
**$p < 0.05$
*$p < 0.10$.

satisfaction due to organizational CSR engagement, received strong support from the data ($\gamma = .632$ in the whole dataset, $p < 0.01$). On the multi-group level, γ was significant for all domains and ranked between .555 and .796. χ^2-difference tests revealed no differences between the domains. H4 received support for all CSR domains.

Hypothesis H5 predicted that a more favourable evaluation of the perceived CSR engagement of the company would positively influence employees' organizational pride. Results confirmed this hypothesis ($\gamma = .541$ in the whole dataset, $p < 0.01$). On the multi-group level, γ ranked between .419 and .672 (all significant). χ^2-difference tests revealed that the γ in the employee-oriented CSR domain was significantly stronger than in the philanthropy-oriented CSR domain ($\Delta\chi^2 = 6.5$, $\Delta df = 1$, $p < 0.05$) and that γ in the environment-oriented CSR domain was significantly stronger than in the philanthropy-oriented CSR domain ($\Delta\chi^2 = 8.2$, $\Delta df = 1$, $p < 0.01$) and the customer-oriented CSR domain ($\Delta\chi^2 = 2.9$, $\Delta df = 1$, $p < 0.10$). H5 was also confirmed for all CSR domains.

Hypothesis H6, which presumed that a more favourable evaluation of the perceived CSR engagement of the company would positively influence employees' expressions of positive WOM regarding the organizational CSR engagement, was confirmed by the data as well ($\gamma = .593$ in the whole dataset, $p < 0.01$). On the multi-group level, γ ranked between .499 and .611 (all significant). χ^2-difference tests did not yield any significant differences with regard to the four CSR domains. H6 was also supported for all CSR domains.

Discussion and implications

We developed a model explaining the influence of a company's CSR communication on employees and tested it in four CSR domains (customer-oriented, employee-oriented, environment-oriented, and philanthropy-oriented CSR), controlling for gender, age, tenure with the company, and job level.

One important result of this study is that perceived cause-company fit of the CSR communication is a major determinant for employees for a positive evaluation of the organizational CSR engagement. This result corroborates findings from Kim, Cheong, and Lim (2015) as well as from Seok Sohn, Han, and Lee (2012). Extending the current literature, our study furthermore shows that perceived cause-company fit is more important than liking of the CSR communication and the message credibility. This proved to be true in all four CSR domains; in the philanthropic CSR domain, cause-company fit was especially important. Thus, the more company employees perceive the organizational CSR engagement as appropriate for and aligned with their company, the more likely they are to judge that their company is acting in a socially responsible manner. Employees are likely to have insider information about CSR initiatives (more than e.g. normal customers), which explains that a good fit between the CSR initiative and the company is vital for employees' evaluation of their company's CSR engagement. From a managerial perspective, this finding clearly indicates that marketers should take into consideration that the CSR initiatives should present a good match between company and cause and should focus on highlighting the fit between performing societally beneficial actions and the company's core activities when talking about CSR to employees. To conclude – and highly relevant for advertising research – when selecting a CSR initiative for communication purposes, marketers should make sure that a high perceived cause-company fit is given. For employees' evaluation of their company's CSR communication, high perceived cause-company fit is particularly important.

The importance of message credibility for advertising effectiveness has been widely demonstrated (e.g. Yilmaz et al. 2011; Eisend and Tarrahi 2016). Results of the current study additionally reveal that a higher perceived message credibility of the company's CSR communication leads to a more positive evaluation of the organizational CSR engagement by employees in the customer-oriented, environment-oriented and philanthropy-oriented CSR domains, but not in the employee-oriented domain. Hence, the more the company's employees perceive the messages about CSR initiatives as believable and trustworthy, the more likely they are to think that their company is serving the greater community and is devoting time, money, and other resources to socially responsible causes. In the philanthropy-oriented and customer-oriented CSR domains, message credibility has the strongest influence, whereas in the employee-oriented CSR domain, message credibility turns out not to be a significant driver of employees' evaluation of organizational CSR engagement. The reason for this is probably that employees can assess the employee-oriented CSR engagement very well as this is directed towards themselves. They do not have to depend on what the communication says as they can verify the credibility of the company's employee-oriented CSR engagement in their daily working life. From a managerial perspective, our research indicates that message credibility in CSR communication is of major importance in the customer-oriented, environment-oriented, and philanthropy-oriented CSR domains, and companies need to pay attention to the use of credible CSR messages. For the employee-oriented CSR domain, message credibility plays a less important role.

The assumption – the more the company's employees like the CSR advertisements, the more positive their evaluation of the organizational CSR engagement tends to be – is only true for the employee-oriented CSR domain. A possible explanation might be that, according to De Cremer and Van Lange (2001), people tend to be self-oriented in the sense that they are inclined to maximize personal outcomes. Thus, it appears reasonable that for the employee-oriented CSR domain it is especially important that employees like the advertisements, as these display positive activities directed towards themselves which allow them to maximize their personal outcome. Consequently, in this CSR domain, liking positively influences employee evaluation of the CSR engagement. For the other CSR domains, credibility and cause-company fit, which can be considered as more cognitive variables, are more important as employees are probably less emotionally involved in these other-directed issues. From a managerial perspective and highly relevant for advertising research, the liking of the CSR communication is important for employee-oriented CSR initiatives, but has no significant influence in the other three CSR domains. Hence, it appears that employees process their company's CSR advertising differently, depending on whether the CSR domain is self-related (i.e. employee-oriented) versus other-related (i.e. customer-oriented, environment-oriented, or philanthropy-oriented). Whereas affective advertising appraisal (ad liking) is particularly relevant for self-related CSR, cognitive advertising appraisal (message credibility) seems to be particularly relevant for other-related CSR. Above all, however, a high fit between cause and company is vital. Practitioners should keep this in mind when conceptualizing CSR communication and advertising material that may also reach their employees or that explicitly targets their employees.

In line with research demonstrating that communication effects, among them advertising, can go well beyond traditional effects such as fostering customers' purchases (e.g., Rosengren and Bondesson 2014), the results of this study point out that a more favourable evaluation of the perceived CSR engagement by employees leads to positive work outcomes in all four CSR domains. As regards job satisfaction, the more the employees perceive their company as socially responsible, the more likely they are to feel satisfied to work for their company. There were only minor, non-significant differences in the strength of the relationship between the four CSR domains. From a managerial perspective, this suggests that a company should strive to inform its employees about its CSR engagement in order to achieve higher job satisfaction. It would also be fruitful to better integrate the communication about the company's CSR initiatives in employees' working lives to increase their awareness of the CSR commitment.

In the same vein, our findings show that a more favourable evaluation of the perceived CSR engagement by employees leads to higher levels of organizational pride, again in all four CSR domains. Hence, the more employees perceive their company to be socially responsible, the more likely employees are to feel proud of being part of this company. Since CSR communication raises individual awareness of organizational CSR engagement and informs employees about ongoing CSR initiatives, it is likely to support this internal process. As for the differences between the four CSR domains, in the environment-oriented domain the influence of employees' evaluation of the organizational CSR engagement on their organizational pride was stronger than in the philanthropy-oriented and the customer-oriented CSR domains. In the employee-oriented CSR domain, the influence of employees' evaluations was higher than in the philanthropy-oriented CSR domain. The finding that employee-oriented CSR engagement is highly important for employees' organizational pride can be explained by referring to social identity theory. Organizational pride is closely related to identification with the company. As people tend to be self-oriented, employees' organizational pride seems to be highly affected by employee-oriented CSR engagement. In addition, environment-oriented CSR engagement is also highly relevant as a factor in increasing organizational pride. Thus, CSR measures directed at employees and at the environment seem to be especially beneficial for employees' identification with the company and for their organizational pride. From a managerial perspective, our findings suggest that companies should communicate about their CSR engagement to their employees and especially highlight their employee-oriented and their environment-oriented CSR engagement in order to foster employees' positive evaluation of the organizational CSR engagement and in turn to increase employees' organizational pride.

A more favourable evaluation of the perceived CSR engagement also leads to greater expressions of positive WOM about the organizational CSR engagement by employees, in all four CSR domains. Hence, employees are more willing to talk positively about their company if they perceive it as being socially responsible. Importantly, from a managerial perspective, companies should try to encourage informal yet credible communication channels such as WOM by stakeholders. Our findings support Dawkins (2005), who emphasized that companies should not underestimate the power of employees as CSR communicators, as in her study roughly every third employee had indeed advised someone to use their company because it had acted responsibly. Since employees typically have a wide reach among other stakeholder groups through their social ties, and are often considered as a source of credible information, companies should tune up their internal CSR communi-cation strategy and find ways to convert employees into CSR advocates. With the help of CSR communication, companies can prompt employees to act as credible spokespersons for their company's CSR engagement.

This article contributes to the advancement of CSR research in several ways: First, by drawing from signaling theory and social identity theory, which have both proved to be valuable in order to explain a company's CSR communication effects, this investigation adds a theoretical foundation to the CSR-communication-outcome-research. Secondly, the conceptualized model proved to be useful in explaining how the liking of the company's CSR communication, their message credibility, as well as their cause-company-fit influence employees' evaluation of the perceived organizational CSR engagement and how this relates to employees' job satisfaction due to CSR, organizational pride, and WOM about CSR. Third, the investigation demonstrates that a company's CSR communication effects may go well beyond traditional effects such as fostering customers' purchases. A company's CSR communication is also able to create favourable employee attitudes and behavior at the workplace. Fourth, our study clearly indicates that it is important to take different CSR domains into consideration. By applying the conceptual model to the different CSR domains, several important differences in the relationship were revealed. In particular, the employee-oriented CSR differed notably from the other three domains with regard to the liking of the communication and message credibility. In addition, in the philanthropic CSR domain, cause-company fit turned out to be especially important for employees' evaluation of their company's CSR engagement.

Limitations and directions for future research

Beyond its significant contributions, our study has some limitations. We used self-reported measures in our survey. Even though self-reported measures are considered to be among the most informative and valid data sources for evaluating individual attitudes, cognitions, feelings, and perceptions (Spector 1994), they can generate common method bias. In our research, we employed the CFA marker-variable technique that suggests that common method bias was probably not a problem in our study. Nevertheless, future research may utilize other methodological approaches (e.g., qualitative interviews, secondary data sour-ces) to corroborate the findings of this investigation. In addition, future researchers may consider employing scenarios or fictional collages to manipulate the different CSR domains in order to extend our research. Besides, despite the fact that we tested different CSR adver-tisements from four different CSR domains, we only tested them in one single company, which works in the energy sector. Hence, future studies may want to test the outlined model in other companies, other industries, and in other countries. This research included gender, age, tenure with the company, and job level as control variables. Future research might want to further explore the role of sociodemographic variables as well as other indi-vidual and contextual boundary conditions, for instance, different levels of importance and value which employees place on CSR, their moral identity, or their motivation for complying with, advocating for, or participation in CSR activities (Rupp et al. 2013; 2018). Future research may also want to put more focus on potential interaction effects that may occur between antecedents of employees' CSR evaluation. For instance, advertising that is liked but not seen as credible may lower evaluations of the organization's CSR engagement.

Acknowledgment

Published with the financial support of the Faculty of Humanities of the Alpen-Adria University of Klagenfurt.

Disclosure statement

No potential conflict of interest was reported by the authors.

ORCID

Sarah Desirée Schaefer ⓘD http://orcid.org/0000-0002-2573-2019
Ralf Terlutter ⓘD http://orcid.org/0000-0003-2284-5816
Sandra Diehl ⓘD http://orcid.org/0000-0002-0422-5579

References

Aguinis, H., and A. Glavas. 2012. What We know and don't know about corporate social responsibility. *Journal of Management* 38 no. 4: 932–68.
Aguinis, H., and A. Glavas. 2017. On corporate social responsibility, sensemaking, and the search for meaningfulness through work. *Journal of Management* 45: 1057–1086.
Ailawadi, K.L., S.A. Neslin, Y.J. Luan, and G.A. Taylor. 2014. Does retailer CSR enhance behavioral loyalty?. *International Journal of Research in Marketing* 31 no. 2: 156–67.
Arnett, D.B., S.D. German, and S.D. Hunt. 2003. The identity salience model of relationship marketing success. *Journal of Marketing* 67 no. 2: 89–105.
Ashforth, B.E., S.H. Harrison, and K.G. Corley. 2008. Identification in organizations: an examination of four fundamental questions. *Journal of Management* 34 no. 3: 325–74.
Ashforth, B.E., and F. Mael. 1989. Social identity theory and the organization. Academy of Management Review 14 no. 1: 20.
Becker-Olsen, K.L., B.A. Cudmore, and R.P. Hill. 2006. The impact of perceived corporate social responsibility on consumer behavior. *Journal of Business Research* 59 no. 1: 46–53.

Berens, G., C. van Riel, and G.H. van Bruggen. 2005. Corporate associations and consumer product responses. *Journal of Marketing* 69 no. 3: 35–48.

Bhattacharya, C.B., D. Korschun, and S. Sen. 2009. Strengthening stakeholder–company relationships through mutually beneficial corporate social responsibility initiatives. *Journal of Business Ethics* 85 no. S2: 257–72.

Bhattacharya, C.B., and S. Sen. 2004. Doing better at doing good. *California Management Review* 47 no. 1: 9–24.

Bhattacharya, C.B., S. Sen, and D. Korschun. 2007. Corporate social responsibility as an internal marketing strategy. *Sloan Management Review* 49: 37–44.

Brunton, M., G. Eweje, and N. Taskin. 2017. Communicating corporate social responsibility to internal stakeholders. Business Strategy and the Environment 26 no. 1: 31–48.

Carvalho, S.W., S. Sen, M. de Oliveira Mota, and R.C. de Lima. 2010. Consumer reactions to CSR. *Journal of Business Ethics* 91 no. S2: 291–310.

Chang, S.-J., A. van Witteloostuijn, and L. Eden. 2010. From the editors: Common method variance in international business research. *Journal of International Business Studies* 41 no. 2: 178–84.

Chaudhary, R. 2017. Corporate social responsibility and employee engagement: Can CSR help in redressing the engagement gap?. *Social Responsibility Journal* 13 no. 2: 323–38.

Collier, J., and R. Esteban. 2007. Corporate social responsibility and employee commitment. *Business Ethics: A European Review* 16 no. 1: 19–33.

Connelly, B.L., S.T. Certo, R.D. Ireland, and C.R. Reutzel. 2011. Signaling theory: a review and assessment. *Journal of Management* 37 no. 1: 39–67.

Crane, A., and S. Glozer. 2016. Researching corporate social responsibility communication: Themes, opportunities and challenges. Journal of Management Studies 53 no. 7: 1223–52.

Dawkins, J. 2005. Corporate responsibility: the communication challenge. *Journal of Communication Management* 9 no. 2: 108–19.

de Cremer, D. and P.A.M. van Lange. 2001. Why prosocials exhibit greater cooperation than proselfs. *European Journal of Personality* 15 no. S1: S5–S18.

del Mar García-De los Salmones, M., and A. Perez. 2018. Effectiveness of CSR advertising. *Corporate Social Responsibility and Environmental Management* 25 no. 2: 194–208.

Dhanesh, G.S. 2014. CSR as organization-employee relationship management strategy: a case study of socially responsible information technology companies in India. *Management Communication Quarterly* 28 no. 1: 130–49.

Diehl, S., R. Terlutter, and B. Mueller. 2016. Doing good matters to consumers: the effectiveness of humane-oriented CSR appeals in cross-cultural standardized advertising campaigns. *International Journal of Advertising* 35 no. 4: 730–57.

Du, S., C.B. Bhattacharya, and S. Sen. 2007. Reaping relational rewards from corporate social responsibility: the role of competitive positioning. *International Journal of Research in Marketing* 24 no. 3: 224–41.

Du, S., C.B. Bhattacharya, and S. Sen. 2010. Maximizing business returns to corporate social responsibility (CSR). *International Journal of Management Reviews* 12 no. 1: 8–19.

Du, S., C.B. Bhattacharya, and S. Sen. 2015. Corporate social responsibility, multi-faceted job-products, and employee outcomes. Journal of Business Ethics 131 no. 2: 319–35.

Duthler, G., and G.S. Dhanesh. 2018. The role of corporate social responsibility (CSR) and internal CSR communication in predicting employee engagement: perspectives from the United Arab Emirates (UAE). *Public Relations Review* 44: 453–462.

Eisend, M., and F. Tarrahi. 2016. The effectiveness of advertising: a Meta-Meta-Analysis of advertising inputs and outcomes. *Journal of Advertising* 45 no. 4: 519–31.

Farooq, M., O. Farooq, and S.M. Jasimuddin. 2014. Employees response to corporate social responsibility. *European Management Journal* 32 no. 6: 916–27.

Flanagin, A.J., and M.J. Metzger. 2000. Perceptions of internet information credibility. *Journalism & Mass Communication Quarterly* 77 no. 3: 515–40.

Flanagin, A.J., and M.J. Metzger. 2007. The role of site features, user attributes, and information verification behaviors on the perceived credibility of web-based information. *New Media & Society* 9 no. 2: 319–42.

Fornell, C., and D.F. Larcker. 1981. Evaluating structural equation models with unobservable variables and measurement error. *Journal of Marketing Research* 18 no. 1: 39–50.

Grewal, R., J.A. Cote, and H. Baumgartner. 2004. Multicollinearity and measurement error in structural equation models: implications for theory testing. *Marketing Science* 23 no. 4: 519–29.

Hopkins, M. 2016. *CSR and sustainability from the margins to the mainstream*. Sheffield, U.K. Greenleaf Pub.

Jellinek, R. 2015. Energy efficiency trends and policies in Austria. http://www.odyssee-mure.eu/publications/national-reports/energy-efficiency-austria.pdf. Accessed May 09, 2017.

Jones, D.A. 2010. Does serving the community also serve the company?. *Journal of Occupational and Organizational Psychology* 83 no. 4: 857–78.

Kim, K., Y. Cheong, and J.S. Lim. 2015. Choosing the right message for the right cause in social cause advertising. *International Journal of Advertising* 34 no. 3: 473–94.

Lee, E.M., S.-Y. Park, and H.J. Lee. 2013. Employee perception of CSR activities: its antecedents and consequences. *Journal of Business Research* 66 no. 10: 1716–24.

Locke, E.A. 1991. The nature and causes of job satisfaction. In *Handbook of industrial and organizational psychology*, ed. M. D. Dunnette and L. Hough, 1297–1349. Chicago: Rand McNally.

May, D.R., R.L. Gilson, and L.M. Harter. 2004. The psychological conditions of meaningfulness, safety and availability and the engagement of the human spirit at work. *Journal of Occupational and Organizational Psychology* 77 no. 1: 11–37.

McShane, L., and P. Cunningham. 2012. To thine own self be true? employees' judgments of the authenticity of their organization's corporate social responsibility program. Journal of Business Ethics 108 no. 1: 81–100.

Nan, X., and K. Heo. 2007. Consumer responses to corporate social responsibility (CSR) initiatives: Examining the role of Brand-Cause fit in Cause-Related marketing. *Journal of Advertising* 36 no. 2: 63–74.

Pérez, A., and I. Rodríguez del Bosque. 2015. The formation of customer CSR perceptions in the banking sector. *International Journal of Business & Society* 16 no. 1: 75–94.

de Roeck, K., G. Marique, F. Stinglhamber, and V. Swaen. 2014. Understanding employees' responses to corporate social responsibility. *The International Journal of Human Resource Management* 25 no. 1: 91–112.

Rosengren, S., and N. Bondesson. 2014. Consumer advertising as a signal of employer attractiveness. *International Journal of Advertising* 33 no. 2: 253–69.

Rupp, D.E., J. Ganapathi, R.V. Aguilera, and C.A. Williams. 2006. Employee reactions to corporate social responsibility: an organizational justice framework. *Journal of Organizational Behavior* 27 no. 4: 537–43.

Rupp, D.E., R. Shao, D.P. Skarlicki, E.L. Paddock, T.-Y. Kim, and T. Nadisic. 2018. Corporate social responsibility and employee engagement: the moderating role of CSR-specific relative autonomy and individualism. *Journal of Organizational Behavior* 39 no. 5: 559–79.

Rupp, D.E., R. Shao, M.A. Thornton, and D.P. Skarlicki. 2013. Applicants' and employees' reactions to corporate social responsibility: the moderating effects of first-party justice perceptions and moral identity. *Personnel Psychology* 66 no. 4: 895–933.

Rupp, D.E., P.M. Wright, S. Aryee, and Y. Luo. 2015. Organizational justice, behavioral ethics, and corporate social responsibility: finally the three shall merge. *Management and Organization Review* 11 no. 01: 15–24.

Rynes, S.L. 1991. Recruitment, job choice, and post-hire consequences: a call for new research directions. In *Handbook of industrial and organizational psychology*, ed. M. D. Dunnette and L. M. Hough, 399–444. Palo Alto, CA: Consulting Psychologists Press.

Schaefer, S. D., R. Terlutter, and S. Diehl. 2019. Is my company really doing good? Factors influencing employees' evaluation of the authenticity of their company's corporate social responsibility engagement. *Journal of Business Research* 101: 128–43.

Seok Sohn, Y., J.K. Han, and S.-H. Lee. 2012. Communication strategies for enhancing perceived fit in the CSR sponsorship context. *International Journal of Advertising* 31 no. 1: 133–46.

Spector, Paul E. 1994. Using Self-Report Questionnaires in OB Research. *Journal of Organizational Behavior* 15 no. 5: 385–92.

Suh, Y.J. 2016. The role of relational social Capital and communication in the relationship between CSR and employee attitudes. *Journal of Leadership & Organizational Studies* 23 no. 4: 410–23.

Sun, L., and T.R. Yu. 2015. The impact of corporate social responsibility on employee performance and cost. *Review of Accounting and Finance* 14 no. 3: 262–84.

Taylor, C.R. 2018. Red alert: on the need for more research on corporate social responsibility appeals in advertising. *International Journal of Advertising* 37 no. 3: 337–9.

Valentine, S., and G. Fleischman. 2007. Ethics programs, perceived corporate social responsibility and job satisfaction. *Journal of Business Ethics* 77 no. 2: 159–72.

Vlachos, P., N. Panagopoulos, and A. Rapp. 2014. Employee judgments of and behaviors towards corporate social responsibility. Journal of Organizational Behavior 35 no. 7: 990–1017.

Williams, L.J., N. Hartman, and F. Cavazotte. 2010. Method variance and marker variables. *Organizational Research Methods* 13 no. 3: 477–514.

Yilmaz, C., E. Eser Telci, M. Bodur, and T. Eker Iscioglu. 2011. Source characteristics and advertising effectiveness. *International Journal of Advertising* 30 no. 5: 889–914.

Zasuwa, G. 2017. The role of Company-Cause fit and company involvement in consumer responses to CSR initiatives. *Sustainability* 9 no. 6: 1016.

Appendix

Table A1. Results from the control variables: age, gender, job level, and tenure with the company.

Path		CSR (Domain)				
		Customer-oriented	Employee-oriented	Environ.-oriented	Philant.-oriented	Total Sample
Control: age	→ Evaluation of perceived CSR	.080	.052	.056	.023	.035
Control: age	→ Job satisfaction due to CSR	.296***	.198**	.215**	.374***	.271***
Control: age	→ Organizational pride	−.083	−.418***	−.060	−.379***	−.251***
Control: age	→ Word-of-Mouth about CSR	-.011	−.496***	.063	−.240***	−.196***
Control: gender	→ Evaluation of perceived CSR	.050	−.022	.114	.043	.014
Control: gender	→ Job satisfaction due to CSR	.053	.251***	.008	.089	.108**
Control: gender	→ Organizational pride	−.038	−.012	−.114	−.159*	−.047
Control: gender	→ Word-of-Mouth about CSR	−.001	.054	−.179*	−.179**	−.059
Control: job level	→ Evaluation of perceived CSR	−.011	−.026	.031	−.160*	−.013
Control: job level	→ Job satisfaction due to CSR	.123	.406***	.156*	.138	.195***
Control: job level	→ Organizational pride	.107	.150*	.124	.262***	.159***
Control: job level	→ Word-of-Mouth about CSR	.188*	.303***	.051	.196**	.174***
Control: tenure	→ Evaluation of perceived CSR	.074	.002	.029	−.119	−.024
Control: tenure	→ Job satisfaction due to CSR	−.209**	−.232***	−.124	−.254***	−.197***
Control: tenure	→ Organizational pride	.120	.243***	.162*	.191**	.185***
Control: tenure	→ Word-of-Mouth about CSR	.143	.450***	.172*	.271***	.253***

Note. The control variables are coded as follows – Age: 0 = up to 35 years, 1 = older than 35 years. Gender: 0 = male, 1 = female. Job level: 1 = with managerial responsibilities, 0 = without managerial responsibilities. Tenure: 1 = up to 1 year, 2 = up to 2 years, 3 = up to 5 years, 4 = up to 10 years, 5 = longer than 10 years.

Table A2. Descriptives of key variables by CSR domain and ANOVA.

	Customer-oriented (N=110)			Employee-oriented (N=110)			Environment-oriented (N=107)			Philanthropy-oriented (N=105)			Total sample (N=432)			ANOVA (4 CSR Domains)		
Variables	M	SD	α	M	SD	α	M	SD	α	M	SD	α	M	SD	α	F	p	p. η^2
1. Liking of the ads	5.55	1.13	0.87	5.40	1.37	0.95	5.59	1.19	0.90	5.23	1.39	0.90	5.44	1.28	0.91	$(3, 428) = 1.76$	.154	.012
2. Message credibility	5.24	1.14	0.86	5.02	1.19	0.92	5.53	1.17	0.82	5.18	0.91	0.77	5.24	1.12	0.76	$(3, 428) = 3.91$	.009	.027
3. Cause-company Fit	5.84	0.97	0.83	5.40	1.14	0.90	5.96	1.14	0.87	5.65	0.96	0.76	5.71	1.07	0.85	$(3, 428) = 5.86$	.001	.039
4. Evaluation of perceived CSR	5.26	1.12	0.91	5.15	1.08	0.84	5.44	1.17	0.92	5.14	1.18	0.86	5.20	1.06	0.88	$(3, 428) = 2.83$	.038	.019
5. Job satisfaction due to CSR	4.52	1.45	0.88	4.56	1.33	0.83	4.87	1.43	0.91	4.47	1.32	0.81	4.60	1.39	0.86	$(3, 428) = 2.58$	.053	.018
6. Organizational pride	6.03	1.16	0.94	6.00	1.14	0.87	6.09	1.12	0.95	6.11	1.06	0.89	6.06	1.12	0.91	$(3, 428) = 0.29$	.835	.002
7. Word-of-Mouth about CSR	5.72	1.20	0.70	5.59	1.15	0.66	5.85	1.10	0.79	5.81	1.17	0.87	5.74	1.16	0.75	$(3, 428) = 1.02$	.383	.007

Note. M = Mean; SD = Standard Deviation; α = Cronbach's Alpha. p. η^2 = Partial Eta Square.

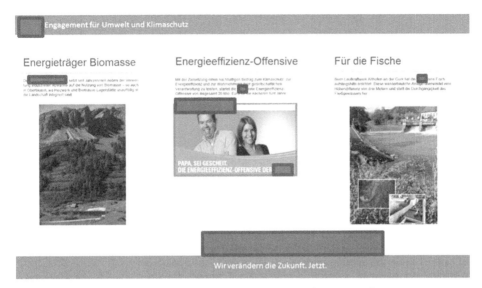

Figure A1. Example of a collage including environment-oriented CSR appeals.

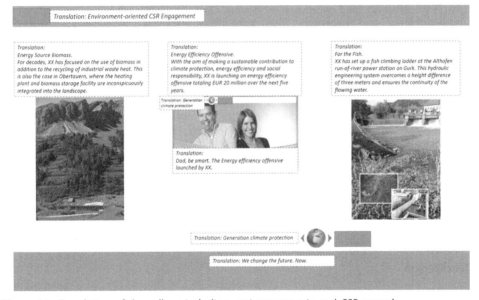

Figure A2. Translation of the collage including environment-oriented CSR appeals.

Celebrity vs. Influencer endorsements in advertising: the role of identification, credibility, and Product-Endorser fit

Alexander P. Schouten, Loes Janssen and Maegan Verspaget

ABSTRACT

In their marketing efforts, companies increasingly abandon traditional celebrity endorsers in favor of social media influencers, such as vloggers and Instafamous personalities. The effectiveness of using influencer endorsements as compared to traditional celebrity endorsements is not well understood. Therefore, the present research investigated the impact of celebrity vs. influencer endorsements on advertising effectiveness (attitudes toward the advertisement and product, and purchase intention), moderated by product-endorser fit. Moreover, this research investigated two potential mediators underlying this relationship: identification (perceived similarity and wishful identification) and credibility (trustworthiness and expertise). Two experiments ($N = 131$, $N = 446$) investigated celebrity vs. influencer endorsers with good vs. poor fit with a beauty and a fitness product (Study 1), or a food and a fashion product (Study 2). Overall, our results showed that participants identify more with influencers than celebrities, feel more similar to influencers than celebrities, and trust influencers more than celebrities. In terms of advertising effectiveness, similarity, wishful identification, and trust mediate the relationship between type of endorser and advertising effectiveness. Product-endorser did not explain the relationship between type of endorser and any of the mediating and dependent variables. In all, our results show the added value of using influencer endorsers over celebrity endorsers and the importance of similarity, identification and trust in this process.

Introduction

Celebrity endorsements are a popular way for marketers to promote their brands, products, and services. By transferring the positive image and characteristics of a celebrity onto the brand, marketers aim to trigger consumers' intent to purchase or use the endorsed product or service (Atkin and Block 1983). Many academic studies have confirmed that celebrity endorsements significantly increase advertising effectiveness (e.g., Atkin and Block 1983; Erdogan 1999; Amos, Holmes, and Strutton 2008; Bergkvist and Zhou 2016). However, in addition to using 'traditional' celebrities such as actors, supermodels, and athletes to add value to their brand, companies increasingly turn to social media influencers (also called 'micro-celebrities'), such as vloggers and 'Instafamous' personalities, to endorse their brands (Marwick 2015). In contrast to traditional celebrities who have gained public recognition because of their professional talent, social media influencers (from now on called 'influencers'), have gained fame by successfully branding themselves as experts on social media platforms (Khamis, Ang, and Welling 2017). By enthusiastically sharing self-generated content on topics like beauty, fitness, food, and fashion, these (mostly female) social media users have gained a large follower base, turning their online social presence into a primary profession such as 'fashionblogger', or 'fitgirl' (Lin, Bruning, and Swarna 2018).

Despite the increasing deployment of influencers for brand endorsement, scientific knowledge on their marketing value is limited. Whereas the effectiveness of traditional celebrity endorsement has been widely investigated (Bergkvist and Zhou 2016), the impact of influencer endorsement on brand responses is relatively understudied. Although recent qualitative research suggests that influencers, compared to celebrities, have a stronger impact on brand attitudes and purchase behaviors of young consumers (Djafarova and Rushworth 2017), no study to date has directly compared the two endorsement types. Scholars as well as practitioners would benefit from more insight into the effects of celebrity versus influencer endorsements on advertising effectiveness.

Therefore, in two experiments, the present research will investigate the effectiveness of endorsement advertising by celebrities versus influencers in terms of attitude toward the advertisement, attitude toward the advertised product, and purchase intention. In addition, we investigate two important mediating processes that may explain potential differences in effectiveness between these two types of endorsements: *identification* (in particular, perceived similarity and wishful identification; cf. Hoffner and Buchanan 2005) and *credibility* (consisting of trustworthiness and expertise; cf. Sternthal, Phillips, and Dholakia 1978). Both identification and credibility have been shown to play a key role in explaining celebrity endorsement effects, and may play a significant role in influencer endorsement as well (Chapple and Cownie 2017; Djafarova and Rushworth 2017).

Finally, since the effectiveness of an endorsed advertisement is inseparably tied to the degree in which the endorser fits the advertised product (e.g., Kamins and Gupta 1994; Till and Busler 2000; Fink, Cunningham, and Kensicki 2004), we will take *product-endorser fit* into account as a moderator in the relationship between type of endorser and marketing outcomes. We will argue that the effect of product-endorser fit on advertising effectiveness may be even more pronounced for influencers than for celebrity endorsers.

Theoretical background

Influencers attract millions of followers by sharing content curated from their daily lives on platforms like Instagram and YouTube, evolving around one particular domain of interest (Chapple and Cownie 2017; MediaKix 2017). Although 'traditional' celebrities have also found their way to social media, influencers built their careers online and were unknown to a general public before. Marketers have eagerly embraced these influencers as spokespersons for their brands, and advertisers are investing large budgets on influencer endorsements (WFA 2018). Influencers do not only have the power to directly influence the purchase decisions of a large audience, but their followers also judge them to be reliable information sources (De Veirman, Cauberghe, and Hudders 2017; Djafarova and Rushworth 2017).

A growing body of academic research is investigating the merits of influencer marketing, and the processes playing a role in influencer effects on brand responses. For example, Lee and Watkins (2016) showed that vloggers positively affect consumer purchase intentions for (luxury) brands promoted in their vlogs. Likewise, in an interview study by Chapple and Cownie (2017), consumers stated to regularly follow lifestyle vloggers' product recommendations, either by buying a product themselves or recommending it to others. In this study, participants considered vloggers as credible sources of information, mainly driven by perceptions of trust and similarity. In another study, Colliander and Dahlén (2011) found that a blog post about a fashion brand resulted in higher brand attitude and increased purchase intent compared to an online magazine article on the same topic, because readers felt closer to the blogger.

Although no study has directly compared the impact of influencer endorsements to more traditional forms of endorsement advertising, interviews with female Instagram users (Djafarova and Rushworth 2017) suggest that influencers are perceived as more credible and relatable than traditional female celebrities, and their product reviews have a significant impact on young females' purchasing behavior. In an earlier study comparing the effectiveness of celebrity endorsements with product reviews of an unknown 'ordinary' customer, female participants were more positive about a promoted experience product when it was promoted by a relatable consumer (Wei and Lu 2013).

Although still in its infancy, scientific research on influencer endorsement seems to corroborate the acclaimed success of influencer endorsements as a marketing tool and suggests that influencers may nowadays have a more significant impact on brand attitudes and purchase behaviors than traditional celebrities. We therefore expect that influencer endorsements will result in higher advertising effectiveness than celebrity endorsements. In this study, we will measure advertising effectiveness in terms of attitude toward the ad, attitude toward the advertised product, and purchase intention (cf. Karson and Fisher 2005). In sum, we hypothesize the following:

H1: Compared to celebrity endorsements, influencer endorsements will lead to higher attitude toward the ad, attitude toward the product, and purchase intention.

The role of identification and credibility

Existing research on endorsement marketing has identified two major processes that may underlie the effect of brand endorsement on advertising effectiveness: identification with the endorser (e.g., Basil 1996) and perceived endorser credibility (e.g., Ohanian 1991). Since both processes have been suggested to play a significant role in influencer endorsements as well (Chapple and Cownie 2017; Djafarova and Rushworth 2017), we will investigate to what extent identification and credibility can explain influencer versus celebrity endorsement effects.

When consumers believe that they share certain interests, values, or characteristics with an endorser, they are more likely to adopt their beliefs, attitudes, and behaviors (Cialdini 1993; Kelman 2006). Identification derives from both actual and perceived similarity, or the degree to which one perceives to have things in common with another person, as well as wishful identification, which is the desire to be like the other person (Hoffner and Buchanan 2005). In the case of celebrity endorsements, identification mostly arises from wishful identification, or an individual's aspiration to be like that celebrity (Kamins et al. 1989). In contrast, we expect identification with influencers to be more strongly determined by perceived similarity (Gräve 2017). In comparison to celebrities, influencers are perceived as more relatable and approachable, like having a long-distance friend (Djafarova and Rushworth 2017). Influencers tend to directly address their followers in their posts, which connotes a certain closeness, and makes followers see them as peers (Erz and Christensen 2018; Gannon and Prothero 2018). The ability to comment on influencers' posts and the possibility for interaction may strengthen the feeling that the influencer is similar to oneself (Schmidt 2007).

In sum, unlike celebrities, influencers present themselves like 'ordinary', approachable, and authentic personalities (Chapple and Cownie 2017), which could make people feel more similar to them. However, when it comes to wishful identification, consumers may be more attracted to the glitter and glamourous fame of traditional celebrities. Since people are more likely to accept product claims communicated by endorsers they can identify with (Basil, 1996), we expect both types of identification to positively affect advertising effectiveness. In this study, we will measure advertising effectiveness in terms of attitude toward the ad, attitude toward the advertised product, and purchase intention (cf. Karson and Fisher 2005). In sum, we hypothesize the following:

H2a: Influencer endorsements lead to a higher perceived similarity with the endorser than celebrity endorsements.

H2b: Celebrity endorsements lead to more wishful identification with the endorser than influencer endorsements.

H2c: Perceived similarity and wishful identification mediate the relationship between influencer vs. celebrity endorsements and attitude toward the ad, attitude toward the product, and purchase intention.

A second process that has been shown to play a role in the relationship between endorser and advertising effectiveness is perceived endorser credibility (Sternthal, Phillips, and Dholakia 1978; Ohanian 1991). In general, research on endorsement effects has shown that consumers are more likely to positively evaluate brands and products endorsed by people that they perceive to be credible (Erdogan 1999; Bergkvist and Zhou 2016). Credibility consists of two components: trustworthiness and expertise (Sternthal et al. 1978). Trustworthiness refers to perceptions of honesty, integrity, and believability of an endorser, whereas expertise refers to the relevant knowledge, skills, or experience the endorser is perceived to be possessing (Erdogan 1999).

For traditional celebrities, trustworthy endorsers seem to have more persuasive power than untrustworthy endorsers (e.g., Priester and Petty 2003), and perceived endorser expertise has been found to positively affect product attitudes and purchase intentions (e.g., Ohanian, 1991; Eisend and Langner 2010). Regarding influencers, studies in the more general domain of electronic word-of-mouth (eWOM) have shown that the effectiveness of eWOM on consumers' product attitudes and purchase intentions is determined by endorser credibility (Reichelt, Sievert and Jacob 2014; Erkan and Evans 2016). For influencers in particular, findings from Chapple and Cownie (2017) and Djafarova and Rushworth (2017) suggest that influencer credibility plays an important role in affecting purchase behavior.

In the present study, we argue that influencers may be perceived as more credible product endorsers than celebrities. First, influencers are known to share user-oriented product reviews, recommendations, and personal experiences on their social media channels, such as beauty influencers demonstrating make-up articles in their vlogs[1]. Although a growing amount of this content is company-sponsored and designed to persuade, the majority of influencer-generated content reflects honest opinions and does not have promotional goals (Evans et al. 2017). In contrast, consumers are generally well aware that celebrities get paid for their endorsements (Friestad and Wright, 1994). Second, influencers generally promote products in authentic, real-life settings, which may increase perceptions of trustworthiness as compared to celebrities. Uzunoğlu and Kip (2014) found that bloggers seem trustworthy because by posting about certain brands they demonstrate that they have tried the products themselves. Russell and Rasolofoarison (2017) found that when celebrities do endorse a product in a more authentic way (being associated with the product in a real-life setting), they are perceived as more credible compared to more commercial forms of endorsement. Hence, when influencers endorse a product, consumers may be more likely to attribute this to the endorser genuinely believing in the positive characteristics of the product than when a celebrity endorser is used (cf. Zhu and Tan 2007). Third, an inherent part of influencers' success is that they have been able to establish a career by devoting themselves to a particular domain of interest and create their own expert profession (Balog, Rijke, and Weerkamp 2008; Erz and Christensen, 2018). Their self-acclaimed expertise could make it more likely for influencers to be perceived as knowledgeable on products and services in their domain of interest than traditional celebrities. Based on these propositions, we state the following hypotheses:

H3a: Influencer endorsements lead to a higher perceived trustworthiness and expertise than celebrity endorsements.

H3b: Perceived trustworthiness and expertise mediate the relationship between influencer vs. celebrity endorsements and attitude toward the ad, attitude toward the product, and purchase intention.

Product-Endorser fit

In addition to identification and credibility as potential explanatory processes of influencer vs. celebrity endorsement effects, we investigate the moderating role of product-endorser fit. Using an endorser in an advertisement does not automatically guarantee a successful advertisement. Previous research has demonstrated that the effectiveness of an endorsed advertisement is inseparably tied to the degree in which the image, personality, or expertise of the endorser fits the advertised product (e.g., Kamins 1990; Kamins and Gupta 1994). Multiple studies have confirmed that when an endorser's perceived expertise matches the product endorsed, this enhances product evaluation and purchase intention (e.g., Till and Busler 2000; Fink et al. 2004). Moreover, endorsers that advertise products that do not fit their expertise are deemed less credible (Dwivedi and Johnson 2013; Lee and Koo 2015).

For influencers, endorser relevance to the product was mentioned by consumers as important to endorsement success as well (Djafarova and Rushworth 2017). Indeed, the effect of product-endorser fit on credibility may be even more pronounced for influencers than for celebrity endorsers. Since influencers have successfully branded themselves as representative of a particular domain of interest, such as 'beautyvlogger', and regularly share product information with their followers (Balog et al. 2008), an associative link between product and endorser may be more easily established. Therefore, as compared to celebrities, influencers may be more likely to be frowned upon when they endorse products that do not fit their specific 'niche' specializations and may only be perceived as credible information sources in endorsements that fit well with their domain of interest. A good fit between the endorser and the product could therefore be of higher importance for influencers than for celebrities, which results in the following hypothesis:

H4: The effect of product-endorser fit on trustworthiness and expertise is more pronounced for influencer endorsers than for celebrity endorsers.

Study overview

We conducted two studies to test our hypotheses, using different endorsers and products in each study. All hypotheses are visualized in the conceptual model in Figure 1. In both studies, we manipulated type of endorsement by creating advertisements with

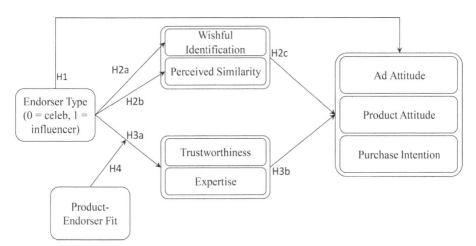

Figure 1. Conceptual Model.

Figure 2. Example of an influencer endorsement with poor fit: A protein shake endorsed by a beauty blogger (blurred for legal & copyright reasons).

Table 1. Sample demographics for Study 1 and Study 2.

	Study 1	Study 2
N	131	446
Mean Age (*SD*)	23.80 (4.07)	31.53 (5.04)
Education level (%)		
College degree (master or professional)	40.5	17.9
College degree (bachelor)	31.3	46.6
Vocational / Associate degree	18.3	27.6
High school	10.0	7.8
Use Instagram (%)[a]	n/a	81.4
Instagram use in hours per week (SD)[b]	n/a	3.43 (3.52)

Note: [a]We did not ask for Instagram use in Study 1.
[b]Calculated for Instagram users by multiplying days used per week and use per active day.

either a celebrity or influencer endorser. Fit was manipulated by pairing the endorser with a product that fit or did not fit with the endorser's profession. The products in both studies were selected to be experience goods as their product characteristics (such as quality) are difficult to determine pre-purchase, so people tend to rely more on the evaluations of others (Park and Lee 2009).

The first study was based on a convenience sample of 131 Dutch adults, consisting mostly of students. The second study used a random sample of 446 US adults collected through Amazon MTurk. Both studies focused on women only as the majority of influencers tailor to a female audience (Gannon and Prothero 2018; IndaHash Labs 2017). Moreover, both studies focused on women between the ages of 18 and 40 as this constitutes the most common Instagram demographic, with 64.1% of women between the ages of 18 and 40 using Instagram compared to only 22.6% of women over 40 (Pew Research Center 2018). Descriptions of both samples can be found in Table 1.

Study 1

Method

Design & manipulation

Study 1 employed a 2 (type of endorsement: celebrity vs. influencer endorsement) X 2 (product-endorser fit: good vs. poor fit) between-subjects design. Moreover, as a within-subject factor, participants were shown both an advertisement for a beauty product (tinted moisturizer) and an advertisement for a fitness product (protein shake). The two manipulated advertisements used in the main experiment consisted of existing advertisements (but unknown to our participants) of the beauty and fitness products, combined with the picture of the endorser.

For both product categories, two influencers and two celebrities were selected based on a pretest (see below). The celebrity good-fit conditions consisted of either an advertisement of a tinted moisturizer (beauty product) combined with the picture of Kate Moss, a famous supermodel, or an advertisement of a protein shake (fitness product) combined with the picture of Fatima Moreira de Melo, a famous Dutch field hockey player. In the influencer good-fit conditions, the advertisement of the tinted moisturizer was shown with a picture of Serena Verbon, a beauty influencer, and the advertisement of the protein shake was combined with a picture of Kayla Itsines, a fitness influencer. The beauty blogger is well known in the Netherlands with 119.000 followers on Instagram and 30.000 unique daily website visitors. The fitness influencer has over 10 million Instagram followers world-wide.

In the poor-fit conditions, we swapped the products that the celebrities or influencers advertised, so that, for example, the beauty influencer was shown advertising the fitness product (see Figure 2 for an example and see the appendix for all stimuli) .

Pretest

A pretest ($n = 33$) was conducted to examine which influencers and celebrities could serve as good and poor fits with beauty and fitness products. Participants were presented with names and pictures of six influencer endorsers and six celebrity endorsers (three for each product category), which were selected based on our own knowledge of famous celebrities and well-known influencers in the beauty and fitness industry and a Google search for famous influencers and celebrities in both industries. For each endorser, participants indicated the perceived fit of the presented celebrity or influencer with beauty products and the perceived fit with fitness products on 7-point scales ($1 = not\ at\ all$, $7 = very\ well$). For the main experiment, for each product category we chose the celebrity and influencer with the highest fit score.

Procedure

All participants were presented with two stimuli, after each of which they filled in a questionnaire. First, participants were randomly presented with either the manipulated advertisement for the fitness product or the advertisement for the beauty product. Thereafter, they were shown the advertisement for the other product category. For each product, participants were randomly assigned to one of the four conditions. Both name and profession of the endorser were shown before presenting the respective advertisement. This way, participants could still evaluate the advertisements even when they did not recognize the endorser.

Measures

Wishful identification and perceived similarity were measured with two subscales from Hoffner and Buchanan (2005), on a scale from 1 (*totally disagree*) to 7 (*totally agree*).

Wishful identification was measured with four items: '[name endorser] is the type of person I want to be like myself,' 'sometimes I wish I could be more like [name endorser],' '[name endorser] is someone I would like to emulate,' and 'I'd like to do the kind of things [name endorser] does'. Perceived similarity was also measured with four items: '[name endorser] thinks like me,' '[name endorser] behaves like me,' '[name endorser] is like me,' and '[name endorser] is similar to me'. Factor analyses showed that all items loaded on their respective factors, for both the fitness ad (similarity: EV = 3.33, R^2 = 41.57%, α = .93; identification: EV = 2.68, R^2 = 33.47%, α = .85) and the beauty ad (similarity: EV = 3.29, R^2 = 41.11%, α = .93; identification: EV = 2.76, R^2 = 34.32%, α = .84).

Endorser credibility was assessed by using the trustworthiness and expertise subscales of the credibility scale by Ohanian (1990). Participants rated the endorser's trustworthiness on five 7-point semantic differential scales: undependable – dependable, dishonest –honest, unreliable – reliable, insincere – sincere, and untrustworthy – trustworthy. Expertise was also measured with five 7-point semantic differential scales: not an expert – expert, inexperienced – experienced, unknowledgeable – knowledgeable, unqualified – qualified, and unskilled – skilled. All items loaded on their respective factors, for both the fitness ad (trust: EV = 3.74, R^2 = 37.38%, α = .91; expertise: EV = 3.62, R^2 = 36.24%, α = .90) and the beauty ad (trust: EV = 3.92, R^2 = 39.24%, α = .93; expertise: EV = 3.92, R^2 = 39.17%, α = .92).

Attitudes toward the advertisement and product were assessed with a scale based on Spears and Singh (2004). Both were rated with five items on 7-point semantic differential scales: unappealing – appealing, bad – good, unpleasant – pleasant, unfavorable – favorable, and unlikable – likable. Factor analyses yielded two factors corresponding with both subscales, for both the fitness ad (Attitude ad: EV = 4.07, R^2 = 40.69%, α = .94; Attitude product: EV = 4.32, R^2 = 43.16%, α = .96) and beauty ad (Attitude ad: EV = 4.34, R^2 = 43.42%, α = .95; Attitude product: EV = 4.38, R^2 = 43.78%, α = .97).

Finally, purchase intention was measured with one item asking 'The next time you are looking to purchase a tinted moisturizer/protein shake, how likely are you to purchase this product?', rated on a 7-point scale from 1 (*very unlikely*) to 7 (*very likely*).

To ensure the validity of our manipulation of product-endorser fit, we asked participants to indicate perceived fit between the presented product and endorser on a 7-point scale ranging from 1 (*totally disagree*) to 7 (*totally agree*). In addition, familiarity with the endorser was measured on a similar scale: 'I know [name endorser].'

Results

Manipulation checks

Of our participants, 54.7% of respondents were at least somewhat familiar (4 or higher on the scale) with the Dutch hockey player, and 68.0% were familiar with the supermodel. In contrast, 37.5% of respondents were familiar with the fitness influencer, and 39.3% were familiar with the beauty influencer. For both the fitness product ($M_{good\ fit}$ = 4.65, SD = 1.54; $M_{poor\ fit}$ = 3.18, SD = 1.64) and the beauty product ($M_{good\ fit}$ = 5.86, SD = 1.24; $M_{poor\ fit}$ = 4.29, SD = 1.61), the data confirmed that the advertisements with

Table 2. Study 1 means and standard deviations (in parentheses) for all mediating and dependent variables for the fitness product and the beauty product, as a function of type of endorsement and product-endorser fit.

	Fitness product			
	Celebrity endorsement		Influencer endorsement	
	Poor fit ($n = 39$)	Good fit ($n = 36$)	Poor fit ($n = 29$)	Good fit ($n = 27$)
Wishful identification	3.03^{ab} (1.19)	2.76^a (1.17)	3.36^{ab} (1.30)	4.02^b (1.29)
Perceived similarity	2.27^a (0.81)	2.33^a (0.94)	3.09^b (1.47)	3.51^b (1.51)
Trustworthiness	4.16^a (0.68)	4.29^a (1.24)	4.66^{ab} (0.88)	4.91^b (0.85)
Expertise	4.66 (0.96)	4.76 (1.19)	4.62 (1.08)	5.02 (1.12)
Attitude toward the advertisement	3.65^a (1.12)	3.80^{ab} (1.07)	3.61^a (1.21)	4.40^b (1.39)
Attitude toward the product	3.50^a (1.23)	3.38 ^{a} (1.34)	3.30 ^{a} (1.35)	4.36^b (1.53)
Purchase intention	2.23^a (1.56)	2.53^a (1.44)	2.66^a (1.52)	4.04^b (1.91)
Influencer familiarity	4.13 (2.47)	4.42 (2.38)	3.07 (2.19)	3.52 (2.56)
Product-endorser fit	3.23^a (1.83)	4.31^b (1.45)	3.10^a (1.37)	5.11^b (1.55)
	Beauty product			
	Celebrity endorsement		Influencer endorsement	
	Poor fit ($n = 39$)	Good fit ($n = 36$)	Poor fit ($n = 29$)	Good fit ($n = 27$)
Wishful identification	3.17^a (1.36)	3.52^{ab} (1.23)	4.19^b (1.49)	3.79 ^{ab} (0.78)
Perceived similarity	2.57^a (1.22)	2.44^a (0.87)	3.59^b (1.48)	3.82^b (1.16)
Trustworthiness	4.48 (1.05)	4.48 (0.87)	4.83 (1.05)	4.97 (0.92)
Expertise	4.58 (1.22)	5.12 (0.90)	4.77 (1.19)	4.88 (0.93)
Attitude toward the advertisement	4.55 (1.18)	4.87 (0.96)	4.68 (1.25)	4.87 (0.89)
Attitude toward the product	4.66 (1.35)	4.99 (1.00)	4.84 (1.07)	4.78 (1.11)
Purchase intention	3.31^a (1.79)	3.83^{ab} (1.44)	3.52^{ab} (1.57)	4.41^{ab} (1.25)
Influencer familiarity	4.72^a (2.09)	4.69^a (2.33)	3.17^b (2.39)	3.63^{ab} (2.17)
Product-endorser fit	4.56^a (1.52)	6.00^b (1.27)	3.93^a (1.69)	5.67^b (1.21)

Note: Different superscripts indicate significant differences between conditions (across rows).

good product-endorser fit were indeed considered a better fit than the advertisements with poor product-endorser fit, $t_{fitnessproduct}(129) = -5.30$, $p < .001$; $t_{beautyproduct}(129) = -6.24$, $p < .001$).

Overview of analysis

First, we tested the main and interaction effects of type of endorser and product-endorser fit on our dependent variables (H1) and our mediating variables (H2a, H2b, H3a, H4). Since product type is a within-subject factor as all participants were presented with both a beauty and fitness advertisement, we conducted a repeated-measures ANOVA on each of our mediating variables, with type of endorsement (celebrity endorsement vs. influencer endorsement) and product-endorser fit (good fit vs. poor fit) as between-subjects variables, and product type (beauty product vs. fitness product) as within-subjects variable. Means and standard deviations are presented in Table 2. Correlations between mediating and dependent variables are presented in Table 3.

In order to test the mediation hypotheses put forward in H2c and H3b, we conducted mediation analysis using the Process v2.15 macro in SPSS (Hayes 2013; model 4, 10,000 samples). Because of our repeated measures design, we had to test the effects of beauty and fitness advertisements with separate analyses. We therefore conducted six mediation analyses, for each of the three dependent variables (attitude toward the ad, attitude toward the product, and purchase intention), for both the fitness and beauty product advertisements separately. For clarity reasons, we only report significant

Table 3 Study 1 Pearson product-moment correlations between all mediating and dependent variables, for both fitness and beauty products.

		1	2	3	4	5	6	7	8
Fitness Product									
1	Wishful identification								
2	Perceived similarity	.604*							
3	Trustworthiness	.448*	.538*						
4	Expertise	.373*	.386*	.665*					
5	Attitude toward the advertisement	.329*	.353*	.374*	.454*				
6	Attitude toward the product	.432*	.495*	.402*	.442*	.686*			
7	Purchase intention	.429*	.601*	.415*	.411*	.492*	.654*		
8	Influencer familiarity	.219*	.247*	.197	.307*	.001	.237	.152*	
9	Product-endorser fit	.236*	.329*	.311*	.406*	.567*	.517*	.481*	.090
Beauty Product									
1	Wishful identification								
2	Perceived similarity	.664*							
3	Trustworthiness	.460*	.454*						
4	Expertise	.327*	.262*	.712*					
5	Attitude toward the advertisement	.230*	.230*	.538*	.437*				
6	Attitude toward the product	.258*	.200*	.611*	.471*	.740*			
7	Purchase intention	.367*	.360*	.417*	.254*	.595*	.584*		
8	Influencer familiarity	.225*	.117	.088	.131	.014	.028	.021	
9	Product-endorser fit	.095	.103	.332*	.422*	.452*	.439*	.428*	.124

Note: $^{*}p < .01$.

mediation effects. In our results below, we first discuss direct effects of endorser type on the mediating (H2a, H2b, H3a) and dependent variables (H1). We then discuss the mediation analyses (H2c, H3b), and effects of product-endorser fit (H4).

Direct effects of endorser type on advertising effectiveness

H1 posed that influencer endorsements would results in a higher effectiveness than celebrity endorsements. This was confirmed for product intention only, $F(1, 127) = 11.42$, $p = .001$, $\eta^2 = .083$. No effects were found for attitude toward the ad, and attitude toward the product, F's < 1.50, p's $> .25$.

Effects of endorser type on mediators

Analyses revealed that influencer endorsements led to higher wishful identification, $F(1, 127) = 14.99$, $p < .001$, $\eta^2 = .106$, perceived similarity, $F(1, 127) = 37.01$, $p < .001$, $\eta^2 = .226$, and trustworthiness, $F(1, 127) = 13.07$, $p < .001$, $\eta^2 = .093$ than celebrity endorsements. Type of endorser did not have a main effect on expertise, $F(1, 127) = 0.07$, $p = .788$, $\eta^2 < .001$. Hence, our results confirm H2a, but for H2b we found the opposite results as expected. H3a was only confirmed for trustworthiness, not for expertise.

Mediation analysis

For the advertised fitness product, only expertise was significantly related to attitude toward the ad, $b = .388$, $t(129) = 3.24$, $p = .002$. However, neither expertise nor any other variable (wishful identification, perceived similarity or trustworthiness) significantly mediated the relationship between endorser type and attitude toward the ad. Expertise was also significantly related to attitude toward the product, $b = .339$, $t(129) = 2.61$, $p = .010$, as well as similarity, $b = .350$, $t(129) = 3.14$, $p = .002$. Similarity, though, was the only variable that mediated the relationship between type of endorser and attitude toward the product, $b = .348$, 95% CI [.136, .675]. For purchase intention, results showed positive effects of both expertise, $b = .364$, $t(129) = 2.41$, $p = .018$, and similarity, $b = .634$, $t(129) = 4.89$, $p < .001$, but again only similarity mediated the relationship between type of endorser and purchase intention, $b = .630$, 95% CI [.297, 1.070].

For the advertised beauty product, only trustworthiness was significantly related to attitude toward the ad, $b = .534$, $t(129) = 4.13$, $p < .001$. Trustworthiness also significantly mediated the relationship between endorser type and attitude toward the ad, $b = .226$, 95% CI [.050, .469]. Similar results were obtained for attitude toward the product. Trustworthiness was the only variable significantly related to attitude toward the product, $b = .730$, $t(129) = 5.73$, $p < .001$, and mediated the relationship between endorser type and attitude toward the product, $b = .309$, 95% CI [.067, .609]. Finally, trustworthiness also was related to purchase intention, $b = .568$, $t(129) = 2.86$, $p = .005$, and mediated the relationship between endorser type and intention, $b = .240$, 95% CI [.039, .594]. In sum, we observe different effects for the fitness and beauty product. For the fitness product, H2c is confirmed for similarity, but we find no support for the mediating effect of trustworthiness and expertise (H3b). For the beauty product, H2c is not confirmed, but we do find that trust is a significant mediator, partly confirming H3b. For a visualization of our mediation analyses, see Figure 3.

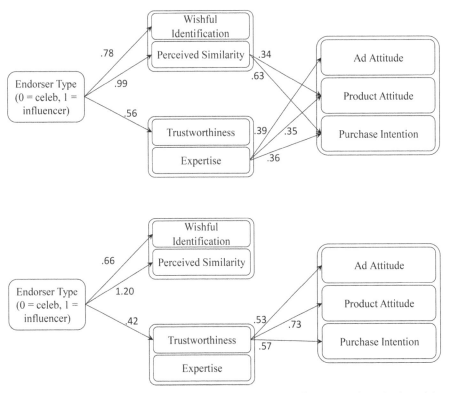

Figure 3. Overview of mediated analyses for Study 1 for the fitness product (top) and beauty product (bottom). Figure only depicts significant results at $p < .05$. Coefficients are unstandardized b's.

Product-Endorser fit

Product-endorser fit was not related to any of the mediating variables, F's < 3.20, p's > .07. A good fit between endorser and product did not result in higher ratings of trustworthiness and expertise than a poor fit. However, additional analyses showed that product-endorser fit did directly affect attitude toward the ad, $F(1, 127) = 5.53$, $p = .020$, $\eta^2 = .042$, and purchase intention, $F(1, 127) = 14.82$, $p < .001$, $\eta^2 = .105$, with well-fitting endorsements resulting in a more positive attitude toward the ad and a higher purchase intention than poor-fitting endorsements. Disconfirming H4, no interaction effects between type of endorser and product-endorser fit were observed for any of the mediating and dependent variables, F's < 3.20, p's > .070.

Study 2

Method

In Study 2, we focused on two other product categories that influencers regularly endorse: food and fashion. The design and procedure for Study 2 were similar to that of Study 1, except that each participant received one stimulus only, resulting in a 2 (type of endorsement: celebrity endorsement vs. influencer endorsement) X 2 (product-endorser fit: good fit vs. poor fit) X 2 (product type: food vs. fashion product) between-subjects design.

A pretest ($n = 46$) was conducted using Amazon MTurk to select the endorsers and products for our stimuli. First, participants were asked to list up to five female endorsers in each of these four categories: celebrities in the food industry, food influencers, celebrities in the fashion industry, and fashion influencers. The four endorsers that were mentioned most often in these four categories were selected for our main experiment, being Rachael Ray (food celebrity, mentioned 32 times), Gaby Dalkin (food influencer, mentioned 10 times), Kendall Jenner (fashion celebrity, mentioned 9 times), and Danielle Bernstein (fashion influencer, mentioned 10 times).

Next, participants were asked to indicate for three food products and three fashion products how well they felt that each product would fit a food/fashion endorser on a five-point scale from 1 (*Terrible*) to 5 (*Excellent*). For our main experiment, we selected the two products with the highest perceived product-endorser fit, which was a stand mixer for the food endorsers ($M = 4.59$, $SD = 0.62$), and a watch for the fashion endorsers ($M = 4.37$, $SD = 0.90$).

In the main experiment, in the good fit conditions the food celebrity or food influencer were paired with the stand mixer and the fashion celebrity or fashion influencer were paired with the watch. In the poor fit conditions, this was the other way around (see the appendix for all stimuli).

Dependent variables were similar to those in Study 1, except for including the attractiveness subscale of Ohanian's (1990) credibility scale. Factor analysis revealed that wishful identification and perceived similarity formed a single factor, but upon forcing the factor analysis in two factors, the two subscales clearly emerged, with all items loading on their respective factors (similarity: EV = 3.54, R^2 = 44.29%, α = .95; identification: EV = 3.30, R^2 = 41.27%, α = .93). For credibility, three factors emerged, representing trustworthiness (EV = 4.24, R^2 = 28.29%, α = .93), expertise (EV = 4.27,

$R^2 = 28.47\%$, $\alpha = .94$), and attractiveness (EV $= 3.25$, $R^2 = 21.65\%$, $\alpha = .88$). Finally, attitude towards the ad (EV $= 4.46$, $R^2 = 44.61\%$, $\alpha = .97$) and product (EV $= 4.41$, $R^2 = 44.12\%$, $\alpha = .97$) also constituted two reliable scales.

Results

Manipulation checks
Of our participants, 91% of respondents were at least somewhat familiar (4 or higher on the scale) with the food celebrity, while 84.5% were familiar with the fashion celebrity. In contrast, only 29% of participants were familiar with the fitness influencer, and 38.1% were familiar with the fashion influencer. The advertisements with a good product-endorser fit ($M = 5.15$, $SD = 1.51$) were indeed considered a better fit than the poor-fitting advertisements ($M = 3.84$, $SD = 1.86$), $t(444) = -8.16$, $p < .001$.

Overview of analysis
Similar to Study 1, we first discuss direct effects of endorser type on the mediating (H2a, H2b, H3a) and dependent variables (H1). We then discuss the mediation analyses (H2c, H3b), and effects of product-endorser fit (H4). To test the main and interaction effects of type of endorser and product-endorser fit on our mediating and dependent variables, we used a between-subjects factorial ANOVA. Next, we tested the mediation hypotheses using the Process v2.15 macro (Hayes 2013; model 4, 10,000 samples) for each of the three dependent variables separately (attitude toward the ad, attitude toward the product, and purchase intention). For clarity reasons, we only report significant mediation effects. Means and standard deviations are presented in Table 4. Correlations between mediating and dependent variables are presented in Table 5.

Direct effects of endorser type on advertising effectiveness
H1 posed that influencer endorsements would results in a higher effectiveness than celebrity endorsements. This was confirmed for product intention only, $F(1, 438) = 7.56$, $p = .006$, $\eta^2 = .017$. No effects were found for attitude toward the ad, and attitude toward the product, F's < 1.00, p's $> .40$.

Effects of endorser type on mediators
Similar to the results of Study 1, analyses revealed that influencer endorsements led to higher wishful identification, $F(1, 438) = 9,69$, $p = .002$, $\eta^2 = .022$, perceived similarity, $F(1, 438) = 27.39$, $p < .001$, $\eta^2 = .059$, and trustworthiness, $F(1, 438) = 5.02$, $p = .026$, $\eta^2 = .011$ than celebrity endorsements, but there was no main effect on expertise, $F(1, 438) = 0.23$, $p = .630$, $\eta^2 = .001$. Therefore, H2a was confirmed, results for H2b were reversed, and H3a was confirmed only for trustworthiness, not for expertise.

Mediation analysis
Identification, $b = .178$, $t(442) = 2.89$, $p = .004$, similarity, $b = .162$, $t(442) = 2.64$, $p = .009$, trustworthiness, $b = .302$, $t(442) = 3.70$, $p < .001$, and attractiveness $b = .423$, $t(442) = 7.20$, $p < .001$, were all positively related to attitude toward the ad. Identification, $b = .085$, 95% CI [.017, .210], similarity, $b = .124$, 95% CI [.020, .262],

Table 4. Study 2 means and standard deviations (in parentheses) for all mediating and dependent variables for the food product and the fashion product, as a function of type of endorsement and product-endorser fit.

	Food product			
	Celebrity endorsement		Influencer endorsement	
	Poor fit ($n = 56$)	Good fit ($n = 55$)	Poor fit ($n = 53$)	Good fit ($n = 54$)
Wishful identification	3.00^a (1.71)	4.06^b (1.66)	3.65^{ab} (1.50)	4.13^b (1.45)
Perceived similarity	2.79^a (1.53)	3.74^b (1.56)	3.89^b (1.62)	4.27^b (1.41)
Trustworthiness	4.11^a (1.57)	5.51^b (1.05)	4.52^a (1.06)	5.29^b (0.98)
Expertise	4.23^a (1.68)	6.03^b (0.81)	4.57^a (1.36)	5.33^c (1.04)
Attractiveness	5.15 (1.24)	5.09 (1.10)	4.85 (1.10)	5.26 (1.03)
Attitude toward the advertisement	4.21^{ab} (1.74)	4.76^{bc} (1.53)	3.92^a (1.87)	5.03^c (1.52)
Attitude toward the product	5.63 (1.26)	5.80 (1.18)	5.31 (1.25)	5.91 (1.17)
Purchase intention	4.23^a (1.57)	4.58^{ab} (1.62)	4.38^{ab} (1.68)	5.02^b (1.32)
Influencer familiarity	5.54^a (1.43)	6.20^a (0.73)	2.79^b (2.11)	3.24^b (2.14)
Product-endorser fit	3.00^a (2.01)	6.11^b (0.99)	3.91^c (1.55)	4.87^d (1.54)
	Fashion product			
	Celebrity endorsement		Influencer endorsement	
	Poor fit ($n = 55$)	Good fit ($n = 55$)	Poor fit ($n = 56$)	Good fit ($n = 62$)
Wishful identification	3.75^{ab} (1.65)	3.34^a (1.59)	4.17^b (1.60)	4.08^b (1.53)
Perceived similarity	3.75^a (1.61)	2.84^b (1.46)	3.94^a (1.57)	4.08^a (1.52)
Trustworthiness	5.11^a (1.27)	4.17^b (1.51)	5.04^a (1.14)	5.11^a (1.25)
Expertise	5.32^a (1.28)	4.21^b (1.56)	5.05^a (1.15)	5.08^a (1.29)
Attractiveness	4.83 (1.27)	5.23 (1.45)	5.21 (1.15)	5.24 (1.23)
Attitude toward the advertisement	4.80 (1.47)	4.72 (1.80)	5.03 (1.54)	4.97 (1.67)
Attitude toward the product	5.16 (1.54)	5.12 (1.61)	5.31 (1.53)	5.31 (1.49)
Purchase intention	3.69 (1.84)	3.71 (1.81)	4.34 (1.96)	4.29 (1.96)
Influencer familiarity	5.47^a (1.77)	5.69^a (1.43)	3.23^b (2.16)	3.27^b (2.08)
Product-endorser fit	3.91^a (1.78)	4.76^b (1.62)	4.54^{ab} (1.77)	4.87^b (1.42)

Note: Different superscripts indicate significant differences between conditions (across rows).

Table 5. Study 2 Pearson product-moment correlations between all mediating and dependent variables, for both fitness and beauty products.

		1	2	3	4	5	6	7	8	9
Food Product										
1	Wishful identification									
2	Perceived similarity	.848*								
3	Trustworthiness	.664*	.633*							
4	Expertise	.578*	.549*	.830*						
5	Attractiveness	.541*	.522*	.646*	.622*					
6	Attitude toward the advertisement	.595*	.618*	.675*	.623*	.626*				
7	Attitude toward the product	.226*	.198*	.338*	.330*	.309*	.439*			
8	Purchase intention	.527*	.523*	.488*	.427*	.383*	.529*	.527*		
9	Influencer familiarity	.243*	.161	.271*	.358*	.271*	.269*	.156	.232*	
10	Product-endorser fit	.540*	.500*	.633*	.560*	.357*	.522*	.259*	.440*	.345*
Fashion Product										
1	Wishful identification									
2	Perceived similarity	.835*								
3	Trustworthiness	.708*	.706*							
4	Expertise	.639*	.610*	.868*						
5	Attractiveness	.566*	.464*	.673*	.692*					
6	Attitude toward the advertisement	.711*	.631*	.718*	.671*	.699*				
7	Attitude toward the product	.524*	.443*	.643*	.616*	.675*	.712*			
8	Purchase intention	.690*	.658*	.584*	.525*	.561*	.707*	.684*		
9	Influencer familiarity	.242*	.172*	.201*	.225*	.282*	.284*	.236*	.261*	
10	Product-endorser fit	.568*	.512*	.480*	.466*	.621*	.624*	.549*	.661*	.217*

Note: $^*p < .01$.

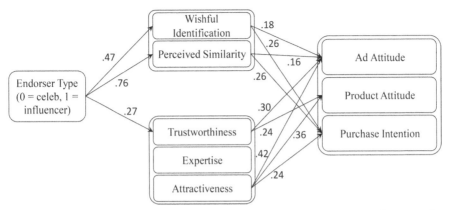

Figure 4. Overview of mediated analyses for Study 2. Figure only depicts significant results at *p* <.05. Coefficients are unstandardized *b*'s. NB. In study 2, attractiveness was included as an additional dimension of credibility.

and trustworthiness significantly mediated the relationship between endorser type and attitude toward the ad, *b* = .083, 95% CI [.010, .204].

Both trustworthiness, *b* = .244, *t*(442) = 2.74, *p* = .006, and attractiveness, *b* = .361, *t*(442) = 5.62, *p* < .001, significantly affected attitude toward the product. However, only trustworthiness mediated the relationship between endorser type and attitude toward the product, *b* = .067, 95% CI [.004, .200].

Finally, purchase intention was positively predicted by identification, *b* = .262, *t*(442) = 3.35, *p* = .001, similarity, *b* = .256, *t*(442) = 3.26, *p* = .001, and attractiveness, *b* = .242, *t*(442) = 3.24, *p* = .001. However, only identification, *b* = .155, 95% CI [.038, .266], and similarity, *b* = .196, 95% CI [.071, .369], mediated the relationship between endorser and purchase intention. For a visualization of our mediation analysis, see Figure 4.

Product-endorser fit

Product-endorser fit positively affected both trustworthiness, *F*(1, 438) = 7.63, *p* = .006, η² = .017, and expertise, *F*(1, 438) = 8.98, *p* = .003, η² = .020. A good fit between endorser and product lead to higher ratings of trust and expertise than poor fit. Product-endorser fit also directly affected attitude toward the ad, *F*(1, 438) = 5.89, *p* = .016, η² = .013, with well-fitting endorsements resulting in a more positive attitude toward the ad than poor-fitting endorsements. No interaction effects between type of endorser and product-endorser fit were observed for any of the mediating and dependent variables, disconfirming H4, *F*'s < 1.00, *p*'s > .400.

Discussion

The goal of our study was to compare the effectiveness of endorsement advertising by social media influencers to traditional celebrity endorsements. We have investigated our hypotheses in two experiments, using different celebrity and influencer endorsers across four popular influencer marketing domains (beauty, fitness, food, and fashion) using different measures of advertising effectiveness.

Overall, our results showed that participants identify more with influencers than with celebrities, feel more similar to influencers than celebrities, and trust influencers more than celebrities. In terms of advertising effectiveness, similarity, wishful identification, and trustworthiness mediate the relationship between type of endorser and advertising effectiveness, albeit not consistently. In contrast to expectations, product-endorser fit did not moderate the relationship between type of endorser and expertise or trust.

Hypothesis 1 was confirmed only for purchase intention. Participants were more willing to buy a product endorsed by an influencer than by a celebrity. No direct effects were observed for attitude toward the advertisement or product. Therefore, although participants are more likely to buy products from an influencer, they do not particularly like advertisements of influencers and the products advertised by influencers more than those of celebrities.

In line with H2a, influencer endorsements led to higher perceived similarity than celebrity endorsements. However, contrary to H2b, influencer endorsements also led to higher wishful identification with the endorser than celebrity endorsements. In hindsight, this may not come as a surprise, as many people now aspire to become a social influencer (Chae 2018). Because influencers are seen as more similar to 'ordinary people' than celebrities, perceived similarity may even make it easier for people to wishfully identify with them, because it is easier to believe they could be like them. Moreover, Uzunoğlu and Kip (2014) previously found that a main reason for following Instagram bloggers was a combination of admiration on the one hand, and the feeling of connectedness to the influencer on the other.

H2c posed that perceived similarity and wishful identification would mediate the relationship between type of endorser and attitude toward the ad, product, and purchase intention. Overall, we found support for this hypothesis. In Study 1, perceived similarity mediated the relationship between type of endorser and attitude toward the product and purchase intention, albeit only for the fitness product. An explanation for why similarity did not mediate the relationship between endorser type and purchase intention for the beauty product may be because people feel they may be able to achieve a similar fitness or shape as the influencer and are therefore more inclined to try the protein shake, whereas obtaining similar beauty by simply using a tinted moisturizer is more difficult.

In Study 2, perceived similarity mediated the relationship between type of endorser and attitude toward the ad and purchase intention. People feel more similar to influencers than celebrities and as a result like their endorsements more and are more inclined to purchase the endorsed product. Similar to the fitness product in study 1, the products endorsed in study 2 (food and fashion) may actually allow the consumer to feel more similar to the endorser, in contract to beauty products, therefore resulting in higher purchase intention. In all, perceived similarity is an important explanation for the success of influencer endorsements, but its role depends on the type of products endorsed. Most likely, when the product endorsed will not lead the consumer to feel more similar, endorsing products will not be as effective as when the product endorsed may actually make the consumer feel more similar to the influencer (e.g., I may feel as fashionable as the influencer by buying a watch, but I'll never become as pretty by wearing make-up).

Wishful identification also mediated the relationship between endorser type and attitude toward the ad and purchase intention, albeit only in Study 2. A possible explanation may be that the products we used in Study 2 (a watch and a stand mixer) are more generally appealing to a larger group of people than the products in Study 1 (a tinted moisturizer and protein shake), and purchase intention is therefore more likely to be affected when people aspire to be like an endorser. This mirrors the explanation given above: It is likely that wishful identification explains the effectiveness of influencers endorsements only when consumers actually feel they may become like the endorser (i.e., genuine aspiration), which is most likely easier in the areas of food and fashion, than it is becoming fit or pretty.

Our third hypothesis (H3a) posed that influencer endorsements would lead to higher perceived trustworthiness and expertise than celebrity endorsements. In both studies, we found that influencer endorsers were indeed seen as more trustworthy, whereas no differences were found on expertise. An explanation for not finding differences in expertise could be that in both studies, we selected influencers and celebrities that are well-known experts in their specific fields. In addition, the expertise subscale used in our experiments assessed generic expertise (e.g., 'this person is knowledgeable') and did not measure specific expertise on the product endorsed. Future research is therefore advised to measure specific expertise, as to gain better insight in the role of expertise in influencer versus celebrity endorsements.

In H3b, we posed that trustworthiness and expertise would mediate the relationship between type of endorser and advertising effectiveness. Expertise was not a significant mediator in any of the tested relationships. However, in both studies, trustworthiness was an important variable explaining why influencers are more effective endorsers than celebrities. Trustworthiness mediated the relationship between type of endorser and attitude toward the advertisement (in Studies 1 and 2), attitude toward the product (in Studies 1 and 2) and purchase intention (in Study 1). Overall, our results are in line with earlier studies that stress the role of authenticity and trust in influencer endorsements (Uzunoğlu and Kip 2014). A reason that trust, not expertise mediated the relationship between type of endorser and advertising effectiveness may be that trust is as much of a social-affective construct than a cognitive construct, in that trust depends on a feeling of integrity, believability, and mutual understanding (Uzunoğlu and Kip 2014). Thus, consumers are most likely to trust an influencer more and are therefore more persuaded by influencer advertisements because an influencer is more like them and hence trustworthy.

H4 was not confirmed. We did not find any interaction effects of product-endorser fit and endorser type on trustworthiness or expertise. We also did not find any main effects of product fit in Study 1. An explanation may be that a fitness influencer endorsing a beauty product may not have been considered a very poor fit, since the fitness influencer was an attractive woman and beauty products are generally endorsed by pretty endorsers. In study 2, we do find main effects of product-endorser fit on expertise and trustworthiness, as the difference between food and fashion products is like to be more marked than the difference between beauty and fitness. Yet, we find no evidence that fit is more important for influencers than celebrities.

Conclusion

The present research is one of the first to directly compare celebrity and influencer endorsements in terms of their advertising effectiveness. We have shown that influencers are deemed more trustworthy than celebrities, and that people feel more similar to influencers and identify more with them than celebrities. These processes, in turn, affect advertising effectiveness. Therefore, a first implication of our study is that influencers may be more effective product endorsers than traditional celebrities and a practical recommendation is therefore to continue to use influencer endorsers in marketing campaigns.

A second implication is the importance of investigating the processes underlying effective product endorsements. Wishful identification, similarity, and trust are important explanations for why product endorsements work and also explain why influencer endorsements are more effective than celebrity endorsements. However, our results also show that the underlying processes explaining advertising effectiveness may depend on specific product-endorser combinations. Specifically, for an influencer endorsement to be more effective than a celebrity endorsement, an endorsed product must be able to enhance feelings of similarity and wishful identification. In all, our results show that when endorsing products, it is important for influencers to be perceived as similar to their audience and that identification with an influencer needs to be based on true aspiration rather than only wishful thinking.

Third, finding no direct effects of endorser type on advertisement and product attitude, while we do find several mediation effects via trust, similarity, and identification may indicate that there may be several other mediators that may explain the relationship between endorser type and advertising effectiveness. Possibly, the positive effect of influencer over celebrity endorsements on advertisement and product attitude via the mediators may be mitigated by other variables, such as likeability of the influencer (De Veirman et al. 2017; Gräve 2017).

Although (or because) our study is one of the first to investigate the effects of influencer endorsements on advertising effectiveness, it is not without drawbacks. First, a potential improvement may be the way we presented the endorsements to our respondents. In all experimental conditions, our stimuli consisted of images of a product next to an endorser, resembling a basic advertising format. Although this makes for an experimentally valid comparison between endorser types, this is not how influencers on social media normally engage with a product. Usually, the product that is endorsed is part of a larger message and is integrated in a social media post, such as a vlog or an Instagram post (Kapitan and Silvera 2016). Theory on product placement teaches us that integration of a product in a storyline in a visually appealing way is positively related to endorsement effectiveness (Russell 1998). We therefore recommend investigating different types of social media endorsements with different levels of product engagement in future studies. On the other hand, that a relatively simple endorsement as ours yielded such effects shows the potential power of influencer endorsements over celebrity endorsements.

Furthermore, future research could examine other moderators than product-endorser fit influencing the relationship between endorser type and advertising effectiveness. For example, as this study only included experience goods, future research could

compare the effects of influencer vs. celebrity endorsements on other types of products, such as search goods. Findings of Wei and Lu (2013) suggest that in contrast to
experience products, search products like a pair of boots are more effectively
endorsed by celebrities than by 'ordinary' consumers. Future research could also distinguish between informational and transformational or utilitarian and hedonic goods.

Finally, in our study we compared endorsements of traditional celebrities with
endorsements by social media influencers. However, in reality, this distinction is not
always so clear-cut. Numerous cases are known of successful social media influencers
transgressing into more 'traditional' celebrities, pursuing a career as talk show pre-
senter or fashion model and making their way to the general public and mass media.
On the other hand, many traditional celebrities have become popular influencers on
social media. This raises the question which type of influencers are the most successful
endorsers, and to what extent popularity of the endorser is an important variable in
explaining endorser effectiveness. In our studies we used well-known influencers with
a large follower base, so-called 'micro-celebrities', but influencers who are relatively
less popular may be even more effective endorsers. As compared to more popular
influencers, 'micro-influencers' may be experts in a relatively small field and engage
with their audience more, and may therefore be seen as more similar to their followers
(De Veirman et al. 2017; Gräve 2017). Nevertheless, even the 'micro-celebrities' we
used in our studies appear to be more aspirable, relatable, and trustworthy than traditional celebrities, and are therefore more effective brand endorsers.

In conclusion, influencer endorsements are more effective than celebrity endorsements, which can be explained by processes of wishful identification, similarity, and
identification. For an influencer endorsement to be more effective than a celebrity
endorsement, an endorsed product must be able to enhance feelings of similarity and
wishful identification. Moreover, an influencer must elicit trust in order to be effective.
Influencers are not deemed more knowledgeable than celebrity endorsers, and expertise does not explain why influencer endorsements may be more effective than celebrity endorsements. Product-endorser fit has no effect on the relationship between type
of endorsement and trust, expertise, or advertising effectiveness, although the effectiveness of influencer vs. celebrity endorsements hinges upon specific influencer-prod-
uct combinations that elicit feelings of similarity, identification, and trust.

Note

1. e.g., http://www.nikkietutorials.com

Disclosure statement

No potential conflict of interest was reported by the authors.

References

Amos, C., G. Holmes, and D. Strutton. 2008. Exploring the relationship between celebrity endorser effects and advertising effectiveness. *A Quantitative Synthesis of Effect Size. International
   Journal of Advertising* 27, 209–34.
Atkin, C., and M. Block. 1983. Effectiveness of celebrity endorsers. *Journal of Advertising Research*
   23: 57–61.
Balog, K., M. D. Rijke, and W. Weerkamp. 2008. Bloggers as experts: Feed distillation using expert
   retrieving models. In *Proceedings of the 31st annual international ACM SIGIR conference on
   research and development in information retrieval*, ed. Syung Hyon Myaeng, Douglas W. Oard,
   Fabrizio Sebastiani, Tat-Seng Chua, and Mun-Kew Leong, 753–54. New York: ACM.
Basil, M.D. 1996. Identification as a mediator of celebrity effects. *Journal of Broadcasting &
   Electronic Media* 40, 478–95.
Bergkvist, L., and K.Q. Zhou. 2016. Celebrity endorsements: a literature review and research
   agenda. *International Journal of Advertising* 35, no. 4: 642–63.
Chae, J. 2018. Explaining females' envy toward social media influencers. *Media Psychology* 21,
   no. 2: 246–62.
Chapple, C., and F. Cownie. 2017. An investigation into viewers' trust in and response towards
   disclosed paid-for-endorsements by YouTube lifestyle vloggers. *Journal of Promotional
   Communications* 5, : 110–36.
Cialdini, R. 1993. *The psychology of influence*. New York: William Morrow & Co.
Colliander, J., and M. Dahlén. 2011. Following the fashionable friend: the power of social media:
   weighing publicity effectiveness of blogs versus online magazines. *Journal of Advertising
   Research* 51, no. 1: 313–20.
De Veirman, M., V. Cauberghe, and L. Hudders. 2017. Marketing through instagram influencers:
   the impact of number of followers and product divergence on Brand attitude. *International
   Journal of Advertising* 36, no. 5: 798–828.
Djafarova, E., and C. Rushworth. 2017. Exploring the credibility of online celebrities' instagram
   profiles in influencing the purchase decisions of young female users. *Computers in Human
   Behavior* 68, 1–7.
Dwivedi, A., and L.W. Johnson. 2013. Trust–commitment as a mediator of the celebrity
   endorser–Brand equity relationship in a service context. *Australasian Marketing Journal* 21, no.
   1: 36–42.
Eisend, M., and T. Langner. 2010. Immediate and delayed advertising effects of celebrity endorsers' attractiveness and expertise. *International Journal of Advertising* 29, no. 4: 527–46.
Erdogan, B.Z. 1999. Celebrity endorsement: a literature review. *Journal of Marketing Management*
   15, no. 4: 291–314.
Erkan, I., and C. Evans. 2016. The influence of eWOM in social media on consumers' purchase
   intentions: an extended approach to information adoption. *Computers in Human Behavior* 61,
   47–55.
Erz, A., and A.B.H. Christensen. 2018. Transforming consumers into brands: Tracing transform-
   ation processes of the practice of blogging. *Journal of Interactive Marketing* 43, 69–82.

Evans, N.J., J. Phua, J. Lim, and H. Jun. 2017. Disclosing instagram influencer advertising: the effects of disclosure language on advertising recognition, attitudes, and behavioral intent. *Journal of Interactive Advertising* 17, no. 2: 138–49.

Fink, J., G. Cunningham, and L.J. Kensicki. 2004. Utilizing athletes as endorsers to sell women's sport: Attractiveness versus expertise. *Journal of Sport Management* 18, no. 4: 350–67.

Friestad, M., and P. Wright. 1994. The persuasion knowledge model: How people cope with persuasion attempts. *Journal of Consumer Research* 21, no. 1: 1–31.

Gannon, V., and A. Prothero. 2018. Beauty bloggers and YouTubers as a community of practice. *Journal of Marketing Management, Online First* 34, no. 7/8: 592. https://doi.org/10.1080/0267257X.2018.1482941

Gräve, J.F. 2017. Exploring the perception of influencers vs. traditional celebrities: Are social media stars a new type of endorser? In Proceedings of the 8th International Conference on Social Media & Society (p. 36). ACM.

Hayes, A.F. 2013. *Introduction to mediation, moderation, and conditional process analysis: a regression-based approach*. London: Guilford Press.

Hoffner, C., and M. Buchanan. 2005. Young adults' wishful identification with television characters: the role of perceived similarity and character attributes. *Media Psychology* 7, no. 4: 325–51.

IndaHash Labs. 2017. Women are the new media: How influencers became publishers. https://labs.indahash.com/wp-content/uploads/2017/06/indaHash_LABS_report_2017.pdf

Kamins, M.A., M.J. Brand, S.A. Hoeke, and J.C. Moe. 1989. Two-sided versus one-sided celebrity endorsements: the impact on advertising effectiveness and credibility. *Journal of Advertising* 18, no. 2: 4–10.

Kamins, M.A. 1990. An investigation into the 'match-up' hypothesis in celebrity advertising: When beauty may be only skin deep. *Journal of Advertising* 19, no. 1: 4–13.

Kamins, M.A., and K. Gupta. 1994. Congruence between spokesperson and product type: a matchup hypothesis perspective. *Psychology and Marketing* 11, 569–86.

Kapitan, S., and D.H. Silvera. 2016. From digital media influencers to celebrity endorsers: Attributions drive endorser effectiveness. *Marketing Letters* 27, no. 3: 553–67.

Karson, E.J., and R.J. Fisher. 2005. Reexamining and extending the dual mediation hypothesis in an on-line advertising context. *Psychology and Marketing* 22, : 333–51.

Kelman, H.C. 2006. Interests, relationships, identities: Three Central issues for individuals and groups in negotiating their social environment. *Annual Review of Psychology* 57, no. 1: 1–26.

Khamis, S., L. Ang, and R. Welling. 2017. Self-branding, 'micro-celebrity' and the rise of social media influencers. *Celebrity Studies* 8, no. 2, 191–208.

Lin, H.C., P.F. Bruning, and H. Swarna. 2018. Using online opinion leaders to promote the hedonic and utilitarian value of products and services. *Business Horizons* 61, no. 3: 431–42.

Lee, J.E., and B. Watkins. 2016. YouTube vloggers' influence on consumer luxury Brand perceptions and intentions. *Journal of Business Research* 69, no. 12: 5753–60.

Lee, Y., and J. Koo. 2015. Athlete endorsement, attitudes, and purchase intention: the interaction effect between athlete endorser-product congruence and endorser credibility. *Journal of Sport Management* 29, no. 5: 523–38.

Marwick, A.E. 2015. Instafame: Luxury selfies in the attention economy. *Public Culture* 27, no. 175: 137–60.

Mediakix 2017. May 5. Instagram influencer marketing is a 1 billion dollar industry. http://mediakix.com/2017/03/instagram-influencer-marketing-industry-size-how-big/#gs.QAEVJdQ

Ohanian, R. 1990. Construction and validation of a scale to measure celebrity endorsers' perceived expertise, trustworthiness, and attractiveness. *Journal of Advertising* 19, no. 3: 39–52.

Ohanian, R. 1991. The impact of celebrity spokespersons' perceived image on consumers' intention to purchase. *Journal of Advertising Research* 31, 46–54.

Park, C., and T.M. Lee. 2009. Information direction, website reputation and eWOM effect: a moderating role of product type. *Journal of Business Research* 62, no. 1: 61–7.

Pew Research Center 2018. Core Trends Survey [SPSS dataset]. http://www.pewinternet.org/dataset/jan-3-10-2018-core-trends-survey/

Priester, J.R., and R.E. Petty. 2003. The influence of spokesperson trustworthiness on message elaboration, attitude strength, and advertising effectiveness. *Journal of Consumer Psychology* 13, no. 4: 408–21.

Reichelt, J., J. Sievert, and F. Jacob. 2014. How credibility affects eWOM reading: the influences of expertise, trustworthiness, and similarity on utilitarian and social functions. *Journal of Marketing Communications* 20, no. 1-2: 65–81.

Russell, C.A. 1998. Toward a framework of product placement: theoretical propositions. *Advances in Consumer Research* 25, 357–62.

Russell, C.A., and D. Rasolofoarison. 2017. Uncovering the power of natural endorsements: a comparison with celebrity-endorsed advertising and product placements. *International Journal of Advertising* 36, no. 5: 761–78.

Schmidt, J. 2007. Blogging practices: an analytical framework. *Journal of Computer-Mediated Communication* 12, no. 4: 1409–27.

Spears, N., and S.N. Singh. 2004. Measuring attitude toward the Brand and purchase intentions. *Journal of Current Issues & Research in Advertising* 26, 53–66.

Sternthal, B., L.W. Phillips, and R. Dholakia. 1978. The persuasive effect of source credibility: a situational analysis. *Public Opinion Quarterly* 43, 285–314.

Till, B.D., and M. Busler. 2000. The match-up hypothesis: Physical attractiveness, expertise, and the role of fit on Brand attitude, purchase intent and Brand beliefs. *Journal of Advertising* 29, no. 3: 1–13.

Uzunoğlu, E., and S.M. Kip. 2014. Brand communication through digital influencers: Leveraging blogger engagement. *International Journal of Information Management* 34, no. 5: 592–602.

Wei, P.S., and H.P. Lu. 2013. An examination of the celebrity endorsements and online customer reviews influence female consumers' shopping behavior. *Computers in Human Behavior* 29, no. 1: 193–201.

WFA 2018. July 20. Brands to invest more on influencers. https://www.wfanet.org/news-centre/multinational-brands-focus-on-influencer-transparency/

Zhu, J., and B. Tan. 2007. Effectiveness of blog advertising: Impact of communicator expertise, advertising intent, and product involvement. In *ICIS 2007 proceedings*. http://aisel.aisnet.org/icis2007/121/

Appendix. **Stimuli used in study 1 and study 2 (blurred for legal and copyright reasons)**

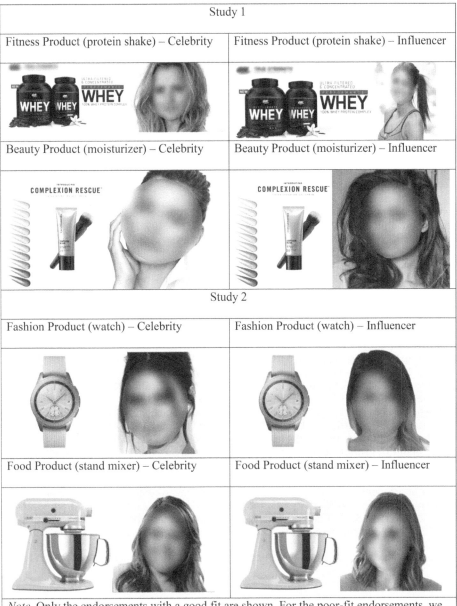

Study 1	
Fitness Product (protein shake) – Celebrity	Fitness Product (protein shake) – Influencer
Beauty Product (moisturizer) – Celebrity	Beauty Product (moisturizer) – Influencer

Study 2	
Fashion Product (watch) – Celebrity	Fashion Product (watch) – Influencer
Food Product (stand mixer) – Celebrity	Food Product (stand mixer) – Influencer

Note. Only the endorsements with a good fit are shown. For the poor-fit endorsements, we simply swapped the fitness & beauty endorsers (Study 1) and the fashion & food endorsers (Study 2).

Index

Figures are in italics and tables are in bold type. Endnotes are indicated by the page number followed by "n" and the endnote number e.g., 75n1 is endnote 1 on page 75. "CRM" refers to "cause-related marketing" and "CSR" refers to "corporate social responsibility".

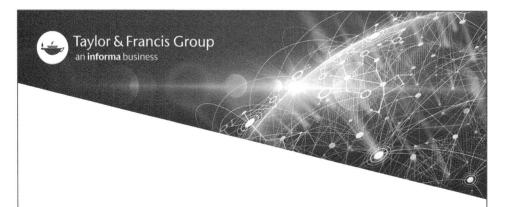